The Mississippi River
Campaign, 1861–1863

ALSO BY BENTON RAIN PATTERSON
The Great American Steamboat Race: The Natchez *and the* Robert E. Lee *and the Climax of an Era*
(McFarland, 2009)

The Mississippi River Campaign, 1861–1863

The Struggle for Control of the Western Waters

BENTON RAIN PATTERSON

McFarland & Company, Inc., Publishers
Jefferson, North Carolina, and London

Photograph research by Victoria Harlow.

Excerpts from *Sarah Morgan: The Civil War Diary of a Southern Woman*, edited by Charles East, Copyright © University of Georgia Press, are reprinted by permission of the University of Georgia Press.

LIBRARY OF CONGRESS CATALOGUING-IN-PUBLICATION DATA

Patterson, Benton Rain 1929–
The Mississippi River Campaign, 1861–1863 : the struggle for control of the western waters / Benton Rain Patterson.
      p.   cm.
Includes bibliographical references and index.

ISBN 978-0-7864-5900-1
softcover : 50# alkaline paper ∞

1. Mississippi River Valley — History — Civil War, 1861–1865 — Campaigns.
2. United States — History — Civil War, 1861–1865 — Campaigns. I. Title.
    E470.8.P38   2010   973.7'31—dc22   2010027261

British Library cataloguing data are available

©2010 Benton Rain Patterson. All rights reserved

No part of this book may be reproduced or transmitted in any form or by any means, electronic or mechanical, including photocopying or recording, or by any information storage and retrieval system, without permission in writing from the publisher.

Front cover: illustrations from Frank Leslie's *The Soldier in Our Civil War*, Vol. II (1885); background imagery ©2010 Shutterstock

Manufactured in the United States of America

McFarland & Company, Inc., Publishers
Box 611, Jefferson, North Carolina 28640
www.mcfarlandpub.com

To the memory of those
who for loyalty to their homeland
gave themselves to a doomed cause
and to the memory of those
who for love of country
gave their all to preserve the Union.

Table of Contents

Introduction 1

Part I: 1861

1. The Drive Begins 5
2. The Defenders 12
3. The Gunboats 17
4. River-Borne Warriors 27

Part II: 1862

5. Target on the Tennessee 35
6. The Assault That Failed 45
7. The Fall of Fort Donelson 54
8. Goodbye, Columbus 64
9. Fortress Island 70
10. The Receding Gray Line 84
11. The Ascension Begins 99
12. The Battle for Passage 111
13. The Defiant City 121
14. The Conquered City 133
15. The Ellet Fleet 140
16. The Confederate Offensive 147
17. Showdown at Memphis 155
18. Up from New Orleans 162
19. The *Arkansas* vs. the U.S. Navy 171
20. A Battle Too Far 182
21. New Attempts at Vicksburg 192

Part III: 1863

22. Tributaries and Distributaries 201
23. New Directions 215

24. The Other Side of the River 223
25. Vicksburg at Last 232
26. Finale at Port Hudson 249

Epilogue 257
Chapter Notes 259
Bibliography 267
Index 271

Introduction

At 4:30 in the morning on Friday, April 12, 1861, with a steeply arching, ten-inch mortar round fired from Fort Johnson on James Island, the army of the Confederate States of America commenced its massive artillery assault on Fort Sumter, guardian of the entrance to Charleston harbor. Rebel batteries at Fort Moultrie, on the opposite side of the harbor, and at Cummings Point, at the signal of the first shot, instantly joined the bombardment. Despite the early hour, curious and excitement-seeking spectators, knowing the deadline given to Fort Sumter's commandant for its surrender, thronged the streets and waterfront of Charleston to witness the awful display of shells bursting brightly in the night sky, raining destruction on the embattled Union stronghold.

Thirty-three hours later, on Saturday afternoon, Major Robert Anderson, Fort Sumter's commandant, raised a white flag of surrender and, to a detail of rebel officers sent to the fort in a small boat, declared that he was accepting the terms offered by the Confederates' commander, Brigadier General Pierre Gustave Toutant Beauregard. At noon on Sunday, April 14, "in an impressive ceremony of prayer and salute," as one nineteenth-century chronicler put it, the tattered, shot-riddled Stars and Stripes[1] was hauled down, and the garrison of nine commissioned officers, sixty-eight noncommissioned officers and privates, eight musicians and forty-three noncombatant workmen evacuated the battered and burned fortress.

The troops of the garrison embarked upon the ships of the relief flotilla that had arrived too late to save or support them, and as the U.S. vessels steamed away from Charleston harbor, headed for New York, the Confederate soldiers who had so recently driven their enemy from the fort hailed and cheered them with artillery salutes.

News of Fort Sumter's fall reached Washington, D.C., later in the day on Saturday, and on Sunday morning newly inaugurated President Abraham Lincoln met with his cabinet members and Lieutenant General Winfield Scott, the U.S. Army's aging general in chief, to discuss the next moves of a nation plunged into war. Before the day's business was done, Lincoln, with his own hand, had written a proclamation addressed to the officials of the states still in the Union and to the country's population at large:

> Whereas, the laws of the United States have been for some time past and now are opposed, and the execution thereof obstructed in the States of South Carolina, Georgia, Alabama, Florida, Mississippi, Louisiana, and Texas, by combinations too powerful to be suppressed by the ordinary course of judicial proceedings, or by the powers vested in the marshals by law; now therefore, I, Abraham Lincoln, President of the United States, in virtue of the power vested by the Constitution and the laws, have thought fit to call forth, and hereby do call forth the militia of the several States of the Union, to the aggregate number of seventy-five thousand, in order to suppress said combinations and to cause the laws to be duly executed.... I appeal to all loyal citizens to favor, facilitate, and aid this effort to maintain the honor, the integrity, and existence of our National Union.[2]

The proclamation was promptly disseminated by telegraph and published in newspapers across the country the next day, Monday, April 15. The response to it was sudden and massive. Governors replied that they were ready to provide the president their full quotas of militiamen. Recruitment of volunteers began in almost every county in the northern states. State legislatures and city governments voted funds to finance the arming, equipping and clothing of the volunteers. According to Lincoln's private secretary, John G. Nicolay, who recorded those early events, more than double the number of men requested in Lincoln's appeal offered their services, and within forty-eight hours of the publication of the proclamation, armed companies and even whole regiments of volunteers formed up and showed themselves ready to be sent into action.[3]

Lincoln's call to arms had effects in the South as well. Virginia had been teetering on the brink of secession, and the call to arms forced it over the edge. On April 17 the convention it had called voted to secede, a decision later ratified by a popular vote, and within five weeks of Virginia's secession Arkansas, Tennessee and North Carolina also voted to secede. Those four states expanded the territory of the Confederate States by nearly one half, making it a country four times the size of France. They also vastly increased the Confederacy's material resources and doubled its population to comprise five and a half million whites and three and a half million blacks.[4]

Even before the bombardment of Fort Sumter the Confederacy's secretary of war, Leroy Walker, anticipating the effects of the bombardment, had asked the seceded states for twenty thousand troops, and on April 16, two days after Fort Sumter's evacuation, he called for thirty-four thousand more. On April 29 Confederate President Jefferson Davis informed the Confederate Congress that he had "in the field, at Charleston, Pensacola, forts Morgan, Jackson, St. Philip and Pulaski, nineteen thousand men, and sixteen thousand are now en

The interior of Fort Sumter on April 14, 1861, the day the fort was evacuated by its Union garrison. Confederate artillery, under the command of Brig. Gen. P.G.T. Beauregard, had opened fire on the fort on the morning of Friday, April 12. The fort's commander, Maj. Robert Anderson, surrendered thirty-three hours later, on Saturday afternoon (National Archives and Records Administration).

route for Virginia." He said further that he planned to organize an additional force of one hundred thousand men to be held in readiness.

As the Union prepared, it was to General Scott that the responsibility fell for plotting the United States's course for the war. A Virginian, he realized better than most the menace presented by the hostility of the Southern states. When asked for his predictions about how the conflict would go and for how long, he told Lincoln's cabinet members he expected the war to continue for three years and after that there would still be a need for the federal government "to restrain the fury of the non-combatants."[5]

In a separate message intended for President Lincoln, written when Lincoln still could have avoided war, Scott had warned that the seceding states might be conquered by an invading army of 300,000 disciplined men, but at a cost of an "enormous waste of life to the North and Northwest, with at least $250,000,000 added thereto." He said that "the destruction of life and property on the other side would be frightful." The result, he predicted, would be "fifteen devastated provinces, not to be brought into harmony with their conquerors, but to be held for generations by heavy garrisons, at an expense quadruple the net duties or taxes which it would be possible to extort from them."[6]

Instead of invading armies, what Scott had in mind was spelled out in a letter he wrote to Major General George McClellan on May 3, 1861:

> We [should] rely greatly on the sure operation of a complete blockade of the Atlantic and Gulf ports soon to commence. In connection with such blockade, we propose a powerful movement down the Mississippi to the ocean, with a cordon of posts at proper points, and the capture of Forts Jackson and Saint Philip [commanding the river below New Orleans]; the object being to clear out and keep open this great line of communication in connection with the strict blockade of the seaboard, so as to envelop the insurgent States and bring them to terms with less bloodshed than by any other plan.

Scott said his plan would require twelve to twenty steam gunboats for the operations on the Mississippi and as many as forty other steam vessels to transport the sixty thousand men assigned to the land force that would capture and hold the river. He told McClellan:

> This army, in which it is not improbable you may be invited to take an important part, should be composed of our best regulars for the advance and of three-years' volunteers, all well officered, and with four months and a half of instruction in camps prior to (say) November 10. In the progress down the river all the enemy's batteries on its banks we of course would turn and capture, leaving a sufficient number of posts with complete garrisons to keep the river open behind the expedition. Finally, it will be necessary that New Orleans should be strongly occupied and securely held until the present difficulties are composed.[7]

When details of Scott's proposed strategy seeped out to the press, newspaper editorialists in the North, eager for the United States government to retaliate against the rebellious South, denounced both the plan and its author, calling the sage old warrior a superannuated dotard and accusing him of being motivated by sympathy for his native South. His strategy was labeled "the Anaconda Plan," since it proposed to encircle the seceded states and slowly squeeze the life out of the rebellion, in the same way the huge South American serpent surrounds, constricts and crushes its prey.

It might more appropriately have been called "the Patience Plan," in recognition of its forbearance in the face of the imminent massive violence threatening the fractured nation. Throughout the North, many heads hotter than the old general's were demanding immediate action against the rebels. The governors of the states of the upper Midwest, in a conference in Cleveland, urged Lincoln's administration to quickly send into action the troops they had just raised and asked Lincoln to call for three hundred thousand more men without delay, saying that, in the words of Wisconsin Governor Alexander Randall, "It is a fact, there is a spirit evoked by this rebellion among the liberty loving people of the country, that is drawing them to action, and if the government will not permit them to act for it, they will act for themselves."[8]

Northern newspapers took up the cry. Across the loyal states of the Union overwhelming public sentiment demanded immediate, forceful action against the seceded states, protesting to President Lincoln and his officials that General Scott's ridiculed Anaconda Plan for subduing and winning back the separated states by economic strangulation was out of the question.

But as the offended nation moved more deeply into conflict, it soon became clear that the Union's objective was indeed, and ought to be, as General Scott proposed, to isolate and squeeze the seceded states into submission and to do so, in large part, by capturing the Mississippi River, thereby cleaving the Confederacy, severing its communication across the mighty and vital river and hastening the end of the war.

By the middle of 1861, General Scott's plan for capturing the Mississippi was being hurried into implementation, though not without the engagement of the Union's armed forces. Forty-eight-year-old Major General John C. Frémont, the Pathfinder of western exploration twenty years earlier, was sent by President Lincoln to St. Louis to take command of U.S. military operations in Missouri as well as in all other states between the Mississippi River and the Rocky Mountains, and Illinois, too. His mission was to hold the strategic state of Missouri in the Union and to launch from Missouri the mighty southward thrust that would seize the Mississippi. "I have given you *carte blanche*," Lincoln told him as he was about to leave. "You must use your own judgment and do the best you can."[9]

On July 25, 1861, General Frémont arrived in St. Louis and assumed command of the army given him for the achievement of his task. The Mississippi River, "the great valley of American empire without which the war could not be won," as the eminent Civil War historian Bruce Catton put it,[10] was about to become the battleground in the monumental struggle for America's destiny.

Part I: 1861

1. The Drive Begins

During the meeting at the three-story mansion that was his St. Louis headquarters, Major General John Frémont, commanding the U.S. Army's Department of the West, saw something he liked in the brand new brigadier general who stood before him. The new general's clubbish fellow West Pointers had pegged him as a loser and a drifter, a man with a serious drinking problem. Frémont, though, had never been part of the West Point crowd and either hadn't heard or didn't care about their gossip. What he saw in the man, as he later wrote, were traits "of unassuming character not given to self elation, of dogged persistence, of iron will."[1] And so, in a decision of immeasurable historic importance, Frémont in August 1861 chose for the Army's command at Cairo, Illinois, not the likeliest prospect — blustering Brigadier General John Pope — but this new general, who just days earlier had served under Pope as a colonel and regimental commander. His name was Ulysses S. Grant.

It was understandable that Frémont made his choice on feeling rather than the record, since there wasn't much in Grant's record to recommend him. He had attended the U.S. Military Academy only because his father wanted him to get the free education that the government provided cadets. At the academy he became known as Uncle Sam, because of his initials, but was more commonly called Sam. Following graduation, in June 1843, at age twenty-one, he had begun serving the time he owed the Army. His first posting was to Jefferson Barracks, Missouri, just outside St. Louis, where nearby lived the family of Grant's West Point roommate, Fred Dent. Grant became a frequent visitor to the Dents' plantation and there met Fred's pretty, seventeen-year-old sister, Julia. Her good looks were almost matched by Grant's. Not tall, slight of build, with uncommonly fair skin, pale-blue eyes and clean-shaven face, young Lieutenant Grant was, as Julia's younger sister described him, "pretty as a doll."

When he returned from the Mexican War, during which he had served mostly as a quartermaster and a commissary, he married Julia in 1848 and remained in the Army. In 1852, after a number of posts in the upper Midwest, serving as a quartermaster, he had been promoted to captain and put in command of an infantry company posted in northern California. Bored stiff in that job and missing his wife and his kids, he had taken to the bottle, apparently more so than most of his fellow officers. In 1854 he had resigned his commission and gone back to Ohio to be with his family. He had tried farming near St. Louis on land his father-in-law had given Julia, had failed at that, had tried selling real estate, had failed again, then, at age thirty-eight, with a wife and three children to support, a pile of debts and no other job prospects, he had gone to work as a clerk in his father's leather-goods store in Galena, Illinois.

Then came Fort Sumter. Caught up in the patriotic fervor of the public response in Galena, he had helped train recruits in the Illinois militia and by appointment of the governor had helped organize the militia as it rapidly expanded. When he volunteered his services to the U.S. Army, though, his letter to the adjutant general in Washington had gone unanswered. When he made a trip to Cincinnati to see Major General George McClellan, a West Point acquaintance who was the newly appointed commander of the Army's Department of Ohio, hoping to get a job on his staff, McClellan was too busy to see him.

While Grant was gone on that trip, the Illinois governor appointed him a militia colonel and gave him command of the militia's Twenty-first Regiment. He assumed command in June 1861, two months after the fall of Fort Sumter, and in less than a month he had shaped the regiment into a disciplined fighting unit. Shortly thereafter the regiment was federalized, making Grant a colonel and a regimental commander in the U.S. Army. Earlier, when he had written to the Army's adjutant general requesting a colonelcy, he had felt, as he said, "somewhat doubtful whether I would be equal to the position," but in the meantime he had managed to reassure himself. "I had seen nearly every colonel who had been mustered in from the state of Illinois, and some from Indiana, and felt that if they could command a regiment properly, and with credit, I could also."[2]

In early July 1861, facing combat for the first time as a regimental commander, he had suffered a new surge of self-doubt. His orders were to take the Twenty-first Regiment across the Mississippi River and relieve an Illinois regiment that was surrounded by a rebel force near Palmyra, Missouri. "I had been in all the engagements in Mexico that it was possible for one person to be in," he remarked, "but not in command. If someone else had been colonel and I had been lieutenant colonel, I do not think I would have felt any trepidation."[3] As his regiment was preparing to cross the river at Quincy, Illinois, the troops that had been surrounded came straggling into town, forcing a postponement of his first test of leadership in combat. "I am inclined to think," he commented, "both sides got frightened and ran away."

Later ordered to move against a rebel unit commanded by Confederate Colonel Thomas Harris, which had encamped along a creek near the town of Florida, Missouri, he began to worry about what lay ahead for him as he approached the enemy. Along with his troops he climbed the hill that overlooked the rebel position, expecting to find Harris's men formed up and ready to do battle. "My heart kept getting higher until it felt to me as though it was in my throat," he confessed, remembering the moment. "I would have given anything then to have been back in Illinois." When his troops topped the hill and he could see the valley below, where he expected to find the rebels, there were signs of a recent encampment, but there was no enemy in sight. "My heart resumed its place," he said. "It occurred to me at once that Harris had been as much afraid of me as I had been of him." After that incident, he said, "I never experienced trepidation upon confronting an enemy, though I always felt more or less anxiety. I never forgot that he had as much reason to fear my forces as I had his. The lesson was valuable."[4]

His promotion to brigadier general had come as a surprise. While encamped near Mexico, Missouri, spending most of his time training his troops and still not having faced combat in his new role, he read in a St. Louis newspaper that his name was at the top of a list of seven officers who had been recommended by the Illinois congressional delegation, the members of which Grant felt he hardly knew well enough to have gained their confidence. A few days later the U.S. Senate confirmed his appointment as brigadier general, along with those of three others from Illinois. His commission was dated May 17, 1861.

The command that General Frémont gave him, the District of Southeast Missouri, comprised all of Missouri south of St. Louis and southern Illinois as well. Moving quickly into the new job, Grant set up a temporary headquarters at Cape Girardeau, Missouri, on the Mississippi River, some one hundred miles below St. Louis, then on September 4 moved his headquarters to Cairo, where the blue Ohio flows into the gray Mississippi. He showed up for duty wearing civilian clothes, the new uniform he had ordered from New York having not yet been received, and the colonel whom he relieved yielded his post without knowing for certain who it was that was relieving him.

The next day Grant received a visitor who identified himself as a scout for General Frémont and claimed to have important intelligence to report. He said he had just come from Columbus, Kentucky, a town on the Mississippi River about twenty-five miles below Cairo, and that a Confederate force had occupied the town and was preparing to move out from Columbus to occupy Paducah, Kentucky, at the confluence of the Ohio and the Tennessee rivers, an important strategic point that commanded the Ohio and the mouth of the Tennessee as well. Union forces could not afford to have Paducah occupied by the enemy, who could block passage of Union vessels on the Ohio before they reached the Mississippi and prevent passage up the Tennessee. Navigable from Paducah eastward as far as Muscle Shoals in northwest Alabama, the Tennessee flowed down through Kentucky and Tennessee, providing access to the South's heartland.

Quickly grasping the significance of the threat, Grant immediately telegraphed General Frémont to inform him of the report and to tell him that he was planning to leave with a force that night so that he could beat the Confederates to Paducah. To speed his troops the forty-five miles up the Ohio to Paducah, Grant scrambled to hire steamboats idled by the conflict, tied up at Cairo's wharves. Receiving no response to his message, he again wired Frémont, telling him that unless he received other orders, he would proceed as planned. There was again no response. With two regiments of infantry and a battery of artillery he embarked on the hired steamers, and escorted by three Union gunboats, the *Lexington*, *Tyler* and *Conestoga*, around midnight of September 5 he steamed off for Paducah, intending to arrive shortly after daybreak the next morning.

Grant's planned invasion of Kentucky and occupation of one of its cities was a ticklish political matter. Although a slave state, Kentucky, with a legislature that was mostly pro–Union and a governor who was a secessionist sympathizer, was tenuously clinging to a policy of neutrality, and President Lincoln was trying his best to avoid offending the people of Kentucky by any word or deed that might drive them out of the Union and into the arms of the Confederacy. A Confederate Kentucky could blockade the Ohio River, which is its northern border, along much of its length and severely impede the planned Union drive down the Mississippi. Lincoln considered Kentucky so important that to lose it, he said, was to lose everything.

Undaunted by the political ramifications, Grant was thinking of the military considerations. His plan was to justify his violation of Kentucky's neutrality by pointing to the fact that the Confederates had already violated it by occupying Columbus and were in further violation as they marched through the state toward Paducah.

Grant's task force of river-borne troops and gunboats arrived at Paducah early on September 6 as planned, completely surprising the town's citizens, who were expecting the arrival not of Union troops but of a Confederate army, which then was in fact but ten to fifteen miles away on its march to Paducah. Grant quickly positioned his troops on the roads leading into the town, blocking the rebels' entrance. The Confederate force approaching Paducah was estimated at nearly four thousand men, substantially outnumbering the Union force; but expecting to occupy the town unopposed and unwilling to engage Grant's troops, the Confederates, on learning of Grant's presence, halted their advance and withdrew back to Columbus.

Once he was satisfied that Paducah was secure, at least for the time being, Grant drew up a proclamation that he printed and posted around town, assuring the people of Paducah that they had nothing to fear from the presence of U.S. troops, that the troops were there to protect Paducah's citizens from the enemies of the United States and that the town's citizens were free to follow their usual pursuits. Then leaving his occupation force behind, along with the gunboats he stationed to guard Paducah's riverfront, he took a steamer back to Cairo, where he found notification of the department's approval of his Paducah plan waiting for him. He then ordered a contingent of troops at Cape Girardeau to reinforce the regiments in Paducah and appointed Brigadier General Charles F. Smith to take command at Paducah and to fortify the Union position.

Still mindful of the delicate political situation, he wrote a letter to the Kentucky legislature explaining his incursion into the state and his occupation of Paducah, prompting the Union-sympathizing legislature to approve Grant's action. Less approving, however, was General Frémont, who for his own reasons reprimanded Grant for corresponding with the Kentucky legislature and warned him against any further such contact.

Frémont was struggling with other problems, largely of his own making. He had gotten himself into hot water with President Lincoln when in a fit of frustration over the lawlessness and rebel threat in Missouri, the state he was desperately attempting to hold for the Union, as ordered, he issued a proclamation decreeing that "all persons who shall be taken with arms in their hands within these lines [the area of the U.S. Army's occupation of Missouri] shall be tried by court martial, and if found guilty will be shot. Real and personal property of those who take up arms against the United States, or who shall be directly proven to have taken an active part with their enemies in the field, is declared confiscated to public use and their slaves, if any they have, are hereby declared free men."[5]

Frémont had the proclamation printed and distributed to the public. He also sent a copy of it to Washington, D.C., where it swiftly came to the attention of President Lincoln. Thinking both practically and politically, Lincoln instantly foresaw the effects of the proclamation and pointed them out to Frémont in a tactful letter, explaining that he was writing to the general "in a spirit of caution and not of censure." The two troublesome points to which he objected were, as he wrote:

> First. Should you shoot a man, according to the Proclamation, the Confederates would very certainly shoot our best men in their hands in retaliation; and so, man for man, indefinitely. It is, therefore, my order that you allow no man to be shot under the proclamation without first having my approbation and consent.
>
> Second. I think there is a great danger that the closing paragraph, in relation to the confiscation of property and the liberating [of] slaves of traitorous owners, will alarm our Southern Union friends and turn them against us; perhaps ruin our rather fair prospect for Kentucky. Allow me, therefore, to ask that you will, as of your own motion, modify that paragraph so as to conform to the first and fourth sections of the act of Congress entitled "An act to confiscate property used for insurrectionary purposes," approved August 6, 1861, a copy of which I herewith send you.[6]

Frémont refused to rescind his order voluntarily. He wrote to the president that he had issued the proclamation when he found himself "between the Rebel armies, the Provisional Government [of Missouri], and home traitors" and said that it was "as much a movement in the war as a battle."[7] Returning Lincoln's tact with bluntness, he told the president:

If your better judgment decides that I was wrong in the article respecting the liberation of slaves, I have to ask that you will openly direct me to make the correction. The implied censure will be received as a soldier always should receive the reprimand of his chief. If I were to retract on my own accord it would imply that I myself thought it wrong, and that I had acted without the reflection which the gravity of the point demanded. But I did not. I acted with full deliberation, and the certain conviction that it was a measure right and necessary, and I still think so.[8]

In further defiance, Frémont dispatched his wife, Jessie, Missouri Senator Thomas Hart Benton's daughter, to carry the letter to Washington and to argue his case to President Lincoln in person. It was all to no effect except to anger the president, stiffen his resistance and draw from him a statement of the principle that he, as a lawyer, believed was involved. A general could rightfully seize and temporarily hold property for strictly military purposes, he wrote in explaining himself to Senator Orville Browning of Illinois, an old friend, but a general could not rightfully determine permanent possession of the property. "That," Lincoln wrote, "must be settled according to the laws made by law-makers, and not by military proclamations." Allowing no further protest, the president gave Jessie Frémont a cold shoulder and promptly and publicly ordered General Frémont to modify the proclamation's statement regarding the liberation of slaves.

In the field things were not going well for Frémont either. He had sent two regiments to strengthen the beleaguered five-thousand-man force of Brigadier General Nathaniel Lyon, which — after capturing Jefferson City, the Missouri capital, running the secessionist governor out of town and allowing a pro–Union state government to be installed — had come up against a daunting Confederate army near Springfield, in southwest Missouri. The two regiments, however, never reached Lyon, and in a desperate move, Lyon ordered his outnumbered force to attack the rebel encampment. In the ensuing fight, known as the Battle of Wilson's Creek, waged about ten miles south of Springfield on August 10, 1861, both sides nearly exhausted themselves in combat, each losing more than two hundred men killed. Among the thirteen hundred total Union casualties — killed, wounded or missing — was General Lyon, who was wounded in the head and then shot through the heart. On his death, the assault ended, and the battered Union troops disengaged and withdrew to Springfield. Fortunately for them, the equally battered Confederates, who suffered some twelve hundred total casualties, did not pursue them.

Six weeks later, on September 20, the Union force guarding an outpost at Lexington, Missouri, a critical location on the Missouri River, about thirty-five miles east of Kansas City, surrendered to an attacking Confederate force after two days of fighting. That battle cost the Union army a hundred casualties and the loss of about twenty-seven hundred troops who became prisoners of war following the surrender. The defeat was so humiliating that it drew reaction directly from the U.S. Army's grand old general in chief, Winfield Scott. President Lincoln, Scott informed Frémont, "expects you to repair the disaster at Lexington without loss of time."[9]

The victorious rebel army became radically diminished as thousands of Missouri militia soldiers, loyal to the militia's commander, Major General Sterling Price, returned to their homes after the Lexington battle, and Price began falling back to the southwest corner of the state. Frémont, meanwhile, anxious for a victory to show for his efforts — and to save his job — emerged from his St. Louis mansion and placed himself at the head of an impressive force comprising five divisions — some thirty-eight thousand men — and began a march to confront the now weakened Price. To let his superiors know of his intended heroics, he fired off a telegram to Washington: "I am taking the field myself. Please notify the President immediately."[10]

In Washington, however, General Frémont's decisive action was coming a bit too late. Ruffled by Jessie Frémont's presumption during her meeting with him and in light of rumors of graft concerning Frémont, plus the general dissatisfaction with the way the war in the West was going, President Lincoln had ordered investigators to discover what they could about Frémont's conduct and competence. Reports came back from the secretary of war and the Army's adjutant general that Frémont was unfit for his position. In St. Louis, Brigadier General Samuel Curtis, one of the investigators, declared in writing that Frémont lacked "the intelligence, the experience, and the sagacity necessary to his command."[11]

Clearly, the president could see, General Frémont had to be removed.

That conclusion, however, was more than Frémont could see. Determined to take possession of the Mississippi River valley—for the glory and whatever other benefits might follow—he did not intend, insiders had warned Lincoln, to relinquish his command at the president's order. Jessie Frémont, in a fit of temper during her meeting with Lincoln, had hinted that Frémont would oppose being relieved and she had threateningly told the president that her husband was no ordinary soldier, that in a test of political strength, Lincoln would find him a worthy adversary.

On October 28, Lincoln sent General Curtis two messages to be delivered to Frémont. One notified Frémont that he was relieved of his command. The other notified him that his replacement was Major General David Hunter, a veteran of the First Battle of Bull Run (or Manassas), fought on July 21, who was on his way to St. Louis to take over. Curtis then gave to a captain the task of delivering the president's orders to Frémont. Meanwhile, news of the orders had found its way to the press, and so Frémont, encamped with his troops outside Springfield, had learned from newspaper reports what was coming.

Pretending to be a local farmer who had valuable information for the general, and disguised to fit the part, the captain bearing the president's orders managed to get past Frémont's line of pickets about five o'clock in the morning on November 1 and arrive at the general's command post. When told he could not see the general then, but that his information would be passed on to him, the captain replied that he would rather wait until he could give the general the information himself. After many hours of waiting, he finally was taken to meet Frémont. The captain then removed from concealment inside the lining of his coat the president's orders and handed them to Frémont, who read them with mounting anger.

Frémont ordered the captain placed under arrest, apparently to keep him and the president's orders quiet, and then roused his troops and readied them for a massive assault on General Price's force, which at last report lay not far in front of the Union camp. A huge victory over the rebel army that had taken Lexington would, Frémont believed, vindicate him and force President Lincoln to back down and rescind his orders. In the excitement of Frémont's troops preparing for the attack, the arrested captain managed to slip out of custody and, having overheard the password of the day, passed quickly through the camp's perimeter guard and fled.

With his army marshaled to fall mightily upon the enemy and ready to move out, Frémont was soon struck by another stark disappointment. Price's entire army had vanished, having stealthily decamped and stolen away without being noticed. There would be no battle, no big victory for General Frémont, no vindication, no recision of the president's orders.

1. The Drive Begins

At last resigned to his new situation, Frémont addressed his troops the next morning and bade them farewell, then turned away and began his lonely retreat back to St. Louis.

He was passing from the scene of the Mississippi's intended conquest, but behind him he was leaving important elements of it, to be useful in the future. Included in the fifteen million dollars of expenditures that he had ordered while in command of the Department of the West were two steamboats that he had had converted into gunboats in preparation for the planned drive down the Mississippi. He had also ordered a flotilla of mortar boats that were planned to assail Confederate fortifications on the river. Moreover, he had dispatched spies into enemy territory to make maps and collect intelligence, the Confederates' plan to occupy Paducah being one result of that gathering of information.

And most significantly, in a rare act of sagacity, he had plucked from the Missouri field of action a brand new, untried brigadier general and had elevated him to the command of the vital post at Cairo, giving to Ulysses Grant historic opportunity and to the Union cause Grant's extraordinary merit.

2. The Defenders

Leonidas Polk, from Raleigh, North Carolina, had thought he wanted to be a soldier when he dropped out of the University of North Carolina after a year and entered the U.S. Military Academy at West Point. He found that he liked military life at the academy well enough and became good friends with his roommate, Albert Sidney Johnston, and several other fellow cadets, including Jefferson Davis. But in his third year at the academy he found a new, superseding interest.

Influenced by the academy's Episcopalian chaplain, Charles McIlvaine, Cadet Polk had a transforming spiritual experience. Upon graduation from West Point in 1827 he laid aside his uniform and his military ambitions, resigned his newly gained commission and enrolled in the Virginia Theological Seminary, to the horror of his father, a Revolutionary War veteran.

He was ordained an Episcopal deacon in 1830, the same year that he married Frances Ann Deveraux and became an assistant to Episcopal Bishop Richard Channing Moore in Richmond. Eight years later, after serving as a priest in Columbia, Tennessee, he was appointed missionary bishop of the Southwest and set about organizing Episcopal congregations in Alabama, Mississippi, Louisiana, Arkansas and the Indian Territory (now Oklahoma). In 1841, at age thirty-five, he was elected Episcopal bishop of Louisiana and he settled down on a large sugar-cane plantation worked by some four hundred slaves, most of whom his wife had inherited. Although warm and charming and possessed of considerable charisma as well as the power of persuasion and beardless good looks, he was not terribly skilled as a manager and he eventually lost the plantation to creditors. After that, he and his family moved to New Orleans.

One of his brightest dreams was to create a university that would compare with Oxford and Cambridge, an institution where young gentlemen of the South's elite families could receive a proper education. It was up to Episcopalians, he figured, to build such a university, believing, as he said, that "Baptists and Methodists have not the bearing or the social position or prestige required to command the public confidence."[1] The dream began to come true when in July 1857 representatives from the dioceses of ten Southern states met with Polk at Sewanee, Tennessee, and founded the University of the South, popularly known as Sewanee.

When the war broke out, Bishop Polk took off his vestments and took up the sword, volunteering for service in the Confederate army. Although he had had no military experience beyond his schooling at West Point and was just barely qualified to be a second lieutenant, his old West Point friend Jefferson Davis, the Confederate States president, in Richmond on June 25, 1861, appointed him a major general and gave him command of the Confederate army's Department No. 2, comprising, roughly, the area between the Mississippi and Tennessee rivers, both of which led into the vital innards of the Confederacy, and down the western side of the state of Mississippi as far south as the mouth of the Red River in Louisiana.

The mission that Davis assigned to Polk, strategically crucial to the Confederacy's survival, was to protect the rebel states from a Union advance down the Mississippi River valley. As someone who had lived in that area for years and was familiar with it and its people, Polk had already realized the vital importance of protecting the Mississippi. In mid–May he had written to Davis about his concerns for it and offered some unsolicited advice, as he was wont to do. "It seems to me that a man of the highest military character should be charged with our defenses," he told Davis. "In a word, what is wanted in the Valley is a head."[2] The man he thought ideal for the responsibility was, as he said, "our old friend Gen'l Johnston," meaning his West Point roommate, Albert Sidney Johnston, who at the time was a brigadier general in the United States Army, posted in California, soon to leave to join the Confederates. Establishing the defense of the Mississippi was too urgent to await his arrival. And since Polk had raised the concern, had intimate knowledge of the territory, was known to Davis and was considered by him to be qualified despite his lack of experience, Polk got the job.

He left Richmond in early July, passed through Nashville, and arrived at Memphis, where he would establish his headquarters, about ten days later. There he immediately ran into the first problem of his new command. Gideon Johnson Pillow, a fifty-five-year-old Tennessee lawyer, politician, farmer and possessor of extensive landholdings in three Southern states, wealthy, willful and self-assertive, was also a soldier of sorts. His military experience had begun in 1833 when he was named adjutant general of the Tennessee militia, with the rank of brigadier general. As a brigadier general of U.S. Army volunteers, he had commanded Tennessee troops during the Mexican War, serving under generals Winfield Scott and Zachary Taylor. During that service he had gained a reputation for ignoring or modifying orders given him and for taking credit for the accomplishments of others. In May 1861, two months before General Polk showed up in Memphis, Pillow had been appointed by the Tennessee governor as senior major general of the Provisional Army of Tennessee, the state's own fighting force, which Pillow had helped recruit and train and which constituted virtually the entire body of troops that Polk had been assigned to command.

Jefferson Davis, president of the Confederate States of America, a West Point graduate, former U.S. Army officer, onetime senator from Mississippi and secretary of war in President Franklin Pierce's administration. Winfield Scott, the U.S. Army's general in chief at the beginning of the war, claimed that he was "amazed that any man of judgment should hope for the success of any cause in which Jefferson Davis is a leader" (National Archives and Records Administration).

Infuriated by his subordination to

Polk and the imposition of Polk over control of *his* army, Pillow resisted relinquishment of its command. The Confederate secretary of war, Leroy Walker, managed to explain to Pillow that General Polk was to command *Confederate* troops in Tennessee, not Tennessee's own army. But without the Tennessee troops, Polk had no army. The Tennessee governor, Isham Harris, then ordered the Tennessee army placed under Polk's command, deftly rendering them Confederate troops. Pillow, too, became a Confederate soldier, receiving an appointment as a brigadier general assigned to serve under Confederate Major General Polk.

Within a matter of weeks following the new arrangement, Pillow demonstrated his willfulness by countermanding an order issued by Polk to one of the units of Pillow's command. Called down by Polk, Pillow lamely claimed that he "had no motive to gratify but to serve the country" and as if justifying his misdeed, he protested that he felt he was "tied down and allowed no discretion."[3] Polk answered that Pillow had ample discretion, but only within his lawful authority.

As the battle of wills continued, General Polk set about his prime task of guarding the lower Mississippi. He determined that he should establish defensive positions as far up the river as possible. On July 27 he ordered Pillow to take a force of six thousand troops from Memphis to New Madrid, Missouri, where they would be reinforced by troops of the Missouri militia's Brigadier General M. Jeff Thompson and those of Confederate army Brigadier General William J. Hardee, all of whom were concentrated in southeastern Missouri. The strength of those combined forces would then total twelve thousand to fifteen thousand men. Polk's plan was, following further reinforcement, to march on Cape Girardeau, built on a sloping bluff that rises from the bank of the Mississippi about a hundred miles below St. Louis. The objective was to capture that commanding position; then, in coordination with another force under Polk positioned on the east side of the river, Pillow would move on to Cairo and take possession of it as well. Firm Confederate strongpoints would thus be planted at the gateway to the lower Mississippi, thereby barring a Union entrance. That was the plan.

By the end of July, Confederate troops under Polk's command had occupied New Madrid and were stalled there, building fortifications and awaiting reinforcements before moving deeper into Missouri. President Davis was reluctant to approve sending more troops to Polk and wanted to know what Polk was doing with the men he had and what he proposed to do with additional men. The correspondence between Polk and Richmond went back and forth for weeks, and while it did, Polk lost interest in Missouri objectives and decided that the defense of the lower Mississippi could best be served by establishing a fortified position on the commanding bluff at Columbus, Kentucky, about twenty-five river miles below Cairo, overlooking the Mississippi River like a forbidding inland Gibraltar.

That move was something that General Pillow had been advocating since shortly after the opening of hostilities—and after the Tennessee legislature had authorized Governor Harris to order a defensive position built at Columbus to provide protection from a Union drive against less defensible Memphis as well as the rest of western Tennessee. Harris, however, was counting on Kentucky's neutrality to block a Union advance on Tennessee, and so when Pillow, as head of Tennessee's own army, had earlier asked the governor's approval to take a force into Kentucky and fortify Columbus, Harris had turned him down. Characteristically, Pillow was prepared to act on his own without the governor's approval and had already written to President Davis to make his case, advising Davis that he, Pillow, would "take the responsibility of acting on [his] own judgment."[4]

Pillow was deterred, however, when Governor Harris specifically instructed him not to send troops into Kentucky or do anything else that could upset Kentucky's neutrality. Now, though, three months after having been initially thwarted, Pillow presented his case to General Polk, Davis's hand-picked military commander, and Polk was persuaded that taking Columbus and fortifying it was a must, despite the fact that he had already assured Kentucky's governor that the Confederate States government had no intention or desire to disturb Kentucky's neutrality.

Meanwhile, Kentuckians were themselves disturbing it. Reports came to President Davis that Kentucky's government was allowing Union loyalists to form and train units of a home guard and to receive weapons supplied to them from across the Ohio River, all of which Davis considered a breach of the state's neutrality and which prompted him to write a cautionary letter to Kentucky's governor. Tennessee Governor Harris was also concerned. On September 2 he telegraphed General Polk to suggest that he hold up on a campaign into the interior of Missouri, in view of the developments in Kentucky.

By then Polk had already decided his objective should not be in Missouri. The day before receiving Harris's telegram, Polk had written a note to Kentucky Governor Beriah Magoffin, giving him the bad news. Polk told him that it was "of the greatest consequence to the Southern cause in Kentucky or elsewhere that I should be ahead of the enemy in occupying Columbus and Paducah."[5] Having decided that the political considerations should not stand in the way of military operations, General Polk determined to move on Columbus. With a contingent of his force he left Memphis and moved up the river to New Madrid, and there he collected General Pillow and his troops, bringing his total strength to about fifteen thousand men, and on September 3 they steamed upriver to Hickman, Kentucky, a tobacco-shipping port about twenty miles below Columbus. Polk disembarked his army there and took over the town of Hickman, then marched northward and occupied Columbus on September 4, setting up an encampment and beginning the construction of fortifications.

It was the next day, September 5, that General Grant, in Cairo, learned from General Frémont's spy that the Confederates had occupied Columbus. That was the same day that news of Polk's action reached Richmond, the Confederate capital, and the news came not from General Polk but from Tennessee Governor Harris, who, horrified at the turn of events, telegraphed President Davis to inform him of Polk's egregious violation of Kentucky's neutrality. At the same time, Harris also wired Polk, telling him that he and President Davis were committed to respecting Kentucky's neutrality and asking if Polk's occupation would be removed.

In his telegram to Davis, Harris pointed out the injury the invasion had done to the Confederate cause in Kentucky and suggested that Davis order Polk to withdraw his troops immediately. Agreeing with Harris, Davis, on the day he received Harris's telegram, passed it along to the Confederate secretary of war, Leroy Walker. On the telegram Davis penned a note to Walker, instructing him to inform Polk that Davis was ordering him to withdraw his troops from Kentucky. Walker promptly wired Davis's orders to Polk.

Later that same day, September 5, Davis received a telegram from Polk, containing a message similar to the one Polk had sent to Governor Harris. Polk claimed that he had acted under "the plenary powers delegated to me by the president" and that the occupation of Columbus was a military necessity. "It is my intention now," he informed President Davis, "to continue to occupy and keep this position."[6]

Davis, who had been ill off and on all summer and days earlier had confessed that he had been too sick even to write a letter, responded to Polk's telegram as if overcome by weakness. The invasion of Kentucky and occupation of Columbus constituted a political catastrophe for the Confederacy, Davis knew, and the troops should be withdrawn. But Polk, his old West Point comrade in whom he had placed so much trust, had declared the occupation a military necessity. Who was he, as president, to gainsay his general? He decided to punt. He would let Polk decide what was necessary and then let him do it. "The necessity," Davis lamely wired back to Polk, "must justify the action." The troops stayed in Columbus.

On September 8, General Polk officially notified Kentucky Governor Magoffin that Confederate troops had moved into Kentucky and were occupying Columbus, as he had warned the governor days earlier. He told Magoffin that the action was made necessary by the presence of Union forces in Kentucky and he offered to withdraw his troops if the Union troops withdrew at the same time. From Magoffin the unhappy news of the occupation was passed on to the Kentucky legislature, then in session, and in response, the legislature on September 14 instructed the governor to demand the withdrawal of the Confederate troops from the state and urged Brigadier General Robert Anderson, the former commandant at Fort Sumter and now commander of the U.S. Army's newly organized Department of the Cumberland, comprising Tennessee and Kentucky, to quickly come to the defense of his native state. The legislature also later outlawed Kentuckians' enlistment in the Confederate armed forces and authorized the recruitment of forty thousand volunteers into the state's home guard to repel the invasion from the South.

Kentucky's critical neutrality, thanks to Leonidas Polk, had come to an end.

On September 14, after Grant had taken Paducah on September 6, thwarting Polk's plan to seize Paducah for the Confederacy, General Polk got around to informing President Davis that the Paducah part of his strategy had gone awry. In that communication he stated his regret that he had not taken Columbus much earlier. "I believe," the bishop-soldier told Davis, "if we could have found a respectable pretext, it would have been better to have seized this place [Columbus] some months ago."[7]

3. The Gunboats

In early May of 1861, mere days after the surrender of Fort Sumter, James B. Eads, a St. Louis engineer, inventor and businessman who had made a fortune by salvaging cargoes from sunken vessels in the Mississippi River using a diving bell he invented, wrote a letter to the U.S. secretary of the Navy, Gideon Welles, offering his ideas for establishing a blockade along the Mississippi and Ohio rivers. He proposed that the Navy build a number of gunboats, or floating artillery platforms, that would patrol the rivers and control traffic. The vessels would be steamboats mounting thirty-two-pounder guns and would be insulated against enemy fire by bales of cotton fastened to the boats' superstructure. He also proposed establishing a protected naval base at Cairo.

Welles, whom President Lincoln called "Old Father Neptune," and who looked the part, with the wavy gray locks of a wig hanging over his ears and a wild gray beard covering his throat, passed Eads's letter along to the War Department, since inland waterways were the jurisdiction of the Army, not the Navy. A few days later the Army's chief executive, Secretary of War Simon Cameron, in response to Eads's proposals, asked Welles to send someone to the Cincinnati headquarters of Major General George McClellan, commanding the Army's Department of Ohio, to confer about organizing a naval force to blockade the Mississippi and Ohio.

The officer Welles picked to send was Navy Commander John Rodgers, the forty-five-year-old son of a distinguished U.S. naval commander. At Rodgers's suggestion, Welles sent along with Rodgers a naval shipbuilder, Samuel Pook. Captivated by the prospects of forming an inland navy, Rodgers and Pook ended up purchasing three steamers, at a bargain total price of $62,000, to be used for the proposed blockade, as envisioned by General Winfield Scott, and requested Navy guns to arm the steamers. Rodgers, however, had taken it upon himself to buy the boats in the name of the Navy and had contracted to have them refitted as warships, all without Welles's knowledge or approval. Following Rodgers's June 8 letter reporting his actions to Welles and requisitioning funds to pay for the boats, Welles fired back two sharp reprimands to the enterprising, enthusiastic Commander Rodgers.

Apparently desiring only a minimal involvement with the proposed inland navy and with his thoughts concentrated on building a sea-going fleet, Welles spelled out for Rodgers the separation of authority and responsibility for a river fleet. The Navy Department would provide armament and crews for the boats but nothing more. Acquisition of the boats was the Army's business. Rodgers was told he had no authority to buy boats or enter into contracts. He was to act, Welles told him, as a "subordinate to the general in command, to aid, advise, and cooperate with him in crossing or navigating the rivers or in arming and equipping the boats required for the army on the western waters."[1]

Welles forwarded Rodgers's report — and the requisitions for payment — to Secretary of War Cameron, who promptly ordered Rodgers to Washington and with more imagination and enthusiasm than Old Father Neptune had shown for the formation of an inland fleet, approved the requisitions and instructed Rodgers that from then on, the Army's quartermaster general would approve whatever Rodgers, acting on General McClellan's authority, would decide was needed to establish a navy on the nation's rivers. By June 23 Commander Rodgers was back on the job of building a fleet for the Mississippi and Ohio rivers.

The protocol for military operations on the rivers thus established, the three steamboats acquired by Rodgers were converted into gunboats, with oaken bulkheads erected to protect the boats' machinery from enemy fire, which earned for them the name "timberclads." They were the *Conestoga*, the *Lexington* and the *Tyler*, the last of which had its name changed to *Taylor* (although it continued to be known as the *Tyler*) because its namesake, former President Tyler of Virginia, had deserted the Union for the Confederacy. The boats' conversion to men-of-war, done swiftly, did not leave them without problems, as revealed in correspondence from Rodgers's assistant, Navy Lieutenant S.L. Phelps, writing to Rodgers from Louisville:

> The more I examine the work on the *Conestoga*, the more disgraceful patching it seems to be. The *Lexington* is best done, but none well; and the joiner-work all around is more like the work of common laborers than of mechanics. The boat davits are not up, and no attempt made to put them up; the same of the iron ties and bars over the boilers. In the *Taylor* you can not get from aft forward without walking over the boilers. No attempt has been made to deck over for a gangway. The contract calls for swinging booms—none are provided.[2]

Besides those items on Phelps's punch list, there was the more fundamental problem of the boats' ability to get down the Ohio River. "I make it my business to gather all the information I can about the river below," Phelps wrote in another report, "and I am satisfied the steamers can not now be floated out in any manner."[3]

In the meantime, the vessels' preparation for war continued. The *Conestoga* took aboard four thirty-two-pounders that fired shot. The *Lexington* was armed with two thirty-pounders and four eight-inch Dahlgrens—smooth-bore guns that fired explosive shells. The *Tyler* was equipped with one thirty-two-pounder and six eight-inch Dahlgrens.

The three made-over vessels finally reported for duty at Cairo in August, in time to escort General Grant's transport steamers to Paducah. None of them was in particularly good shape after having repeatedly run aground on their voyage down the Ohio from Cincinnati, and all looked exactly like what they were—hastily cobbled, makeshift men-of-war. They were commanded by young Navy lieutenants and manned by crews of riverboatmen, who with training, it was believed, would make good artillerists.

Enlisting crews to man the gunboats presented another problem for Rodgers. The Navy Department could provide officers to place in command of the three vessels, but junior officers and ordinary crewmen would have to be recruited from among whatever experienced riverboatmen were available along the Mississippi and Ohio and other Western rivers. With General McClellan's authorization, Rodgers in the summer of 1861 began a recruitment program, conducted by three naval officers in Cincinnati, Louisville and St. Louis. The men signing up for gunboat duty would be serving under officers and regulations of the U.S. Navy, but they would be classified as Army personnel and paid by the U.S. War Department, except for the Navy's officers. Those officers would continue to be paid by the Navy Department.

The enlistment program did not move swiftly. Many men who would have been potential enlistees had already volunteered for service in the Army. Many others were dissuaded from volunteering by rumors that serving on the gunboats would be especially dangerous. And many among those who were willing to volunteer failed to meet the Navy's physical-fitness standards. Less problematic was the recruitment of officers. Experienced riverboatmen who wished to volunteer their services to the Union preferred to serve in jobs they already knew and therefore eagerly stepped forward to serve on a river warship. Veteran river captains signed on as first mates aboard Rodgers's gunboats, and experienced riverboat mates signed on as second and third officers.

Rodgers also hired pilots for the gunboats, two for each one of the vessels. He decided it was cheaper to employ licensed pilots than to teach the pilots' skills to those who had no experience steering steamers across the rivers' treacherous shallows and along their ever-changing courses. He balked at paying them what the pilots' union (the Cincinnati Pilots' Association) demanded, which was the going rate for pilots on commercial riverboats, and the union at last agreed to accept the salary that Rodgers offered — $150 a month, about 60 percent of the pilots' usual pay.

Gideon Welles, a newspaper editor and politician appointed by President Lincoln to be secretary of the Navy despite his scant naval experience. Lincoln called him "Old Father Neptune." Welles assigned the task of building an inland navy to Commander John Rodgers, who began the U.S. river fleet with the purchase of three steamboats for $62,000 (Library of Congress).

One nineteenth-century account pictured the personnel problem as severe: "Great difficulty continued to be experienced in raising men to man the fleet, and, at last, strenuous requisitions had to be made upon the West, upon barge-men, river-men, lake-men, and landsmen of all sorts (and some of the worst), to fill up the vacancies."[4] Admiral Henry Walke, who served with the Western rivers fleet, described the agglomeration of personnel that manned the boats as "fresh-water sailors from our great lakes, and steam-boat hands from the Western rivers. Of the seamen from the East, there were Maine lumbermen, New Bedford whalers, New York liners, and Philadelphia sealawyers. The foreigners enlisted were mostly Irish, with few English and Scotch, French, Germans, Swedes, Norwegians, and Danes. The Northmen, considered the hardiest race in the world, melted away in the Southern sun with surprising rapidity."[5] Aboard the *Carondelet*, the gunboat Walke commanded, he said there "were more young men perhaps than on any other vessel in the fleet. Philadelphians were in the majority; Bostonians came next, with a sprinkling from other cities, and just enough men-o'-war's men to leaven the lump with naval discipline."[6]

Not all the gunboat commanders were fortunate enough to have such leaven assigned to their vessels, and lacking a sufficient cadre of old Navy hands to indoctrinate his new recruits, Rodgers, with some humor, came up with an unusual proposal he thought might help shape up the new men, whom he considered a poorly disciplined lot: "I shall read the Articles of War every Sunday until they know them, and get a parson at them whenever I can so as to break down their spirit—and let their wives come on board to lecture them on week days. With all these helps and hard drill they will have no time to give trouble."[7]

Commander Rodgers soon fell victim to his own efficiency, offending area businessmen who vainly expected him to favor them with naval contracts. General Fremont, then still in command of the Department of the West in St. Louis and hearing protests against Rodgers, asked the Navy Department to replace Rodgers with a naval officer who would command all naval forces on the Western rivers and who would report to Fremont instead of McClellan. The Navy Department quickly complied.

While hastily assembling its makeshift gunboat fleet, the War Department was also considering James Eads's proposal for constructing new gunboats, designed especially for use on the rivers. The Army's veteran chief engineer, Joseph Totten, was called in for consultation. His recommendation was that the river gunboats should be built like a bateau, with a flat bottom and with bow and stern curved upwards, and should be driven by two steam-powered side-wheels. He suggested that the vessels be no more than 170 feet long and 28 feet in the beam and draw no more than five feet of water. Naval shipbuilder Samuel Pook was also consulted. He came up with a different idea, and Totten deferred to Pook's concept of how the river gunboats should be designed.

In the end, the design specified a vessel 175 feet long and 50 feet in the beam. It would draw six feet of water and would make about nine miles an hour. The hull would have a flat bottom, and its sides would be inclined at a 45-degree angle and would rise just twelve inches above the surface of the water. Atop the hull would be built a casemate—an artillery enclosure—150 feet long and 50 feet wide, the sides of which would be eight feet high, sloping up to a flat roof. The casemate, open at the stern, would be made of wood, and its sides would be covered with iron plate two and a half inches thick. Inside the casemate would be the vessel's steam-driven machinery and its armament—a total of thirteen guns, including three nine- or ten-inch guns, four thirty-two pounders mounted on each side, and lighter guns mounted at the stern. The vessel's boiler and engines would be protected not only by the two-and-a-half-inch-thick iron plates but also by a twenty-inch-thick oak shield. The paddle wheel would be mounted at the stern, protected in an iron-plated enclosure. On top of the casemate would be a conical pilothouse, also covered with iron plate.

Those gunboats, specially designed for war on the river, would be like nothing anyone had ever seen before. The War Department ordered seven of them, to be built by Eads in his boatyards at Carondelet, Missouri, outside St. Louis, and Mound City, Illinois, near Cairo. The War Department's contract with Eads specified that the cost of the gunboats would be $89,000 each, that they would be completed within sixty-five days of the signing of the contract (which made them due by October 10, 1861) and that they would be delivered to the government at St. Louis.

In September, while construction proceeded, the plans were modified to increase the amount of iron cladding to embrace all parts of the vessel above the waterline. After some delays, the seven vessels were finally delivered on December 5, 1861. They were named after cities on the Ohio and Mississippi rivers—the *Pittsburg* (spelled without the city's final "h"), the *Cincinnati*, *St. Louis*, *Louisville*, *Cairo*, *Carondelet* and the *Mound City*.

By then the Union had acquired two other ironclads for use on the rivers—the *Benton* and the *Essex*, both former snag boats, designed to remove obstacles from the river, that were converted into warships. Also added to the Union's river fleet were thirty-eight mortar

3. *The Gunboats* 21

The U.S. ironclad gunboat *St. Louis,* one of seven revolutionary vessels designed and built by St. Louis bridge builder and engineer James Eads. The vessels were especially designed and fitted for wartime service on the Mississippi River and other rivers in what was called the country's Western waters (National Archives and Records Administration).

boats that were towed — actually pushed — by steam tugs, and a large number of vessels of various sorts that had been seized from the Confederates.

While the Union fleet was growing, a more modest Confederate fleet was also being assembled, under the direction of the Confederate secretary of the navy — chunky, melon-faced Stephen Russell Mallory, a forty-seven-year-old lawyer from Key West, Florida, who, after marrying the daughter of a prominent Pensacola family, was elected a United States senator from Florida in 1850. In 1853 he was named chairman of the Senate's Committee on Naval Affairs and was instrumental in the modernization of the U.S. Navy through a shipbuilding program that began in 1854. His experience on the committee turned him into something of an expert on naval affairs and made him a prime candidate for the job of Confederate secretary of the navy, to which President Jefferson Davis appointed him on March 4, 1861, following Mallory's resignation from the U.S. Senate.

To build the Confederacy's navy, Mallory had to start from scratch. At the time of his appointment the Confederate States had no navy whatever — no ocean-going ships, no river-going boats. Some individual states, such as Louisiana, North Carolina and Virginia, were forming naval forces of their own, but doing so without coordination between states or with the central government. Although he had no vessels, Secretary Mallory did have a pool of naval officers. More naval officers from the South stayed with the Union than left it (350 staying; 321 leaving), but some 20 percent of the U.S. Navy's officers, all of them Southerners and most of them graduates of the U.S. Naval Academy, resigned their commissions and were offering their services to the Confederacy.[8] Most would soon have their offers of service accepted. An act of the Confederate congress on March 16 authorized President Davis to appoint to the Confederate navy four captains, four commanders, thirty lieutenants, five surgeons, five assistant surgeons, six paymasters and two chief engineers. It also provided for the hiring of as many masters, midshipmen, engineers, naval constructors, boatswains, gunners, carpenters, sailmakers and other petty officers and seamen as the president deemed necessary, up to a total of three thousand naval personnel. Those numbers were increased by an amendatory act of the congress on April 21 to provide for four admirals, ten captains, thirty-one commanders, one hundred first lieutenants, twenty-five second lieutenants, twenty masters, twelve paymasters, twenty-two surgeons, fifteen past assistant surgeons, thirty assistant surgeons, one engineer in chief and twelve engineers.

Experienced officers from the pool available to Mallory were appointed to head and staff the bureaus that Mallory, following the U.S. Navy Department model, swiftly organized within the Confederacy's Navy Department — the Bureau of Orders and Detail, Bureau of Ordnance and Hydrography, Bureau of Provisions and Clothing, and Bureau of Medicine and Surgery.

Two weeks into his job, on March 17, 1861, Mallory sent a team of three officers, headed by Captain Lawrence L. Rousseau, a veteran of the War of 1812, to New Orleans to determine the possibility of purchasing a number of steamers that could be quickly converted into warships. The team's report was discussed in a historic meeting held in Mallory's improvised office in Montgomery on April 17, and out of that meeting came a decision to buy two vessels, the packet *Florida* and the steam-and-sail vessel *Havana*, which would be speedily converted into the notorious Confederate raider CSS *Sumter*, the firstborn of Mallory's navy.

Under the command of Admiral Raphael Semmes, the *Sumter* steamed out of an Algiers shipyard, across the river from New Orleans, on June 18, 1861. It slipped past the Union blockader *Brooklyn*, raced out into the Gulf of Mexico on June 30 and outran the pursuing *Brooklyn* to begin its relentless harassment of Northern merchant shipping on the high seas, capturing or destroying eighteen vessels, which continued until it was captured by U.S. warships at Gibraltar in January 1862.

Stephen R. Mallory, the Confederate secretary of the navy. As a U.S. senator from Florida and chairman of the Senate's Committee on Naval Affairs, he was instrumental in the modernization of the U.S. Navy prior to the war. At the time of his appointment by President Davis, the Confederate States had no navy, neither ocean-going ships nor river-going boats (Library of Congress).

Captain Rousseau's orders from Secretary Mallory were to buy and outfit as many steamers as possible at New Orleans. Another of his acquisitions was the former Mexican vessel *Marques de la Habana*, a screw-driven steamer, like the *Sumter*, which was converted into a ship of war and renamed the CSS *McRae*. Unlike the *Sumter*, it was unable to slip past the Union blockader patrolling the mouth of the Mississippi and so became destined for service on the river. Other purchases included the side-wheeler tug *Yankee*, which was converted into the gunboat CSS *Jackson* and placed in service on June 17, the *Ivy*, the *Calhoun*, the *Oregon* and the *Arrow*, the latter two of which had been seized by the state of Louisiana.

Mallory was assembling an instant navy, composed of whatever suitable vessels could be found and quickly pressed into service, coping as best it could with the South's lack of industry that was capable of quickly producing, as the Union could, the armed vessels needed for its defense. The South's industrial disadvantage, with which the Confederacy was soon confronted, was described by Brigadier General Josiah Gorgas, chief of ordnance for the Confederate army, in his diary:

> We began in April, 1861, without an arsenal, laboratory or powder mill of any capacity, and with no foundry or rolling-mill except at Richmond.... During the harassments of war, while holding our own in the field defiantly and successfully against a powerful enemy; crippled by a depreciated currency; throttled with a blockade that deprived us of nearly all the means of getting material or workmen; obliged to send almost every able-bodied man to the field; unable to use slave-labor, with which we were abundantly supplied, except in the most unskilled departments of production; hampered by want of transportation even of the commonest supplies of food; with no stock on hand even of articles such as steel, copper, leather, iron, which we must have to build up our establishments— against all these obstacles, in spite of all these deficiencies, we persevered at home, as determinedly as did our troops on the field against a more tangible opposition; and in that short period [two years] created, almost literally out of the ground, foundries and rolling mills at Selma, Richmond, Atlanta and Macon, smelting works at Petersburg, chemical works at Charlotte, North Carolina; a powder-mill far superior to any in the United States ... and a chain of arsenals, armories and laboratories ... stretching link by link from Virginia to Alabama.[9]

Despite the handicaps he faced, Mallory, while buying up suitable vessels, was thinking all along of constructing new warships for the Confederate fleet. Having studied the use of iron cladding on ships in England and France, he was particularly interested in building iron-clad vessels. On May 8, 1861, he wrote to the Confederate senate's naval committee to urge approval for the ironclads he intended to build, telling committee members:

> I regard the possession of an iron-armored ship as a matter of the first necessity. Such a vessel could traverse the entire coast of the United States, prevent all blockades, and encounter, with a fair prospect of success, their entire navy.
> If to cope with them upon the sea, we follow their example and build wooden ships, we shall have to construct several at one time, for one or two ships will fall an easy prey to her comparatively numerous steam frigates. But inequality of numbers may be compensated by invulnerability....[10]

Upon the secession of Virginia on April 17, 1861, the U.S. Navy's Gosport shipyard at Norfolk fell into Confederate hands, and among the items captured was the steam frigate USS *Merrimack*, which though burned to its waterline and scuttled by its crew on April 20, still had its hull and machinery intact. Raised and salvaged by the Confederates, it was converted into the ironclad CSS *Virginia* (although still remembered as the *Merrimack*) and, according to the design of Confederate navy Commander John M. Brooke, became both ram and gunboat, 275 feet long and thirty-eight and a half feet in the beam, with an iron ram mounted on its bow and carrying ten guns, four on each broadside and one at each end. Virtually invulnerable within its shell of two layers of two-inch-thick iron plates, one mounted horizontally and one vertically on an oak frame with sloping sides, and its armament in casemates, it made a fearsome foe when it entered the fray in Hampton Roads on March 8, 1862, and destroyed two Union warships.

While the *Merrimack* was being repaired and converted, Secretary Mallory's Navy Department was so impressed they believed the *Merrimack* should be the prototype for other ironclads the Confederates planned to build. However, Mallory had in the meantime learned about the U.S. Navy's contract with James Eads for the construction of seven ironclad river gunboats, and he sent a number of experienced mechanics to St. Louis to find jobs at Eads's boatyards and report back to Mallory on the vessels' design and specifications. Their report on the ironclads that Eads was building helped Mallory change his mind about the boats the Confederacy should be building.

Not long after the Confederate capital was moved from Montgomery to Richmond, Mallory received a visit from the Tift brothers, Nelson and Asa, who came carrying a wooden model of a boat they proposed building for the Confederate navy. Asa was a wrecker—a salvager of cargoes from wrecked ships—who lived in Key West and operated a shipyard there. Nelson was a businessman, newspaper publisher and politician who lived in Albany, Georgia, the town he had founded. The vessel that the Tifts had designed and had made a model of captured the imagination of Secretary Mallory. On September 1, 1861, he wrote in his diary: "I have concluded to build a large warship at N. Orleans upon Nelson Tift's plan, & I will push it."[11] The result was the construction of the CSS *Mississippi*, 260 feet long, fifty-eight feet in the beam, weighing more than six thousand tons, drawing fourteen feet of water, driven by three eleven-foot propellers, powered by three steam engines, designed to mount twenty guns and to make fourteen knots, and clad with three-inch-thick iron plates. Above the main deck was a gallery from which sharpshooters could fire small arms on the crewmen of enemy vessels. Final plans for the boat were drawn up in September, and the first plank was laid on October 14, 1861.

At the same time, work was proceeding on another large Confederate ironclad, the *Louisiana*, according to a design conceived by Kentucky boatbuilder E.C. Murray. The Confederate congress in August had approved the $126,000 needed for the vessel's construction, which was to take place at Jefferson City, Louisiana, near New Orleans, in a boatyard adjacent to where the hull of the *Mississippi* was taking form. Machinery to propel the *Louisiana* was to be made by the Patterson Iron Works in New Orleans, where the *Mississippi*'s machinery was also being built, but the drive shafts had to be cast at three different foundries and transported to New Orleans, all those manufacturing efforts constituting a monumental undertaking. The *Louisiana* was designed to be 264 feet long, sixty-four feet in the beam, weigh more than two thousand tons and draw six feet of water. The casemate containing the twenty-two guns planned for it would slope up at a 45-degree angle, and the boat's sides, bow and stern would be shielded by two layers of interlocking railroad rails, the best the builder could do without a rolling mill to flatten iron into plates. The vessel would be driven by two twenty-seven-foot paddle wheels, mounted one behind the other in the stern half of the boat and within the casemate enclosure. Under the terms of the contract, the boat was to be completed by January 1862.

In August 1861 the Confederate congress ordered the construction of two ironclad rams, their design to copy that of the *Merrimack* (or *Virginia*). The two new ironclads were to be 165 feet long and thirty-five feet in the beam, with an eleven-and-a-half-foot draft, driven by twin propellers powered separately by two steam engines. Each vessel was to be armed with nine guns and carry a crew of two hundred men. The two boats, named the *Tennessee* and the *Arkansas*, were intended to be completed by December 24, 1861, but the shortage of materials and skilled workmen delayed the start of construction until October, making the December launch date impossible.

In the meantime, Secretary Mallory had relieved the aging Captain Rousseau as commander of Confederate naval forces on the Mississippi and appointed Captain George N. Hollins, like Rousseau, a veteran of the War of 1812, to replace him. Hollins ordered the construction of three wooden gunboats, which were never completed, and purchased seven wooden, side-wheeler river steamers that he planned to convert into gunboats. Other steamboats were drafted into service, some as transports, some to carry troops who would engage the enemy with small-arms fire or board the Union vessels in hand-to-hand combat, and others to join the Confederate fleet as gunboat-rams.

On October 7, 1861, Major General Mansfield Lovell, a native of Washington, D.C., took over the job of commanding Confederate forces in what was designated Department No. 1, comprising the gulf coast from Florida to Louisiana, up to the Texas line. Upon assuming his post in New Orleans, he immediately assessed the situation there as troubling, finding the city ill equipped to defend itself or to provide supplies for other points likely to need them. He lacked confidence in the ability of the forts that stood guard on opposite sides of the Mississippi below New Orleans, Fort Jackson and Fort St. Philip, to protect the city against an attack from the Gulf of Mexico. He was further bothered by the Confederate navy's failure to speedily prepare to meet the increasing threat of the Union fleet upriver.

Those weaknesses in the Confederates' defense system on the lower Mississippi Lovell pointed out to Judah Benjamin, the newly appointed Confederate secretary of war and a native of Louisiana, in a letter dated October 18. Replying, Benjamin asked Lovell to offer suggestions. Lovell proposed acquiring river steamers—towboats—and converting them to warships by mounting guns on them and building onto their bows large rams that could pierce the wooden hulls of the Union's slower-moving ironclad gunboats.

On January 9, 1862, the Confederate congress passed two bills authorizing the fleet that Lovell proposed. The legislation spelled out that the vessels to be acquired — by purchase or impressment — were

> not to be part of the navy, for the [congress's] acts intend a service on the rivers, and will be composed of the steamboat-men of the Western waters. The expedition is to be subject to the general command of the military chief of the department where it may be ordered to operate, but the boats will be commanded by steamboat captains and manned by steamboat crews, who will be armed with such weapons as the captains may choose, and the boats will be fitted out as the respective captains may desire. The intention and design are to strengthen the vessels with iron casing at the bows, and to use them at high speed to run down, or run over and sink, if possible, the gunboats and mortar rafts prepared by the enemy for attack at our river defenses.
>
> These gunboats and mortar rafts have been protected so far by iron plates and by their peculiar construction as to offer ... but small chances our being able to arrest their descent of the river by shot or shell, while at the same time, their weight, their unwieldy construction and their slow movement, together with the fact that they show very little surface above the water-line, render them peculiarly liable to the mode of attack devised by the enterprising captains who have undertaken to effect their destruction by running them down....
>
> It is not proposed to rely on cannon, which these men are not skilled in using, nor on fire-arms. The men will be armed with cutlasses. On each boat, however, there will be one heavy gun, to be used in case the stern of any of the gunboats [rams] should be exposed to fire, for they are entirely unprotected behind; and if attempting to escape by flight, would be very vulnerable by shot from a pursuing vessel.[12]

The legislation also appropriated one million Confederate dollars to pay for the vessels, to be spent at the discretion of the secretary of war or secretary of the navy. Thus was created the River Defense Fleet, the Confederacy's civilian navy which was intended to defend the Mississippi River and its vital ports against the constriction of General Scott's anaconda. For the sake of effectiveness and common sense, General Lovell urged that the fleet be placed under the overall command of an experienced navy officer. He worried that "fourteen Mississippi captains and pilots would never agree about anything after they once got under way."[13]

His plea went unheeded. Time would soon show with what effects it was ignored.

4. River-Borne Warriors

To replace John Rodgers as commander of the Union's slowly swelling Western river fleet, Navy Secretary Gideon Welles chose Captain Andrew Hull Foote, a career naval officer whose father was a former Connecticut governor and senator, Samuel A. Foot, the "e" being added to the family name by his son. In 1822, at age sixteen, Foote was appointed a midshipman and on his first cruise sailed aboard the *Grampus* to hunt down pirates in the Caribbean Sea. He later served in the Pacific, the Mediterranean and the Atlantic and in 1839 sailed around the world aboard the warship *John Adams*.

Responding to the influence of one of the officers aboard the *Natchez*, on which he was stationed when he was twenty-one, Foote had a life-changing spiritual experience, so deeply felt that he began wondering if he should remain in an occupation that could place him in war and cause him to kill his fellow man. When he spoke with his father about the matter, his father asked him if he thought a navy was necessary for the country. "Certainly," young Foote answered.

"Then should the navy be in the hands of good men or bad men?" his father asked.

The answer he gave his father was the answer he himself needed to hear. "Of good men," he replied. He decided to stay in the Navy.

His increased sensitivity fostered in him an intense abhorrence of slavery and the slave trade, which he saw for himself when stationed in West Africa as commander of the *Perry* in 1849 and 1850. "If there is anything on earth which, for revolting, filthy atrocity, might make the devil wonder and hell recognize its own likeness," he wrote in describing his experiences, "it was on one of the decks of the old slavers."[1] In 1850 he was complimented for putting out of business the slave ship *Martha*, which he seized off the African coast.

His religious convictions also made of him an advocate of temperance, to the point that, encouraged by the ship's captain, he organized an abstinence society aboard the frigate *Cumberland*. First the officers and then the crewmen joined it, all but one seaman agreeing to forgo his grog ration in exchange for its cash equivalent. The idea was officially deemed such a good one that in 1862 the Navy abolished the obligatory grog ration.

On occasion, Foote also preached sermons to the crews of vessels on which he served. His religious fervor, however, made him no less a warrior. In China in November 1856, Foote was ordered to withdraw the flotilla he commanded, the flagship *Portsmouth* and two other warships, from the vicinity of Whampoa (Huangpu), situated on an island in the Pearl River, below the city of Canton, where the flotilla had been stationed to protect American property during the Opium War between China and England. The withdrawal was ordered to avoid having the U.S. ships drawn into the conflict. While the U.S. vessels were withdrawing, their American flags flying, two of them were twice fired upon by the four Chinese forts guarding the river. Receiving no explanation or apology from the Chinese for their attack on the American vessels, Foote, on his own initiative, put ashore a force of more than two hundred Marines and seamen that stormed the forts and destroyed them after three days of fighting.

At the time that Fort Sumter was surrendered, Foote, fifty-five years old, his broad, weathered face framed by dark, wavy hair and a short, gray beard, was commandant of the Brooklyn Navy Yard. In July he was promoted to captain and in August he was ordered to take over the Western rivers fleet. He reported to General Frémont on September 5 and on September 12 arrived in Cairo to relieve Commander Rodgers, who declined Foote's invitation to remain with the river squadron and instead requested a transfer to the Navy's Atlantic fleet, which was granted.

By then, warfare on the rivers had already begun. On September 4 the Confederate gunboat *Jackson*, the converted tugboat *Yankee*, had fired on the Union timberclad gunboats *Tyler* and *Lexington* while they were reconnoitering the Mississippi below Cairo. The same two timberclads, along with the *Conestoga*, had escorted General Grant's transports to Paducah, and on September 10 the *Conestoga* and the *Lexington* were sent down the Mississippi to cover the movement of Union troops from Norfolk, Missouri, and had fired on a rebel force gathered at Lucas Bend, Missouri. Lieutenant S.L. Phelps, commanding the *Conestoga*, described the action in his report to Captain Foote, his new commander:

> I ... discovered the enemy in force ... and immediately opened fire upon their artillery and cavalry. The enemy had about sixteen pieces of field artillery, and, it is believed, one heavy piece in battery. Several of their pieces were rifled cannon, and ranged to and beyond this vessel, striking all about her. In a short time Commander Stembel, hearing our guns, came down with the *Lexington*, and joined the fight.
>
> The rebels moved their batteries from point to point, while we availed ourselves of our motive power to move up stream as the enemy would attempt to move up.... Their force of cavalry was considerable, and I fired several shells among them with great apparent effect. The shell and shot of both our vessels were lodged among their batteries....
>
> Two steamers of the enemy had come up from Columbus, one of them the gun-boat *Yankee*, which also opened fire on us; but I found our guns could not reach them where they lay below the batteries. At about two o'clock I again dropped down with this vessel, determined to try a shot again at the rebel gun-boat. The first shot must have struck her on the ricochet, as it touched the water close alongside, and she at once started down stream.
>
> The *Lexington* again came up, and, it is believed, succeeded in landing an 8-inch shell in the *Yankee*'s wheel-house and side, where it burst. At all events, the vessel appeared to be greatly injured, and went off with but one engine working. She retired under the batteries at Columbus, where the other one had previously gone. Our boats again opened fire on the enemy's batteries, and before five o'clock we had silenced them entirely, driven their force out of reach, and without any injury to ourselves. I am satisfied we did great damage to the enemy....[2]

Four days after arriving at Cairo, Foote was sent a note from General Frémont, indicating that he was to get on with the river fleet's mission as speedily as possible and without much direction from headquarters. "In consequence of the duties which press upon my attention," Frémont wrote on September 16, "I am necessarily forced to trust much to your discretion. You will, therefore, in the duty confided to you, use your own judgment in carrying out the ends of government. Spare no effort to accomplish the object in view with the least possible delay."[3]

Within a week of receiving that message, Captain Foote himself steamed into the war. On the steamer *Bee*, escorted by the *Lexington*, and under instructions from General Grant, he left from Cairo on a mission to dispose of a reported rebel artillery emplacement at Owensboro, Kentucky, which threatened to block passage on the Ohio. He found no artillery batteries, however, and returned to Cairo from a fruitless mission.

During the following weeks, Foote's gunboats were feeling their way into the conflict and their role in it, probing the Tennessee and Cumberland, patrolling the lower Ohio and reconnoitering the Mississippi. On October 18 Lieutenant Phelps, the most vigorous of Foote's gunboat commanders, having ascended the Tennessee River aboard the *Conestoga*, reported vital intelligence on Fort Henry, the rebel fortification on the Tennessee, soon to become an important strategic objective in the Union's intended drive down the Mississippi valley. On October 28 Phelps reported to Foote the gunboats' involvement in the raid at Eddyville, Kentucky:

> On the afternoon of the 26th instant, by order of General [Charles F.] Smith, I left this place in company with the steamer *Lake Erie*, No. 2, on board of which were three companies of the Ninth Illinois Regiment, under command of Major Phillips, and proceeded up the Cumberland River upon an expedition to surprise a rebel camp near Eddyville, Kentucky, and have the honor to make known to you that the result was in the main successful....
>
> The rebels have a complete system of runners established in that section of the country. The transport was, therefore, sent up the Ohio a few miles, and the *Conestoga* followed, an hour later, with two heavy barges in tow. These were cast off on reaching the transport, which was then taken in tow, with the lights out, fires screened, and engines stopped, by which precautions we succeeded in dropping down to Smithland and passing into the Cumberland, without its being suspected, in the darkness of the night, that we had the steamer in tow.
>
> The two boats, after passing to a safe distance, made all speed up the narrow and crooked stream, but did not reach and disembark the troops at the point selected, two miles below Eddyville, till half-past three o'clock A.M. I then had the transport moved to near the town and concealed behind a wooded point, while this boat was quietly anchored off the main street....
>
> As soon as I felt satisfied that Major Phillips had had time to reach the rebel camp ... I threw a force on shore and surrounded the town with picket-guards, to prevent the escape of rebel citizens, or the entrance and concealment of refugees from the rebel camp.
>
> About 10 A.M., Major Phillips reached town with a number of prisoners, horses, wagons, arms, etc. He had got to within four hundred yards of the enemy after daylight before being discovered, when the rebels formed in line. Our troops were moved at a double-quick to within one hundred yards, when they delivered their fire and charged bayonets upon the rebels, who broke and fled in every direction, leaving seven killed on the field. Two of our soldiers were severely wounded, and one or two slightly....
>
> There were taken in the rebel camp and brought to this place, where we returned last evening, twenty-four prisoners, seven Negroes, thirty-four horses, eleven mules, two transport wagons, a large number of saddles, muskets, rifles, shot-guns, sabres, knives, etc....[4]

On November 5, General Grant received information that the Confederates were preparing to send a large force from Columbus down the Mississippi by boat and then up the White River in Arkansas to reinforce the army of Major General Sterling Price in southern Missouri. Grant had already ordered a detachment under the command of Colonel Richard Oglesby to march south to prevent Price from being reinforced, and now General Fremont ordered him to prevent the rebels' movement from Columbus if possible. Grant promptly instructed Brigadier General Charles F. Smith, in command at Paducah, to move all the troops he could spare immediately toward Columbus, halt them a few miles outside the town and await further orders.

Grant then, on November 6, embarked on steamers at Cairo some three thousand troops, including five infantry regiments, two cavalry companies and a detail of artillerymen to service the two guns that were also loaded aboard the steamers. Escorting the transports would be two of the three timberclad gunboats under Captain Foote's command, the *Taylor* and the *Lexington*. The convoy steamed down the Mississippi to a spot on the Kentucky side about six miles above Columbus, where Grant sent ashore a detail to set up a line of pickets that would make contact with the troops coming from Paducah.

Although he had no thoughts of attacking the Confederate position at Columbus, it being strongly fortified, armed with more than a hundred pieces of artillery and manned by a garrison estimated at forty thousand troops, Grant, seeing the elation of his officers and men at the prospect of at last confronting the rebels, realized that he would have to make some sort of move against the enemy. "I did not see how I could maintain discipline," he wrote in his memoir, "or retain the confidence of my command, if we should return to Cairo without an effort to do something."[5]

Early the next day, November 7, at about two o'clock in the morning, he learned that Confederate troops from Columbus were crossing the Mississippi, presumably to catch up to Oglesby's column and attack it. Grant decided to hit the rebels' rear, diverting their attention from the Union column. He hastily planned a lightning assault on the camp the Confederates had established at Belmont, Missouri, opposite Columbus, where Confederate General Polk had positioned an infantry regiment, a squadron of cavalry and a battery of artillery. Grant's intention was to overwhelm and destroy the camp, then reboard his transports and head back to Cairo.

A drawing of the Battle of Belmont. The battle, the first waged on the Mississippi River, was fought on November 7, 1861, after Brig. Gen. U.S. Grant landed twenty-five hundred troops on the Missouri shore opposite the Confederate fortification at Columbus, Kentucky, in order to prevent a rebel attack on a Union column moving southward through Missouri (Library of Congress).

He quickly began retrieving the pickets from outside Columbus and sent the *Taylor* and the *Lexington* down the river to engage the Confederate batteries at Columbus to draw their attention from the landing near Belmont. The gunboats, however, ran into heavy fog before reaching Columbus and were forced to turn around and return to the spot where they had started. There they waited until six A.M., then moved out from the Kentucky shore in the early daylight, taking the lead as the convoy of troop-carrying transports steamed down the river. About an hour later the transports pulled up to the west bank, out of range of the Confederate guns at Columbus. There, a mile or more above Belmont, Grant disembarked some twenty-five hundred men, his eager troops surging ashore under the protection of Foote's gunboats.

General Grant described the landing site: "The ground on the west shore of the river, opposite Columbus, is low and in places marshy and cut up with sloughs. The soil is rich and the timber large and heavy. There were some small clearings between Belmont and the point where we landed, but most of the country was covered with the native forests. We landed in front of a cornfield."[6]

While the troops were still streaming off the transports, Grant led one regiment down along the river and positioned the men in a hollow in the woods below a clearing. Along with Foote's gunboats, they would guard the transport steamers and prevent the main body of Grant's troops from being taken by surprise by the rebels below them. By now the boats disgorging Union troops had been observed from Columbus, but facing a possible threat from the force that had arrived from Paducah, the Confederates at Columbus made no immediate response to Grant's movements.

About eight A.M. Grant began marching the main body of his force westward through the woods, intending to flank the rebel encampment. After about a mile and a half, he halted the troops in a marshy, densely wooded area, faced them to the left and sent out a large detail of skirmishers to move ahead of the main body. They soon encountered the Confederate skirmishers sent out to confront Grant's force. With a sudden exchange of gunfire, the Battle of Belmont began.

The two Union gunboats meanwhile slipped closer to Columbus and opened fire on the Confederate gun emplacements. The Confederates returned the fire, directing their fire not only at the gunboats but at the transports. "Their shot passed over us," Commander Henry Walke, captain of the *Taylor*, reported, "though in some instances coming very close to us. At this time, with their long-range rifled cannon, they sent a large number of shot half a mile above the transports."[7] At that, the gunboats withdrew back to the transports and advised the captains to move farther up the river, out of range of the rebel guns.

Growing steadily more fierce, the fighting ashore raged for four hours as the rebels were slowly forced back toward their camp. When Grant's horse was shot from under him, he borrowed a mount from one of his staff officers and continued to press his men forward until at last the Confederates were forced back to the clearing where their tents were pitched. At that point they bolted for the riverbank, which rose high and steep from the river and shielded them from the sight and fire of the pursuing Union troops.

The gunboats had moved farther downriver, stopping nearly a quarter of a mile closer to the rebel guns, and were firing again on the Confederate gun positions. One of the rebels' 24-pounders struck the *Taylor*'s starboard side, decapitating one of the crewmen and wounding two others, one seriously. The *Taylor* got off several more rounds, then headed upriver again, firing its stern guns as it withdrew.

When Grant's men, having made their way through the Confederates' abatis, reached the rebel campsite, instead of forcing the surrender of the Confederate troops, who lay trapped between the steep riverbank and the water's edge, they put aside their weapons and went on a wild rampage through the camp, ransacking the enemy's tents, scavenging whatever trophies and souvenirs they thought worth grabbing. "Some of the higher officers," Grant complained, "were little better than the privates."[8]

Unable to bring order back to the reveling troops, Grant finally called his staff officers together and ordered them to set fire to the rebel camp. Soon flames and smoke were rising into the air, and the Confederate guns at Columbus for the first time opened fire on the campsite, the rebel gunners realizing the site had fallen into enemy hands. At the same time, transports laden with gray-clad Confederate soldiers were steaming from Columbus and landing below Belmont, rushing troops across the river to reinforce and rescue their trapped comrades. A report that they were surrounded spread rapidly through the scattered mass of Union troops, and suddenly their attention was arrested. "The guns of the enemy and the report of being surrounded brought officers and men completely under control," Grant related. "At first some of the officers seemed to think that to be surrounded was to be placed in a hopeless position, where there was nothing to do but surrender. But when I announced that we had cut our way in and could cut our way out just as well, it seemed a new revelation to officers and soldiers."[9]

Grant ordered the men into formation, sent out skirmishers and took his force, now outnumbered by three thousand rebel reinforcements under the command of General Pillow and Brigadier General B.F. Cheatham, back through the thick woods and through the field of towering cornstalks, hurriedly moving them toward the transports and gunboats waiting for them upriver, the pursuing Confederates, concealed by the woods and the cornfield, at their back and on their flank.

The Union troops poured onto the waiting transports, the wounded being among the last to be taken aboard. As one contingent of Confederates drew close to the transports, threatening them, the *Taylor* and the *Lexington* turned their guns on the rebel troops, firing grape shot, canister shot and five-inch shells into them, stopping their advance and silencing their guns.

One of the last to board the boats was General Grant himself. Arriving at the river's edge on his horse, Grant was recognized by the captain of a steamer that had already shoved off from the riverbank but stopped and ran out a gangplank for Grant to come aboard. "My horse put his fore feet over the bank without hesitation or urging," Grant related, "and with his hind feet well under him, slid down the bank and trotted aboard the boat, twelve or fifteen feet away, over a single gang plank."[10] Having safely reached the deck of the departing steamer, Grant swung out of the saddle of his plucky mount and climbed the steps to the upper deck as rebel rifle fire riddled the smokestack and peppered the superstructure while the vessel, along with the other transports, sped out into the river and Captain Foote's gunboats vigorously returned the Confederates' fire.

"We were very soon out of range," Grant wrote in his memoir — neglecting to note that the steamers later had to stop and take aboard the Twenty-seventh Illinois Infantry Regiment, which had got itself separated from the main body — "and went peacefully on our way to Cairo, every man feeling that Belmont was a great victory and that he had contributed his share to it."[11]

Grant's casualties totaled 120 men killed, 104 captured and 383 wounded, many of whom fell into enemy hands. The Confederates, who claimed victory after having routed the Union force from the field, suffered 105 killed, 419 wounded and 117 missing.

Although Grant was criticized by Northern newspapers for having waged an unnecessary fight that had no lasting results, he was convinced that it was a worthwhile success. "The two objects for which the battle of Belmont was fought were fully accomplished. The enemy gave up all idea of detaching troops from Columbus" to attack Colonel Oglesby's force, and "the National troops acquired a confidence in themselves at Belmont that did not desert them through the war."[12] He insisted that if the battle had not been fought, "Colonel Oglesby would probably have been captured or destroyed with his three thousand men. Then I should have been culpable indeed."[13]

On the day after the battle General Grant met with some of the officers of General Polk's command and arranged to have Grant's men bury their dead. An exchange of prisoners was also worked out by officers of the two sides, their friendly meeting being hosted by the Confederates, who served lunch to the Union officers and joined them in the meal.

Meanwhile, changes were occurring in the Union's chain of command. On October 31, the gallant old general in chief of the Army, Winfield Scott — seventy-five years old, in rapidly failing health and physical condition, his voice no longer heeded or believed needed, upstaged by the vigorously ambitious Major General George B. McClellan — wrote and dispatched a letter to Secretary of War Simon Cameron, stating, "I am compelled to request that my name be placed on the list of army officers retired from active service."[14] The next morning Lincoln and his cabinet met and unanimously agreed to honor General Scott's request. Later that day the president and the cabinet members held a brief ceremony for the general in Scott's quarters. Lincoln read the document that released General Scott from active duty and that expressed a "profound sense of the important public services rendered by him to his country during his long and brilliant career, among which will ever be gratefully distinguished his faithful devotion to the Constitution, the Union and the flag when assailed by parricidal rebellion."[15]

To replace Scott as general in chief, President Lincoln selected not Major General Henry W. Halleck, as Scott had expected, but instead gave the appointment to McClellan, who earlier had expressed his feelings about General Scott in a letter to his wife, Ellen McClellan, saying, "I do not know whether he is a dotard or a traitor! I can't tell which. He cannot or will not comprehend the condition in which we are placed and is entirely unequal to the emergency.... He is a perfect imbecil [sic]. He understands nothing, appreciates nothing, and is ever in my way."[16]

Before dawn on November 2, the morning following the simple retirement ceremony, General Scott, accompanied by Secretary of War Cameron and a clutch of supporters, boarded a train at Union Station in Washington and left for New York. In the company of a mounted escort, General McClellan, who had done his best to undermine Scott, was one of the many who came to see him off.

Two days after the Battle of Belmont, on November 9, 1861, Major General Henry Wager Halleck, known to fellow officers as "Old Brains," a nickname applied in disparagement, was appointed to replace Major General David Hunter as commander of the Department of the Missouri, the former Department of the West having been reorganized into two departments, the Missouri and the Ohio. Grant and Foote now would be reporting to General Halleck. Old Brains.

Foote, who was promoted to the rank of flag officer on November 13, considered Halleck's appointment so great a grievance that he asked to be transferred to a coastal command. General Grant's distress over Halleck's appointment, surpassing Foote's, was soon to come.

Part II: 1862

5. Target on the Tennessee

As General Grant studied his maps, he could see that the Confederates had established a line of defense that ran through Kentucky from Columbus, where it was anchored on the bluffs above the Mississippi River, eastward to Bowling Green and on to Mill Springs. Each of those three locations had been heavily fortified by the rebels. Grant could also see the paths of the Tennessee and Cumberland rivers streaming toward him at Cairo, highways into the South, twisting through Kentucky and into the state of Tennessee, the two rivers at times running practically parallel, the Cumberland diverging and sweeping across northern Tennessee, the Tennessee plunging through Tennessee and into northern Alabama.

Near the Kentucky-Tennessee state line, west of Clarksville, Tennessee, the two rivers, less than fifteen miles apart at that point, were defended by Confederate fortifications, Fort Heiman and Fort Henry opposite each other on the Tennessee River, and Fort Donelson on the Cumberland, all three positioned to forbid passage to Union forces coming up the rivers. Rebel engineers had begun laying them out within a month after the Confederate assault on Fort Sumter.

"These positions were of immense importance to the enemy," Grant concluded, "and of course correspondingly important for us to possess ourselves of. With Fort Henry in our hands we had a navigable stream open to us up to Muscle Shoals, in Alabama. The Memphis and Charleston Railroad strikes the Tennessee at Eastport, Mississippi, and follows close to the banks of the river up to the shoals. This [rail] road, of vast importance to the enemy, would cease to be of use to them for through traffic the moment Fort Henry became ours.

"Fort Donelson," Grant went on, "was the gate to Nashville — a place of great military and political importance — and to a rich country extending far east into Kentucky. [With] these two points in our possession the enemy would necessarily be thrown back to the Memphis and Charleston [rail] road, or to the boundary of the cotton states, and, as before stated, that road would be lost to them for through communication."[1]

By early January of 1862 Grant's military jurisdiction had been shifted eastward from southeast Missouri to an area designated the District of Cairo, which included the mouths of the Tennessee and Cumberland rivers. On January 6, with that area now within the scope of his responsibility, he was ordered by the Army's new general in chief, General McClellan, through General Halleck's headquarters, to make a show of strength in western Kentucky. Brigadier General Don Carlos Buell, commander of the Union Army's Department of the Ohio, was expected to engage a large Confederate force, commanded by Major General Simon Bolivar Buckner, at Bowling Green, and Grant was to make menacing moves to prevent rebel reinforcements from Columbus or Fort Henry or Fort Donelson from reaching Buckner.

Responding to his instructions, Grant ordered Brigadier General Charles F. Smith to take a force from Paducah up the west bank of the Tennessee River to threaten Fort Heiman and Fort Henry while a six-thousand-man brigade under Brigadier General John A. McClernand marched south from Cairo and then split into two columns, one heading for Columbus, the other proceeding up along the Tennessee River. At the same time, another Union brigade, commanded by Brigadier General Eleazar A. Paine, would march from Bird's Point, Missouri, on the Mississippi River opposite Cairo, to a position directly across the river from the Confederate fortification at Columbus.

It was mostly for show. Grant had no orders to actually engage the rebels. Even so, as eager for action as were his men, Grant accompanied McClernand's force, suffering, along with the troops, bad weather and difficult roads that turned into soft, wet mud under the steady rain and snow. After more than a week of slogging through the muddy mush he and his troops returned to Cairo without having done much, but with Grant satisfied that their mission had been accomplished. "The enemy did not send reinforcements to Bowling Green, and," he wrote, citing an unrelated but important Union victory, "[Brigadier] General George H. Thomas fought and won the battle of Mill Springs before we returned."[2]

The expedition had achieved another result, of greater significance. General Smith had returned from his reconnaissance up the west bank of the Tennessee River and reported to Grant that from what he had seen of Fort Heiman, which was still under construction, he thought it could be captured. It stood on high ground on the west bank of the river, commanding Fort Henry on the east side of the river, and its possession by Union forces would likely ensure the capture of Fort Henry as well.

Smith's report confirmed what Grant had already determined. His maps showed that "the true line of operations for us," as he said, "was up the Tennessee and Cumberland rivers. With us there, the enemy would be compelled to fall back on the east and west entirely out of the state of Kentucky."[3] Before being ordered on the recent expedition, Grant had written to General Halleck on January 6 asking permission to come to St. Louis so that he could present to Halleck his plan to gain control of the Tennessee and Cumberland.

The request had gone unanswered. Now, encouraged by General Smith's report, Grant tried again. This time General Halleck granted him leave, "but not graciously," Grant related. Grant had known Halleck, as he said, "but very slightly in the old army, not having met him either at West Point or during the Mexican war."[4] He was about to know him better.

Forty-seven years old at the time, Halleck — Old Brains — had a reputation as a scholar and a military theoretician. A lawyer as well as an Army officer, he had authored a book on international law and the law of war. He had made money as a land developer in California and had been instrumental in gaining California's admission as a state. He had ability as an administrator, but as a commander of troops, he proved to be overcautious and indecisive, better at evading responsibility than at commanding an army or understanding strategy. President Lincoln, who developed a low opinion of him, described Halleck as "little more than a first-rate clerk."[5] Photographic portraits show him with a high forehead, gray, wavy hair that fell over the tops of his ears, long sideburns, a stocky build and an expression of bemusement on his fleshy face.

Grant's meeting with Halleck did not go well. "I was received with so little cordiality that I perhaps stated the object of my visit with less clearness than I might have done," Grant recounted, "and I had not uttered many sentences before I was cut short as if my plan was preposterous. I returned to Cairo very much crestfallen."[6]

In Cairo, Grant discussed the proposal with Flag Officer Foote, with whom he got along well, the two of them making a sort of philosophical odd couple, as one Civil War author observed, Foote's two strongest hatreds being slavery and strong drink and Grant having an aversion to neither.[7] "He and I consulted freely upon military matters," Grant allowed, "and he agreed with me perfectly as to the feasibility of the campaign up the Tennessee."[8]

Foote's river squadron by now had grown to include not only the three timberclad gunboats but the seven Eads-built ironclad gunboats as well as the *Benton* and the *Essex*, the two snag boats that had been converted into ironclad gunboats, plus thirty-eight mortar boats, or barges, a number of tow boats and sundry other vessels. It had become a formidable fleet, although so short of crewmen that not all the vessels could be manned. Grant's plan was to make full use of the fleet in his proposed campaign up the Tennessee and Cumberland, and Foote, no less aggressive or energetic than Grant, was eager to participate.

Foote would be operating with the benefit of the intelligence gathered by Lieutenant Phelps, commander of the *Conestoga*, who at least three times had steamed up the Tennessee as far as Fort Henry, about sixty miles upriver from Paducah. Those reconnaissances had been made on October 12 and more recently on January 7 and on January 16 through 18. The January 7 reconnaissance had included a feint attack on Fort Henry to discover the location and strength of its defenses.

Having recovered from his rebuff by General Halleck, Grant on January 28 renewed his request for permission to attack Fort Henry, telegraphing Old Brains and telling him that "if permitted, I could take and hold Fort Henry on the Tennessee."[9] On the same day, Flag Officer Foote also wired Halleck: "General Grant and myself are of the opinion that Fort Henry, on the Tennessee River, can be carried with four iron-clad gun-boats and troops, and be permanently occupied. Have we your authority to move for that purpose when ready?"[10]

The next day, January 29, Grant again wrote to Halleck, this time providing more detail about the proposed expedition. On February 1 Grant received, as he said, "full instructions from department headquarters to move upon Fort Henry." Old Brains apparently had finally seen the light.

On the morning of Sunday, February 2, the expedition force started out from Cairo. The little fleet that bore it was composed of seven of Foote's gunboats and the several transports that would carry Grant's 17,000 troops. Grant had learned that there were not enough steamers, or crewmen, in Cairo to take the entire force up the Tennessee in one convoy, and so he embarked more than half his troops and sent them up to Paducah, where the transports would disembark them and then return to Cairo for the remainder of the force. The first division was under the command of General McClernand. The second was commanded by General Smith. Grant followed the first division in a vessel at its rear. Steaming ahead of the transports were the gunboats of Flag Officer Foote.

Grant wanted to land the troops as close to Fort Henry as possible but still stay beyond the range of its guns. He particularly wanted to put the men ashore on the fort side of a stream that emptied into the Tennessee north of the fort. Ordinarily, Grant guessed, the stream would be easily fordable, but now, swollen from weeks of rain, it presented a significant obstacle to his troops. To see for himself if putting them ashore where he wanted was feasible, Grant boarded the gunboat *Essex* to move up the river toward Fort Henry and draw fire from the fort. The *Essex* steamed past the mouth of the stream and after a distance farther came under fire from Fort Henry. The shots fell way short, splashing into the muddy river far in front of the vessel, letting Grant believe he could put his first division ashore at that point, on the fort side of the creek. The rebel fort then opened fire with a rifled gun that sent a shot far beyond the *Essex* and beyond the stream. Another shot passed close to where the gunboat's captain — Commander William Porter — and Grant were standing. It struck the vessel near the stern, passed through the cabin and fell into the river.

The *Essex* immediately turned around and hurried back downstream. Grant had learned what he needed to know. He ordered the troops of the first division to be landed on the side of the stream farthest from the fort, out of the rifled gun's range.

Fort Henry stood in a dog-leg bend of the Tennessee River on its east bank in Stewart County, Tennessee, and was connected to Fort Donelson, eleven miles away on the west bank of the Cumberland, by a road that led also to the town of Dover, the county seat, about two miles up the river, or south, from Fort Donelson. Built on low, marshy ground, Fort Henry was subject to flooding when the Tennessee River rose out of its banks, as it had now, engorged by weeks of rain. Part of the ground on which the fort stood was now two feet deep in water. Below the fort, the floodwater extended from the river into the woods for a distance of several hundred yards.

Fort Henry was a strong, skillfully built, five-sided earthwork covering ten acres, with ramparts about twenty feet thick at their base and tapering up to a thickness of ten feet at their top. Its five bastions were four to six feet high, and its artillery embrasures were stoutly framed with sandbags. Its armament consisted of seventeen heavy guns, including one ten-inch (120-pounder) columbiad, one 24-pounder rifle, twelve 32-pounders, two 12-pounders and one 24-pounder siege gun. Six of the guns were placed to protect the fort from an assault by land. The eleven others protected the river, commanding a stretch of the Tennessee below the fort, as Grant had discovered, up to a distance of about two miles.

Within the fort's walls were barracks and tents to accommodate as many as fifteen thousand men, although the garrison now numbered only about three thousand, including those men entrenched in rifle pits and outworks that extended some two miles back along the road to Fort Donelson and Dover. In addition, according to General Grant's intelligence, a sizeable body of reinforcements from Fort Donelson stood waiting on that road several miles away.

In command of Fort Henry was Confederate Brigadier General Lloyd Tilghman, a dashing figure in his tailored, pearl-gray uniform, dark hair hiding his ears, mustached and goateed. He was forty-six years old, born in Claiborne, Maryland, in January 1816, the son of a Revolutionary War lieutenant colonel. A West Point graduate who had finished near the bottom of his class in 1836, he had resigned his commission after three months of service, had worked as a construction engineer for several railroads, had re-entered the Army as an artillery captain, had resigned again after a year and in 1852 had moved to Paducah, where he was living when General Grant captured the city in September of 1861. He was commissioned colonel of the Third Kentucky Infantry Regiment on July 5, 1861, and was made a brigadier general in the Confederate army on October 18, 1861.

Because of his construction experience, Tilghman was given the job of supervising the construction of Fort Henry and Fort Donelson, although he had had nothing to do with the selection of the sites. "Wretched" was the way he described the Fort Henry site. On completion of the forts, he remained as commandant of Fort Henry.

Once all of his troops had been brought up from Paducah by the steamers, Grant planned to move them against Fort Henry and Fort Heiman simultaneously, in concert with the gunboats' artillery assault. As late as ten o'clock on the night of February 5, however, his troops still had not all arrived. Despite that, he continued with his plan, eager to get the operation started before the Confederates had time to reinforce the forts. He issued orders for his army's advance to begin at eleven o'clock the next morning, February 6, feeling sure that the rest of his troops would have arrived by then.

"The plan," he explained, "was for the troops and gunboats to start at the same moment. The troops were to invest the garrison and the gunboats to attack the fort at close quarters. General Smith was to land a brigade of his division on the west bank during the night of the 5th and get it in rear of [Fort] Heiman."[11]

In anticipation of the movement against Fort Henry, Flag Officer Foote had reported to Navy Secretary Gideon Welles on February 3:

> I have the honor to inform you that I left Cairo yesterday with this vessel [the *Taylor*], having ordered the armored gun-boats *Essex*, *Carondelet*, *Cincinnati*, and *St. Louis* to precede me to Paducah, and arrived here [Paducah] last evening.
>
> Today I propose ascending the Tennessee River with the four new armored boats, and the old gun-boats *Taylor*, *Conestoga*, and *Lexington*, in convoy of the troops under General Grant, for the purpose of conjointly attacking and occupying Fort Henry and the railroad bridge connecting Bowling Green with Columbus.... I am ready with the seven gun-boats to act offensively whenever the Army is in condition to advance; and have every confidence, under God, that we shall be able to silence the guns of Fort Henry and its surroundings....
>
> I inclose a copy of my orders to the commanders of the gun-boats in anticipation of the attack on Fort Henry; also a copy of orders to Lieutenant-Commanding Phelps, who will have more especial charge of the old gun-boats, and operate in a less exposed condition than the armored boats. I have the honor to be, etc.,
>
> A.H. FOOTE, Flag-Officer[12]

Foote had carefully thought out how the gunboats should proceed in the assault on Fort Henry. Leaving little to chance, guesswork or the imagination of his gunboat commanders, he spelled out in detail what they were to do:

Order No. 1

The captains of the gun-boats, before going into action, will always see that the hoods covering the gratings of the hatches at the bows and sterns, and elsewhere, are taken off; otherwise great injury will result from the concussion of the guns in firing. The anchors also must be unstocked if they interfere with the range of the bow guns....

In attacking the fort, the first order of steaming will be observed, as by the vessels being parallel they will be much less exposed to the enemy's range than if not in a parallel line; and by moving ahead or astern, which all the vessels will do by following the motions of the flag-ship, it will be difficult for the enemy to get an accurate range of the gun-boats.

Equal distances from one another must be observed by all the vessels in action. The flag-ship will, of course, open the fire first, and then others will follow when good sight of the enemy's guns in the fort can be obtained. There must be no firing until correct sights can be obtained, as this would be not only throwing away ammunition, but it would encourage the enemy to see us firing wildly. The captains will enforce upon their men the absolute necessity of observing this order; and let it be also impressed upon every man firing a gun that, while the first shot may be either of too much elevation or too little, there is no excuse for a second wild fire, as the first will indicate the inaccuracy of the aim of the gun... .

The great object is to dismount the guns in the fort by the accuracy of our fire, although a shell in the mean time may occasionally be thrown in among a body of the enemy's troops.

When the flag-ship ceases firing, it will be a signal for the other vessels also to cease. As the vessels will be all so near one another, verbal communication will be held with the commander-in-chief when it is wanted. The commander-in-chief has every confidence in the spirit and valor of the officers and men under his command, and his only solicitude arises lest the firing should be too rapid for precision, and that coolness and order, so essential to complete success, should not be observed; and hence he has, in this general order, expressed his views, which must be observed by all under his command.

A.H. FOOTE,
Flag-Officer Commanding Naval Forces on Western Waters[13]

His two other general orders specified the positions the gunboats were to take in the river, the ironclads closest to the fort and the timberclads a distance behind them. He also cautioned his commanders against mistaking Union troops for the enemy, and directed the *Conestoga*, *Taylor* and *Lexington*, under the command of Lieutenant Phelps, to steam upriver as soon as Fort Henry surrendered and destroy the railroad bridge above the fort and capture as many Confederate gunboats and other vessels as possible before running into water too shallow for the three timberclads to operate.

During the day on February 5, on the eve of the planned assault, Flag Officer Foote inspected his officers and crews, addressed them and offered a prayer. Later that day a severe storm swept through the area with heavy rain, causing the river to rise higher and to further flood the ground where Grant's troops were bivouacked, compounding the misery of their wet and cold conditions. The bloated river also affected the gunboats, riding at anchor as the swift current threatened to tear them loose and carry them downriver. The *Carondelet* became caught in a mass of debris and fallen trees surging in the flow and was swept down the river, dragging its two anchors for more than half a mile before it could recover and rejoin the other vessels.

The storm waters revealed another menace — torpedoes that the rebels had planted in the river, but which had been torn loose from their moorings by the current and were floating in the stream, their white color making them look, as then–Commander Walke remarked, like polar bears coming down the stream through the fog. They were iron cylinders, five and a half feet long, eighteen inches in diameter, pointed at both ends, each cylinder containing a seventy-five-pound bag of gunpowder, which was exploded by a percussion cap set off when struck by a vessel. They were anchored in the river, just below the surface. To find out if there were more such devices upstream, Flag Officer Foote ordered the *Conestoga* and the *Taylor* to put their lifeboats into the river to search for them and pluck them from the water. Six were found and hauled aboard the lifeboats. On examination, all but one proved ineffective, water having leaked into the cylinders and soaked the gunpowder.

The next morning, Thursday, February 6, dawned cold and wet, and the movement of troops and gunboats began as planned. General McClernand's division advanced up the eastern side of the river to be in position to attack Fort Henry from the rear and to block the flight of the rebel garrison if they attempted to retreat toward Fort Donelson. Two brigades of General Smith's division started moving up the west side of the river to capture Fort Heiman and turn its guns on Fort Henry. The troops on both sides of the river had to march some five miles to reach the forts, and their progress, through mud and water, was slower than expected. The storm had turned every stream into a torrent, repeatedly forcing the men to halt long enough to build hastily erected bridges for the artillery to cross the raging water.

At 10:50 that morning the gunboats received Foote's order to get under way and steam up to Panther Island, which rose from the middle of the river about two miles north of the fort. They steamed along the west side of the island, the four ironclads in the lead, the three timberclads following about a half mile behind. The *Carondelet*'s captain recounted the action:

At 11:35, having passed the foot of the island, we formed in line and approached the fort four abreast—the *Essex* on the right, then the *Cincinnati, Carondelet,* and *St. Louis.* The last two, for want of room, were interlocked, and remained in that position during the fight.

As we slowly passed up this narrow stream, not a sound could be heard or a moving object seen in the dense woods which overhung the dark swollen river. The gun-crews of the *Carondelet* stood silent at their posts, impressed with the serious and important character of the service before them.

About noon the fort and the Confederate flag came suddenly into view, the barracks, the new earthworks, and the great guns well manned.[14]

At half-past noon, after vainly waiting for the arrival of Grant's troops, who were delayed by the floodwater flowing across their line of march, Foote's boats at seventeen hundred yards opened fire with their bow guns, the *Cincinnati,* to which Foote had transferred his flag, firing first and the others immediately following. The fort's guns quickly responded. Steaming to within six hundred yards of Fort Henry's batteries, the ironclads let loose their broadside guns while the fort's gunners vigorously answered. Brigadier General Lewis Wallace, with General Smith's division on the west side of the river, recounted the spectacle of the awesome exchange of fire:

> The guns of the fleet opened while we were yet quite a mile from our objective. Our line of march was nearly parallel with the line of fire to and from the gun-boats. Not more than seven hundred yards separated us from the great shells, in their roaring, fiery passage. Without suffering from their effect, we had the full benefit of their indescribable and terrible noise. Several times I heard the shots of the fort crash against the iron sides of the boats. You can imagine the excitement and martial furor the circumstances were calculated to inspire our men with.[15]

The fort's guns sent shot pounding against the sides of the ironclads. The *Cincinnati,* standing closest to the fort and conspicuous as the flagship because of its pennant, became the main objective of the rebel gunners, who blasted a steady stream of heavy shot against it. One shot hit the side of the boat and ricocheted off, crashing into the front of the *Cincinnati*'s pilothouse while Foote and the boat's captain, along with a midshipman and the vessel's two pilots, were standing in it. The shot failed to penetrate the vessel's iron plating, but left a deep dent in it. The most damaging shots struck the unplated forward upper deck of the vessel. A 32-pound shot came through the ends of the plating at the starboard bow on the lower deck and killed a seaman, then passed through the entire length of the vessel without causing any other damage. The boat's two smokestacks, forward of the pilothouse, were struck as many as ten times, each shot leaving a gaping hole in the metal. Several of the *Cincinnati*'s crewmen were seriously wounded, but only one was killed.

The ironclad *Carondelet* was struck thirty times. The ironclad *St. Louis* was struck seven times. The *Essex,* another of the ironclads, took a hit from a 32-pound shot that struck near one of its bow guns and killed a young officer before penetrating the bulkhead protecting the boiler. It pierced the flue of the center boiler, causing an eruption of scalding steam and water to spray onto everyone on the forward gun deck as well as the two pilots, who were standing directly over the front of the boilers. Twenty-nine of the vessel's officers and crew were scalded, including the captain, Commander Porter. The vessel itself was completely disabled and began drifting downstream, forced out of the fight.

It was Fort Henry though, that took the heaviest beating. With devastating accuracy the gunboats' unceasing fire of shot and explosive shell smashed through the earthworks and sandbags, dismounting and crippling the fort's heavy guns, crumpling buildings and setting others ablaze, toppling trees within the fort's compound, relentlessly raining shot and shrapnel down onto the fort's defenders. Less than an hour after the bombardment had begun, "the scene in and around the fort exhibited a spectacle of fierce grandeur," according to one nineteenth-century account. "Many of the cabins were in flames. Added to this were the curling and dense wreaths of smoke from the guns; the constant whizzing of fragments of crashing and bursting shells; the deafening roar of artillery; the black sides of five or six gun-boats, belching fire at every port-hole; the volumes of smoke settled in dense masses around the back-waters; and up and over that fog on the heights, the army of General Grant deploying around our small army."[16]

An hour and fifteen minutes after the gunboats' assault had begun, General Tilghman decided it was time to end it. "It is vain to fight longer," he is reported to have said to his men. "Our gunners are disabled, our guns dismounted. We can't hold out five minutes longer."[17] He ordered the Confederate flag lowered and a white flag of surrender raised in its place. When the crewmen of Foote's gunboats saw it, they broke into "the wildest excitement," as one account has it, and loud cheers. It was their victory, the U.S. Navy's victory, stunning in its achievement.

The gunboats drew up to Fort Henry and received a deputation from General Tilghman. Flag Officer Foote recorded the events in his report to Navy Secretary Welles:

> A boat, containing the [Confederate] adjutant-general and a captain of engineers, came alongside after the flag was lowered, and reported that General Lloyd Tilghman, the commander of the fort, wished to communicate with the flag-officer, when I dispatched Commander Stembel and Lieutenant-Commanding Phelps, with orders to hoist the American flag where the Secession ensign had been flying, and to inform General Tilghman that I would see him on board the flag-ship. He came on board soon after the Union had been substituted by Commander Stembel for the rebel flag on the fort, and possession taken.
>
> I received the general, his staff, and some sixty or seventy men as prisoners; and a hospital ship containing sixty invalids, together with the fort and its effects ... which I turned ... over to General Grant, commanding the army, on his arrival in an hour after we had made the capture.[18]

Admiral Walke described the scene inside the fort after the Navy had taken possession of it:

> The Confederate surgeon was laboring with his coat off to relieve and save the wounded; and although the officers and crews of the gun-boat gave three hearty cheers when the Confederate flag was hauled down, the first inside view of the fort sufficed to suppress every feeling of exultation and to excite our deepest pity. On every side the blood of the dead and wounded was intermingled with the earth and their implements of war. Their largest gun, a 128-pounder, was dismounted and filled with earth by the bursting of one of our shells near its muzzle; the carriage of another was broken to pieces, and two dead men lay near it, almost covered with heaps of earth; a rifled gun had burst, throwing its mangled gunners into the water. But few of the garrison escaped unhurt.[19]

General Tilghman, having despaired of receiving sufficient reinforcements to help him hold Fort Henry and observing the menace facing him on the river and the overwhelming numbers of Grant's troops threatening him to his rear, on the night of February 5 had ordered all his troops, except for about a hundred men needed to man the fort's guns, out of Fort Henry and had them take a position at the fort's outworks on the road to Fort Donelson and Dover, moving them out of range of the guns of Foote's gunboats. The next morning, before the U.S. Navy's assault began, he ordered them to retreat to Fort Donelson, nearly three thousand men, leaving without a fight. In his report of the battle, General Tilghman stated that his defense of Fort Henry was intended merely to allow his troops time to withdraw to Fort Donelson. Tilghman and ninety of the fort's surviving defenders became Grant's prisoners. Although pursued by Grant's cavalry, Tilghman's retreating troops, with the exception of a few stragglers, managed to escape.

Also escaped was the garrison of Fort Heiman. When General Smith reached the fort, he discovered that it had been abandoned.

Following the capture of Fort Henry, Lieutenant-Commanding Phelps, as ordered by Foote, took the three timberclad gunboats up the Tennessee River. Some twenty-five miles upriver of Fort Henry Phelps left the *Taylor*, the slowest of the three timberclads, at the bridge over which rail traffic between Bowling Green and Columbus must pass. He gave the *Taylor*'s crew the task of ripping up the tracks to prevent the bridge's use by the Confederates, then proceeded farther up the Tennessee with the *Conestoga* and the *Lexington* in pursuit of the rebel vessels that had clustered in the river above Fort Henry and were now fleeing to escape the Union gunboats.

After a five-hour chase, the *Conestoga*, Phelps's vessel, leading the pursuit, closed the distance with several Confederate steamers, and as it drew near to them, the rebel crews set fire to three of their transports and abandoned them. "The first one fired ... very soon exploded," Phelps recorded in his report to Foote. "The second was freighted with powder, cannon, shot, grape, balls, etc. Fearing an explosion from the fired boats ... I had stopped at a distance of one thousand yards; but even there our skylights were broken by the concussion, the light upper deck was raised bodily, doors were forced open, and locks and fastenings every where broken. The whole river, for half a mile about, was completely 'beaten up' by the falling fragments and the shower of shot, grape, balls, etc...."[20]

Phelps ascended the Tennessee all the way to Muscle Shoals and along the way seized three rebel steamers — the *Eastport*, which was in the process of being converted into an ironclad gunboat, the *Sallie Wood* and the *Muscle*. Another Confederate vessel known to be somewhere on the Tennessee escaped capture by hiding in one of the river's tributaries.

The outstanding, history-making performance of Foote's gunboats in the Union's water-borne victory at Fort Henry drew praise from all over the United States, their story detailed in newspapers and their commander fulsomely lauded by the government. Secretary of the Navy Welles, recognizing the significance of the ironclad gunboats in the conduct of the war, sent Foote his official congratulations. "The labor you have performed," Welles wrote, "and the services you have rendered in creating the armed flotilla of gun-boats on the Western waters, and in bringing together for effective operations the force which has already earned such renown, can never be overestimated. The [Navy] Department has observed with no ordinary solicitude the armament that has so suddenly been called into existence, and which under your well-directed management has been so gloriously effective."[21]

From a fellow warrior in the expedition, another tribute came to Foote, which perhaps he found the most gratifying of all:

> Dear Sir, As an acknowledgment of the consummate skill with which you brought your gun-boats into action yesterday, and of the address and bravery displayed by yourself and your command, I have taken the liberty of giving the late "Fort Henry" the new and more appropriate name of "Fort Foote."

Please pardon the liberty I have taken without first securing your concurrence, as I am hardly disposed to do, considering the liberty which you took in capturing the fort without my co-operation.
Very respectfully yours, etc.,
John A. McClernand, Brig.-Gen., Com. First Division[22]

General Grant's report to General Halleck, giving early news of the battle, was brief and hasty: "Fort Henry is ours. The gunboats silenced the batteries before the investment was completed. I think the garrison must have commenced the retreat last night. Our cavalry followed, finding two guns abandoned in the retreat. I shall take and destroy Fort Donelson on the 8th and return to Fort Henry."[23]

On the day after the capture of Fort Henry, Grant and his staff, escorted by a detachment of cavalry, made a reconnaissance to within a mile of the fortified perimeter of Fort Donelson, guardian of the Cumberland, and there he began to plot the next assault on the Confederates' river defenses.

6. *The Assault That Failed*

On Friday morning, February 7, the day after the fall of Fort Henry, the battered, battle-scarred ironclad gunboats *Cincinnati*, *St. Louis* and *Essex* steamed triumphantly into Cairo, their whistles screaming, a captured Confederate flag flapping upside down on the staff of the flagship *Cincinnati*, and a crowd of cheering spectators watching as the returning victors glided up to wharves and docked.

An assessment of the boats' damages was soon made and repairs begun. The *Essex* was found to have suffered damage more extensive than could be repaired at Cairo's limited naval facility, and it was towed to St. Louis to undergo rebuilding there. Idled crewmen from the *Cincinnati* and *Essex* were transferred to the *Louisville* and *Pittsburg* to provide those two undermanned vessels a full complement.

On the Sunday after Fort Henry's capture, February 9, Flag Officer Foote attended the morning worship service at the Presbyterian church in Cairo, as was his custom, and after the congregation had gathered in the pews, it was discovered that the church's pastor was absent. Taking the matter into his own aggressive hands, Foote went to the church elders and suggested that they conduct the service without the preacher. They were not moved to do so. With no further discussion, he turned and strode to the pulpit himself, stood and read from the Scriptures, offered a prayer and launched into a sermon drawn from the words of Jesus recorded in Saint John's gospel, chapter 14, verse 1: "Let not your heart be troubled; ye believe in God, believe also in me."

The congregation listened attentively, apparently pleased with the job Foote was doing. Foote himself, however, was not altogether positive about his impromptu sermonizing and when an Army chaplain, who had slipped into the service after it was under way, congratulated him at the conclusion of the service, Foote, with humility, told the chaplain that he wished he had come forward and volunteered to take over.

The story of his preaching performance spread throughout the community and elsewhere and won him a brief fame. His old friend Commodore [later Admiral] Joseph Smith wrote to him after hearing about it: "My dear Foote.... I hardly know for which vocation to award you the meed of greatest praise, as a first-rate flag-officer, or as a 'preacher'—no matter which, as you are in high estimation in both."[1]

Meanwhile, General Grant was making plans for Foote's flotilla to take part in a massive attempt to capture Fort Donelson. Grant's reconnaissance had given him a clear picture of the fort and the ground on which it was situated, and he later described it:

> Fort Donelson is two miles north, or down the river, from Dover. The fort ... embraced about one hundred acres of land. On the east it fronted the Cumberland; to the north it faced Hickman's creek, a small stream which at that time was deep and wide because of the back-water from the river; on the south was another small stream, or rather a ravine, opening into the Cumberland. This also was filled with back-water from the river.

The fort stood on high ground, some of it as much as hundred feet above the Cumberland. Strong protection to the heavy guns in the water batteries had been obtained by cutting away places for them in the bluff. To the west there was a line of rifle-pits some two miles back from the river at the farthest point. This line ran generally along the crest of high ground, but in one place crossed a ravine which opens into the river between the village [Dover] and the fort.

The ground inside and outside of this intrenched line was very broken and generally wooded. The trees outside of the rifle-pits had been cut down for a considerable way out, and had been felled so that their tops lay outwards from the intrenchments. The limbs had been trimmed and pointed, and thus formed an abatis in front of the greater part of the line.

Outside of this intrenched line, and extending about half the entire length of it, is a ravine running north and south and opening into Hickman creek at a point north of the fort. The entire side of this ravine next to the works was one long abatis.[2]

Grant's plan was to have Foote's gunboats engage the fort on the east side, facing the Cumberland, while Grant's army attacked from the west. Knowing the Confederates would reinforce Fort Donelson after the fall of Fort Henry, Grant was, as he said, "very impatient to get to Fort Donelson.... I felt that 15,000 men on the 8th would be more effective than 50,000 a month later."[3] He therefore asked Foote to order the serviceable ironclad gunboats that were at Cairo to steam up the Cumberland and prepare to do battle without waiting for the arrival of the three timberclads that were on their way back from their mission up the Tennessee River.

More rain and increased flooding that wiped out the two roads leading from Fort Henry to Fort Donelson frustrated Grant's intention to open his attack on Fort Donelson on February 8, as he had informed General Halleck he would do. He would have to wait for the floodwaters to recede.

On February 8, Fort Donelson's defenders, reinforced by the escaped garrison of Fort Henry, numbered but six thousand troops, including the Forty-ninth Tennessee Infantry, the Fiftieth Tennessee Infantry, the Forty-second Tennessee Infantry and the Tenth Tennessee Infantry regiments, all composed of men from the area around Clarksville and elsewhere in northwestern Tennessee. But reinforcements, as Grant had foreseen, were coming. In St. Louis General Halleck had received intelligence that the Confederates had available some sixty regiments positioned at Bowling Green, and there was a report that ten thousand of those troops were already on their way to Fort Donelson.

Old Brains had never actually ordered Grant to attack the fort, but had merely acquiesced to Grant's stated plan. He did not, as Grant put it, "approve or disapprove on my going to Fort Donelson. He said nothing to me on the subject."[4] Having given at least tacit approval, Halleck suddenly grew anxious about the Fort Donelson expedition. He urgently asked help from the commander of the Department of the Ohio, Brigadier General Don Carlos Buell, in Louisville, who was of no mind to take part in what he saw as an impending disaster for Grant and his army. "This whole move," Buell told his friend General McClellan, the Army's chief general, "right in its strategic bearing, but commenced by Halleck without proper appreciation — preparation — or concert — has now become of vast magnitude."[5] Reinforcement of Grant's army, Buell said, would "have to be made in the face of 50,000 if not 60,000 men and is hazardous."[6] Besides being pessimistic about the campaign, Buell, whose department adjoined Halleck's, was miffed that Halleck had launched it without the courtesy of notifying Buell in advance.

When McClellan suggested that Buell send reinforcements despite his reservations,

Buell turned aside the suggestion. "I cannot on reflection," he told his commander, "think a change in my line would be advisable. I shall want eighteen rifled siege guns and four companies of experienced gunners to man them."[7] Those guns and experienced gunners were in such short supply that Buell felt safe in offering the need of them as an excuse to refuse help to Grant.

Halleck, too, wired the general in chief. He urged McClellan to send reinforcements from wherever they could be found. In response, McClellan ordered new recruits from the Western states to be assembled into regiments and sent to bolster Grant's forces. Those newly formed regiments would soon add about eight thousand troops to Grant's army.

Not yet having given up on help from Buell, Halleck suggested that command of the Fort Donelson expedition be turned over to the reluctant general, apparently hoping that the prospect of glory would entice Buell into bringing his troops to the battle. McClellan agreed that having someone supersede Grant might be a good idea. "Either Buell or yourself," he wired Halleck, "should soon go to the area of operations."[8]

Unaware of what was going on behind his back, Grant was now in danger of losing his command. Replacing Grant was not a new idea to Halleck. He had been thinking about it for some time. He considered Grant not merely daring but reckless. Besides that, as a hesitant though ambitious armchair general, Halleck doubtless harbored feelings of jealousy toward a subordinate who was at once decisive, confident and successful — and, what was more, who had a terrible tendency to draw official and public attention to his successes. Such a general could prove a powerful rival.

On February 9, while Grant continued to wait for the floodwaters to recede, Fort Donelson received a new commander. He arrived by steamer at the Dover landing and established a headquarters in the Dover home of one of his staff officers. He was Brigadier General Gideon Pillow, assigned by the commander of the Confederate army's Western Department, Major General Albert Sidney Johnston, to take over the threatened fort, at least temporarily.

On learning of Pillow's arrival, General Grant was less than intimidated. "I had known General Pillow in Mexico," Grant asserted, "and judged that with any force, no matter how small, I could march up to within gunshot of any intrenchments he was given to hold."[9] Grant also held a low opinion of the man who on February 13 would succeed Pillow as commander, Brigadier General John B. Floyd, the former United States secretary of war under President James Buchanan who had resigned when the cotton states began seceding from the Union. "I knew that Floyd was in command," Grant later wrote, "but he was no soldier, and I judged that he would yield to Pillow's pretensions."[10]

Pillow quickly set about putting the fort's big guns in effective order and inspecting the line of entrenchments that had been established by Major Henry Gilmer of the Confederate army engineers. "When I arrived," Pillow wrote, "I found the work on the river battery unfinished and wholly too weak to resist the force of heavy artillery. I found a 10-inch columbiad and a 32-pounder rifled gun which had not been mounted. Deep gloom was hanging over the command, and the troops were greatly depressed and demoralized by the circumstances attending the surrender of Fort Henry and the manner of retiring from that place. My first attention was given to the necessity of strengthening this work, mounting the two heavy guns, and to the construction of defensive works to protect the rear of the river battery. I imparted to the work all the energy which it was possible to do, working day and night with the whole command...."[11]

Pillow also made a stab at raising morale by issuing a written rallying call to the troops:

"Drive back the ruthless invader from our soil and again raise the Confederate flag over Fort Henry.... With God's help we will accomplish our purpose. Our battle cry, 'Liberty or death.'"[12]

As the attack on Fort Donelson grew imminent, General Halleck, bypassing Grant, on February 11 wired Flag Officer Foote the following message: "FLAG-OFFICER FOOTE— You have gained great distinction by the capture of Fort Henry. Every body recognizes your services. Make your name famous in history by the immediate capture of Fort Donelson and Clarksville. The taking of these places is a military necessity. Delay adds strength to them more than to us. Act quickly, even though only half ready. Troops will soon be ready to support you."[13]

Halleck had wired Foote his congratulations and thanks following the victory at Fort Henry, but to Grant, the designer and initiator of the operation, Halleck had said little or nothing about the operation's success. Now Halleck may have been hoping that Foote and Foote's gunboats could repeat at Fort Donelson what they had achieved at Fort Henry — victory without Grant and his troops. If they could, the praise and celebrity would go not to Grant but to Flag Officer Foote of the Navy, a non-rival to Old Brains.

On the night of February 11, Grant moved General McClernand's division several miles out on the road from Fort Henry to Fort Donelson in preparation for the drive that would begin the next day. On the morning of the 12th, as his army was about to start its march, Grant's first reinforcements, a brigade of six regiments under the command of Colonel John Thayer of Nebraska, arrived on steamer transports. Grant instructed Thayer to reboard the transports and join the convoy of Foote's gunboats that was moving up the Cumberland to Fort Donelson.

Foote was again being urged on by General Halleck, who sent the flag officer another telegraph message on Wednesday the 12th: "FLAG-OFFICER FOOTE— Push forward the Cumberland expedition with all possible dispatch. In addition to the land forces at Paducah and on their way from Michigan, Ohio, Indiana, and Illinois, I shall send one regiment from here [St. Louis] on Thursday, one on Friday, and one on Saturday. Push ahead boldly and quickly. I will give you plenty of support in a few days' time. Now every thing for use. Don't delay an instant."[14]

Foote was on the move, steaming out of Cairo with three ironclad gunboats and two timberclads. The ironclad *Carondelet*, captained by Commander Henry Walke, at Grant's request had left for the Cumberland two days earlier to begin a diversionary attack on the fort. Foote's other gunboats were unavailable for the main assault, either still undergoing repairs or stationed on the Mississippi.

Leaving some twenty-five hundred men under the command of Brigadier General Lewis (Lew) Wallace to guard Fort Henry, Grant began his march on Fort Donelson with fifteen thousand troops, including eight batteries of artillery and part of a regiment of cavalry. "Meeting with no obstruction to detain us," Grant reported, "the advance arrived in front of the enemy by noon. That afternoon and the next day [Thursday, February 13] were spent in taking up ground to make the investment as complete as possible."[15]

By February 12, reinforcements had swelled the Confederate force protecting Fort Donelson to an estimated thirteen thousand to twenty-one thousand men, the lower estimate being General Pillow's, the higher being General Grant's. Pillow had spent much of the time since his arrival correcting the deficiencies he had found and making sure the fort's big guns were properly mounted, that they were served by competent artillerymen and were well supplied with ammunition. The guns included, according to Pillow's account, eight 32-pounders, three 32-pounder carronades (similar to howitzers), one ten-inch columbiad and one rifled 32-pounder.

Commander Walke of the gunboat *Carondelet*, viewing the fort from the river, described the fort's armament as emplaced in three tiers on the bluff that rose from the water's edge: "It had three batteries, mounting in all sixteen guns; the lower battery, about twenty feet above the water, had eight 32-pounders, and one 128-pounder; the second, about fifty feet above the water, was of about equal strength; the third, on the summit, had three or four heavy field-guns, or siege-guns."[16]

The *Carondelet* had arrived just above the fort around noon on February 12, having been towed there by the transport steamer *Alps* to conserve the *Carondelet*'s fuel. Nearing the fort, the gunboat cast off from its towboat and soon came in sight of the fort, menacingly situated atop the 120-foot-high bluff. "Not a living creature could be seen," Walke recounted. "The hills and woods on the west side of the river hid part of the enemy's formidable defences, which were lightly covered with snow. But the black rows of heavy guns, pointing down on us, reminded me of the dismal-looking sepulchers cut in the rocky cliffs near Jerusalem, but far more repulsive."[17]

Shortly before one o'clock that afternoon Walke attempted to draw fire from the fort. "To unmask the silent enemy," he related, "and to announce my arrival to General Grant, I ordered the bow-guns to be fired at the fort. Only one shell fell short. There was no response except the echo from the hills. The fort appeared to have been evacuated. After firing ten shells into it, the *Carondelet* dropped down the river about three miles and anchored.... We were isolated and beset with dangers from the enemy's lurking sharp-shooters."[18]

On the west side of Fort Donelson the *Carondelet*'s booming guns had been heard by the men of Grant's army, who broke into repeated cheers at the sound of them. The vessel's arrival set off a flurry of skirmishes by eager Union troops, who were determined that the Navy would not get ahead of them again, as it had at Fort Henry.

In the early morning of Thursday, February 13, Walke received a dispatch from Grant informing him that the Union troops were in position, having almost entirely invested the rebels' entrenchments. "Most of our batteries," Grant told Walke, "are established, and the remainder soon will be. If you will advance with your gun-boat at ten o'clock in the morning, we will be ready to take advantage of any diversion in our favor."[19]

At 9:05 A.M. the *Carondelet*, under cover of a heavily wooded point on the Cumberland, commenced its assault, firing the first of the one hundred and thirty-nine 70-pound and 64-pound shells with which it would assail the batteries of Fort Donelson. Commander Walke described the action:

> We received in return the fire of all the enemy's guns that could be brought to bear on the *Carondelet*, which sustained but little damage, except from two shots. One, a 128-pound solid, at 11:30 struck the corner of our port broadside casemate, passed through it, and in its progress toward the center of our boilers glanced over the temporary barricade in front of the boilers. It then passed over the steam-drum, struck the beams of the upper deck, carried away the railing around the engine-room and burst the steam-heater, and, glancing back into the engine-room, "seemed to bound after the men," as one of the engineers said, "like a wild beast pursuing its prey...." When it burst through the side of the *Carondelet*, it knocked down and wounded a dozen men, seven of them severely. An immense quantity of splinters was blown through the vessel. Some of them, as fine as needles, shot through the clothes of the men like arrows. Several of the wounded were so much excited by the suddenness of the event and the sufferings of their comrades that they were not aware that

they themselves had been struck until they felt the blood running into their shoes. Upon receiving this shot we ceased firing for a while.[20]

At a quarter past noon, after the wounded crewmen had been transferred to the transport *Alps* and some repairs had been made, the *Carondelet* resumed its assault, continuing the bombardment until dusk. By then all of the vessel's 10-inch and 15-inch shells had been expended, and the guns of Fort Donelson had fallen silent for the night.

A half hour before midnight Flag Officer Foote arrived with the ironclads *St. Louis*, *Louisville* and *Pittsburg* and the timberclads *Taylor* and *Conestoga*. In daylight on February 14 the gunboats' crews worked to cover the upper decks with all the hard material they could find — chains, lumber, sacks of coal — to protect the vessels from the rebels' plunging shot, fired from the heights of the bluff. That makeshift task done, at 3 P.M. the fleet advanced to renew the assault on Fort Donelson. The *Louisville* took a position on the west side of the river, with the flag vessel *St. Louis*, with Foote aboard, beside it. On the starboard side of the *St. Louis* steamed the *Pittsburg* and the *Carondelet*, the four boats forming a line across the breadth of the Cumberland. The two timberclads trailed about a thousand yards to the ironclads' rear.

At 3:30, when the ironclads were about a mile and a half from the fort, the guns of the fort opened fire, their first two shots falling short. When within a mile of the fort, the flagship *St. Louis* commenced firing in return, and the three other ironclads immediately joined the *St. Louis*'s bombardment, their guns firing slowly at first, then more rapidly as the fleet drew closer to the fort and the rebel guns increased their fire. Aboard the gunboats the crews could hear, as Commander Walke described it, "the deafening crack of the bursting shells, the crash of the solid shot and the whizzing of fragments of shell and wood as they sped through the vessel."[21] A 128-pounder shot struck the *Carondelet*'s anchor, smashing it into pieces that flew over the deck, then bounded across the boat, taking away a part of the smokestack. Another shot cut the iron boat davits, and the vessel's lifeboat dropped into the water. Another shot ripped up the iron plating on the side of the *Carondelet* and ricocheted overboard. One shot struck the pilothouse, shattered the iron plating and drove fragments of iron and wood into the pilots, one of whom was mortally wounded. Another shot penetrated the iron plating and lodged in the thick casemate. The rebel fire was coming, as Walke reported, "harder and faster, taking flag-staffs and smoke-stacks, and tearing off the side armor as lightning tears the bark from a tree."[22]

In the heat of the battle, the rifled gun on the *Carondelet*'s port side was loaded too hastily and exploded. A crewman gave his account of the tragic accident:

> I was serving the gun with shell. When it exploded it knocked us all down, killing none, but wounding over a dozen men, and spreading dismay and confusion among us. For about two minutes I was stunned, and at least five minutes elapsed before I could tell what was the matter. When I found out that I was more scared than hurt, although suffering from the gunpowder which I had inhaled, I looked forward and saw our gun lying on the deck, split in three pieces.
>
> Then the cry ran through the boat that we were on fire, and my duty as pump-man called me to the pumps. While I was there, two shots entered our bow-ports and killed four men and wounded several others. They were borne past me, three with their heads off. The sight almost sickened me, and I turned my head away. Our master's mate came soon after and ordered us to our quarters at the gun. I told him the gun had burst, and that we had caught fire on the upper deck from the enemy's shell. He then said: "Never mind the fire; go to your quarters." There I took a station at the starboard tackle of another rifled bow-gun and remained there until the close of the fight.[23]

The *St. Louis*, about three hundred fifty yards from the fort, was also under heavy fire and was hit not only by rebel gunners but by an errant round from one of the timberclads. A solid shot from the fort struck the pilothouse, penetrated the inch-and-a-quarter-thick iron plating and the thirteen-inch-thick timber behind it and sprayed deadly iron and wood fragments throughout the pilothouse. The pilot was instantly killed, and Flag Officer Foote, standing beside him, was wounded in the foot. Then a moment later a shot fired from the *Taylor*, at the rear of the *St. Louis*, came tearing into the *St. Louis*, severing its tiller ropes, making the vessel unsteerable. The tiller ropes of the *Louisville* were shot away by rebel fire, and both the *Louisville* and the *St. Louis*, helpless in the river's swift current and swirling eddies, began drifting downstream, away from the battle.

The *Carondelet* was struck a second time in its pilothouse, wounding another pilot, smashing the vessel's wheel while shells from the timberclads were bursting menacingly over the crippled ironclads. All of the gunboats were falling back, their lines broken. The *Pittsburg*, in a hasty move to withdraw along with the two drifting gunboats, turned about too close to the *Carondelet* and crashed into its stern, breaking the *Carondelet*'s starboard rudder. "There was no alternative for the *Carondelet* in that narrow stream," Commander Walke recounted, "but to keep her head to the enemy and fire into the fort with her two bow-guns, to prevent it, if possible, from returning her fire effectively. The enemy saw that she was in a manner left to his mercy, and concentrated the fire of all his batteries upon her."[24]

Most of the shots from the fort, Walke said, were fired to ricochet into the *Carondelet*'s hull and could be seen skipping on the water before striking the vessel. "The enemy's object," he observed, "was to sink the gun-boat by striking her just below the water-line. They soon succeeded in planting two thirty-two pound shots in her bow, between wind and water, which made her leak badly, but her compartments kept her from sinking until we could plug up the shot-holes. Three shots struck the starboard casemating; four struck the port casemating forward of the rifle-gun; one struck on the starboard side, between the water-line and plank-sheer, cutting the planking; six shots struck the pilot-house, shattering one section into pieces and cutting through the iron casing. The smoke-stacks were riddled."[25]

Commander Walke continued:

Some of the young men from a spirit of bravado or from a belief in the doctrine of fatalism, disregarded the instructions [to drop to the deck when the words "Look out!" or "Down!" were shouted], saying it was useless to attempt to dodge a cannonball, and then would trust to luck. The warning words, 'Look out!' 'Down!' were again soon heard; down went the gunner and his men, as the whizzing shot glanced on the gun, taking off the gunner's cap and the heads of two of the young men who trusted to luck, and in defiance of the order were standing up.... This shot killed another man also, who was at the last gun of the starboard side, and disabled the gun. It came in with a hissing sound; three sharp spats and a heavy bang told the sad fate of three brave comrades. Before the decks were well sanded, there was so much blood on them that our men could not work the guns without slipping.[26]

As the *Carondelet* continued to fall back it kept up a steady fire from its bow guns, hoping to cloud the vessel in the smoke of its guns so that the fort's gunners could not get a clear view of it. Finally it was out of the range of Fort Donelson's guns and, with the others of Flag Officer Foote's gunboat fleet, was out of action.

General Pillow seemed well pleased with the performance of the fort's gun crews and the effectiveness of their efforts:

> My orders to the officers ... were to hold their fire until the enemy's boats should come within point-blank range of their guns. This they did, though the ordeal of holding their fire while the enemy's shot and shell fell thick around their position was a severe restraint to their patriotic impulses; but, nevertheless, our batteries made no response until the enemy's gunboats got within range of their guns. Our entire line of batteries then opened fire. The guns of both parties were well served, the enemy constantly advancing, delivering direct fire against our batteries from his line of five gunboats, while the sixth boat, moving up in rear of the line, kept the air filled with shells, which fell thick and close around the position of our batteries.
>
> The fight continued, the enemy steadily advancing slowly up the river, the shot and shell from fifteen heavy rifled guns tearing our parapets and plunging deep into the earth around and over our batteries. Having come in such close conflict, I could distinctly see the effects of our shot upon his iron-cased boats. We had given two or three well-directed shots from the heavy guns to one of his boats, when she instantly shrank back and drifted helpless below the line. Several shot struck another boat, tearing her iron case and splintering her timbers and making them crack as if by a stroke of lightning, when she, too, fell back. Then a third received several severe shots, making her metal ring and her timbers crack, when the whole line gave way and fell rapidly back from our fire until they passed out of range.
>
> Thus ended the first severe and close conflict of our heavy guns with the enemy's gunboats, testing their strength and the power of our heavy guns to resist them.... These gunboats never renewed the attack....[27]

Flag Officer Foote, however, believed his gunboats, despite disadvantages, had come within fifteen minutes of achieving a success at Fort Donelson similar to their victory at Fort Henry, as he wrote in his report to Secretary of the Navy Welles:

> SIR—I have the honor to report to the Department that, at the urgent request of General Halleck and General Grant, who regarded the movement as a military necessity, although not, in my opinion, properly prepared, I made an attack on Fort Donelson yesterday, the 14th instant, at three o'clock P.M., with four iron-clad and two wooden gun-boats....
>
> There were fifty-four killed and wounded in the attack, which, notwithstanding our disadvantages, we have every reason to suppose would, in fifteen minutes more, could the action have been continued, have resulted in the capture of the two forts bearing upon us. The enemy's fire had materially slackened, and he was running from his batteries, when the two gun-boats helplessly drifted down the river from disabled steering apparatus, as the relieving tackles could not control the helm in the strong current; and the fleeing enemy, returning to their guns, again boldly opened fire upon us from the river batteries, which we had silenced....
>
> On consultation with General Grant and my own officers, as my services, until we can repair damages by bringing up a competent force from Cairo to attack the fort, are much less required here than they are at Cairo, I shall proceed to that point with two of the disabled boats, leaving the two others here to protect the transports, and with all dispatch prepare the mortar-boats and the *Benton*, with other boats, to make an effectual attack upon Fort Donelson....
>
> Very respectfully, your obedient servant,
>
>   A.H. Foote,
>
> Flag-Officer, commanding U.S.N. Forces, Western Waters[28]

To his wife, Foote wrote with more candor:

> MY DEAR WIFE—I telegraphed you from Paducah last night that Fort Donelson was not taken, but that I was slightly wounded, once at a gun and once in the pilot-house. It was by a piece of spent shot once, and a splinter once, but only slightly, on my left arm and left foot, which puts me on crutches for a few days; but I will be running about in less time

than a week. I will not go so near again, although at Fort Henry I produced an effect by it. We ought to have been victorious at Donelson, as we fought harder than at Henry. I went into it against my judgment by order of Halleck....

I don't feel depressed much about Fort Donelson, only in its effect upon our cause; for I fought desperately, but against my judgment, and I am above all blame....

Ever affectionately yours,
A.H.F.[29]

Fort Donelson's Confederate gunners, many of them newly pressed into service, deserved far more of the blame for Foote's failure than he was willing to assign them.

7. The Fall of Fort Donelson

For weeks the weather had been miserable — rain, sleet, snow, freezing temperatures. On Wednesday — February 12 — the day of Grant's march to the entrenchments of Fort Donelson, the weather had dramatically turned for the better, with sunshine and warmth arriving suddenly, leading many of the troops to believe that spring had come. Many of them decided that the encumbrances of blankets and overcoats they were carrying were no longer necessary and they dropped them from their backs, discarding them as they marched in the sun. Then, at the end of the day, when Grant's army had reached the fort, the wintry cold had returned. The men were in the field before the line of entrenchments, in the open. "The greatest suffering," Grant wrote, "was from want of shelter.... It would not do to allow camp-fires except far down the hill out of sight of the enemy, and it would not do to allow many of the troops to remain there at the same time.... There was therefore much discomfort and absolute suffering."[1]

Grant had placed General Smith's division, minus the twenty-five hundred men left with General Wallace at Fort Henry, on the left of the Union's front, which extended as far as Hickman's Creek, and positioned General McClernand's division on the right, which extended as far as the backwater in the ravine that opened into the Cumberland south of Dover and included the road that ran southeast from Dover to Charlotte, Tennessee, and toward Nashville. "The troops were not intrenched," Grant wrote, "but the nature of the ground was such that they were just as well protected from the fire of the enemy as if rifle-pits had been thrown up. Our line was generally along the crest of ridges. The artillery was protected by being sunk in the ground."[2]

When McClernand attempted to stretch his line across his assigned length of the rebel front, it was discovered there was too much distance for his brigades to cover adequately, and the fact that he had to block the road from Dover, over which the rebels might march out from the fort at will if left unimpeded, only added to the inadequacy of his numbers. Grant quickly realized he needed more troops. He knew he had reinforcements coming up the river with Foote's convoy. He also had the brigade he had left behind at Fort Henry, composed of the Eighth Missouri Infantry and the Eleventh Indiana Infantry regiments and Illinois's artillery Battery A.

A courier was dispatched to General Wallace at Fort Henry with an order to bring his command to Fort Donelson. That night Wallace ferried his troops across the Tennessee and reported with them at headquarters before noon on the next day, February 14. Wallace's brigade from Fort Henry was restored to General Smith's division, and General Wallace was assigned to command a third division, composed of Colonel Thayer's brigade, which had arrived with Foote's convoy, and other reinforcements that arrived on the 14th, and Grant placed that new division at the center of his line, allowing the two flanking divisions to close up and strengthen their positions.

"The plan," Grant explained, "was for the troops to hold the enemy within his lines, while the gunboats should attack the water batteries at close quarters and silence his guns if possible. Some of the gunboats were to run the batteries, get above the fort and above the village of Dover.... That position attained by the gunboats it would have been but a question of time — and a very short time, too — when the garrison would have been compelled to surrender."[3] With luck, Grant figured, the besieged fort, once its commanders could see that their communications and escape route on the river was cut off, would surrender without further loss to the troops of either side.

For the Union troops the battle for Fort Donelson had begun on Thursday with the deployment of skirmishers and snipers, both bent on effecting Grant's plan to hold the rebels within their lines. "As always in situations where the advancing party is ignorant of the ground and of the designs of the enemy," General Wallace explained, "resort was had to skirmishers, who are to the main body what antennae are to insects. Theirs is to unmask the foe."[4] Advancing in teams, the skirmishers moved ahead of Grant's main body, probing the wooded area held by the Confederates, attempting to discover their locations and strength.

The snipers, or sharp-shooters, had a different task. "Theirs was a peculiar service," Wallace wrote. "Each was a preferred marksman, and carried a long-range Henry rifle, with sights delicately arranged as for target practice. In action each was perfectly independent. They never manoevred as a corps. When the time came they were asked, 'Canteens full?' 'Biscuits for all day?' Then their order, 'All right; hunt your holes, boys.' Thereupon they dispersed, and, like Indians, sought cover to please themselves behind rocks and stumps, or in hollows. Sometimes they dug holes; sometimes they climbed into trees. Once in a good location, they remained there all day. At night they would crawl out and report in camp."[5]

On the morning of Saturday, February 15, shortly before dawn, while the main body of the Union forces remained in place before the two- to three-mile-long Confederate line, the snipers of General Grant's army dispersed to find hidden places where the rebel fortifications would be within easy range of their sharpshooters' rifles.

General Grant also was up and moving in the early morning of the 15th. The weather had turned intensely cold during the night, bringing new snow, and Grant had retired the evening before, as he said, "not knowing but that I would have to intrench my position, and bring up tents for the men or build huts under the cover of the hills."[6] He was still thinking not of attack, but of a long wait, a patient and strangling siege.

Bad news was coming to change that plan. A messenger from Flag Officer Foote brought Grant a note asking him to come to a meeting on Foote's flagship, the *St. Louis*. Foote explained that he had been wounded the day before, to the extent that he was unable to come to Grant. "I at once made my preparations for starting," Grant related. "I directed my adjutant-general to notify each of the division commanders of my absence and instruct them to do nothing to bring on an engagement until they received further orders, but to hold their positions."[7]

The ground was frozen solid from the night's plummeting temperature, making travel by horseback even slower than it had been across merely muddy roads. "When I reached the fleet," Grant said, "I found the flag-ship was anchored out in the stream. A small boat, however, awaited my arrival and I was soon on board with the flag-officer. He explained to me in short the condition in which he was left by the engagement of the evening before, and suggested that I should intrench while he returned to Mound City with his disabled boats, expressing at the time the belief that he could have the necessary repairs made and be back in ten days."⁸ Grant agreed to that new course of action and was soon back in the small boat, being rowed to shore, there to receive the next piece of bad news.

"Just as I landed I met Captain Hillyer of my staff, white with fear, not for his personal safety, but for the safety of the National troops. He said the enemy had come out of his lines in full force and attacked and scattered McClernand's division, which was in full retreat."⁹

On the night before — the night of Friday the 14th — after the intense artillery battles fought on the Cumberland River and along the entrenchment west of the fort, General Floyd, commanding the Confederate forces, had held a council of war in the hotel on the waterfront in Dover, calling together his general officers and regimental commanders. He had told them that despite the Confederates' heroic repulse of Foote's gunboat flotilla, he considered the defenders' position, in the face of what Floyd and others believed was an overwhelming and growing Union army, was untenable. Floyd had earlier been instructed by the area commander, Major General Albert Sidney Johnston, to fall back to Nashville by way of Charlotte if the situation at Fort Donelson became hopeless. To Floyd it now seemed hopeless. Floyd suggested an attack on the right side of the Union line to recapture the road to Charlotte and force open a path for a massive withdrawal of the Confederate forces from Fort Donelson.¹⁰ The plan called for General Pillow to launch an assault against the right side of the Union line at dawn, with General Buckner supporting Pillow by attacking the right center of the Union line and taking a position beyond the rebel trenches to cover Fort Donelson's retreating garrison. Floyd's proposal had been unanimously accepted by the officers at the meeting.

During the frigid night of February 14–15 the rebel commanders had taken some ten thousand or more of their troops— infantry, cavalry and artillery — out of the snow-covered rifle pits and massed them on the Confederate left, moving so quietly that Union sentries had not detected them. Explaining that failure, General Wallace said, "The pickets of the Federals were struggling for life against the [wintry] blast, and probably did not keep good watch."¹¹ Wallace then described the rebels' surprise attack:

> Here and there the musicians were beginning to make the woods ring with reveille, and the numbed soldiers of the line were rising from their icy beds and shaking the snow from their frozen garments. As yet, however, not a company had fallen in. Suddenly the pickets fired, and with the alarm on their lips rushed back upon their comrades. The woods on the instant became alive.
>
> The regiments formed, officers mounted and took their places; words of command rose loud and eager. By the time Pillow's advance opened fire on [Colonel Richard] Oglesby's right [positioned on General McClernand's extreme right], the point first struck, the latter was ready to receive it. A rapid exchange of volleys ensued.... An hour passed, and yet another hour, without cessation of the fire. Meantime the woods rang with a monstrous clangor of musketry, as if a million men were beating empty barrels with iron hammers.
>
> Buckner flung a portion of his division on McClernand's left, and supported the attack with his artillery.... McClernand, watchful and full of resources, sent batteries to meet Buckner's batteries.... The roar never slackened. Men fell by the score, reddening the snow with their blood. The smoke, in pallid white clouds, clung to the underbrush and tree-tops as if to screen the combatants from each other....
>
> The pressure on the front grew stronger. The "rebel yell," afterward a familiar battle-cry on many fields, told of ground being gained.... At last he [Colonel Oglesby] realized that the end was come. His right companies began to give way, and as they retreated, holding up their empty cartridge-boxes, the enemy appeared emboldened, and swept more fiercely

around his flank, until finally they appeared in his rear. He then gave the order to retire the division.[12]

By eleven o'clock that morning, General Pillow held the road to Charlotte, as well as the entire position that General McClernand's division had occupied. The way out of Fort Donelson was now clear for its Confederate defenders.

Hurrying as fast as the ice-glazed roads would allow his mount to move, General Grant passed the left side of his line, held by General Smith's division, then passed the center of the line, held by Wallace's division. Along both sections he saw, as he said, "everything favorable." Then at last, during a lull in the battle, he reached the right side of his line.

"Even the cannonading ceased," Wallace recounted, "and everybody was asking, 'What next?' Just then General Grant rode up to where General McClernand and I were in conversation. He was almost unattended. In his hand were some papers, which looked like telegrams. Wholly unexcited, he saluted and received the salutations of his subordinates.... He was then informed of the mishap to the First Division, and that the road to Charlotte was open to the enemy.... His face flushed slightly. With a sudden grip he crushed the papers in his hand.... In his ordinary quiet voice he said, addressing himself to both officers, 'Gentlemen, the position on the right must be retaken.' With that he turned and galloped off."[13]

Grant discovered that although McClernand's division had broken, only some of the troops had fled. "Most of the men," he said, "as they were not pursued, only fell back out of range of the fire of the enemy. It must have been about this time that [Colonel] Thayer pushed his brigade [from Wallace's division] in between the enemy and those of our troops that were without ammunition. At all events the enemy fell back within his intrenchments and was there when I got on the field."[14]

Grant also discovered that although many of McClernand's men had run out of ammunition, there were "tons of it," as Grant said, "close at hand." Having surveyed the situation, Grant turned to Colonel J.D. Webster, a member of his staff, and told him, "Some of our men are pretty badly demoralized, but the enemy must be more so, for he has attempted to force his way out, but has fallen back. The one who attacks first now will be victorious—and the enemy will have to be in a hurry if he gets ahead of me."[15]

Grant quickly decided he would immediately make an assault on his left, sending General Smith's force against the section of the Confederate line commanded by General Buckner. "It was clear to my mind," Grant recalled, "that the enemy had started to march out with his entire force, except a few pickets, and if our attack could be made on the left before the enemy could redistribute his forces along the line, we would find but little opposition except from the intervening abatis."[16]

Riding swiftly to General Smith's command post, Grant explained the situation to him and ordered him to charge the rebels' works in front of him with his entire division, telling him that he would find only a thin line to oppose him. Smith almost immediately had his units on the move. General Wallace described the action:

Taking [Colonel Jacob] Lauman's brigade, General Smith began the advance. They were under fire instantly. The guns in the fort joined in with the infantry who were at the time in the rifle-pits, the great body of the Confederate right wing being with General Buckner. The defense was greatly favored by the ground, which subjected the assailants to a double fire from the beginning of the abatis. The men have said that "it looked too thick for a rabbit to get through."

General Smith, on his horse, took position in the front and center of the line. Occasionally he turned in the saddle to see how the alignment was kept. For the most part, however, his face [was] steadily toward the enemy. He was, of course, a conspicuous object for the sharp-shooters in the rifle-pits. The air around him twittered with minie-bullets. Erect as if on review, he rode on, timing the gait of his horse with the movement of his colors....

On to the abatis the regiments moved without hesitation, leaving a trail of dead and wounded behind. There the fire seemed to get terribly hot, and there some of the men halted, whereupon General Smith put his cap on the point of his sword, held it aloft, and called out, "No flinching now, my lads! Here, this is the way! Come on!"

He picked a path through the jagged limbs of the trees, holding his cap all the time in sight; and the effect was magical. The men swarmed in after him, and got through in the best order they could — not all of them, alas!

On the other side of the obstruction they took the semblance of re-formation and charged in after their chief, who found himself then between the two fires. Up the ascent he rode; up they followed. At the last moment the keepers of the rifle-pits clambered out and fled. The four regiments engaged in the feat — the 25th Indiana, and the 2d, 7th, and 14th Iowa — planted their colors on the breastwork.

Later in the day, Buckner came back with his division; but all his efforts to dislodge Smith were vain.[17]

"The outer line of rifle-pits was passed," General Grant related, "and [on] the night of the 15th General Smith, with much of his division, bivouacked within the lines of the enemy. There was now no doubt but that the Confederates must surrender or be captured the next day."[18]

While Smith engaged the rebels on the left of Grant's line, General Wallace and General McClernand were doing their best to retake the ground lost on the Union's right. Wallace's eye-witness account recreates the fight:

Riding to my old regiments — the 8th Missouri and the 11th Indiana — I asked them if they were ready. They demanded the word of me. Waiting a moment for [brigade commander Colonel] Morgan L. Smith to light a cigar, I called out, "Forward it is, then!" They were directly in front of the ascent to be climbed. Without waiting for his supports, Colonel Smith led them down into a broad hollow, and catching sight of the advance, [Colonel Charles] Cruft and [Colonel Leonard] Ross also moved forward. As the two regiments began to climb, the 8th Missouri slightly in the lead, a line of fire ran along the brow of the height. The flank companies cheered while deploying as skirmishers. Their Zouave practice [of loading their weapons while lying prone on the ground] proved of excellent service to them. Now on the ground, creeping when the fire was hottest, running when it slackened, they gained ground with astonishing rapidity, and at the same time maintained a fire that was like a sparkling of the earth. For the most part the bullets aimed at them passed over their heads and took effect in the ranks behind them.

Colonel Smith's cigar was shot off close to his lips. He took another and called for a match. A soldier ran and gave him one. "Thank you. Take your place now. We are almost up," he said, and, smoking, spurred his horse forward.

A few yards from the crest of the height the regiments began loading and firing as they advanced. The defenders gave way. On the top there was a brief struggle, which was ended by Cruft and Ross with their supports.

The whole line then moved forward simultaneously, and never stopped until the Confederates were [back] within the[ir] works. There had been no occasion to call on the reserves. The road to Charlotte was again effectually shut, and the battle-field of the morning, with the dead and wounded lying where they had fallen, was in possession of the Third Division, which stood halted within easy musket-range of the rifle-pits. It was then about half-past 3 o'clock in the afternoon....

When night fell, the command bivouacked without fire or supper. Fatigue parties were told ... to look after the wounded; and in the relief given there was no distinction made between friend and foe. The labor extended through the whole night, and the surgeons never rested.[19]

Within the Confederate lines the situation was rapidly deteriorating. General Pillow gave his account of the mounting desperation:

> The operations of the day had forced the entire command of the enemy around to our right and in front of General Buckner's position in the intrenchments, and when he reached his position he found the enemy advancing rapidly to take possession of his portion of our works. He had a stubborn conflict, lasting one and a half hours, to regain his position, and the enemy actually got possession of the extreme right of his works, and held them so firmly that he could not dislodge him.
>
> The position thus gained by the enemy was a most important and commanding one, being immediately in rear of our river batteries and field work for its protection. From it he could readily turn the intrenched work occupied by General Buckner and attack him in reverse, or he could advance, under cover of an intervening ridge, directly upon our battery and field work. While the enemy held the position it was manifest we could not hold the main work or battery.
>
> Such was the condition of the two armies at night-fall, after nine hours of conflict, on the 15th instant, in which our loss was severe, and leaving not less than 1,000 of the enemy dead upon the field. We left upon the field nearly all of his wounded, because we could not remove them. We left his dead unburied, because we could not bury them. Such carnage and conflict has perhaps never before occurred on this continent. We took about 300 prisoners and a large number of arms.
>
> We had fought the battle to open the way for our army and to relieve us from an investment which would necessarily reduce us and the position we occupied by famine. We had accomplished our object, but it occupied the whole day, and before we could prepare to leave, after taking in the wounded and dead, the enemy had thrown around us again in the night an immense force of fresh troop and reoccupied his original position in the line of investment, thus again cutting off our retreat.
>
> We had only about 13,000 troops all told; of these we had lost a large proportion in the three battles. The command had been in the trenches night and day for five days, exposed to the snow, sleet, mud, and ice-water, without shelter and without adequate covering and without sleep. In this condition the general officers held a consultation, to determine what we should do.[20]

What Pillow and Floyd decided to do was save themselves from capture by Grant's forces. Floyd in particular had reason to fear capture. General Grant explained why:

> General Floyd, the commanding officer, who was a man of talent enough for any civil position, was no soldier and, possibly, did not possess the elements of one. He was further unfitted for command, for the reason that his conscience must have troubled him and made him afraid. As Secretary of War he had taken a solemn oath to maintain the Constitution of the United States and to uphold the same against all its enemies. He had betrayed that trust.
>
> As Secretary of War he was reported through the northern press to have scattered the little army the country had so that the most of it could be picked up in detail when secession occurred. About a year before leaving the Cabinet he had removed arms from northern to southern arsenals. He continued in the Cabinet of President Buchanan until about the 1st of January, 1861, while he was working vigilantly for the establishment of a confederacy made out of United States territory. Well may he have been afraid to fall into the hands of National troops. He would no doubt have been tried for misappropriating public property, if not for treason, had he been captured.[21]

General Pillow at first proposed holding out in the trenches for another day, arguing that by Sunday night — February 16 — the steamer transports that had evacuated the Confederates' prisoners and the mounted troops would have returned and could move the rebel army across the river and allow it to escape to Clarksville. Buckner, the professional soldier and realist, resisted that proposal, saying, "Gentlemen, you know the enemy occupy the rifle pits on my right, and can easily turn my position and attack me in rear or move down on the river battery. I am satisfied he will attack me at daylight, and I cannot hold my position half an hour."[22]

Having suffered heavy losses in his own command on Saturday and thus unwilling to reinforce Buckner's command, Pillow accepted Buckner's assessment of the situation and told his comrades, "Gentlemen, if we cannot cut our way out nor fight on, there is no alternative left us but capitulation, and I am determined that I will never surrender the command nor will I ever surrender myself a prisoner. I will die first."[23]

General Floyd, according to Pillow's account, said he felt the same way — that he would die before he would surrender himself or his troops. Buckner then told his two superiors that taking such a stand was a personal matter and that personal considerations should never influence official action. "General Floyd," Pillow related, "said he acknowledged it was personal with him, but nevertheless such was his determination."[24]

At that, General Buckner said he was satisfied that nothing else could be done and that if he were placed in command, he would surrender the fort and its army of defenders and would accept whatever fate awaited them.

Quick to accept that offer, Floyd immediately responded, "General Buckner, I place you in command. Will you permit me to draw out my brigade?"

"Yes," Buckner answered, "provided you do so before the enemy act upon my communication [of surrender]."

Floyd then turned to Pillow and said, "General Pillow, I turn over the command." "I pass it," Pillow replied.

Command of the Fort Donelson troops then passed into General Buckner's hands. "I assume it," he said. "Bring on a bugler, pen, ink, and paper."[25] When the articles were brought to him, Buckner sat down at a table and began to write his message of surrender.

Upon the meeting's conclusion, General Floyd swiftly prepared for his departure. He ordered his brigade assembled, and following the arrival of two steamboats shortly before daylight on Sunday, February 16, he hurried to the riverfront, embarked his troops, numbering some three thousand men, and quickly steamed off to Nashville. "He never satisfactorily explained," General Wallace reported, "upon what principle he appropriated all the transportation on hand to the use of his particular command."[26]

Pillow procured the assistance of J.W. Smith of Dover, who during the night rowed him and his staff across the Cumberland in a twelve-foot flatboat. He fled to Clarksville and later was united with his horse, servant and baggage. From Clarksville he trooped off to Nashville.[27] Also during the night other elements of the Confederate force slipped away, some evading the Union line by passing between its right end and the river, slogging across the flooded ravine above the fort and escaping. Among those were Lieutenant Colonel Nathan Bedford Forrest and an estimated one thousand cavalrymen.

Some who were among the fort's garrison told of the Confederates' hasty withdrawal and surrender. One of them was Judge Tyler, who related his experiences in a Clarksville newspaper story: "At midnight we evacuated the fort and marched two miles up to Dover. There we stood shivering in the cold for hours while three generals — Buckner, Floyd and Pillow — held a council of war in the old hotel on the river bank. The enemy's campfires blazed brightly all around us. We expected orders to cut our way through, but instead were ordered back to the fort. In a short while a courier came with an order to raise a white flag over the fort. Curses both loud and deep followed this intelligence. There was no white flag in the regiment, nobody expecting to need one, but Ordinance [sic] Sergeant R.L. Cobb had a white sheet, which was run up at daylight. Nearly half the regiment escaped from the fort."[28]

Another was Lewis R. Clark of Clarksville: "The rumors came that we were about to be surrendered. Some of the men escaped and joined other commands, but the majority were so tired and exhausted that they slept in spite of efforts to keep awake, and the next morning, February 16, we found ourselves prisoners."[29]

Thomas A. Turner of the Forty-second Tennessee Infantry Regiment said that "though Friday was a busy day, the enemy were repulsed wherever they made an attack, and every Confederate soldier's heart beat high in anticipation of a glorious victory. Saturday the same feeling prevailed, and there was never greater surprise in the camp than when we learned we were to be surrendered."[30]

Buckner's message of capitulation was received by General Grant shortly before daylight on Sunday. It read:

> HEADQUARTERS, FORT DONELSON
> February 16, 1862
>
> Sir — In consideration of all the circumstances governing the present situation of affairs at this station, I propose to the Commanding Officer of the Federal forces the appointment of Commissioners to agree upon terms of capitulation of the forces and fort under my command, and in that view suggest an armistice until 12 o'clock today.
>
> I am, sir, very respectfully,
> Your ob't se'v't.
> S.B. Buckner,
> Brig. Gen. C.S.A.

Grant was not inclined to negotiate. He replied to Buckner with a terse and threatening note:

> HEADQUARTERS ARMY IN THE FIELD
> Camp near Donelson,
> February 16, 1862
>
> General S.B. Buckner,
>   Confederate Army.
>   Sir: Yours of this date, proposing armistice and appointment of Commissioners to settle terms of capitulation, is just received. No terms except an unconditional and immediate surrender can be accepted. I propose to move immediately upon your works.
>
> I am, sir, very respectfully,
> Your ob't se'v't,
> U.S. Grant,
> Brig. Gen.

With obvious irritation but resignation, General Buckner responded to Grant's demand:

> HEADQUARTERS, DOVER, TENNESSEE
> February 16, 1862
>
> To Brig. Gen'l U.S. Grant,
>   U.S. Army.
>   Sir — The distribution of the forces under my command, incident to an unexpected change of commanders, and the overwhelming force under your command, compel me,

notwithstanding the brilliant success of the Confederate arms yesterday, to accept the ungenerous and unchivalrous terms which you propose.

    I am, sir,
    Your very ob't se'v't,
    S.B. Buckner,
    Brig. Gen. C.S.A.[31]

Even before he had received Grant's reply, Buckner had dispatched notes to the rebel commanders along the line of entrenchment, notifying them that he had sent the capitulation proposal to General Grant and ordering the commanders to "refrain from hostile demonstrations with a view to preventing a like movement on the enemy's part."[32] White flags soon began appearing along the Confederate line.

General Wallace's division, at the center of the Union line, was up early that Sunday morning, getting into formation in preparation for an attack on the Confederate breastworks south of Dover. "In the midst of the preparation," Wallace recounted, "a bugle was heard and a white flag was seen coming from the town toward the pickets. I sent my adjutant-general to meet the flag half-way and inquire its purpose. Answer was returned that General Buckner had capitulated during the night, and was now sending information of the fact to the commander of the troops in this quarter, that there might be no further bloodshed. The [third] division was ordered to advance and take possession of the works and of all public property and prisoners."[33]

From his command post Wallace then rode to Dover, encountering no challenges as he passed the Confederate positions. "I found General Buckner with his staff at breakfast," Wallace wrote. "He met me with politeness and dignity. Turning to the officers at the table, he remarked: 'General Wallace, it is not necessary to introduce you to these gentlemen; you are acquainted with them all.' They arose, came forward one by one, and gave their hands in salutation. I was then invited to breakfast, which consisted of corn bread and coffee, the best the gallant host had in his kitchen. We sat at the table about an hour and a half, when General Grant arrived and took temporary possession of the tavern as his headquarters. Later in the morning the army marched in and completed the possession."[34]

Immediately after receiving Buckner's second note, Grant had mounted his horse and begun his ride to Buckner's headquarters in Dover, where Wallace, Buckner and Buckner's staff were waiting. Grant was cordially received. "I had been at West Point three years with Buckner and afterwards served with him in the army, so that we were quite well acquainted," Grant related. "In the course of our conversation, which was very friendly, he said to me that if he had been in command I would not have got up to Donelson as easily as I did. I told him that if he had been in command I should not have tried in the way I did. I had invested their lines with a smaller force than they had to defend them, and at the same time had sent a brigade full 5,000 strong, around by water. I had relied very much upon their commander to allow me to come safely up to the outside of their works."[35]

When Grant asked Buckner about the number of troops he was surrendering, Buckner answered that he couldn't give accurate figures, explaining that "the sick and weak," as Grant put it, had been sent to Nashville during the siege, that Floyd and Pillow had left and taken many men with them, that Forrest and others had also fled with their troops and that the number of casualties was still unknown. As best as he could guess, Buckner said, Grant would find not fewer than twelve thousand and not more than fifteen thousand remaining in the trenches and within the fort.

Grant himself made an estimate of the number of Confederate troops at Fort Donelson, conceding, however, that the actual number could never be given with complete accuracy. "The largest number admitted by any writer on the Southern side," he said, "is by Colonel Preston Johnston. He gives the number at 17,000. But this must be an underestimate. The [U.S.] commissary of prisoners reported having issued rations to 14,623 Fort Donelson prisoners at Cairo, as they passed that point. General Pillow reported the killed and wounded at 2,000; but he had less opportunity of knowing the actual numbers than the officers of McClernand's division, for most of the killed and wounded fell outside their works, in front of that division, and were buried or cared for by Buckner after the surrender and when Pillow was a fugitive. It is known that Floyd and Pillow escaped during the night of the 15th, taking with them not less than 3,000 men. Forrest escaped with about 1,000 and others were leaving singly and in squads all night. It is probable that the Confederate force at Donelson, on the 15th of February, 1862, was 21,000 in round numbers.

"On the day Fort Donelson fell," Grant said, "I had 27,000 men to confront the Confederate lines and guard the road four or five miles to the left, over which all our supplies had to be drawn on wagons. During the 16th, after the surrender, additional reinforcements arrived."[36]

General Pillow wrote in an official report to assistant adjutant-general Captain Clarence Derrick on February 18, 1862: "Our total force in the field did not exceed 10,000 men, while, from what I saw of the enemy's force and from information derived from many prisoners of the enemy, we are sure he had between 30,000 and 40,000 men in the field."[37]

Later, on March 14, 1862, when he had had time to reflect on the public-relations aspect of his acquiescence to the surrender of Fort Donelson, Pillow wrote to Confederate assistant adjutant general Colonel W.W. Mackall:

> It may be asked if I was in favor of cutting our way out, why, when the command was turned over to me, I did not take it out. My reply is that, though technically speaking the command devolved on me when turned over by General Floyd, it was turned over to General Buckner in point of fact. All parties so understood it....
>
> In addition to this, General Floyd was my senior, and of high character and acknowledged ability. General Buckner, though my junior in rank, possessed high reputation as an officer of talent and experience. With the judgment of both against my position, if I had acted upon my own convictions and had failed or involved the command in heavy loss, I was apprehensive it would be regarded as an act of rashness, and brought upon me the censure of the Government and the condemnation of the country....
>
> Again, I believe we could have maintained our position another day, and have saved the army by getting back our boats and setting the command across the river; but inasmuch as General Buckner was of [the] opinion that he could not hold his position half an hour and I could not possibly do more than hold my own portion of the line, I had no alternative but to submit to the decision of a majority of my brother general officers.
>
> While I thus differed with them in opinion, I still think I did right in acquiescing in opinion with them. We all agreed in opinion that we could not long maintain the position against such overwhelming numbers of fresh troops as were daily arriving. We all agreed that the army had performed prodigies of valor, and that, if possible, further sacrifice should be avoided. Men will differ or agree according to their mental organizations. I censure not their opinions nor do I claim merit for my own. The whole matter is submitted to the judgment of the Government.[38]

General Pillow, the man whom Grant considered the de facto commander in the defense of the fallen Fort Donelson, was living up to his reputation. In Grant's conversation with Buckner after the surrender of the fort, when Pillow's escape came up, Grant is reported to have told Buckner, "If I had captured him, I would have turned him loose. I would rather have him in command of you fellows than a prisoner."[39]

8. Goodbye, Columbus

General Beauregard was making the most of his celebrity. Fort Sumter had made him a hero throughout the South, and he played the hero's role with melodramatic style. Before leaving to take a new assignment, he stood before his troops at Charleston in late May and grandly promised them that "whatever happens at first, we are certain to triumph at last, even if we had for arms only pitchforks and flintlock muskets, for every bush and haystack will become an ambush and every barn a fortress. The history of nations proves that a gallant and free people, fighting for their independence and firesides, are invincible."[1]

Greeted by cheering throngs at nearly every station along the way, he traveled by train from Charleston to Richmond, the new capital of the Confederacy, and there received a huge welcome from the crowd that had gathered to await his arrival. The carriage that delivered him to his hotel was triumphantly escorted by a band to herald his passage. He declined, however, repeated calls for speechmaking before checking into his suite at the Spotswood.

On the day after his arrival, May 31, he met with President Davis and General Robert E. Lee, then the acting commander of all Confederate troops in Virginia. Davis was thinking of giving Beauregard an assignment in Virginia, which Union forces were threatening to overrun, but he hadn't decided exactly where to send him. Lee, who had recently returned from northern Virginia, was thinking of the critical situation there, where Union troops had crossed the Potomac and occupied Alexandria. To Lee it looked as if a Union army was now about to move on Manassas, about twenty-five miles southwest of Washington. Hardly big enough to be called a town, Manassas was a rail center important to the Confederates. It was the junction of the Orange & Alexandria Railroad and the Manassas Gap Railroad. The former ran from Alexandria through Manassas southwest to Gordonsville, Virginia, then southeast to Richmond. The latter ran northwest to Winchester, Virginia, then down through the Shenandoah valley. Those two rail lines allowed the Confederates to be supplied and reinforced from their rear. Their loss would not only deprive the Confederates of their lines of communication but would provide Union forces rail access to the Confederate capital and the heart of the state. Lee suggested that Beauregard be sent to Manassas and be placed in command of the Confederate forces assembled to defend that strategic site. Davis agreed to Lee's idea and offered Beauregard the command.

Beauregard accepted. He arrived at Manassas on the night of June 2, 1861, and the next day took over its defense. Troops who had served with him at Charleston reportedly shouted, as if raising a battle cry, "Ol' Bory's come!" He immediately went to work inspecting his troops and ordering the building of defensive sites along the south side of Bull Run, the stream that flowed from northwest to southeast on the east side of Manassas.

By mid-July the gathering Union army was ready to launch its attack on the rebel defenses. On July 21 a force of some thirty thousand men under Brigadier General Irvin

McDowell assaulted Beauregard's line. With about as much luck as skill, Beauregard, his supporting commanders and his troops repelled repeated Union attacks, turned the Union's right flank and routed the attackers, sending them fleeing back to Washington. That stunning victory, gained in the first major battle of the war, brought Beauregard still more acclaim across the South.

It was what he had been living for. Born in 1818 to an aristocratic Creole family that owned a sugar cane plantation in St. Bernard Parish, Louisiana, just below New Orleans, Pierre Gustave Toutant Beauregard at age eleven had been sent by his father to New York City to attend the French School, run by the two Peugnet brothers, who had been officers in the army of Napoleon Bonaparte. Under the influence of the Peugnets and hearing their oft-told tales of service with Napoleon, Pierre, a bright and energetic student, decided he would be a soldier, too, with Napoleon as his model. With persistence he talked his reluctant father into securing a political appointment to West Point for him. He graduated in 1838 at age twenty, finishing second in a class of forty-five cadets and receiving a commission as a second lieutenant in the Army's corps of engineers. He was assigned a series of posts working on coastal defenses on the Atlantic and the gulf, including sites in Louisiana. While he was back in Louisiana he met and fell in love with the sister of his friend Charles Villere, Marie Laure Villere, and married her in September 1841.

Gen. Pierre G.T. Beauregard. He became a Southern hero after bombarding Fort Sumter into submission in April 1861 and winning a stunning victory over Union forces at the Battle of Manassas on July 21, 1861. His criticism of his superiors led to his being assigned to duty in the West, where he would no longer have easy access to the press and the Confederate congress (Library of Congress).

Service in the Mexican War followed five years later, which at last gave him a chance at glory. He seized the opportunity and came out of the war with a distinguished record for valor, leadership and tactical judgment. Back in the U.S. after the capture of Mexico City, he received new engineering assignments, remarried after suffering the loss of Marie Laure, who died giving birth to their third child, and in January 1861, thanks to the influence of his new wife's brother-in-law, Senator John Slidell, he was appointed superintendent of the U.S. Military Academy at West Point.

On January 24, 1861, the day after he assumed the superintendency, the Army, having suddenly realized its mistake in appointing a secessionist sympathizer to that position, revoked the appointment. On January 26, Louisiana's secession convention voted to withdraw the state from the Union. On January 28, five days after taking over the position, Captain Beauregard, at the War Department's request, resigned as superintendent of West Point. He left for New Orleans shortly thereafter. On February 20 his resignation from the United States Army became effective.

In a long, late-night meeting with Confederate President Davis in Montgomery on February 26, 1861, Beauregard was given command of all Confederate and South Carolina armed forces at Charleston, where the crisis over Fort Sumter had become explosive, and the next day, before leaving for Charleston, he learned he had been appointed the Confederacy's first brigadier general. He was on his way to fame.

In early 1862 he was forty-three years old, his birthday being the twenty-eighth of May. To most who saw him, according to his biographers, he looked French, or at least foreign. Perhaps his obviously French name helped some make that observation. He was five feet seven inches tall and weighed about a hundred and fifty pounds, with his hair cut above his ears and parted down the left side of his head. His hair, according to one report, had been jet black when he served at Charleston, but now, since the Union blockade had cut off the supply of imported hair dye, it had turned white. He had a broad forehead and high cheekbones, and a dark, bushy mustache across the entire width of his mouth. His eyes, large and melancholy seeming, were perhaps his most arresting feature. He was characterized by those who knew him as courteous, solemn, sometimes reserved and sometimes abrupt. His expression was usually impassive, but he could rise to eloquent passion when aroused, speaking with a faint French accent. One of his worst faults was his lack of careful attention to vital details. Another was his predilection for judging the actions of his superiors and putting his criticisms into writing.

His criticisms, some of them made public in Richmond newspapers, had so antagonized Secretary of War Judah Benjamin and President Jefferson Davis that they decided to send him someplace where he would not be so troublesome and would not have the easy access to the press and to the Confederate congress that he enjoyed in Virginia. A full general now, in January 1862 he was offered a post in the West, serving under General Albert Sidney Johnston, the Confederates' over-all commander in the West. Beauregard would command the left wing of the Confederate defensive line that stretched across nearly half of Kentucky, from Columbus on the Mississippi River to Bowling Green in south central Kentucky. The situation in the West had become critical, he was told, and it was there that he was needed. He accepted the transfer, saying, "I am a soldier of the cause and of my country, ready ... to do my duty cheerfully, wherever placed by the constituted authorities."[2]

He left Manassas for the new assignment on February 2, traveling by train first to Nashville, where as the Confederacy's war hero he was presented to the Tennessee legislature. From Nashville he went on to Bowling Green, which he reached on February 4. There he conferred with General Johnston, whom he was meeting for the first time. Johnston was an impressively handsome giant of a man, more than six feet tall, broad in the shoulders, thick in the chest, fifty-nine years old, dignified and solemn, a highly regarded former general of the United States Army.

Johnston's command included not only the forty-eight thousand troops positioned along the one-hundred-and-fifty-mile-long Kentucky line, anchored at Columbus and at Bowling Green, but also some twenty thousand troops in Arkansas under the command of Major General Earl Van Dorn. Perhaps because he considered his greatest threat to be the reported (and hugely exaggerated) eighty-thousand-man Union force of Major General Don Carlos Buell positioned at Louisville, General Johnston had established his command post at Bowling Green, which stands athwart the road to Nashville, a city that Johnston deemed vital to the Confederacy and its war effort. Nashville was not only the capital of Tennessee but was the site of an important gunpowder plant and two large supply depots and was the trade center for much of the food the South required. To protect it Johnston had but about twenty-five thousand troops. Seeing himself woefully undermanned to defend against the Union threats, from Buell in the north and Grant to the west, Johnston had repeatedly asked for reinforcements, making pleas that had gone unheeded.

The day after his arrival at Bowling Green, February 5, Beauregard, with Johnston, made an inspection of the works that had been erected to defend the city and was unimpressed with them. He believed they could be easily turned and defeated. Beauregard had a reputation for expertise in fortifications, and his advice to Johnston was to abandon Bowling Green and move its defending troops to forts Henry and Donelson. His argument was that the city would have to be evacuated anyway if the concentrated Union forces were to advance against it. Johnston rejected that advice, clinging to the idea that Bowling Green was essential to the defense of Nashville.

It was on February 6, the day following Beauregard's inspection of Bowling Green's fortifications, that Flag Officer Foote and his Union gunboats captured Fort Henry and turned it over to General Grant and his troops. Oddly, a rumor that Beauregard was coming from Virginia and bringing with him fifteen regiments of reinforcements was what had spurred General Halleck into approving Grant's proposed assault on Fort Henry, resulting in its capture. News of the fall of the fort was delivered to Beauregard on February 7, while he was sick in bed, suffering from the effects of an operation on his throat, which he had undergone shortly before leaving Virginia. Beauregard and Johnston and Brigadier General William J. Hardee, one of Johnston's Arkansas troop commanders and the bearer of the news about Fort Henry, held a war council to decide what should be done about Fort Donelson now that Fort Henry was in Union hands.

Beauregard argued for concentrating Johnston's forces at Fort Donelson, which was Grant's obvious next objective, but in the end he signed on to Johnston's plan to give up on Fort Donelson, believing it could no longer be held, and move the army at Bowling Green to Nashville, where it would establish a defensive position on the south side of the Cumberland River. With the Union's expected capture of Fort Donelson would come the threat of Union control of the Cumberland, and Johnston feared having his army trapped on the north side of the river, with Foote's gunboat fleet behind him, Buell's army in front of him and Grant on his left flank. Johnston's hope was that the garrison at Fort Donelson could hold out long enough to allow his Bowling Green army to get to Nashville and erect fortifications that could turn back Foote's gunboats. Apparently to that end, Johnston ordered twelve thousand troops — nearly half of his force — sent to Fort Donelson, despite having conceded it could not be held and believing that it could be taken, like Fort Henry, with gunboats alone.

With Grant and Foote now on the Tennessee River, Johnston's troops at Bowling Green were cut off from the seventeen-thousand-man Confederate force at Columbus, commanded by General Polk. Johnston's command for the time being would have to operate as two independent units, with Johnston commanding the Bowling Green troops and Beauregard the troops at Columbus. In a note sent to Richmond, Johnston reported that both Beauregard and Hardee agreed that in light of the fall of Fort Henry and the threat to Fort Donelson, the Confederates' line of defense had to be shifted southward. The plan to which the three generals agreed called for the troops at Columbus to be moved to Humboldt, Tennessee, leaving only a small garrison to man the Columbus fortifications.

Johnston's evacuation of Bowling Green began on February 11, and on February 13, Beauregard, struggling to overcome a throat ailment, left for Columbus, taking time first to write to Johnston that he proposed to abandon Columbus completely and that the western anchor of the new Confederate line of defense be established at Island No. 10, a small land mass in the Mississippi River about sixty miles below Columbus, and at Fort Pillow, Tennessee, on the Mississippi some forty-five miles above Memphis. The main body of the troops to be evacuated from Columbus, he suggested, would be sent to Jackson, Tennessee, rather than Humboldt, placing them in a more advantageous position to defend the railroad lines of western Tennessee. Johnston replied that he would meet Beauregard in Nashville to discuss his proposal.

The two of them met on February 14, Beauregard still suffering with his throat. Apparently uninterested in assuming over-all management of western operations, Johnston told Beauregard that he would have to make decisions on his own and that he was free to abandon Columbus if the government in Richmond approved.

That concession failed to cheer the ailing Beauregard. In a letter he wrote to Roger A. Pryor, one of his friends in the Confederate congress, Beauregard complained that "I am taking the helm when the ship is already on the breakers, and with but a few sailors to man it. How it is to be extricated from its present perilous condition Providence alone can determine."[3] From Nashville, Beauregard traveled southwest to Corinth, Mississippi, where during his stop he received a message from Johnston reporting that Fort Donelson had fallen on February 16.

From Corinth he went to Jackson, Tennessee, where he became so ill that he had to halt his travel. On February 18 Johnston wired him that he, Johnston, was withdrawing his troops from Nashville and falling back in the face of Buell's advancing army. With no plan of his own, he told Beauregard to do whatever he saw fit. Beauregard decided to evacuate Columbus immediately, while there was still a way out. He wired the Confederate army's adjutant general in Richmond to inform him of his intention. Secretary of War Benjamin notified Beauregard that his decision to abandon Columbus was approved and on February 20 ordered General Polk, the commander at Columbus, to effect the evacuation.

By February 23 the evacuation was well under way, most of the garrison and other troops, the fort's supplies and many of its one hundred and forty big guns being transported down the river on barges.

On March 1, Flag Officer Foote reported to U.S. Secretary of the Navy Welles what was occurring at Columbus:

> SIR,—Lieutenant-Commanding Phelps, sent with a flag of truce today to Columbus, has this moment returned, and reports that Columbus is being evacuated. He saw the rebels burning their winter-quarters, and removing their heavy guns on the bluffs; but the guns in the water-batteries remain intact. He also saw a large force of heavy cavalry drawn up ostentatiously on the bluffs, but no infantry were to be seen as heretofore; and the encampment seen in our armed reconnoissance [sic] a few days ago has been removed. Large fires were visible in the town of Columbus and upon the river banks below, indicating the destruction of the town, military stores, and equipment.[4]

On March 2, Polk set fire to the last of his buildings and abandoned the site. On the morning of March 4, Foote's gunboats, accompanied by transport steamers carrying two regiments of Union infantry under the command of Brigadier General William T. Sherman, made an armed reconnaissance down to Columbus and finding it evacuated, took possession of the works. A news correspondent, Alexander Simplot, in a report published in *Harper's Weekly*, described the ruined Confederate fortress:

> The river batteries have been almost entirely demolished — three tiers of them — their guns dismounted and thrown into the river, the gun-carriages mutilated and magazines demol-

ished, leaving nothing to mark their former presence save ruined breast-works and huge piles of cannon-balls and shells.

Just below the upper river battery, a huge chain, which has been christened "Pillow's Folly," emerges from the water, extends up the almost perpendicular bank a hundred feet or more, and disappears under the soil, where it extends to—the Lord only knows where. This is the Kentucky end of the chain which the valiant inside-ditchdigger had stretched across the river to obstruct the passage of our gun-boats. A few feet above the chain and below the battery I counted five sixty-four pound guns which had been thrown over the breast-works, with the intention of sinking them in the river; but they had lodged in the yielding earth and become unmovable. Two others lay a few rods below, which had been taken from the batteries on the bluff.

Within the breast-works on the hill there was nothing to be seen but the wildest desolation. Burning piles of rubbish, smouldering heaps of grain — the remnants of burned warehouses—charred timbers of what were once quarters for the troops, broken gun-carriages and disabled ordnance, completed the picture.

Leaving the lower town and ascending the hill in the rear, we get the most comprehensive view of the rebel works. From one point near the top of the hill my guide pointed out to me the locality of no less than eight different batteries, besides the positions of forty-five or fifty isolated pieces of heavy artillery. In all, I computed that a month ago there could not have been less than one hundred and thirty pieces of artillery, of the calibre of twenty-four pounders and upward, added to which there were over seventy pieces of light field artillery. Most of these heavy guns are now in the river, or disabled upon the works.[5]

The Confederates had stretched an enormous chain, its links weighing twenty pounds apiece, its weight supported by anchored barges, across the breadth of the river. The chain was secured by a six-ton sea anchor buried in the ground on the Columbus side of the river and attached to a capstan on the Missouri side. Explosive mines, or torpedoes, had been placed upriver of the chain. In addition to the main earthworks, which had been named Fort DeRussy in honor of General Polk's chief engineering officer, Lewis G. DeRussy, there were two smaller sets of works situated on the bluff, which was surrounded by miles of trenches and abatis. Electrically fired land mines had been placed along the roads leading to Columbus.

Now the menacing fortress and its outworks and defensive devices lay ruined and forsaken. Its big guns no longer forbade passage down the river. Their line ruptured by the seizure of forts Henry and Donelson, their flank in western Kentucky turned, the Confederates had withdrawn to form a new line of defense. The first major barrier to the Union's reach down the Mississippi had been removed.

9. Fortress Island

Now vanished, swept away by the irresistible force of the river's current, Island No. 10 was a huge sandbar in 1862, about a mile long and 450 yards wide at its widest point, rising about ten feet above the surface of the river at low water. Designated No. 10 because in the nineteenth century islands in the river below Cairo were numbered sequentially beginning at the mouth of the Ohio, it was situated near the bottom of a U-shaped turn that created almost parallel courses of the river, each about twelve miles long, one flowing south and one flowing north, about eight miles apart. The river's northbound course, lying west of the southbound, made a counterclockwise hairpin turn at New Madrid and resumed a southward direction.

The island provided an almost ideal defensive position. Vessels coming down the Mississippi had to negotiate a slow, tight turn to the right as they approached and attempted to pass the island, making them vulnerable to the artillery mounted on two sides of the island and on the shore above and below the island. It was situated diagonally in the river, with its narrow northern tip in midstream and its wide southern end about half a mile off the Tennessee shore. From the riverbank, across a natural levee, a road led to Tiptonville, Tennessee, a riverfront town about ten miles to the south. That road provided the only practicable land approach to the island — and the only route of retreat. The swamp that lay between the road and Reelfoot Lake, to the east, rendered Island No. 10 otherwise inaccessible, except from the river.

On February 23, 1862, Brigadier General John Pope, the man who had been Grant's commanding officer in Missouri and who had been passed over by General Frémont for appointment to the command at Cairo, had been named by Frémont's replacement, Major General "Old Brains" Halleck, to command the Union's Army of the Mississippi. He was given some twenty-six thousand troops and ordered to eliminate the fortified barriers erected by the rebels on the Mississippi River. His first objective: Island No. 10.

Dark-haired and black-bearded, General Pope would observe his fortieth birthday during his campaign to capture the island. Born in Louisville, the son of a federal judge, he was a graduate of the U.S. Military Academy at West Point, class of 1842, had served as a topographical engineer in Florida and along the Canadian border, then had fought under General Zachary Taylor during the Mexican War and been brevetted to the rank of captain. After the war, he had served as a surveyor in Minnesota, had been chief engineer of the Army's Department of New Mexico and had surveyed a route for the Pacific Railroad. He was one of four officers chosen to escort Abraham Lincoln, a friend of Pope's father, to Washington, D.C., for the inauguration. On June 14, 1861, he was appointed a brigadier general of volunteers and sent to Illinois to recruit volunteers, then was named to assume command, under General Frémont, of the Army's District of North and Central Missouri.

Aggressive, impatient, boastful and self-assured to the point of being obnoxious, Pope had become disgruntled with Frémont and had attempted to pull political strings to have him removed from his command. After Frémont had been replaced for other reasons, Pope's success at driving back the Confederate force of General Sterling Price and taking twelve hundred prisoners in a battle at Blackwater, Missouri, had attracted the attention of General Halleck and won Pope the assignment to attack the Confederate strongpoints down the Mississippi.

Pope began his campaign against Island No. 10 shortly before the rebels evacuated Columbus. He took a transport steamer down to Commerce, Missouri, below Cape Girardeau, where the troops assigned to him were assembling, coming from St. Louis, Cairo and Cincinnati. After organizing them into brigades and divisions, Pope on February 28 began a march down the tip of southeastern Missouri, treading rough corduroy roads that traversed the swampy lowlands along the Mississippi, on the way to New Madrid. On the way, he routed a rebel force commanded by Brigadier General M. Jeff Thompson that had attempted to block the march, and his muddied army reached the vicinity of New Madrid on the morning of March 3.

The leading elements of his army, units of the division commanded by Brigadier General Schuyler Hamilton, deployed as skirmishers and advanced on the town, driving the Confederate pickets back into their trenches and drawing the fire of the Confederates' artillery emplaced along the town's eastern fortification, a works the rebels called Fort Thompson. Soon the gunboats of Captain George N. Hollins, commander of Confederate naval forces on the Mississippi, also opened fire.

General Pope quickly decided against making a direct attack on the rebel fortifications. He believed he could take them by a swift assault, but could not hold them so long as the rebel gunboats could rake the field with their guns. He then determined to lay a siege on the town and its defending fortifications. He ordered his troops to encamp about two miles back from the river and dispatched a message to Cairo, urgently requesting that heavy artillery, big siege guns, be sent to him.

He also ordered three infantry regiments— the Eleventh Missouri, the Twenty-sixth Illinois and the Forty-seventh Illinois— plus four guns of the First Missouri Light Artillery, one company of engineers and two cavalry companies to move south under the command of Colonel Joseph B. Plummer and occupy the town of Point Pleasant, some thirteen miles below New Madrid and almost directly opposite Island No. 10. Their mission was to use their artillery to prevent rebel transports from bringing reinforcements to New Madrid and Island No. 10 and to do what they could to hold the Confederate gunboats at bay. Captain Hollins had come up from New Orleans with five wooden gunboats— the *McRae*, the *Livingston*, the *Maurepas*, the *General Polk* and the *Ivy*— which were now stationed at Island No. 10 and New Madrid. The ironclad *Manassas* had also been part of Hollins's flotilla, but had to be sent back to New Orleans.

Plummer's troops began their march toward Point Pleasant on the morning of March 5, taking a circuitous route to avoid the river and the fire of the Confederate gunboats. They halted within about three miles of the town and bivouacked for the night. The next day a rebel gunboat harassed Plummer's cavalry and artillery units and prevented their occupying the town, but it was eventually driven off by rifle fire. By the morning of March 7 Plummer's men, working during the night, had dug emplacements for the four artillery pieces, which were positioned a short distance from the river, and had dug lines of rifle pits that connected the artillery emplacements. Later on the 7th General Pope telegraphed Halleck to report that Plummer and his troops had established their position at Point Pleasant. Their artillery would block the passage of rebel transports beyond Point Pleasant. Confederate gunboats attempting to knock out Plummer's artillery were met by the fire of Union sharpshooters in the rifle pits who picked off rebel crewmen with deadly accuracy, eventually forcing the gunboats to hug the Tennessee shore and keep their distance as they moved past the line of rifle pits.

When he requested heavy artillery, Pope had specified rifled thirty-two-pounders, but Brigadier General George W. Cullum, Halleck's chief of staff, who was posted at Cairo and was in charge of sending reinforcements, equipment and supplies to the troops in Halleck's command, had been unable to find thirty-twos and had instead procured three twenty-four-pounders and one eight-inch howitzer. Colonel Josiah W. Bissell, commander of Pope's engineer regiment, was sent to Cairo to await the guns' arrival, and on March 1, when the four pieces were delivered, he promptly had them shipped across the river to Bird's Point, then sent by rail to Sikeston, about twenty miles north of New Madrid. At Sikeston they were received by Pope's artillerymen and Bissell's engineers, who mounted them on carriages and had them hauled by horses down the swampy road that had been recently improved by Union engineers. The guns arrived at the Union position outside New Madrid around sunset on March 12.

By three o'clock the next morning the guns' emplacements had been laboriously dug under the cover of darkness. The big guns, still in the dark, were then mounted in position and as the sun rose on March 13, they commenced firing on Fort Thompson.

It was only then that the Confederate commander at Fort Thompson learned that the Union forces now had heavy artillery. The guns of both rebel fortifications quickly returned the fire and were joined by the guns of the Confederate gunboats, firing from a distance. More eager to knock out the rebel boats than the rebel fortifications, General Pope ordered his artillerymen to turn their guns on the gunboats, which withdrew after suffering a number of hits but little damage.

That evening, after a day of pounding by Pope's siege guns, Brigadier General John P. McCown, the Confederate commander at New Madrid and Island No. 10, went aboard Hollins's flagship and met with Hollins in a council of war that included Brigadier General A.P. Stewart, commanding the rebels' two fortified works at New Madrid. Surprised by the sudden appearance of the siege guns, Hollins said he had been assured that heavy artillery could not be brought through the swamp above New Madrid and said his vessels were not equipped to deal with heavy artillery. General McCown remarked that it seemed obvious that Pope intended to capture Fort Thompson by using traditional siege tactics, moving the Union trenches and artillery ever closer. No help, no reinforcements, he said, could be expected to reach the Confederates in less than ten days. At that, General Stewart replied that he could not hold out for even three days.

The three Confederate leaders agreed then that the rebel fortifications, manned by some thirty-five hundred troops facing an overwhelming Union force, would have to be abandoned. About ten o'clock that night three gunboats and two transport steamers drew up beside the rebel works in darkness and a driving rain, and the embattled New Madrid defenders spiked their artillery pieces with rat-tail files, boarded the transports and slipped across the river without being detected.

On the morning of March 14, around six o'clock, two rebel deserters, feeling their way through a thick fog, approached the Union siege line under a white flag and reported that New Madrid had been evacuated. The officers in command of the two Union companies manning the heavy guns, Captain Mowrer and Lieutenant Fletcher, then entered the deserted Fort Thompson and hoisted the Stars and Stripes above it.

Pope's troops were now in control of the west side of the river. The next move would be against Island No. 10 itself and its supporting batteries.

The fortifications on and beside the island were formidable. Under the direction of Confederate Captain Asa B. Gray, construction of the island's forbidding batteries had begun in August 1861. Gray positioned the uppermost battery, known as Battery No. 1, or the Redan Battery, on the Tennessee shore about a mile and a half above the island. It commanded the approach to the first of the two turns that enemy vessels had to make to proceed down the river. For more than a mile, approaching boats would be headed directly toward the menacing maws of the heavy artillery mounted at Battery No. 1.

Work on the fortifications had been interrupted later in 1861, but had resumed after the fall of forts Henry and Donelson, events that had given Island No. 10 additional importance for the Confederates. When General McCown took over command of the island on February 26, 1862, he continued the work of Captain Gray. By the time Pope and his troops arrived, five batteries comprising twenty-four artillery pieces had been established on the Tennessee shore above the island. Five batteries on the island itself mounted a total of nineteen big guns, and a floating battery of nine guns was set up on a barge, the *New Orleans*, moored at the north end of the island, in midstream. Besides that armament, the rebels also had mounted guns at the two works they had built at New Madrid: Fort Thompson, armed with fourteen guns, on the east side of the town, and Fort Bankhead, with seven guns, on the west side, the two fortifications now in Union hands.

Once the rebels' evacuation of New Madrid was confirmed, Pope moved General Hamilton's division into the abandoned works. Finding that not all of the rebel artillery pieces had been effectively spiked, Pope's artillerymen turned the captured guns toward the river. During the night of March 14 new battery positions were dug and established along a lengthy stretch of the river, just back from the riverbank, extending Pope's line facing the Tennessee shore and Island No. 10 to seventeen miles, from New Madrid to just below Point Pleasant.

When daylight on March 15 revealed the muzzles of the Union army's big guns protruding over the riverbank, facing toward the rebels, the five Confederate gunboats soon set out to destroy them. They moved to within three hundred yards of the west bank of the river and opened a furious cannonade against the Union gun positions, which immediately returned the gunboats' fire. In the intense exchange of fire, one gunboat was sunk and others damaged, and several of Confederate gunners were shot by sharpshooters posted in the rifle pits along the river. After an hour and a half the gunboats broke off the engagement and withdrew down the river.

Eager to move against Island No. 10, Pope devised a plan to cross the river by boat just below the island and land troops on the Tennessee shore, capture the Confederates' defensive positions and isolate the island's garrison. To effect the plan, however, he needed Flag Officer Foote's armored gunboats to protect the troops from Confederate gunboats during the crossing and to destroy the rebel gun emplacements along the riverbank before making the landing. He also needed transport steamers to ferry the troops across the river.

Repeated calls for Foote to send his fleet to Island No. 10 were turned aside by the flag officer. His reasons were set out in a March 4 letter he wrote to Navy Secretary Welles:

Sir,—I have the honor to forward a copy of the telegram sent to the Department to-day announcing the fall of Columbus.

The fleet not being in a condition to proceed down to Island No. Ten and to New Madrid, where the rebels are represented as fortifying, I leave for Cairo immediately to make the necessary preparation for going down the river with a suitable force of gun-boats and mortar-boats in a proper condition for effective service. I am fully impressed with the importance of proceeding to New Madrid as soon as possible, where General Pope has arrived with ten thousand men; but such is the condition of my command that I shall decline moving, as I informed Generals Sherman and Cullum, unless I am ordered to do so by the Secretary of the Navy, as I must be the judge of the condition of the fleet, and when it is prepared for the service required.[1]

Foote was determined not to be rushed by the impatient Pope, in the way he felt he had let Halleck rush him to Fort Donelson, a lingering regret in Foote's mind. And so it was not until the morning of March 14 that Foote's fleet of seven ironclad gunboats and ten mortar boats at last left Cairo, steaming for Island No. 10. Along the way, at Columbus, the fleet was joined by Union transports carrying twelve hundred troops commanded by Colonel John Buford, and together the boats reached Hickman, Kentucky, that evening. The next morning they continued the voyage toward Island No. 10. Commander Henry Walke, captain of the *Carondelet*, one of the seven ironclads, provided an eyewitness account:

On March 15th the flotilla and transports continued on their way to Island Number Ten, arriving in its vicinity about nine in the morning. The strong and muddy current of the river had overflowed its banks and carried away every movable thing. Houses, trees, fences, and wrecks of all kinds were being swept rapidly down-stream. The twists and turns of the river near Island Number Ten are certainly remarkable. Within a radius of eight miles from the island it crosses the boundary line of Kentucky and Tennessee three times, running on almost every point of the compass. We were greatly surprised when we arrived above Island Number Ten and saw on the bluffs a chain of forts extending for four miles along the crescent-shaped shore, with the white tents of the enemy in the rear. And there lay the island in the lower corner of the crescent, with the side fronting the Missouri shore lined with heavy ordnance, so trained that with the artillery on the opposite shore almost every point on the river between the island and the Missouri bank could be reached at once by all the enemy's batteries.[2]

The threat posed by the Confederates' big guns daunted Flag Officer Foote. He was no longer willing to send his gunboats into the face of heavy artillery believing their iron cladding would keep them safe. He had learned the hard way at Fort Donelson that the ironclads could be crippled by shot or shell. At Island No. 10 the danger was even greater. Unlike the situation at Fort Donelson, where his gunboats attacked the rebel fortification from downriver, moving against the current, at Island No. 10 his boats would be attacking from upriver, moving in the direction of the current. At Fort Donelson the disabled Union gunboats had drifted *away* from the enemy. At Island No. 10 a disabled vessel would helplessly drift with the current into further enemy fire and into enemy water, where it would certainly be either destroyed or captured. This time, Foote had resolved, his assault on rebel fortifications would be more cautious, made from a prudent distance.

His first move against the island came on March 15 when through a dense fog and heavy rain he managed to position two of the mortar boats within range of the rebel positions. Early the next morning he opened fire. "I placed the mortar-boats in as good a position as the circumstances would admit," he reported to Secretary Welles, "when[ce] they shelled several regiments out of their encampments, and, at extreme range, reached the batteries on No. Ten, the floating battery, and the five batteries on the Tennessee shore."[3] The mortar boats were actually rectangular barges on which a thick, wooden, seven-foot-high protective bulkhead had been built to surround the monstrous, stubby mortar mounted in the center of the barge, one mortar per barge. The mortar fired a shot thirteen inches in diameter and weighing 215 pounds. The mortar was loaded with the aid of a derrick, which dropped the enormous ball into the gaping mouth of the mortar. Twenty-three pounds of gunpowder were then required to blast the shot into a parabola that carried it into the sky and onto its target. When the mortar was fired, the men serving it protected themselves from the massive concussion by standing or squatting outside the protective bulkhead.

The bombardment resumed on March 16 (General Pope's birthday). A nineteenth-century account recorded the dramatic scene and action:

> Five [Union] gunboats and four mortar-boats moved down to within two thousand yards of the upper battery or redan, and opened fire. The batteries on main-land and island replied. One hundred pieces of heavy ordnance rent the quivering air with their thunder. The rampart of the redan had been constructed twenty-four feet thick, but the high water beating against it had washed it, and, by percolation, softened it. The heavy shot from the gunboats passed through it.
>
> Thirteen-inch shells exploding in the ground made caverns in the soil. Water stood on the ground within, and the artillerists wade in mud and water. The conflict lasted till evening. The staff of the signal-flag used in the redan was shattered by a shot; but the officer, Lieutenant Jones, picking up the flag, and using his arm as a staff, continued signalling. The rampart of the redan was torn and ridged, and one sixty-four gun was dismounted and another injured, an officer killed, and seven enlisted men wounded. On the island a one hundred and twenty-eight pound gun burst. In the fleet a gun burst on the Pittsburg, killing and wounding fourteen men.[4]

On the morning of March 17 Foote tried a new technique. To prevent a disabled vessel from drifting toward the rebels, he had his flag steamer, the ironclad *Benton*, tied between two other gunboats. If one boat lost propulsion or steering, the others would provide it. Foote reported the details of the action that followed:

> Soon after daylight, the mortar-boats being in position, I had the *Benton* lashed between two other steamers—the *Cincinnati* and the *St. Louis*—and with the remaining iron-clad steamers made an attack on the forts, at a distance of two thousand yards or more, on account of the rapid current rendering the boats too unmanageable to come within a shorter range, without endangering their being carried under the enemy's guns, and as a nearer approach would expose the bows and quarters of the vessels—their most vulnerable points—to a fire of six other batteries, mounting forty-three guns. We opened fire on the upper fort on the Tennessee shore at meridian, and continued to give and receive quite a brisk fire from this and also four other batteries on the same shore until darkness obscured the forts from view. The ten mortars, in the mean time, shelled the troops out of range, excepting those manning the batteries.
>
> The upper fort was badly cut up by the *Benton* and the other boats with her. We dismounted one of their guns, and the men, at times, ran from the batteries....
>
> In the attack of to-day this vessel (*Benton*) received four shots, while a rifle-gun burst aboard the *St. Louis*, killing and wounding fifteen, officers and men. I inclose a list of casualties. The *Cincinnati* has had her engines injured, which may render it necessary for me to send her to Cairo for repairs....[5]

The gunboats, firing once every minute, as instructed by the flag officer, had managed to silence all but one of the guns in the upper fort, Battery No. 1. When he reported the action, Foote included a complaint about the ammunition the Navy had provided. "Our shells," he told Welles, "bursting prematurely, we have to drown them before loading the guns. The fuses—many of which, I am informed, were made before the Mexican War—

ought to have been condemned." Commander Walke also complained. In his account of the first engagement at the island, he cited the explosion of the *St. Louis*'s rifled gun as "another proof of the truth of the saying that the guns furnished the Western flotilla were less destructive to the enemy than to ourselves."

Foote realized his bombardment was generally ineffectual. On March 19 he admitted as much in a letter to his wife, telling her, "We are not making much progress, firing almost beyond the enemy's range." His futile efforts to batter the Confederates into submission became an object of ridicule among Pope's officers. One of them, Colonel Gilmore of Chillicothe, Ohio, when a question was asked about Foote's fleet at an officers' meeting, reportedly answered, "Oh, it is still bombarding the state of Tennessee at long range." The Confederates claimed that the fire of Foote's gunboats had caused no casualties or damage at Island No. 10.

Above New Madrid a stream—called John's Bayou by the Confederates and Wilson's Bayou by U.S. engineers—emptied into the Mississippi, coming out of the swamp that lay across the peninsula formed by the first of the two big turns at New Madrid and Island No. 10. General Hamilton suggested to Pope that a channel might be cleared to allow that bayou to connect with the river water that flowed into a slough some ten miles above the first turn, creating a twelve-mile-long waterway that would allow the transport steamers and gunboats that Pope needed for his intended attack to cut across the peninsula and reach New Madrid without having to brave the island's guns.

On March 19, Pope proposed that plan to General Halleck, who swiftly and enthusiastically endorsed it, replying to Pope, "If you can in this way turn and capture the enemy, it will be one of the most brilliant feats of the war." The task of constructing the channel was turned over to Colonel Bissell and his regiment of engineers. Pope instructed Bissell to call for help from the rest of the troops if needed, and he immediately sent a request to Cairo for four light-draft steamers and the tools and equipment needed to get the project started. It required cutting a swath through the trees and underbrush to create a channel fifty feet wide and four and a half feet deep. Where the swamp water was too shallow, the channel had to be excavated. Tree trunks had to be sawed off underwater and then dragged out of the channel. The work would be long and laborious, done by men on the decks of two steamer tugs and two barges or standing in the frigid water of the swamp.

The impatient Pope was taking other measures to circumvent Foote's continued obstruction. He ordered the construction of floating batteries to be manned by his troops. Each battery would be made up of three heavy barges, bolted together. On the middle barge a four-foot-thick timber bulkhead was erected at both ends and on both sides. Three heavy guns were mounted in the center of the bulkheads, and each carried eighty sharpshooters. The decks of the barges attached to either side of the center barge were covered by watertight barrels lashed together, and on top of the barrels were laid wooden rails with bales of cotton packed tightly between the rails. A shot fired at the floating battery would have to penetrate a flanking barge, passing through twenty feet of wooden rails and cotton bales to reach the center barge. The flanking barges, loaded with buoyant barrels, were virtually unsinkable. The barges were to be towed by steamers to a spot opposite New Madrid.

Meanwhile, the garrison at Island No. 10 and its outworks was being shifted. On the night of March 17, General McCown had taken six regiments of infantry, two units of artillery and two cavalry units and left Island No. 10's defenses, heading for Fort Pillow and then to Corinth, where they would join the gathering force of General Albert Sidney Johnston. Confederate gunboats in the river below the island by now had been reduced to the function of dispatch boats and transports, carrying supplies each night to Tiptonville, despite the fire from Union batteries on the west bank of the river. Captain Hollins had decided that it was useless to fight artillery batteries with wooden gunboats, since the guns on shore were protected by parapets and nothing was to be gained by firing into them except perhaps the killing of a few Union artillerymen.

At last moved by Pope's repeated appeals to send gunboats and transports to New Madrid, Foote on March 20 polled his gunboat captains to find out if they thought it practicable to try to take a gunboat past the rebel fortifications on Island No. 10 and along the Tennessee shore in order to reach New Madrid. All opposed the idea, believing it to be a suicide mission, except for Commander Walke of the *Carondelet*. "I did not think so," Walke recalled, "but believed with General Pope that, under the cover of darkness and other favorable circumstances, a gunboat might be run past the enemy's batteries, formidable as they were with nearly fifty guns. And although fully aware of the hazardous nature of the enterprise, I knew that the aid of a gunboat was absolutely necessary to enable General Pope to succeed in his operations against the enemy, and thought the importance of this success justified the risk."[12]

Walke felt a rising urgency to take Island No. 10, knowing that Pope's officers were becoming increasingly impatient and that the Confederates were building several large, powerful ironclad gunboats that could ascend the Mississippi, silence Pope's big guns, relieve the embattled garrison at Island No. 10 and maintain the island as a formidable obstruction to a Union fleet attempting to descend the Mississippi from Cairo or above.

Foote was becoming resigned to making an attempt to run past the island, but he wanted to be sure the object was worth the gamble of his ironclads and be certain there was no other way to take the island. On March 20, after polling his captains, he wrote to Secretary Welles:

> I have been seriously disposed to run the blockade myself with this vessel [the *Benton*], which is better protected than the other boats, although she is slow, and works sluggishly; but, upon reconsideration, as her loss would be so great if we failed, and my personal services here are considered so important with the fleet and transports, I have, for the present abandoned the idea.
>
> When the object of running the blockade becomes adequate to the risk, I shall not hesitate to do it.

He was hoping against hope that something would happen to allow his ironclads to avoid the daunting mission. "The place may be occupied by us in a short time without an assault," he told Welles, "as the rebels must be cut off from their necessary supplies. Still, if this do [*sic*] not soon take place, it may become necessary to force the blockade, or adopt some other measures which have not yet suggested themselves."

Walke felt none of Foote's reluctance. On March 29 the flag officer held a council of war aboard the *Benton* and again called for his captains to give their opinions on the prospect of running past Island No. 10. Again all agreed that it was too hazardous a mission — except for Walke, who again was in favor of trying it. When asked if he was willing to make the attempt himself, he said he was. Foote accepted Walke's offer and told his captains that he felt relieved of a heavy responsibility, since he was determined to send none but volunteers on an expedition he regarded as perilous and of very doubtful success.

On March 30 Foote issued his order formally directing Walke to undertake the mission:

Sir,—You will avail yourself of the first fog or rainy night, and drift your steamer down past the batteries on the Tennessee shore and Island No. Ten until you reach New Madrid.

I assign you this service, as it is vitally important to the capture of this place that a gunboat should soon be at New Madrid for the purpose of covering General Pope's army while he crosses at that point to the opposite shore, or to the Tennessee side of the river, that he may move his army up to Island No. Ten, and attack the rebels in rear while we attack them in front.

Should you succeed in reaching General Pope, you will freely confer with him, and adopt his suggestions, so far as your superior knowledge of what your boat will perform and enable you to do, for the purpose of protecting his force while crossing the river.

You will also, if you have coal, and the current of the river will permit, steam up the river while the army moves, for the purpose of attacking their fortifications. Still, you will act cautiously here, as your own will be the only boat below....

If you successfully perform the duty assigned you, which you so willingly undertake, it will reflect the highest credit upon you and all belonging to your vessel....

Commending you and all who compose your command to the care and protection of God, who rules and directs all things, I am, respectfully, your obedient servant,

A.H. Foote, Flag-Officer.

P.S.—Should you meet with disaster, you will, as a last resort, destroy the steam machinery; and, if impossible to escape, set fire to your gun-boat or sink her, and prevent her from falling into the hands of the rebels.

A.H.F.

While Walke was making preparations for his mission, Foote continued to attack the Confederate defenses. At eleven o'clock on the night of April 1 the crews of the *Benton* and four other of Foote's gunboats joined some fifty soldiers in a joint operation under the command of Colonel George W. Roberts of the Second Illinois Volunteer Regiment. They rowed down the eastern shore of the river to the uppermost rebel battery, chased off a group of Confederate sentries, landed their small boats, spiked the battery's eleven guns before the rebels had a chance to respond and speedily withdrew back to the west side of the river without losing a man. On the morning of April 4 the *Benton*, the *Cincinnati* and the *Pittsburg*, along with three mortar boats, opened fire on the *New Orleans*, the Confederates' floating battery moored at the north end of Island No. 10. After enduring an hour of constant bombardment, the battery's crew cut the *New Orleans* free of its moorings and let it drift down the river about three miles.

By April 4 Commander Walke had completed the *Carondelet*'s preparations, which he described:

All the loose material at hand was collected ... and the decks were covered with it, to protect them against plunging shot. Hawsers and chain cables were placed around the pilothouse and other vulnerable parts of the vessel, and every precaution was adopted to prevent disaster. A coal-barge laden with hay and coal was lashed to the part of the port side on which there was no iron plating, to protect the magazine. And it was truly said that the old *Carondelet* at that time resembled a farmer's wagon prepared for market. The engineers led the escape-steam, through the pipes aft, into the wheel-house, to avoid the puffing sound it made when blown through the smoke-stacks.... In order to resist boarding parties in case we should be disabled, the sailors were well armed, and pistols, cutlasses, muskets, boarding-pikes, and hand-grenades were within reach. Hose was attached to the boilers for throwing scalding water over any who might attempt to board.

If it should be found impossible to save the vessel, it was designed to sink rather than burn her, as the loss of life would probably be greater in the latter case by the explosion of her magazine.

Satisfied that the *Carondelet* was as ready as his makeshift efforts could make it, Walke informed Foote that he planned to attempt the run that night, April 4, and Foote gave his approval.

As the sun was going down, twenty-three sharpshooters from the Forty-second Illinois Infantry Regiment came aboard the *Carondelet*, men who had volunteered to defend the gunboat on its mission. The time for departure having drawn near, Commander Walke, gaunt-faced and Lincolnesque, addressed the officers and crew of the *Carondelet*, impressing on them the importance of the boat's mission and giving them an idea of what they would be facing. All expressed their readiness to carry on.

At ten o'clock the moon had gone down, and a thunderstorm had swept in and spread a uniform blackness over sky, land and river, relieved only by quick flashes of brilliant lightning. Deciding that the time had come, Walke ordered the vessel's first-master to cast off its lines. With its barge of hay and coal tied to its port side, the *Carondelet* started down the river slowly, then speeded up to drive itself through the storm. Standing on the deck, suffering the wind, the cold and the driving rain and hazarding rebel gunfire was the *Cincinnati*'s first-master, William Hoel, a veteran Mississippi River steamboat captain. Under the flashes of lightning Hoel would pick out the features of the shore and guide the *Carondelet*'s pilot down the surging river.

For the first half mile all went well, and Commander Walke began to think the *Carondelet*, its engine noise lost in the wind, its presence unseen in the blackness, might just be able to pass the rebel batteries undetected. Then suddenly a bright, tall flame burst from each of the vessel's two smokestacks, as if the boat were carrying a huge pair of blazing torches to light its way. The soot inside the smokestacks, ordinarily kept wet by escaping steam — which now had been diverted through the wheelhouse — had dried and caught fire. The flames soon died, and strangely, they brought no notice from the shore.

Minutes later, as the *Carondelet* was passing the Confederates' shore Battery No. 2, the smokestacks blazed up again. Though the flames were quickly extinguished, this time they were noticed, and rebel sentries fired their muskets to sound an alarm. Almost immediately signal rockets from the island and from the shore soared into the dark sky. Moments later an artillery shot came from Battery No. 2 above the island. Walke immediately called for full speed, knowing all possible rebel guns were being manned and aimed at the fleeing gunboat, elusive as a ghost in the darkness and torrential, blowing rain. The shot and shell and rifle and musket balls passing across the *Carondelet* were so loud and so close that they could be heard over the noise of the storm. In the moments that the lightning illuminated the Confederate fortifications Walke could see the rebel soldiers at their guns, loading and firing.

Those gunners could see the *Carondelet* only for a split second, which gave them little chance for accurate firing. In the split second when the *Carondelet* was visible, it apparently appeared farther out in the river than it actually was, and the rebels' fire consistently passed harmlessly over the boat. With the gunboat moving as swiftly as it was in the fast current, and the rebels' limited ability to get a shot off before it disappeared again in the blackness, only a lucky shot would hit it.

The greatest danger came not from the rebel batteries, but from the hazards of the river. The current was not only swollen and fast, but shifted from side to side within the curve of the stream. Bars of sand and mud jutted out from either shore. Hoel and the pilots were relying on the lightning to show them the shape of the shore and depending also on the vessel's crewmen who from the forecastle continuously threw out weighted lines to measure the depth of the dark water before them. At one frightening moment Hoel shouted a loud, sudden order—"Hard a-port! Hard a-port!"—and the vessel and its barge swerved agonizingly slowly toward mid river, away from shoal water that would have grounded them, stranding them as a stationary target for the Confederate gunners.

At another point, the *Carondelet* passed so close to a Confederate battery that a rebel officer could be heard giving orders to his gun crews, shouting, "Elevate your guns!" As the gunboat neared the spot where the rebels' floating battery on the barge *New Orleans* had drifted, which was marked by a light on the barge, Commander Walke braced for an onslaught from its nine guns. He ordered the *Carondelet*'s pilot to keep as close as possible to the Missouri shore. As the vessel glided past the battery, the Confederates fired a half dozen or so shots at it, but with no effect. One cannonball struck the barge, and one buried itself in a bale of hay.

Once out of range of the Confederate guns, the *Carondelet* continued steadily downriver and rounded the counterclockwise turn of the river above New Madrid. The end was in sight, the men aboard the vessel noticing the bonfires that were blazing a welcome beside the New Madrid landing. The crew and their soldier passengers burst into shouts and cheers, and signal guns were fired to announce the boat's arrival. Suddenly the vessel abruptly stopped, the river rushing past it. It had run hard aground in the shallows above the landing. After about an hour of work, hauling the bow guns to the stern and assembling all hands aft, the bow of the vessel lifted from the muddy bottom, and the pilot was able to back the boat up and continue to the landing.

At one o'clock in the morning on April 5, the daring voyage of the intrepid *Carondelet* was over. It had completed its mission and arrived at New Madrid safe and unscarred, as were its crew and passengers. Paymaster Nixon called for a celebration with drinks all around, and all hands, in naval parlance, spliced the main brace.

Commander Walke sent a dispatch to Flag Officer Foote reporting the good news:

> U.S. Gun-boat "Carondelet," New Madrid,
> April 5, 1862
>
> Sir,—I have the honor to report my arrival here last night about one o'clock—all well. On our way all of the rebel batteries and a large number of infantry opened fire upon us, which was continued until we were out of range. Providentially, no damage was done to the vessel or the officers and crew, who conducted themselves with admirable courage and fidelity. The terrible storm which prevailed at the time rendered it impossible to make any reliable observation.
>
> Most respectfully, sir, your obedient servant,
> H. Walke, Commander U.S. Navy

By April 4, the channel across the swamp above New Madrid had been opened. It ended up taking nineteen days to saw, hack and dig through the forested swamp and create what General Pope called a canal, and when it was done, it could float transports but was too shallow for the deep-draft gunboats. On April 5 a number of steamers and barges came through the channel and landed near New Madrid at a spot where they could not be seen by the rebels across the river.

To Foote's dispatch, sent to Pope in New Madrid, asking whether the *Carondelet* had arrived, the general promptly replied that it had and that all were safe. He then requested that Foote send down a second gunboat, making it all the safer to ferry his troops and land them across the river.

With a reluctance that had become customary for him, Foote resisted the request. In protest, he wrote to General Halleck on April 6 saying he considered it "injudicious to hazard another boat in attempting to reach New Madrid." Thomas Scott, the U.S. assistant secretary of war, who was in St. Louis overseeing the war's Western operations, took the matter to Secretary of War Edwin Stanton, pleading General Pope's case, telling Stanton that a gunboat's running past Island No. 10 "can be done with comparative safety any night, and might save the lives of thousands of our soldiers. The risk of the boat is trifling compared with that of Pope's army." He asked if Stanton could arrange to have Navy Secretary Welles issue an order for a second gunboat, thereby relieving Foote of the burden of responsibility for the decision.

Before Stanton could act on that suggestion, Foote had a change of heart, for whatever reason. At 5:15 P.M. on April 6, Secretary Stanton received a telegraph message informing him that Foote had agreed to send a second gunboat if the night was dark.

On the morning of April 6, a Sunday, after a service of prayer and thanksgiving, Walke took the *Carondelet* on a reconnaissance voyage some twenty miles down the river from New Madrid, past Point Pleasant and nearly as far as Tiptonville. On board with him were three of General Pope's officers— Brigadier General Gordon Granger, commanding the cavalry division composed of the Second and Third Michigan Cavalry regiments; Colonel J.L.K. Smith, commander of the Forty-third Ohio Infantry Regiment; and Captain L.H. Marshall, a member of Pope's staff. The *Carondelet* came under nearly constant fire from the Confederate batteries along the Tennessee shore, returning the fire as it went, while Walke and the Army officers took note of the locations of the rebel guns. On the return trip, the *Carondelet* silenced the guns of the rebel battery opposite Point Pleasant, and Captain Marshall then took a detail ashore and spiked the battery's two guns, a thirty-two-pounder and a twenty-four-pounder.

The night of April 6 was another dark, stormy night, apparently just the kind that Flag Officer Foote required for a second run to New Madrid. At two hours past midnight the gunboat *Pittsburg*, commanded by forty-one-year-old Lieutenant Egbert Thompson, slipped its moorings and began a descent of the embattled river, heading toward Island No. 10. With even less difficulty than the *Carondelet* had encountered, it steamed past the Confederate batteries untouched and arrived safely at New Madrid about five o'clock on the morning of the 7th. A gracious and apparently genuinely grateful General Pope telegraphed Flag Officer Foote to give him the news of the *Pittsburg*'s safe arrival and to tell him, "With the aid of the two boats you have sent, and of the gallant officers who command them, I shall be able to effect the passage of the river with the necessary force and without increasing the tremendous hazard which must otherwise have attended such an operation."

On the morning of April 7, under a gray sky and in the continuing heavy rain, the operation began. At dawn Pope's thirty-two-pounder guns opened fire on the Confederate batteries at Watson's Landing, the spot on the Tennessee shore where Pope intended to land his troops. At eight o'clock the *Carondelet* and forty-five minutes later the *Pittsburg* joined the bombardment. Walke ran his vessel down past the rebel guns, blasting them with port broadsides, then turned the boat about and opened up with his starboard guns, concentrating his fire on the battery with the heaviest guns and receiving answering fire. The *Carondelet* was struck in its starboard quarter by a shot that severed a steering rope, but it was quickly repaired. At times the gunsmoke over the river became so thick that Walke ceased firing until the smoke dissipated enough for the targets to be clearly seen.

By 8:45, when the *Pittsburg* entered the fray, the rebels' fire had slacked off. With the *Carondelet* leading, the two gunboats moved in closer to the heavy-gun battery and hit the site with explosive shells and grapeshot, driving the defenders from the gun emplacements and rifle pits, deserting their artillery to flee from the murderous cannonades. Walke then ordered a party ashore to spike the guns. It was soon discovered that rebel batteries all along the shore were being deserted, and Walke moved his vessel along the riverbank, stopping at each battery to spike the guns that the withdrawing rebel troops had not already spiked.

About eleven o'clock Walke took the *Carondelet* back across the river and personally reported to General Pope that the Tennessee shore had been cleared of the enemy and that the gunboats were ready to cover the crossing of river and the landing of Pope's army.

Meanwhile, Confederate Captain Hollins declined to have his gunboats engage Foote's ironclads, despite pleas from the garrison commander at Island No. 10 to come to his aid and requests from the commanders of the *Pontchartrain*, the *Maurepas* and the *Polk* to let them attack the *Carondelet*. Hollins was convinced that his wooden boats would be no match for the *Carondelet* or *Pittsburg* and he resolutely held his vessels out of the action. (Hollins's temperament may have been revealed in a rebuke he made to a junior officer who tried to explain his actions off Island No. 10 and began with, "I thought, sir —-" Hollins cut him off. "You dared to think, sir? I will have you understand I am the only man in this fleet who is allowed to think!")

At noon the four Union transports moved to begin disgorging the troops onto the Tennessee shore below Island No. 10 as the *Carondelet* and the *Pittsburg* stood guard under clearing skies. By then, however, Pope had received intelligence that the bulk of the Confederate force was in retreat, heading for Tiptonville. Only one regiment remained at Island No. 10. Pope promptly ordered the troops aboard the transports to quickly disembark and immediately pursue the retreating rebel army.

Colonel J.D. Morgan's brigade, composed of the Tenth and Sixteenth Illinois infantry regiments, swiftly moved into the head of the column of pursuers, followed by the brigade of Colonel G.W. Cumming, commanding the Twenty-sixth and Fifty-first Illinois infantry regiments, the First Illinois Cavalry and the Sixty-fourth Illinois Infantry (Yates' Sharpshooters). In their race toward Tiptonville, the Union troops passed deserted camps and abandoned artillery, and some units stopped long enough to take prisoners. As the Union column approached it, a unit of Confederate cavalry sped away.

After several miles, the column came upon the rebel troops, now commanded by Brigadier General William W. Mackall, who had relieved General McCown on March 31. The troops were drawn up in a defensive position, with infantry, cavalry and artillery in place. When the lead regiment of Colonel Morgan's brigade deployed in line, however, threatening an assault, Mackall withdrew his men and continued the march toward Tiptonville. Twice more Mackall halted and formed in a line as if to make a stand, then retreated again as the Union force approached.

Just outside Tiptonville the road divided into two branches, one taking a direct route to the town, the other taking a slightly longer route. While Mackall's troops were delayed on the short route, threatened by the sudden appearance of the ironclads as the road ran beside the river, Colonel Morgan's brigade, advancing rapidly on the longer route, reached Tiptonville at nightfall, took shelter in an abandoned camp and waited for the retreating rebel army to arrive.

General Mackall now found himself boxed in. To the east and southeast were Reelfoot Lake and an impassable swamp; to the north was the bulk of General Paine's army; to the west were the river and the ironclads; and to the south, in Tiptonville, was Morgan's brigade. In the early morning of April 8 General Mackall surrendered his rebel army.

Lieutenant Colonel John Cook, commander of the Twelfth Arkansas Infantry Regiment, had been appointed by General Mackall as commandant at Island No. 10 on the morning of April 7, before the main body of the Confederate defenders began their flight. That evening, realizing the hopelessness of his position, Cook had passed the command to an artillery officer, Captain Humes, and with most of his regiment Cook had fled to the edge of Reelfoot Lake. He and his men waited in the cold and rain for their turn to have two small flatboats and hastily constructed rafts to ferry them across the lake. By noon of April 9 all had crossed over and had begun a desperate march toward Memphis. Back at their forsaken fortress, Captain Humes on the afternoon of April 8 had surrendered Island No. 10 to Flag Officer Foote, who had drawn his flag-steamer safely up under the silenced guns.

In his final report of the operation, General Pope assayed what had been captured from the Confederates: "Three generals [Mackall, Lucius. M. Walker and Edward W. Gantt], two hundred and seventy-three field and company officers, six thousand seven hundred privates, one hundred and twenty-three pieces of heavy artillery, thirty-five pieces of field artillery, all of the very best character and of the latest patterns, seven thousand stand of small arms, tents for twelve thousand men, several wharf-boat loads of provisions, an immense quantity of ammunition of all kinds, many hundred horses and mules, with wagons and harness, etc., are among the spoils." The Confederates also lost six steamers, two of them sunk, and the floating battery.

Casualties on both sides were remarkably light. The Union lost seventeen men killed and thirty-four wounded, including the fifteen casualties incurred when a gun burst on the gunboat *St. Louis*. Confederate casualties are estimated to have been about thirty, including killed and wounded.

Old Brains Halleck, his attention divided at the moment between the conflict at Island No. 10 and the drama taking place beside Shiloh Church in Tennessee, was pleased. "I congratulate you and your command on your splendid achievement," he wired Pope. "It exceeds in boldness and brilliancy all other operations of the war. It will be memorable in military history, and will be admired by future generations."

Halleck was partly right. Foote's gunboats and Pope's army had indeed performed a memorable achievement, removing an immense and forbidding obstacle from the Mississippi, opening the Union's way to further descent. But Island No. 10's fame in military history was about to be eclipsed by the battle fought beside that rough little Methodist churchhouse in Tennessee.

10. The Receding Gray Line

General Beauregard, the admirer of Napoleon, wanted a Napoleonic victory, the kind that came from massing large numbers of troops into an overwhelming force. As early as February 21, less than three weeks after arriving on the scene of the Confederates' Western operations, though still suffering from his throat ailment, he had proposed marshaling a vast army and launching an offensive that would recapture Paducah, regain the mouths of the Tennessee and Cumberland rivers and take Cairo and even St. Louis as well. To effect the plan he dispatched letters to the governors of Tennessee, Mississippi and Louisiana asking each to send him five thousand troops to reinforce the fifteen thousand he already had. Writing also to Major General Earl Van Dorn, the Confederate commander in Arkansas, he outlined his plan and urged Van Dorn to bring ten thousand troops and join him.

"What say you to this brilliant programme," Beauregard asked Van Dorn, "which I know is fully practicable if we can get the forces? At all events, we must do something or die in the attempt; otherwise all will shortly be lost."[1]

The governors responded with promises of help, but with little else. General Albert Sidney Johnston, the Confederates' commander in the West and Beauregard's superior, offered no encouragement at all, and Beauregard's plan for a grand Confederate offensive came to naught.

General Johnston was thinking defense, not offense. Having lost Fort Henry and Fort Donelson, he had evacuated Bowling Green and withdrawn to Nashville; and threatened by the approach of General Buell's army and Foote's gunboats, he then had retreated from Nashville to establish a new defensive line, this one stretching westward from Corinth, an important rail junction in northeast Mississippi, to New Madrid and Island No. 10. When those two latter positions fell to the Union, the western anchor of the line became Fort Pillow and Memphis, the new line roughly following the route of the Memphis & Charleston Railroad. Johnston's repeated flights from a confrontation with the enemy soon turned public opinion in the South against him. "Bounds could scarcely be set to the fury and despair of the people," Johnston's son, Confederate Colonel William Preston Johnston, wrote. "General Johnston was the special target of every accusation, including imbecility, cowardice and treason."[2] Many of the general's critics urged President Davis to fire him, which Davis refused to do, steadfastly sticking by him. "My confidence in you has never wavered," Davis wrote to Johnston in late March.[3] Davis himself then became an object of public wrath in the South.

Dissatisfaction with Johnston's cheerless performance was understandable enough among Southerners, but in the North, criticism of the performance of the victorious General Grant, coming as it did from within the Union Army's chain of command, was mystifying — and unsettling to Grant. On March 2, supposedly acting on an anonymous written complaint, General Halleck irritatedly wired General McClellan, the Army's general-in-chief, in Washington and told him, "I have had no communication with General Grant for more than a week. He left his command without my authority, and went to Nashville. His army seems to be as much demoralized by the victory at Fort Donelson as was that of the Potomac by the defeat at Bull Run. It is hard to censure a successful general immediately after a victory, but I think he richly deserves it. I can get no reports, no returns, no information of any kind from him. Satisfied with his victory, he sits down and enjoys it without any regard to the future. I am worn out and tired by this neglect and inefficiency. C.F. Smith is almost the only officer equal to the emergency."[4]

Without waiting for corroboration of Old Brains's complaints, McClellan swiftly replied to Halleck the next day, March 3: "The future success of our cause demands that proceedings such as General Grant's should at once be checked. Generals must observe discipline as well as private soldiers. Do not hesitate to arrest him at once if the good of the service requires it, and place C.F. Smith in command. You are at liberty to regard this as a positive order, if it will smooth your way."[5]

Halleck immediately removed Grant from command, notifying him in a dispatch Grant received on March 4: "You will place Maj.-Gen. C.F. Smith in command of expedition, and remain yourself at Fort Henry. Why do you not obey my orders to report strength and positions of your command?"[6]

On March 6 Grant received another wire from Halleck: "Your going to Nashville without authority, and when your presence with your troops was of the utmost importance, was a matter of very serious complaint at Washington, so much so that I was advised to arrest you on your return."[7]

Grant answered that message the next day. "Troops will be sent under command of Major-General Smith, as directed," he told Halleck. "I am not aware of ever having disobeyed any order from your headquarters—certainly never intended such a thing. I have reported almost daily the condition of my command, and reported every position occupied."[8] In his response Grant also asked to be relieved from any further duties under Halleck.

President Lincoln himself then entered the controversy. The U.S. Army's adjutant general, General Lorenzo Thomas, on March 10 wrote to Halleck, telling him, "It has been reported that, soon after the battle of Fort Donelson, Brigadier-General Grant left his command without leave. By direction of the President, the Secretary of War directs you to ascertain and report whether General Grant left his command at any time without proper authority, and if so, for how long; whether he has made to you proper reports and returns of his forces; whether he has committed any acts which were unauthorized or not in accordance with military subordination or propriety, and if so, what?"[9] Unlike McClellan, President Lincoln wanted specifics. He demanded that Halleck provide details of the charges made against Grant.

And in a stunning development the next day, March 11, the president, fed up with McClellan's lethargic pursuit of the war in the East, fired McClellan from his job as general-in-chief of the United States Army.

Halleck then, seemingly in fearful reaction to the president's intervention, began speedily back-pedaling. On March 13 Old Brains telegraphed Grant, telling him, "You cannot be relieved from your command. There is no good reason for it. I am certain that all which the authorities at Washington ask is, that you enforce discipline and punish the disorderly.... Instead of relieving you, I wish you, as soon as your new army is in the field, to assume the immediate command and lead it on to new victories."[10] Halleck had gulped and swallowed down the crow. Grant replied to him with dignity and firmness: "After your [earlier] letter enclosing copy of an anonymous letter upon which severe censure was based, I felt as though it would be impossible for me to serve longer without a court of inquiry. Your telegram of yesterday, however, places such a different phase upon my position that I will again assume command, and give every effort to the success of our cause. Under the worst circumstances, I would do the same."[11]

On March 15, Halleck responded to the order sent him by the adjutant general and completely exonerated Grant. The whole affair was much ado about nothing, merely false accusations trumped up by Old Brains Halleck, all apparently in an effort to defame Grant and replace him with General Smith. "General Halleck unquestionably deemed General C.F. Smith a much fitter officer for the command of all the forces in the military district than I was," Grant later wrote, "and, to render him available for such command, desired his promotion [to major general] to antedate mine and those of the other division commanders.... But this did not justify the dispatches which General Halleck sent to Washington, or his subsequent concealment of them from me when pretending to explain the action of my superiors."[12] As for General Smith, he was apparently unaware of Halleck's manipulations and was embarrassed by them when they came to light.

In Richmond the Confederate government responded to Beauregard's appeal for reinforcements by ordering five thousand troops sent from New Orleans and more from Pensacola and Mobile. When Beauregard learned that Major General Braxton Bragg had been ordered to take ten thousand men from Pensacola to reinforce him, Beauregard exultantly wrote to his Richmond superiors that rather than run the risk of missing Bragg's help at the moment, he would be agreeable to serving under Bragg even after he, Beauregard, recovered his health. And to his brother-in-law, Charles Villere, a member of the Confederate congress, Beauregard wrote a don't-rock-the-boat message, instructing him not to let Beauregard's name be used in any way that was critical of the Confederate government. "United we may stand," he told Villere. "Divided we must fall."[13]

A united stand was now what Beauregard eagerly sought. He and Johnston were both moving toward Corinth, Johnston perhaps at Beauregard's suggestion and Beauregard probably on his own initiative, seeing Corinth as a natural massing point. Corinth was where the east-west Memphis & Charleston Railroad crossed the tracks of the north-south Mobile & Ohio Railroad, two lines that were vital to the South, providing rapid movement of troops and supplies. Corinth furthermore is situated some thirty miles from where the Tennessee River, flowing out of east Tennessee and north Alabama, makes a big turn to the north. Beauregard and Johnston assumed, correctly as it turned out, that Grant would push up the Tennessee with troop transports and gunboats and attempt to destroy the railroad bridges that crossed the Tennessee, thereby interdicting vital communication lines.

Johnston's force included his troops from Bowling Green, plus those that had escaped Fort Donelson before its capture and, among others, some four thousand Arkansas troops commanded by Major General William J. Hardee. Altogether the force totaled about twenty-three thousand men, about sixteen thousand of whom were considered effectives fit for battle. Johnston moved that army into Corinth during the last week of March.

Beauregard had posted some ten thousand troops of his command along the west side of the Tennessee River, to the north of Corinth, and with Bragg's troops, plus the five thousand from New Orleans, commanded by Brigadier General Daniel Ruggles, Beauregard's remaining force totaled some thirty thousand men, about twenty-four thousand of whom were effectives.

Meeting with Johnston in Corinth on March 24, Beauregard reported that Grant's army had come up the Tennessee River and had debarked on the west side of Pittsburg Landing, Tennessee, about twenty-five miles above Corinth. Intelligence had also revealed that General Buell was marching south to join Grant with twenty-five thousand troops. With that knowledge, Beauregard had moved most of his army to the vicinity of Corinth. Now, after discussing their next possible moves, Johnston and Beauregard agreed that they should attack Grant as soon as possible, before Buell arrived with his army.

In preparation for their attack, Beauregard devised a reorganization scheme for the forces he and Johnston commanded. Under Beauregard's table of organization, which Johnston approved, the forces were divided into four corps, with General Polk commanding the First Corps, composed of 9,136 men, General Bragg commanding the Second Corps, with 13,589 men, General Hardee commanding the Third Corps, with 6,789 men, and Major General John C. Breckinridge commanding the Fourth Corps, with 6,439 men. Johnston was in over-all command; Beauregard was second in command, and Bragg was chief of staff. With the organization done, Johnston began drafting his plan of attack.

Grant reassumed command of the Union forces on March 17, having made his way to Savannah, Tennessee, to join his army immediately upon being restored. At Savannah, a town on the Tennessee River about twenty-five land miles northeast of Corinth, he took over from General Smith, who although sick in bed with what proved a fatal illness, seemed delighted to see Grant and expressed his disgust with the way Grant had been treated.

Grant quickly assessed his army's situation. "I found the army divided," he related, "about half being on the east bank of the Tennessee at Savannah, while one division was at Crump's landing on the west bank about four miles higher up, and the remainder at Pittsburg landing, five miles above Crump's. The enemy was in force at Corinth, the junction of the two most important railroads in the Mississippi valley — one connecting Memphis and the Mississippi River with the East, and the other leading south to all the cotton states. Still another railroad connects Corinth with Jackson, in west Tennessee.

"If we obtained possession of Corinth," Grant observed, "the enemy would have no railroad for the transportation of armies or supplies until that [railroad] running east from Vicksburg was reached. It [Corinth] was the great strategic position at the West between the Tennessee and the Mississippi rivers and between Nashville and Vicksburg."[14]

Knowing the Confederates were massing at Corinth, Grant quickly began moving his troops from Savannah to Pittsburg Landing, the river port nearest Corinth, about eight miles southwest of Savannah. Around the end of February Beauregard had ordered a battery of field artillery, including at least six field pieces, emplaced on the bluff overlooking the river at the landing, hoping the rebel guns could command the river at that point and protect the landing. He had also posted two regiments of infantry to support the artillery. But on March 1 the U.S. Navy timberclad gunboats *Lexington* and *Tyler* (*Taylor*), under the command of Lieutenant William Gwin and carrying a detachment of sharpshooters from the Thirty-second Illinois Infantry Regiment, steamed up to the Confederate position and attacked it. After a furious exchange of fire, the gunboats had silenced the rebel guns and then under the cover of canister and grapeshot, landed a force of sailors and soldiers that drove back the defenders. The Union force had then steamed away and when it returned a few days later, it found the Confederates had abandoned the position and Pittsburg Landing was undefended. Now the area around the landing suddenly bustled with continuing arrivals of Union troops and boatloads of equipment and supplies and wagons and horses that crowded the waterfront and the nearby roads.

Grant planned to position Buell's troops, when they arrived, at Hamburg Landing, about six miles upriver from Pittsburg Landing. He intended to wait for the arrival of Buell's army, comprising some twenty-five thousand troops, before launching his attack on the Confederate position at Corinth. On March 19, Buell was still eighty-five miles away at Columbia, Tennessee.

It was Grant's opinion that Johnston and Beauregard would simply wait for him to make his move and that he could take his time to make it. "I regarded the campaign we were engaged in as an offensive one," Grant admitted, "and had no idea that the enemy would leave strong intrenchments to take the initiative when he knew he would be attacked where he was if he remained."[15]

Guided by that belief, Grant declined to entrench his men or construct fortifications. His decision was aided by the report from his chief military engineer, who told him that if he were to entrench the troops, the trenches would have to be dug along a line that would move the troops farther back from their present position, closer to the river, farther from the enemy.

Meanwhile, Johnston and Beauregard were planning to attack Grant as soon as expediency would permit. On the night of April 2, Beauregard received a telegraph message from the commanding officer of Confederate troops posted near Bethel, Tennessee, about twenty miles north of Corinth and about the same distance west of Savannah. The message reported that Union troops were maneuvering in strength to his front, which to Beauregard meant that the Union commander had divided his army in preparation for a drive on Memphis, eighty miles farther west. Beauregard immediately dashed off a note on the bottom of the telegram: "Now is the moment to advance, and strike the enemy at Pittsburg Landing."[16] He then handed the telegram to his chief of staff, Colonel Thomas Jordan, and told him to take it to General Johnston.

Jordan found Johnston in his quarters and delivered the telegram to him. Johnston read it and told Jordan that he wanted to confer with General Bragg about Beauregard's proposal. He and Jordan then crossed the street and met with Bragg in his rooms. Bragg favored making the attack that Beauregard suggested, but the ever cautious Johnston resisted, claiming, among other objections, that the troops needed more training. Taking what he knew to be Beauregard's position, Jordan argued that any delay would allow Grant's army to be strengthened with reinforcements and that an attack now would take Grant's troops by surprise. At last Johnston gave in and instructed Jordan to prepare a written order for the attack.

Jordan promptly penned orders addressed to generals Polk, Hardee, Bragg and Breckinridge directing them to be ready to move their troops out by six o'clock the next morning, April 3. Jordan then instructed an aide to wake up Beauregard at five A.M. and inform him that orders had been issued for the Confederate troops to be ready to move.

Beauregard called Jordan to his quarters shortly after sunrise the next day and told him to prepare orders for the movement of troops on Pittsburg Landing, handing him notes that Beauregard, coping with a paper shortage, had written on the backs of telegrams and envelopes. Jordan's drafting of the orders was interrupted when he was called back to Beauregard's quarters for a conference attended by Johnston, Bragg, Hardee and Beauregard, at which the orders were a major topic of discussion. When Jordan commented that drawing up the orders required time, Beauregard, his battle plan clear in his head, rose and sketched the proposed troop movements on the top of a camp table, explaining to his fellow generals the routes of their advance and the positions they would take in the assault against the Union line. Written orders were to come later, but the corps commanders now knew what their assignments were and they were instructed to have their troops on the move by noon, two hours from then.

Flanking Pittsburg Landing were two roughly parallel creeks, streaming toward the Tennessee River about three miles apart, both flowing southwest to northeast. One of them, Owl Creek, ran through a swamp and merged with another stream, Snake Creek, which emptied into the Tennessee River north of the landing. The other, Lick Creek, joined the river south of the landing. Enclosed by those three creeks was a plateau that rose eighty to a hundred feet above the level of the river and ended at the river in sloughs and ravines and the bluff on which stood Pittsburg Landing. The plateau was mostly wooded, with a dozen or so cleared fields of about eighty acres each that formed giant patches on the expanse of high ground.

The roads in the area were little more than dirt trails, one of which paralleled the river, although a distance away from it to avoid the sloughs, and connected Pittsburg Landing with Crump's Landing, about five miles to the north, and with Hamburg Landing, about six miles to the southeast. Two roads led to the landing from Corinth. One, called Ridge or Bark Road, ran north and then curved eastward; the other ran east and then turned northward to join Ridge Road about four miles from Pittsburg Landing. On the way to the landing, the easternmost road ran past a hamlet named Monterey, and from Monterey two other small roads, the roads to Savannah and Purdy, ran northward and crossed Ridge Road. At the intersection of the Savannah road and Ridge Road stood a house known as Mickey's, about eight miles from Pittsburg Landing.

The written orders issued by Beauregard called for General Hardee to advance along Ridge Road on the afternoon of April 3 and bivouac at Mickey's during the night. At three o'clock the next morning, April 4, Hardee's troops were to move out and deploy into battle formation as they approached the Union line, about three miles from the landing. Bragg's troops were to assemble at Monterey and proceed in two sections along the Savannah and Purdy roads to Ridge Road, one stopping to bivouac at Mickey's before dark and the other stopping sometime during the night of April 3. On the morning of the 4th Bragg's troops were to fall in behind Hardee's and deploy into a second line of battle behind Hardee's corps. Polk's two divisions were split between Corinth and a position at Bethel. His division at Corinth was to begin marching up Ridge Road a half hour behind Hardee's corps, bivouac along the way, then form up at Mickey's on the morning of the 4th and stand by as a reserve force, which would be joined by Polk's other division, coming down from Bethel.

For raw troops, the movements were hopelessly intricate, and it wasn't long before Beauregard's attack plan and timetable began to go awry, becoming even more complicated. Because of a late realization that Bragg's troops and Polk's Corinth division might reach the Ridge Road–Purdy Road intersection at the same time — creating a massive traffic jam of men, horses, wagons, field pieces and caissons — new orders were issued calling for Polk to halt his men at the intersection and wait for Bragg's troops to pass. Then Polk's units were to assemble at Monterey and proceed to Mickey's by whatever route seemed best or else move to wherever they were needed once the engagement with Union forces took place.

At the moment of engagement the attacking Confederates would be arranged in four lines, one behind the other, Hardee's corps first, then Bragg's, Polk's and Breckinridge's, and move simultaneously across a three-mile front, each commander having to observe the entire front rather than a segment of it. The formation furthermore was highly susceptible to having units of one corps become mixed with units of another corps during the advance and the course of the battle.

The plan called for the Confederates to turn the Union's left flank and force it away from the river and back it up into the swamp through which Owl Creek flowed. Driven into that hopeless position, with no good means of escape, Grant's army would be forced to surrender. However, as Beauregard had arranged it, the Confederate attack would be equally strong all along the three-mile front, rather than being weighted with more strength on its right side to drive back the Union left.

Johnston apparently had in mind a more conventional plan of attack, whereby Polk's units would be placed on the Confederate left, Bragg's at the center and Hardee's on the right, but in haste he had unknowingly allowed Beauregard and Jordan to design a different plan and to order it in the written orders that were issued to the corps commanders.

Little, if anything, went according to plan. Men, horses and wagons so clogged the streets of Corinth that the scheduled march came to a standstill. Beauregard blamed Polk; Polk blamed Hardee, who instead of moving out by noon, didn't get his troops moving until late afternoon. It was nearly dark before Polk's units moved out and they halted for the night just nine miles out of Corinth. Seeing the delays, Beauregard altered his schedule. Instead of commencing the attack on April 4, he would launch it on April 5, shifting everything back twenty-four hours. That wasn't the end of the problems, however.

On the night of the 4th, while the mass of the rebel army was bedded down around Mickey's, Polk's division marching from Bethel still had not arrived, and was not expected until early in the morning of the 5th. Polk's other troops, which were supposed to be behind Bragg's men, were actually in front of Bragg's, requiring Bragg's units to move through Polk's troops before they could take their planned place behind Hardee's units. Shortly after midnight the clouds burst with a heavy rain, which continued past three A.M., the hour at which Hardee's men were supposed to move forward and form the leading line of battle. Hampered by the rain and darkness, Hardee's troops were not ready to advance until dawn. Because Hardee didn't have enough men to stretch his line across the entire front, Beauregard authorized him to take one of Bragg's brigades and place it on the right side of Hardee's line. By the time that was done and Hardee's line was in position to start the attack, it was ten o'clock. Then more time was required to get Bragg's units into position behind Hardee's.

Johnston and Beauregard had left Corinth on April 4 and had spent most of the night at Monterey. By sunrise on the 5th they were on their way to Mickey's. Johnston arrived there in time to see Bragg forming up his line and discovering that he was missing a division. When Johnston sent a staff officer over to Bragg to ask where the division was, Bragg answered that it was somewhere in the rear and that he was trying to find it. At half past noon, with the missing division still not found, Johnston, his patience exhausted, protested, "This is perfectly puerile! This is not war!" and rode off to search for the absent division himself. He found it still on the road, its way to the front blocked by some of Polk's troops.

Johnston ordered the road cleared, which took till two in the afternoon to accomplish. The lost division then was able to move up and join the deployment of Bragg's troops along their line. Polk was then able to begin forming up his line behind Bragg's. That movement took until four o'clock, when Polk's division from Bethel finally arrived.

Like Johnston, Beauregard had reached the end of his patience. He called Polk to him and let him know that he was far from pleased with the delays, and while Polk tried to

10. The Receding Gray Line

dodge responsibility, Beauregard told him that the entire plan had come apart and that the Confederate force would have to return to Corinth, its mission unaccomplished. As Beauregard delivered that verdict to Polk, General Johnston approached with several other officers. When Johnston asked what the problem was, Beauregard made his case for calling off the attack, claiming that the element of surprise had been lost in the delays, that the Union forces were growing in numbers and that having learned of the Confederates' planned assault, "Now they will be entrenched to the eyes."

Johnston disagreed. He said he didn't think their presence was known and even if the enemy did know the Confederates were about to attack, the operation was too far along to cancel it. "We shall fight them tomorrow," he declared, ending the discussion, then turned and walked off, telling a staff officer as he strode away, "I would fight them if they were a million."[17]

General Grant had set up his headquarters at Savannah and had developed a routine of spending the day at Pittsburg Landing, less than ten miles away, and returning to Savannah by horseback and by steamer in the late afternoon or evening. He intended to transfer his headquarters to Pittsburg Landing once Buell arrived, which he was expecting to happen any day now. He was aware that the Confederates were positioned west of him along the line of the Mobile & Ohio Railroad, and he believed both Crump's and Pittsburg landings were threatened by them. "My apprehension was much greater for the safety of Crump's landing than it was for Pittsburg," he related. "I had no apprehension that the enemy could really capture either place. But I feared it was possible that he might make a rapid dash upon Crump's and destroy our transports and stores, most of which were kept at that point."[18]

The rebels' skirmishing along the Union lines outside Pittsburg Landing, however, which had intensified since April 3, was a big part of the reason he wanted to shift the site of his headquarters, and he was spending more time at the landing, leaving for Savannah each evening at a later hour than he had been, wanting to make sure before he left that there was no danger of enemy action until the following morning.

The nightly trips from the landing to Savannah finally exacted a price from him. On the night of April 5, as the Confederate army lay waiting for daylight to launch their attack, Grant was riding through the darkness, his way illumined only by flashes of lightning as a torrential rain pounded down on him, when his horse lost its footing on the sodden ground and fell, trapping Grant's leg under the animal's big body. Grant's ankle was so severely injured that his boot had to be cut off him, and he was forced to use crutches to walk.

During the day on the 5th, the first of Buell's troops, the division commanded by Brigadier General William Nelson, had reached Savannah, and Grant, notified of its arrival, had written an order to Nelson to take a position on the east bank of the Tennessee River, where the division could be quickly ferried to Pittsburg Landing or to Crump's Landing, as the developing situation required. Grant's orders from General Halleck required him to link up with Buell's army and capture the Memphis & Charleston Railroad, and on the night of the 5th, Grant seemed satisfied that he could afford to wait for Buell. He telegraphed Halleck to report, "I have scarcely the faintest idea of an attack (general one) being made upon us, but will be prepared should such a thing take place."[19] In the meantime, Buell arrived in Savannah during the night.

Early the next morning — Sunday, April 6 — Grant was at breakfast in Savannah, intending to meet with Buell later, when in the distance he could hear sounds of heavy firing coming from the direction of Pittsburg Landing. He dashed off a hurried note to

General Buell, explaining that he would be unable to meet with him in Savannah, then swiftly made his way to Savannah's river landing and boarded his dispatch steamer, the *Tigress*. His first stop was Crump's Landing, where he briefly met with the commander of his Third Division, newly promoted Major General Lew Wallace, who was aboard the steamer he used as his headquarters and was waiting for Grant, having anticipated his coming in response to the noise of battle. Grant instructed Wallace to form up his troops and be ready to execute whatever orders he might be given. Wallace replied that his men were already under arms and were prepared to move out.

At about eight A.M. Grant arrived at Pittsburg Landing and took not many minutes to conclude that the Confederates had opened a major assault on his position.

The morning had begun with the sun breaking through the misty fog that had clouded the lines of the two opposing forces, and the clearing sky gave promise of the coming of a crisp spring day. General Johnston had composed what he hoped was a stirring, pep-rally speech, and as the rebel troops formed up for the attack, Johnston's words were read out to each of the regiments. The men in the ranks—most of them more boy than man—were exhorted to remember their mothers, their wives and children, those precious ones at home whose lives were hanging in the balance, awaiting the outcome of the battle now imminent. Johnston's words urged the troops to remember their "fair, broad, abounding land" and their happy homes, all threatened with devastation if the enemy should prevail.

At about five-thirty the Confederates began to advance with Hardee's troops in front and Bragg's following five hundred yards behind them. Beauregard, not yet resigned to the fight before them, protested once more to Johnston, as did a couple of fellow officers, but Johnston was undeterred by their argument. "The battle has opened, gentlemen," Johnston responded, dismissing their objections. "It is too late to change our dispositions." He then mounted his horse, and turning toward his aides, he promised them, "Tonight we will water our horses in the Tennessee River."[20]

Johnston rode up to the front of the advancing troops, and Beauregard, who would be responsible for directing the reserve forces, rode off to the rear of the formations. In the rear the men had been told to place their knapsacks in piles and leave details to guard them while the rest stood ready to march off to the fighting. Some objected to being left out of the action. One eager rebel soldier, according to one report, offered to hand over all his rations to any of his comrades who would let him take his place on the front line. The great mass of Confederate troops moved deeper into the woods, Hardee's corps in the leading edge of the attack, the men pushing their way through two miles of thickets and brush, driving back the scattered enemy pickets and at last coming upon the Union lines, and the musket fire that had been sporadic soon became continuous, punctuated by blasts of artillery.

The wave of Confederate attackers crashed all along the Union's front, striking Grant's encamped and surprised troops. The Union line had the brigade commanded by Colonel David Stuart on the extreme left, the division commanded by Brigadier General Benjamin Prentiss on Stuart's right, General McClernand's division on Prentiss's right and Brigadier General William T. Sherman's division to the right of McClernand. Behind that forward line were the division of Brigadier General Stephen A. Hurlbut and, positioned on Hurlbut's right, the division commanded by Brigadier General W.H.L. Wallace, who had taken over for the injured and incapacitated General Smith.

"The position of our troops," General Grant recounted, "made a continuous line from Lick Creek on the left to Owl Creek, a branch of Snake Creek, on the right, facing nearly south and possibly a little west. The water in all these streams was very high at the time and contributed to protect our flanks. The enemy was compelled, therefore, to attack directly in front. This he did with great vigor, inflicting heavy losses on the National side, but suffering much heavier on his own. The Confederate assaults were made with such a disregard of losses on their own side that our line of tents soon fell into their hands."[21]

About two miles from the landing, standing on the ridge that divided the water draining from the plateau into Snake and Lick creeks, was a Methodist meetinghouse, a rough, rectangular log structure called Shiloh Church. Grant saw that church house as the key to his position. That section of the front was held by the troops of General Sherman. Sherman's division, Grant wrote, "was at that time wholly raw, no part of it ever having been in an engagement; but I thought this deficiency was more than made up by the superiority of the commander."[22]

The ferocity of the Confederate assault forced parts of the Union line backward, toward the river, some fleeing the battle, some retreating to new positions to oppose the attack. "In two cases, as I now remember," Grant recounted, "colonels led their regiments from the field on first hearing the whistle of the enemy's bullets. In these cases the colonels were constitutional cowards, unfit for any military position; but not so the officers and men led out of danger by them."[23] Grant described the condition of the Union troops. "Three of the five divisions engaged on Sunday were entirely raw, and many of the men had only received their arms on the way from their States to the field. Many of them had arrived but a day or two before and were hardly able to load their muskets according to the manual. Their officers

Shiloh Church. This crude log structure was a Methodist meetinghouse that stood atop a ridge about two miles from Pittsburg Landing, a steamboat stop on the Tennessee River. General Grant saw the church as the key to his position as his army faced a massive attack by General Beauregard's Confederate force (Library of Congress).

were equally ignorant of their duties. Under these circumstances it is not astonishing that many of the regiments broke at the first fire."[24]

Prentiss's division braved the assault and attempted to hold its line while troops on either side of it fell back, exposing Prentiss's flanks. It was forced to give ground gradually, falling back to a spot in a heavily wooded area where the depression created by an old roadway formed a trench that provided cover for Prentiss's desperately embattled fighters as their general rallied them to maintain their resistance. The struggle went on for hours, the stubborn troops of General Prentiss repelling eleven rebel assaults on their line and exacting a staggering toll on their attackers. So intense was the prolonged combat there that the spot became known as the Hornets' Nest.

On his horse close to the front, General Johnston could see a problem developing. The Union forces, rather than being wheeled back toward the swamp below the landing, according to the battle plan, were instead being driven straight back to Pittsburg Landing. Around noon he rode out to the right side of his line to spur new effort by his troops to hammer the Union left flank hard and push it out of its path to the landing, where Grant's transport steamers and two timberclad U.S. gunboats awaited.

Around two-thirty Johnston, astride his horse while he observed the battle, suddenly reeled. Tennessee Governor Isham Harris, serving as a volunteer aide to the general, saw him reel and galloped over to his side and asked him, "General, are you hurt?"

"Yes," Johnston answered. "And I fear seriously." A bullet had severed the femoral artery in his right leg, and he was bleeding profusely.

Harris maneuvered his mount beside Johnston's, held Johnston up in the saddle and guided the two horses away from the front and into a ravine, where he lowered Johnston, now unconscious, from his saddle and laid him on the ground as other officers huddled around him. Moments later General Johnston was dead.

Harris then remounted and sped off to find Beauregard and give him the awful news. He reached Beauregard, at the rear of the Confederate lines, a little after three o'clock.

As the Confederate troops advanced, Beauregard had repeatedly shifted his command post forward. About an hour before he was told of Johnston's death he had established a new command post near Shiloh Church. He had been sending aides across the battlefield to observe the progress of the attack and had kept himself well informed by their reports. Taking over command from the fallen Johnston, Beauregard ordered the attack to continue all along the front. He ordered General Bragg to command the Confederate right and ordered General Ruggles to command the center.

Both of those sections of the Confederate line continued to press Prentiss's position at the Hornets' Nest. Ruggles moved in more than sixty field pieces and steadily blasted the Union position with artillery fire. About five-thirty General Prentiss, isolated and all but surrounded by persistent rebel troops, finally gave up the fight and surrendered some twenty-two hundred men as prisoners of war, about half the number he had had at the beginning of the day.

Steadfastly resisting the rebel onslaught, Prentiss's troops had stalled the Confederate advance and allowed time for the right side of the Union line to move back toward the landing and form a tight new semicircular perimeter. As if the plan of Beauregard and Johnston to force his army into the Snake River swamp had been divined, Grant had strengthened his left side with fifty artillery pieces to turn back the Confederates while the two Union gunboats, the *Lexington* and the *Tyler*, stood in the river firing broadsides into the rebel ranks.

"The nature of the battle was such that cavalry could not be used in front," Grant wrote. "I therefore formed ours into line in rear, to stop stragglers—of whom there were many. When there would be enough of them to make a show, and after they had recovered from their fright, they would be sent to reinforce some part of the line which needed support, without regard to their companies, regiments or brigades. On one occasion during the day I rode back as far as the river and met General Buell, who had just arrived; I do not remember the hour, but at that time there probably were as many as four or five thousand stragglers lying under cover of the river bluff, panic-stricken."[25] Grant reported that he later learned the panic in the Confederate lines was not much different from what his army was experiencing and that he had heard from civilians in the area that the number of stragglers from Johnston's army was as high as twenty thousand, a number he considered an exaggeration.

Before the day was done, the Confederates made one more desperate attempt to turn Grant's left flank but were repulsed. After thirteen hours of fighting, the troops of both sides were exhausted both in body and spirit. Beauregard at last ordered his troops to disengage, pull back a short distance and bivouac for the night, which was fast coming on and bringing with it more rain. For his shelter Beauregard moved into the tent that had been Sherman's command post near Shiloh Church and had been abandoned as the rebel attack pushed Sherman's division back to the right side of the new Union position.

Maj. Gen. William T. Sherman. He earned special regard from General Grant for his fighting ability, but at the Battle of Pittsburg Landing, or Shiloh, his position at the Shiloh church house was overrun in the furious Confederate assault, and at the end of the first day's fighting his hastily abandoned command-post tent provided shelter for General Beauregard (National Archives and Records Administration).

The famished Confederates that evening dined on the food left behind in the tents of Union soldiers. "Our mess had that night," a Confederate soldier from Tennessee later wrote, "all the tea, coffee, sugar, cheese, hardtack and bacon they could want."[26] Many of the rebel soldiers quit the field after coming across the abandoned food and belongings of Grant's men. By midnight, one Confederate officer reported, "half of our army was straggling back to Corinth loaded down with belts, sashes, swords, officers' uniforms, Yankee letters, daguerreotypes of Yankee sweethearts ... some on Yankee mules and horses, some on foot, some on the ground prostrate with Cincinnati whiskey."[27] Others, however, not so fortunate in discovering the spoils of the Union troops, did the best they could to cope with their hunger and the rain during a long, stormy night as the bodies of their dead comrades and foes alike lay scattered forlornly across the muddy terrain.

Still, to Beauregard it seemed a day of success. He instructed his chief of staff, Colonel Jordan, to wire Richmond and report that every enemy position had been captured and that the Confederate army had gained "a complete victory." President Davis, receiving the news, then proudly announced to the Confederate congress that the Union army had been practically destroyed.[28]

Not quite. "The situation at the close of Sunday was as follows," Grant related. "Along the top of the bluff just south of the log-house which stood at Pittsburg landing, Colonel J.D. Webster, of my staff, had arranged twenty or more pieces of artillery facing south or up the river. This line of artillery was on the crest of a hill overlooking a deep ravine opening into the Tennessee. Hurlbut with his division intact was on the right of this artillery, extending west and possibly a little north. McClernand came next in the general line, looking more to the west. His division was complete in its organization and ready for any duty. Sherman came next, his right extending to Snake Creek. His command, like the other two, was complete in its organization and ready, like its chief, for any service it might be called upon to render. All three divisions were, as a matter of course, more or less shattered and depleted in numbers from the terrible battle of the day.

"The division of W.H.L. Wallace, as much from the disorder arising from changes of division and brigade commanders, under heavy fire, as from any other cause, had lost its organization and did not occupy a place in the line as a division. Prentiss' command was gone as a division, many of its members having been killed, wounded or captured; but it had rendered valiant services before its final dispersal, and had contributed a good share to the defence of Shiloh."[29]

In the meantime Brigadier General Lew Wallace, having been delayed in moving down from Crump's Landing, arrived with some five thousand effective troops after the firing had ceased for the day, and Grant placed them on the right side of the line. "Thus night came, Wallace came, and the advance of Nelson's division came," Grant remarked, "but none — unless night — in time to be of material service to the gallant men who saved Shiloh on that first day against large odds."[30]

Grant made a point of discrediting any reports that Buell's arrival had helped save the day for him. "Before any of Buell's troops had reached the west bank of the Tennessee, firing had almost entirely ceased; anything like an attempt on the part of the enemy to advance had absolutely ceased," Grant stated. "Buell's loss on the 6th of April was two men killed and one wounded, all members of the 36th Indiana infantry. The Army of the Tennessee [Grant's army] lost on that day at least 7,000 men. The presence of two or three regiments of Buell's army on the west bank before firing ceased had not the slightest effect in preventing the capture of Pittsburg landing."[31]

While Beauregard slept in Sherman's tent, Grant sought shelter from the torrential rain under a tree several hundred yards from the river. Unable to sleep because of the downpour and the pain in his injured ankle, he moved to a log cabin beside the river to get relief at least from the rain. The building was being used as a hospital, and all night long the wounded were brought in to have their wounds dressed or to have an arm or leg amputated. The sight of those suffering soldiers Grant found more unendurable than facing the enemy's fire, and before long he grabbed his crutches, hobbled outside and returned to the tree he had earlier left.

Shortly after sunrise on Monday, April 7, the action resumed. "At daylight on Monday,"

Sherman recounted, "I received General Grant's orders to advance and recapture our original camps."[32] Moving forward over the ground that the Confederates had won and had withdrawn from when the engagement was ended late Sunday afternoon, Sherman's troops soon reached the extreme right of McClernand's former position. There Sherman encountered artillery fire and halted, waiting for sounds that Buell's units were coming down the Ridge Road to join the battle. Lew Wallace, as ordered, moved west and then south. McClernand also moved forward, and then Hurlbut, too.

At seven o'clock that morning Lieutenant Gwin, commanding the gunboats standing at Pittsburg Landing, received a note from Grant saying that the gunboats were not to fire anymore, that the Army was attacking. By ten o'clock Sherman could tell from the sounds of battle that Buell was advancing, and Sherman started forward again. Nearing the Ridge Road, he and his troops could see, he wrote, "the well-ordered and compact columns of General Buell's Kentucky forces, whose soldierly movements at once gave confidence" to Sherman's wearied men.[33]

As the Union forces converged, the area around Shiloh Church became the focus of their attack, the fighting growing in intensity as the morning wore on. "The battle raged furiously for four hours," Confederate Colonel Jacob Thompson, one of Beauregard's aides, related, "and the enemy was completely silenced on the right and in the center. About 11:30 o'clock it was apparent that the enemy's main attack was on our left, and our forces began to yield ground to the vigor of his attack."[34]

"In a very short time," Grant related, "the battle became general all along the line. This day everything was favorable to the Union side. We had now become the attacking party. The enemy was driven back all day, as we had been the day before."[35]

Sometime after noon, realizing he was facing a superior force, now aware that substantial Union reinforcements had arrived, Beauregard began preparations to retire from the field. His forty-thousand-man army, having suffered enormous casualties as well as desertions, had shrunk to a force about half its original size and now numbered no more than Buell's troops alone. Those that he still had were worn out. Colonel Jordan observed the men, then came back to Beauregard and remarked, "General, do you not think our troops are very much in the condition of a lump of sugar thoroughly soaked with water, but yet preserving its original shape, though ready to dissolve? Would it not be judicious to get away with what we have?"

"I intend to withdraw in a few moments," Beauregard replied.[36] He instructed members of his staff to ride and tell the corps generals to retire, slowly and in good order, maintaining an attitude of dignity rather than defeat. He positioned a strong rear guard, including artillery units, near Shiloh Church to cover the withdrawal, and by four o'clock Beauregard's dispirited army was on the road to Corinth, its victory of April 6, paid for at high cost, having been seized from its grasp on the morning of April 7.

The Confederates had suffered 10,699 casualties, including 1,728 killed, 8,012 wounded and 959 missing or captured. Union casualties totaled 13,047, including 1,754 killed, 8,408 wounded and 2,885 missing or captured. Wounded Confederates were taken from the bloody field and transported by the wagonload down the rugged road to Corinth. There they overflowed the public buildings—schools, churches, hotels, train depots—and were placed in private homes that, like the town's other buildings, were turned into hastily prepared hospitals and aid stations.

General Grant decided not to pursue the retreating rebel army. "After the rain of the night before," he later wrote, "and the frequent and heavy rains for some days previous, the roads were almost impassable. The enemy carrying his artillery and supply trains over them in his retreat, made them still worse for troops following. I wanted to pursue, but had not the heart to order the men who had fought desperately for two days, lying in the mud and rain whenever not fighting, and I did not feel disposed to positively order Buell, or any part of his command, to pursue."[37]

Instead of pressing after Beauregard and the retreating rebels, Grant had his army take time to bury the dead of both sides. "After the battle," he related, "I gave verbal instructions to division commanders to let the regiments send out parties to bury their own dead, and to detail parties, under commissioned officers from each division, to bury the Confederate dead in their respective fronts and to report the numbers so buried."[38]

Outside Corinth, Beauregard established a strong defensive position to protect the town and its rail lines from the Union advance that he knew would soon come from Pittsburg Landing. When he learned that General Old Brains Halleck, unhappy with the way Grant had conducted the engagement, was coming with reinforcements to take command himself, Beauregard began planning to abandon Corinth.

Seven weeks after its fight at Pittsburg Landing and its withdrawal to Corinth, Beauregard's rebel army moved fifty miles south to Tupelo, Mississippi. The gray line of Confederate opposition that once had stretched across the Mississippi River from Missouri eastward through Kentucky had, with the fall of Columbus, New Madrid and Island No. 10, receded down from Missouri and Kentucky and now from most of Tennessee. The Union victory at Pittsburg Landing had completely flanked Memphis and the last rebel defensive position above it, Fort Pillow—at which the Union drive down the big river was now directed.

11. The Ascension Begins

Gustavus Vasa Fox, the United States assistant secretary of the Navy, was especially glad to hear the news that reached Washington on November 13, 1861. Six days earlier a fleet commanded by Captain Samuel DuPont had achieved a feat thought impossible by some of the Navy brass. With wooden warships he had steamed into Port Royal Sound in South Carolina, defying the guns of the two Confederate forts that guarded the harbor, one on the left of the channel at Hilton Head and the other on the right at Bay Point, and with repeated broadsides from seventeen vessels turning huge ellipses in single file, had blasted both forts into submission and captured Port Royal, to be used as an important base for the Navy's Atlantic blockading squadron.

The action against Port Royal was Fox's idea, which he pushed despite warnings that the two protective forts were too strong, that their forty-one guns trained on the harbor passage would demolish wooden ships. Easier objectives were suggested instead for the wanted Navy base on the Confederate coast — Fernandina, in north Florida, or Bulls Bay in South Carolina, both more lightly defended than Port Royal. But Port Royal was the most strategic location, situated midway between Charleston and Savannah, and the biggest harbor, big enough to accommodate the combined fleets of several navies.

Fox had seemed sure that the moving targets that the steam-driven warships presented would prove hard to hit, while at the same time the stationary land fortifications would be vulnerable to relentless bombardment by the floating batteries. DuPont's success had proved him right. The assault on the Confederate forts had begun at nine A.M. on November 7. At two P.M. the rebels had abandoned Fort Walker, on Hilton Head, and by three-thirty they had abandoned Fort Beauregard, on Bay Point. DuPont's vessels had incurred only slight damage in the six-hour-long exchange of fire. Their crews had suffered thirty-one casualties. They had gained two forts and a harbor. Fox was well pleased.

Fox, husky, balding and black-bearded, had had the good fortune to marry Virginia Woodbury, the daughter of a New Hampshire judge who also had a daughter who had married Montgomery Blair, whom President Lincoln had appointed postmaster general and whose voice was one of the most influential and forceful in Lincoln's cabinet. Fox had other credentials as well. He had been appointed a Navy midshipman in 1838 at age seventeen and later had received a commission and had served during the Mexican War on a ship carrying troops to Vera Cruz. He had been promoted to lieutenant in 1852, but in 1856 he had resigned from the Navy and gone to work for a woolen mill in Lawrence, Massachusetts.

His interest in naval affairs remained, however, so much so that when Fort Sumter was threatened by the rebels in the spring of 1861, he devised a plan to reinforce and supply the beleaguered garrison that was defending it. Through his connection with Montgomery Blair, who vigorously championed the plan and its originator, he was able not only to have

Lincoln's government approve the plan but to have himself, although a civilian, put in charge of its execution. The plan called for a fleet of small, open boats and steam tugs, supported by warships, to carry a quantity of provisions and a small force of men to the fort by running past the rebel guns on some dark night. Scattered and delayed by a storm en route from New York, the fleet, commanded by civilian Fox, arrived outside Charleston harbor too late to prevent its surrender to the Confederates, and the best that Fox's fleet could do then was to evacuate the garrison and take the men back to New York.

Although Fox's plan had failed, his naval expertise and his ideas continued to be valued, particularly by Navy Secretary Welles, whose knowledge of things nautical had begun only after Lincoln appointed him to his job. Fox was given a position as chief clerk to Secretary Welles and on August 1, 1861, he was appointed assistant secretary, an office created specifically for him. In contrast to Welles, Fox knew a great deal about naval matters, including many of the Navy's ablest officers, one of whom, in Fox's estimation, was controversial Commander David Dixon Porter, a forty-eight-year-old veteran of the naval service, the son of a former admiral, full of ideas, the sort of energetic person who habitually strives for recognition.

Encouraged by DuPont's success, Fox began thinking again that New Orleans, the Confederacy's major seaport and the key to control of the Mississippi River, could be captured, like Port Royal, by ships that would blast past New Orleans's protective forts and then fall on an otherwise lightly defended city. At the same time, he thought, too, of Commander Porter. Fox knew New Orleans and its approaches from the Gulf of Mexico. The merchant steamers he had commanded as a civilian had made New Orleans a port of call going to and from Panama. Porter, though, knew them even better. He was then captain of the USS *Powhatan*, a side-wheel steam frigate that had been engaged in blockading gulf ports. From his blockade experience he knew the passes that led from the wide waters of the gulf into the channels that gave access to the mainstream of the Mississippi. He furthermore knew the two forbidding forts, one on either side of the river, that guarded New Orleans against a naval approach from the gulf, Fort St. Philip on the east bank and Fort Jackson on the west bank.

Besides valuing Porter's expertise, Fox admired Porter's attitude and ideas, which were similar to his own. Like Fox, Porter believed forts St. Philip and Jackson could be

Adm. David Dixon Porter. His knowledge of the passes into the Mississippi River from the Gulf of Mexico helped him in developing a plan to run past Fort Jackson and Fort St. Philip, which guarded the lower river. He was instrumental in the selection of David Farragut, his adoptive brother, as commander of the naval force that captured New Orleans (Library of Congress).

passed by wooden warships, making New Orleans vulnerable. Fox and Welles had already sketched out a plan for getting warships past the forts, and Porter had taken their plan several steps farther with his own version of it. During the week that the Port Royal news was received, Porter was in Washington and was summoned to Welles's office.

In the anteroom of Welles's office suite on November 12, Porter met two members of the Senate Committee on Naval Affairs, James W. Grimes of Iowa and John P. Hale of New Hampshire, the committee chairman (and father of John Wilkes Booth's fiancée), and took advantage of the opportunity to speak to influential persons about the plan he had devised. He then, with the senators, was ushered into Secretary Welles's office, where he once more presented his version of the plan, which interested Welles.

The two senators then left, and Welles took Porter, along with Fox, into the presence of the president himself. The three men sat down with President Lincoln — and later with the then brand-new commanding general of the Army, General McClellan — and Porter again laid out the plan. The idea of *ascending* the Mississippi to capture it was a new one to the president, who had been thinking only of the drive *down* the river. But after hearing the plan, he was all for it, commenting, "This should have been done sooner."[1] McClellan, although expressing some doubts about the Navy's wooden-hulled ships being able to survive the guns of forts Jackson and St. Philip, also bought into it after Welles huffily told the general that the operation's ships were the Navy's concern and that the Army was only being asked to provide troops for the occupation of the city.

The plan, as submitted to President Lincoln, was described by Porter: "A naval expedition was to be fitted out, composed of vessels mounting not fewer than two hundred guns, with a powerful mortar-flotilla, and with steam transports to keep the fleet supplied. The army was to furnish twenty thousand troops, not only for the purpose of occupying New Orleans after its capture, but to fortify and hold the heights above Vicksburg. The navy and army were to push on up the river as soon as New Orleans was occupied by our troops, and call upon the authorities of Vicksburg to surrender. Orders were to be issued to Flag-Officer Foote, who commanded the iron-clad fleet on the upper Mississippi, to join the fleet above Vicksburg with his vessels and mortar-boats."[2]

A primary element of the plan of attack was the creation of a fleet of mortar boats — Porter's main contribution to the plan originally devised by Welles and Fox. The mortar boats would be scows and converted schooners that would be towed by steamboats, each vessel mounted with a stubby, mammoth mortar that from a safe distance in the river would lob monstrous thirteen-inch shells onto forts Jackson and St. Philip, battering them relentlessly while a flotilla of seagoing sloops and frigates, together carrying at least two hundred big guns, blasted their way past the embattled forts in darkness and sailed up the river to New Orleans. Confronted by an overwhelming Union naval force at its front door, capable of pounding the city into ruins, New Orleans would have no choice but to surrender. The city would then be occupied by the Union troops carried aboard the fleet's transports.

Having gained the president's go-ahead, Welles, Fox and Porter together turned their attention to the next steps, one of the most important of which was the selection of a commander for the expedition. Their choice was Porter's remarkable sixty-year-old adoptive brother, Captain David Glasgow Farragut, a fifty-year veteran naval officer who had been informally adopted by Porter's father (also named David Porter) and had begun his career at age nine as an acting midshipman aboard the ship that Porter's father had captained.[3] Farragut had a solid but not particularly distinguished record. The fact that he was a Southerner, a native of Tennessee and a resident of Virginia until Virginia seceded, was a point against him. If the mission should fail, rabid Unionists such as Senator Hale would be quick to blame Farragut's supposed Southern sympathies and the men who had picked him for the task. Welles and Fox, however, were steadfast in their support of him.

Farragut was interviewed first by Porter, who sounded him out about leading a naval operation but apparently without telling him what the operation's objective was. Farragut was interested. He was then interviewed by Fox and Montgomery Blair over breakfast at Blair's house. According to one account, Fox seemingly off-handedly asked Farragut if he thought New Orleans, where Farragut had once lived, could be captured by an attack from the gulf. "Yes, emphatically," Farragut replied. "The forts are well down the river. Ships could easily run them. And New Orleans itself is undefended. It would depend somewhat on the fleet, however."

"Well," Fox offered, "with such a fleet as, say, two steam frigates, five screw sloops of the Cities class, a dozen ninety-day gunboats and some mortar vessels to shell the forts from high angle?"

"Why, I would engage to run those batteries with two-thirds of such a force," Farragut responded. "Leave out the mortars, though. They only delay things."

Fox then had another question for Farragut. "What would you say if appointed to head such an expedition?"

"What would I *say*?" Farragut exclaimed, rising abruptly from his chair. "What would I *say*?" He would, it was obvious, be delighted.[4] His histrionic reaction had a negative effect on Blair, but Fox was able to persuade Blair that Farragut was the man for the job.[5]

On December 23, 1861, Captain Farragut received his official orders and immediately went to work assembling and preparing the fleet he would command. To Porter went the responsibility for creating the mortar-boat force, which he would command — and which, despite Farragut's objection, would not be eliminated from the plan. Aggressively ambitious, Porter had carved out for himself a prominent place in the operation and apparently saw himself as its de facto leader, with Farragut in nominal command, executing Porter's wishes.

The building of the fleet would take all winter, mainly because of the time required to fit out the mortar boats. Porter detailed the preparation process:

> The Assistant-Secretary of the Navy, Mr. G.V. Fox, selected the vessels for the expedition, and to me was assigned the duty of purchasing and fitting out a mortar-flotilla, to be composed of twenty large schooners, each mounting one heavy 13-inch mortar and at least two long 32-pounders. It was not until December 1861, that the Navy Department got seriously to work fitting out the expedition. Some of the mortar-vessels had to be purchased; the twenty mortars, with their thirty thousand bomb-shells, had to be cast at Pittsburg [*sic*] and transported to New York and Philadelphia, and the mortar-carriages made in New York. It was also necessary to recall ships from stations on the coast and fit them out; also to select officers from the few available at that time to fill the various positions where efficiency was required — especially for the mortar-flotilla, the operation of which imposed unfamiliar duties.[6]

Farragut's objection to the inclusion of mortar boats in the operation was becoming understandable, and the delay they caused in getting the operation under way was growing increasingly dangerous. It was well known that the large, powerful ironclads that the Confederates were building, the *Louisiana* and the *Mississippi*, were nearing completion at New Orleans, and the destruction that those vessels, when completed, could wreak on wooden warships was daunting to contemplate. The operation could end in a monumental disaster for the Union Navy and for the entire campaign to capture the Mississippi River.

To the operation's advantage, however, the *Louisiana* and the *Mississippi* were suffering delays of their own. The *Mississippi* had been launched, and the framing of its superstructure was completed, but the fifty-foot drive shaft needed to propel it still had not been delivered to the boatyard, and the boat had been armored only below the gun-deck. The *Louisiana* was in worse shape. Its embrasures were too small to allow its guns to be sufficiently elevated or aimed. The steering propellers were not ready, and the rudder was insufficient to steer the boat without them. Besides that, and other deficiencies, the engines that had been removed from the steamer *Ingomar* would not work after being installed in the *Louisiana*. More time was needed to overcome the problems.

The fleet being assembled and prepared by Farragut would include: the steam frigate *Colorado*, carrying fifty guns; four screw sloops, one of which, the *Hartford*, was to be Farragut's flagship, each armed with twenty-four nine-inch, bottle-shaped Dahlgren guns, two six-inch rifled guns and two howitzers; a side-wheel frigate with one ten-inch and fifteen eight-inch guns; three large screw gunboats carrying six to ten guns each; and nine paddle-wheel gunboats, each with one eleven-inch gun, one light rifled gun and two howitzers. Altogether Farragut's fleet would carry 243 guns, even more than the 200 asked for. Also joining the fleet would be the sailing sloop *Portsmouth*, armed with sixteen eight-inch guns, to provide protection for the schooner mortar boats while at sea, and the revenue cutter *Harriet Lane* and five steam ferryboats that would tow the mortar boats.

Adm. David Glasgow Farragut. His career in the U.S. Navy began when, as a nine-year-old, he became an acting midshipman on a ship captained by David Porter's father. By the time he was chosen to lead the perilous mission to capture New Orleans, he had served in the Navy for 50 years (Library of Congress).

With all in readiness, Farragut, aboard the *Hartford*, set out from Philadelphia on January 19, 1862. He steamed down to Hampton Roads, where he received his final instructions:

> There will be attached to your squadron a fleet of bomb-vessels, and armed steamers enough to manage them, all under the command of Commander D.D. Porter, who will be directed to report to you. As fast as these vessels are got ready they will be sent to Key West to await the arrival of all and the commanding officers, who will be permitted to organize and practice with them at that port.
>
> When these formidable mortars arrive, and you are completely ready, you will collect such vessels as can be spared from the blockade, and proceed up the Mississippi River, and reduce the defenses which guard the approaches to New Orleans, when you will appear off that city and take possession of it under the guns of your squadron, and hoist the American flag therein, keeping possession until troops can be sent to you. If the Mississippi expe-

dition from Cairo shall not have descended the river, you will take advantage of the panic to push a strong force up the river to take all their defenses in the rear.[7]

Farragut reached Key West on February 11 and from there he set off a wave of doubt in Fox's mind about his ability to handle the mission. As commander of the West Gulf Blockading Squadron, directing blockade operations along the west gulf coast, the job from which he had been plucked to lead the attack against New Orleans, Farragut in Key West learned that blockade runners were having success operating out of rivers and bayous too shallow for the deep-draft, sea-going Navy ships that were intended to stop and seize them. And so he quickly wrote a note to Fox asking for shallow-draft naval vessels to combat the blockade runners. But he neglected to tell Fox why he wanted them.

Stricken by misgivings on receiving Farragut's request, Fox promptly wrote Porter, then en route to the operation's rendezvous, and told him:

> We have dispatches from your Flag, a cold shudder ran through me at the time. He wants a lot of 4-foot draft boats. This is not the time for such requests. There are no boats under 7-foot draft and they are good for nothing, and if he does the work laid out for him there will be no use for these frail boats, not one of which would get to the Gulf at this season of the year. I trust we have made no mistake in our man but his dispatches are very discouraging. It is not too late to rectify our mistake. You must frankly give me your views from Ship Island. I shall have no peace until I hear from you.[8]

Swift to make Farragut look bad and himself look good, Porter replied:

> If you suppose there is any want of the proper abilities in the Flag Officer it is now too late to rectify the mistake. I never thought Farragut a Nelson or a Collingwood; I only considered him the best of his rank and so consider him still; but men of his age in a seafaring life are not fit for important enterprises, they lack the vigor of youth. He talks very much at random at times and rather underrates the difficulties before him without fairly comprehending them. I know what they are, and as he is impressible hope to make him appreciate them also. I have great hopes of the mortars if all else fails.[9]

That note revealed the character flaw that made Secretary Welles wary of Porter. "David was not always reliable on unimportant matters, but amplified and colored transactions, where he was personally interested especially," Welles wrote. "I did not always consider David to be depended upon if he had an end to attain, and he had no hesitation in trampling down a brother officer if it would benefit himself."[10]

John Russell Bartlett was a midshipman serving aboard the *Brooklyn*, one of the blockading vessels that Farragut drew into his fleet after he reached Pass à l'Outre at the mouth of the Mississippi on March 7. Bartlett described Captain Farragut as he soon came to know him:

> I had never met Farragut, but had heard of him from officers who were with him in the *Brooklyn* on her previous cruise. He had been represented as a man of most determined will and character—a man who would assume any responsibility to accomplish necessary ends. I saw a great deal of him at the Head of the Passes.... Often, when I came on board the *Hartford* with a message from the captain of the *Brooklyn*, Farragut sent me somewhere to carry an order or to do certain duty. I was much impressed with his energy and activity and his promptness of decision and action. He had a winning smile and a most charming manner and was jovial and talkative.
>
> He prided himself on his agility, and I remember his telling me once that he always turned a handspring on his birthday, and should not consider that he was getting old until he was unable to do it. The officers who had the good fortune to be immediately associated with him seemed to worship him.

He had determination and dash in execution, but in planning and organizing he appeared to want method.... He had, however, the good fortune to have on his staff two of the best organizers and administrators of detail in the service....[11]

With great difficulty and the strenuous exertions of men and towboats, the assembled fleet at last crept over the bar at Southwest Pass, one by one, although the *Colorado*, the mammoth frigate that drew twenty-three feet of water, was sent back to Ship Island because it became obvious it would never make it across the mud at any of the passes at the river's mouth. Some of *Colorado*'s guns were removed and distributed among the other ships. The *Mississippi* and the *Pensacola*, two other deep-draft vessels, also returned to Ship Island, where they were lightened by removing whatever weight could be spared. They then rejoined the fleet.

To his commanders Farragut issued elaborate instructions. Spars and rigging at the forward end of the ships were removed to provide clear lines of fire; grapnels were positioned on the deck to be ready for towing away fire-ships; each vessel was to be trimmed so that if it went aground, it would not swing helplessly around in the river, with its stern upstream. Methods of plugging shot-holes and serving guns in battle were described. Huge blankets of chain mail with iron links an inch and a half in diameter were devised and fastened to the sides of the vessel, extending down to two feet below the water line. Protective sandbags were piled up around exposed parts of the ships machinery. The ships' holds were cleared out to create makeshift hospitals for the ships' surgeons to attend the wounded. Hawsers were hauled out and placed where they could be quickly thrown out to take in tow the ship immediately astern. Preparations also included drilling the crews, taking target practice with the ships' guns, and taking aboard provisions and coal.

One of the first things Farragut did on reaching the Mississippi was to send out his chief of staff, Captain Henry H. Bell, with two gunboats to reconnoiter the vicinity of the two forts. Bell returned to report that eight hulks were moored in line across the river, with heavy chains extending from one to the other, and rafts of logs were also positioned to block passage up the river. Passage between the forts, Bell said, was entirely closed.

Leaving as little as possible to chance or last-minute decision, surveyors aboard the Coast Survey vessel *Sachem*, which had accompanied the fleet, braved the fire of Confederate snipers along the river banks to map the river near the forts and post markers to indicate where the mortar boats should be anchored to bombard the forts. All the while, Bartlett reported, Farragut "was about the fleet from early dawn until dark, and if any officers or men had not spontaneous enthusiasm he certainly infused it into them."[12]

By April 16, Farragut, Porter and the fleet were at last ready to begin their assault.

Fort St. Philip, built during the Spanish administration of Louisiana in the mid-eighteenth century, was formidable enough to deter the British from approaching New Orleans by way of the river during the War of 1812, in the days before steam warships. Fort Jackson, named for Andrew Jackson, who proposed its construction, was built in 1822, seven years after Jackson's heroic defense of New Orleans in January 1815. Commander (later Admiral) Porter described them:

Forts Jackson and St. Philip had been much strengthened since the expedition was started. Situated in a most commanding position, at a turn in the river, the former on the west bank and the latter on the east, they commanded the stream above and below; Fort St. Philip being particularly well placed to rake the lower approach.

The works themselves were of masonry. Fort Jackson was of pentagonal form, with bastions, its river front being about one hundred yards from the levee, above which its casemates just appeared. The armament consisted of a total of seventy-five guns.... The water battery of this fort, having the command of the lower approach, was a powerful work, mounting seven guns....

Fort Jackson was altogether in a good condition; its citadel, in the centre of the works, contained large amounts of war stores and provisions, while the bomb-proofs had been made more secure by sand bags piled upon them to a depth of some six feet, and all vulnerable parts protected in like manner.

The guns of Fort St. Philip were all in barbette, and numbered a total of fifty-three pieces of ordnance.... Each of the forts was garrisoned by some seven hundred men, and both, with their adjuncts, were under command of Brigadier General Johnson K. Duncan.[13]

Duncan, commander of the coast defenses of the Confederate army's Department No. 1, which included the lower Mississippi, had hurried to Fort Jackson in late March after being informed that the Union fleet was steaming up the river from the gulf. When he arrived at Fort Jackson, he discovered that floodwaters from the river, at a seasonal high, had inundated the fort. The parade ground and the casemates were covered with muddy water three to eighteen inches deep and rising. Only by continual pumping was the garrison able to keep the fort's magazine dry enough to preserve its ammunition and gunpowder. The officers and men of the garrison, under the constant threat of attack by the Union fleet, were forced to live in the flooded casemates and struggled with the discomfort of wet clothes and feet, enduring the unhealthy conditions thrust upon them. Across the river at Fort St. Philip conditions were little better, the high water of the Mississippi having also covered much of it as well.

In such soggy conditions the men of the garrisons worked in shifts, toiling day and night, to keep both forts in operating order and in readiness for the attack that was surely coming. To protect their main magazines against the vertical bombardment of the mortars, the men filled sandbags and stacked them into a covering shield several feet high. Platforms were speedily built to provide for the mounting of the additional heavy guns that General Duncan had requested.

To reinforce the lower Mississippi's defenses, General Duncan had asked Major General Mansfield Lovell, the Confederate army commander in New Orleans, for more troops, too, and Lovell had responded by sending the five hundred men of the Chalmette Regiment, commanded by Colonel Ignace Szymanski, to the quarantine station on the river six miles above the forts, to guard against the approach of Union troops coming through the bayous that join the river near there. A company of scouts and sharpshooters, some 125 men, commanded by Captain W.G. Mullen, was posted in the woods below Fort Jackson.

Lovell also ordered down to the forts four rams of the River Defense Fleet — the *Warrior*, *Defiance*, *Resolute* and the *Stonewall Jackson*— two steamers that had been fitted out by the state of Louisiana, the *Governor Moore* and the *General Quitman*, and two other vessels, the *Jackson* and the *Manassas*. To the commander of the River Defense Fleet vessels, Captain John A. Stevenson, Lovell gave explicit orders, telling him that he must keep his rams constantly on the alert for the movement of the enemy. "Should he attack," Lovell instructed, "all of your fleet must be kept above the raft, and such of your boats as have stern guns should lie in the middle of the stream, above the raft and without the field of our fire [from the forts], and use these guns against the enemy. Should any boat of the enemy by any means get above the raft, you must instantly ram it with determination and vigor at all risks and every sacrifice."[14]

The raft and its strategic placement in the river were described by Porter: "Less current and fewer eddies existed close under the west bank, near Fort Jackson; consequently the best passage up river was in that channel. The Confederates had obstructed this way by means of a heavy raft of logs, which closed the only part of the river not blockaded by the hulks and their chain connections, anchored across, below the forts, almost from bank to bank. The raft was fitted to act as a gate, opening or closing at the pleasure of the defenders."[15]

The major obstruction, as noted by Porter, was the heavy chain fastened to hulks, derelict schooners, stretching across the river, the hulks' bows facing upstream, their rigging and cables dangling overboard and trailing in the current to ensnare the propeller-driven ships of Farragut's fleet.

As a further deterrent, the Confederates had assembled a large number of fire rafts—flatboats piled high with wood saturated with tar and resin—and had tied them to the banks of the river above the forts, whence they could be quickly towed into midstream, set on fire and sent on the current to collide with the advancing Union vessels and set them ablaze. The flaming rafts were also used to light up the river at night and allow the forts' garrisons to observe the Union fleet's movements during the hours of darkness.

On April 16, Farragut moved his fleet to within three miles of the forts and told Porter that he could begin the mortar bombardment as soon as he was ready. Porter had positioned two divisions of his mortar flotilla under the lee of thick woods on the west bank of the river. The forts could be seen from the tops of the mortar boats' masts, but the boats, camouflaged with brush and blending in with the woods beside them, would be difficult for the Confederate gunners to spot. The vessels of the flotilla's third division were positioned on the east side of the river, the first in line being about two miles from Fort Jackson.

On the morning of April 18, Porter gave the order to commence firing, each mortar boat being instructed to fire once every ten minutes. Commander Porter described the bombardment's opening hours:

> The moment that the mortars belched forth their shells, both Jackson and St. Philip replied with great fury; but it was some time before they could obtain our range, as we were well concealed behind our natural rampart. The enemy's fire was rapid, and, finding that it was becoming rather hot, I sent Lieutenant Guest up to the head of line to open fire on the forts with his 11-inch pivot [gun]. This position he maintained for one hour and fifty minutes, and only abandoned it to fill up with ammunition.
>
> In the meantime the mortars on the left [east] bank ... were doing splendid work, though suffering considerably from the enemy's fire. I went on board the vessels of this division to see how they were getting on, and found them so cut up that I considered it necessary to remove them, with Farragut's permission, to the opposite shore, under cover of the trees, near the other vessels, which had suffered but little. They held their position, however, until sundown, when the enemy ceased firing.[16]

By then Fort Jackson was on fire, the flames being noticed from the mortar boats around five o'clock, and some of the fort's gun crews had abandoned their guns when the blaze began to spread. When Porter's tiring gunners saw the effects of their bombardment, they redoubled their efforts and began firing a shot every five minutes, a rate, Porter calculated, of two hundred and forty shells an hour. "During the night," Porter recounted, "in order to allow the men to rest, we slackened our fire, and only sent a shell once every half hour."[17] The next morning the faster pace of bombardment was resumed, continuing all day and into the night.

On the third day of the bombardment a Confederate deserter managed to make his way to Porter's boats and told of the havoc created by the mortar shells, which had smashed the bomb-proofs, set fire to the fort's citadel and cut a breach in the levee, which had flooded the interior of the fort. He claimed that his comrades were demoralized and desperate. Porter tended to doubt the deserter's report, but nevertheless took him to Farragut to have him repeat his claims. Farragut found them interesting, but was reluctant to attempt to take advantage of the reported deteriorating condition of the forts and their garrisons, believing the barrier created by the line of hulks was too formidable to permit his ships to pass it.

As the fleet lay anchored along the west bank, the Confederates made repeated attempts to damage or destroy it by sending fire rafts downriver, but the current and eddies channeled the flaming vessels along the east side of the river, and they drifted by harmlessly or ran aground beside the river bank. Some of them got caught in the obstructions in the stream. "If there had been any one man to direct the enemy's operations," Midshipman (later Commander) Bartlett remarked, observing the rebel efforts from the deck of the *Brooklyn*, "and so secure concert of action, we should have fared badly; for half a dozen rafts chained together and pushed into position by their gunboats would have made havoc with the fleet. One night five rafts were sent down, one of which had been towed over to the right bank and came almost directly into the fleet; the *Westfield* made for it and pushed it out into the stream; but it came so near that even with hose playing on the side and rigging the *Brooklyn*'s paint was badly blistered."[18]

Continual fire from the forts' rifle guns was kept up on the mortar boats and the ships of Farragut's fleet, occasional shots coming close to the *Brooklyn*. To suppress the fire, one of the fleet's sloops or two of its gunboats would charge out from under the cover of the trees on the east bank and blast away at the forts with their eleven-inch pivot guns, steaming downstream and presenting a moving target, difficult to hit, as they did so.

On the night of April 20, Farragut sent out a party to breach the barrier of chained hulks under the cover of darkness. The mission was headed by Farragut's chief of staff, Captain Henry H. Bell. About ten o'clock that night Bell boarded the gunboat *Pinola* and directed it and the gunboat *Itasca* toward the barrier, slipping quietly up the river through rain and blustery headwinds, hoping to avoid detection. With Bell aboard the *Pinola* was Julius Kroehl, reputed to be an explosives expert who would be in charge of placing petards on the hulks and exploding them to blast one of the hulks free from the cables that held it in place and thereby open a gap in the barrier. Kroehl brought along five 180-pound charges of gunpowder, several reels of insulated wire and batteries to provide an electric charge to ignite the explosives.

At ten-thirty the *Pinola*, creeping along in the dark, made an abrupt, unexpected contact with the barrier, and crewmen swiftly boarded the nearest hulk and placed the petards, as instructed by Kroehl, over the hulk's bow and stern mooring cables and fastened a container of gunpowder onto the cable that bound the vessel at midships. "At this moment," one of the crewmen related, "a rocket went up on shore, lights were shown along the batteries, and immediately they opened fire in the direction which we were. We kept perfect silence knowing it to be our only safety. They fired high, though the shot came whizzing by very disagreeably. Soon they ceased firing, thinking no doubt it was a false alarm, particularly as they could not distinguish our vessels from their own hulks."[19]

After about ten minutes, the time required to prepare the explosive charges, the *Pinola* backed away from the hulk, but in doing so it became fouled with the hulk and had to take anxious minutes to free itself. When at last it had disengaged, Captain Bell gave Kroehl the awaited order: "Explode!" Nothing happened. "The conductor is broken," Kroehl told Bell.

"Explode the second one then," Bell replied. Again there was nothing. "That one is also broken," Kroehl limply explained.

Thwarted and with some feeling of exasperation, Bell ordered the *Pinola* toward the line of hulks again. As it neared the barrier a small boat from the *Itasca* drew up beside the *Pinola*, and an officer aboard it announced that the *Itasca* needed help. It had run aground near the east bank of the river and was stuck fast in the mud. There was good news to report, too. Eschewing explosives and the explosives expert, the *Itasca*'s commander, Lieutenant Charles H.B. Caldwell, had slipped up to one of the hulks and had his crewmen unshackle the chains that held the derelict schooner in place and had opened a channel through which the Union ships could pass.

After the *Pinola* had gone to the *Itasca* and pulled it free, the *Itasca* steamed away to return to the fleet, but, Caldwell wrote in his ship's log, "in running close by another schooner ran on a chain and carried it away, breaking the schooner partially adrift and carrying away some booms astern moored by chains to the schooner, thus still more effectually clearing the passage."[20]

Meanwhile, where the *Hartford* and the other ships of the fleet lay, Flag Officer Farragut was suffering anxious hours, which he wrote about in a letter to his wife. "Captain Bell went up last night to cut the chain across the river. I never felt such anxiety in my life as I did until his return. I was as glad to see Bell ... as if he had been my boy. I was up all night, and could not sleep until he got back to the ship."[21] It was well past midnight when the *Pinola* and the *Itasca* came steaming down the river, lights at their bows penetrating the gloom, and returned to their anchorages within the cluster of Union vessels.

As if in retaliation for breaching their barrier, the Confederates launched an enormous fire raft that bore down on the Union fleet's position about two-thirty in the morning of April 21, not long after the return of the *Pinola* and *Itasca*. The gunboats scrambled to get out of its way, and the burning raft, with flames reaching as high as the tops of the ships' masts, passed between the *Hartford* and the *Richmond* as it drifted downriver and caused so much confusion among the vessels trying to avoid it that the gunboats *Kineo* and *Sciota* collided and then the two of them crashed into the *Mississippi*. Two small boats from the *Iroquois* were launched to grapple the raft and tow it out of the way, and while they were doing so, the *Westfield* managed to run into the *Iroquois*, completing the chaos of the night.

On April 23, after five days of continual bombardment by the mortars, despite which the forts were still able to command the river with the deadly fire of their guns, Commander Porter, who had had such grandiose ideas about the importance of the mortar boats in the operation, against the objections of Captain Farragut, reported to Farragut that his men were exhausted from lack of sleep and rest and that his ammunition was nearly depleted.

Farragut had been holding councils of war aboard the *Hartford* every day, keeping in touch with his ship commanders and discussing how their ultimate move would be made. Now that the line of obstructing hulks had been broken and there was no reason for further delay, a plan for running past the forts was developed and discussed. "Some of the captains thought it suicidal and believed that the whole fleet would be annihilated; others, that perhaps one or two vessels might get by, but they would be sunk by the rams," Bartlett related. "All this time Farragut maintained that it must and should be done, even if half the ships were lost."[22]

On the afternoon of the 23rd a final council was held, and it was decided to attempt to run past the forts that night. Porter described the plan:

> The original and best plan of Farragut was that the heavier vessels of the squadron should lead the attack, as they would more easily overcome any obstruction to be met afloat. According to this plan he was to lead in the "Hartford," being followed immediately by the "Brooklyn," "Richmond," "Pensacola," and "Mississippi." The senior commanders interposed the objection to this that wisdom would not permit the Commander-in-chief to receive the greatest shock of the battle; and he was finally induced, very reluctantly, to consent to an arrangement whereby the fleet would be separated into three divisions, with his immediate position in the centre of the line.[23]

The arrangement of the fleet put seven ships comprising the first division, commanded by Captain Theodorus Bailey, in single file on the east side of the river, five ships comprising the third division, commanded by Captain Bell, in single file on the west side, and three ships—*Hartford*, *Brooklyn* and *Richmond*—comprising the center division, commanded by Farragut, in single file in the middle of the river. As the vessels steamed ahead, the mortar boats were to move forward from their position two miles below Fort Jackson and pound the heavy guns of Fort Jackson's water battery, considered the most dangerous of the Confederate guns, while the fleet attempted to get past the forts.

At two A.M. on April 24, the *Hartford*'s signal officer, who was also a correspondent for the New York *Herald*, hoisted two red signal lights high atop the *Hartford*'s mast, and the vessels of the fleet hauled up their anchors to get under way.

12. The Battle for Passage

The blustery winds and rain had ended, leaving the night still and the river spread over with a haze, the air heavy with humidity and only the slightest breeze to move it, the moon yet to appear. Aboard the *Brooklyn*, which would follow in line immediately behind the *Hartford*, Farragut's flagship, all hands had been on the deck since midnight, making sure the guns and all else were ready for the impending fray. The decks were wet down and sanded, prepared for the spilling of blood. At the signal of the two red lights raised high atop the *Hartford*, the anchor was heaved up as noiselessly as possible, and at two-thirty in the morning the *Brooklyn* steamed ahead, in the wake of the *Hartford*.

The vessels would be moving no faster than four miles an hour against the Mississippi's high water and three-and-a-half-knot current. At that rate, it would take more than an hour to reach safety on the far side of the forts. From where the ships would start it was about two miles to the forts, where they would be under the forts' guns for a mile, and it would be another two miles before the ships were out of range of those guns, a total distance of five miles to success and survival.[1]

Keeping the fleet's machinery quiet was an impossible task, and the noise of seventeen capstans raising anchors signaled to the forts' gunners that the fleet was preparing to get under way. Around three A.M., when the moon had at last lightened the sky, the forts' gunners, aiming at shadowy, moving shapes, opened fire as Captain Bailey's lead ship, the *Cayuga*, in the line advancing along the east side of the river, passed through the opening in the row of hulks, and came into range of the forts' guns. Bailey's division advanced for nearly a mile under the rebel barrages and suffered considerable damage while returning fire as its guns came to bear on Fort St. Philip, finally blasting the fort with broadsides of grape and canister shot. Meanwhile, Commander Porter's mortars opened fire on Fort Jackson, the bombardment so intense that no fewer than five of their enormous shells were in the air at the same moment, sometimes as many as eleven, according to one account.[2]

By Porter's account, "No grander or more beautiful sight could have been realized than the scenes of that night. From silence, disturbed now and then only by the slow fire of the mortars— the phantom-like movements of the vessels giving no sound — an increased roar of heavy guns began, while the mortars burst forth into rapid bombardment, as the fleet drew near the enemy's works. Vessel after vessel added her guns to those already at work, until the very earth seemed to shake from their reverberations. A burning raft adding its lurid glare to the scene, and the fiery tracks of the mortar-shells as they passed through the darkness aloft, and sometimes burst in mid-air, gave the impression that heaven itself had joined in the general strife."[3]

Flag Officer Farragut had climbed into the rigging on the mizzen mast and through opera glasses that he had borrowed from his signal officer, B.S. Osbon, the *Herald* corre-

Farragut's fleet assaulting Fort Jackson. Union vessels kept up a steady fire on the Confederates' protective forts below New Orleans as the fleet, arranged in three columns, steamed up the river and passed the two forts, one on each side of the river, in the early morning darkness of April 24, 1862 (Library of Congress).

spondent, he was peering into the dark before him when the first shots struck the *Hartford*. The *Hartford* returned the rebel fire with two guns mounted on the ship's forecastle, and when the vessel came to within a half mile of Fort Jackson, it sheered off and blasted back at the fort's water battery with broadsides of grape and canister, forcing rebel gunners to run for cover. From the fort's casemates, though, the *Hartford* continued to receive steady fire.

The *Brooklyn* took its first hit as it approached the break in the line of hulks. "With our own smoke and the smoke from the vessels immediately ahead, it was impossible to direct the ship," then–Midshipman Bartlett recounted, "so that we missed the opening between the hulks and brought up on the chain. We dropped back and tried again; this time the chain broke, but we swung alongside of one of the hulks, and the stream-anchor, hanging on the starboard quarter, caught, tore along the hulk, and then parted its lashings. The cable secured us just where the Confederates had the range of their guns, but somebody ran up with an axe and cut the hawser, and we began to steam up the river."[4]

The *Richmond*, in line behind the *Brooklyn*, passed within a stone's throw of Fort Jackson, raking it with grape and canister, then swerved across the river to fire on Fort St. Philip as the rebel guns were turned on it. A gun-crew captain aboard the *Richmond* was decapitated by a solid shot, and a gunnery officer had his right arm ripped off by an exploding shell. A crewman carrying a message to the ship's captain, Commander James Alden, had just reached him on the forecastle when a rifle shot struck the sailor in the forehead and killed him instantly.

On the *Pensacola*, steaming behind the *Cayuga*, Lieutenant Francis Roe was standing on the bridge, piloting the vessel, when the signal quartermaster, standing beside him, had a leg shot off and a young aide standing nearby was blown away by a shot. The right leg of

Poe's uniform pants was slashed by a shot, and the skirt of his coat was ripped, but Poe escaped injury.

The *Brooklyn* was blasting shells into Fort Jackson as fast as the guns could be loaded and fired. Just as the ship came abreast of the fort, a shot struck one of its port-side guns, and at the same time a shell burst directly over the gun. The gun-crew captain's head was cut off, and nine of the gun's crew were wounded. Minutes later the *Brooklyn* was attacked by the Confederate ram *Manassas*. The *Brooklyn*'s commander, Captain Thomas T. Craven, described the encounter:

> She came butting into our starboard gangway, first firing from her trap-door when within about ten feet of the ship, directly toward our smoke-stack — her shot entering about five feet above the water-line, and lodging in the sand-bags which protected our steam-drum. I had discovered this queer-looking gentleman [the *Manassas*] while forcing my way over the barricade lying close in to the bank, and when he made his appearance the second time, I was so close to him that he had not an opportunity to get up his full speed, and his efforts to damage me were completely frustrated, our chain-armor proving a perfect protection to our sides. He soon slid off and disappeared in the darkness.[5]

Farragut was at last persuaded to come down from the rigging, and no sooner had he put his feet back on the deck than a shell exploded above him and tore away much of the rigging where he had been standing. The New York *Herald* correspondent, Signal Officer Osbon, described the horrific scene:

> It is quite out of the question to give any idea of the fire at this time, or of the night picture we made there in the midst of flame and smoke and iron hail.... A shell burst on our deck.... I ran forward to see what damage had been done, when the wind of another shell carried away my cap.... We were struck now on all sides. A shell entered our starboard beam, cut our cable, wrecked our armory and exploded at the main hatch, killing one man instantly, and wounding several others. Another entered the muzzle of a gun, breaking the lip and killing the sponger who was in the act of "ramming home." A third entered the boatswain's room destroying everything in its path, and exploding, killed a colored servant who was passing powder.
>
> Death and destruction seemed everywhere. Men's faces were covered with powder — blacked and daubed with blood. They had become like a lot of demons in a wild inferno, working fiercely at the business of death.[6]

The *Hartford* came into the sights of the Confederate tug *Mosher*, which pushed a burning fire raft alongside the *Hartford*, the flames quickly leaping from the raft to the *Hartford*'s sides and rigging and setting the sails of the mizzen mast aflame. Desperate moments followed, as described by Albert Kautz, then a lieutenant serving on the blazing Union flagship:

> No sooner had Farragut given the order "Hard-a-port," than the current gave the ship a broad shear, and her bows went hard up on a mud-bank. As the fire-raft came against the port side of the ship, it became enveloped in flames. We were so near to the shore that from the bowsprit we could reach the tops of the bushes, and such a short distance above Fort St. Philip that we could distinctly hear the gunners in the casemates give their orders; and as they saw Farragut's flag at the mizzen, by the bright light, they fired with frightful rapidity. Fortunately, they did not make sufficient allowance for our close proximity, and the iron hail passed over our bulwarks, doing but little damage.
>
> On the deck of the ship it was as bright as noonday, but out over the majestic river, where the smoke of many guns was intensified by that of the pine-knots of the fire-rafts, it was dark as the blackest midnight. For a moment it looked as though the flag-ship was

indeed doomed, but the firemen were called away, and, with the energy of despair, rushed aft to the quarter-deck. The flames, like so many forked tongues of hissing serpents, were piercing the air in a frightful manner, that struck terror to all hearts.

As I crossed from the starboard to the port side of the deck, I passed close to Farragut, who, as he looked forward and took in the situation, clasped his hands high in the air, and exclaimed, "My God, is it to end in this way!"

Fortunately, it was not to end as it at that instant seemed, for just then Master's Mate Allen, with the hose in his hand, jumped into the mizzen rigging, and the sheet of flame succumbed to a sheet of water. It was but the dry paint on the ship's side that made the threatening flames, and it went down before the fierce attack of the firemen as rapidly as it had sprung up.

As the flames died away, the engines were backed "hard," and, as if providentially, the ram *Manassas* struck the ship a blow under the counter, which shoved her stern in against the bank, causing her bow to slip off. The ship was again free; and a loud, spontaneous cheer rent the air as the crew rushed to their guns with renewed energy.[7]

While the blaze was still roaring, Farragut, standing on the poop deck, cooly watching the ship's firemen working under the direction of Commander Richard Wainwright, noticed the gun crews moving back from their guns to avoid the heat of the flames and he called out to them, "Don't flinch from that fire, boys! There's a hotter fire than that for those who don't do their duty!" Then rallying the gunners to strike back at the attacking Confederate tug-ram *Mosher*, he shouted, "Give that rascally little tug a shot and don't let her get off with a whole coat!"[8] Nevertheless, the *Mosher* did escape.

Some of the Confederates' vessels, upriver of the forts, had quickly responded at the first sounds of firing below their position. The *Manassas* and the *Governor Moore*, along with the tug *Belle Algerine*, headed rapidly downstream from above Fort St. Philip to attempt to ram the oncoming Union vessels. Aboard the immobile *Louisiana*, gunners on the starboard side tensely awaited the command to fire as the Union vessels came up to the spot where the rebel gunboat lay moored upstream of Fort St. Philip. Other Confederate vessels, standing in their berths near Fort Jackson, were set ablaze by their crews and abandoned. The *McRae*, also swiftly responding to the sounds of battle, soon came under fire from the Union gunboat *Iroquois* and hurried to the opposite side of the river, where it became the target of more Union fire. An officer aboard the *McRae*, Lieutenant Charles W. Read, described the vessel's plight:

> One of their shells striking us forward, and exploding in the sail-room, set the ship on fire. The engine and deck pumps were immediately started, but owing to the combustible nature of the articles in the sail-room, the fire burned fiercely. The sail-room was separated from the shell lockers by a third bulkhead. The commander directed the ship to be run close into the bank, and ordered me to inform him when the fire should reach the shell locker bulkhead. I repaired to the scene of fire, and succeeded in smothering and extinguishing it. Two large ships and three gunboats were now engaging us, at a distance of about 800 yards. We backed off the bank with the intention of dropping down near the forts, when the *Manassas* came to our relief. She steered for the enemy's vessels, and as soon as they discovered her, they started up the river.
>
> Just as we were backing off the bank, Lieut. Commanding T.B. Huger fell severely wounded. I now directed the course of the vessel across and up the river, firing the starboard guns as rapidly as possible, and, I think, with much accuracy. We soon reached a position which furnished a view of the river around the first bend above the forts, where I discovered eleven of the enemy, and not deeming it prudent to engage a force so vastly superior to my own, I determined to retire under the guns of the forts.
>
> Having dropped a short distance, and getting into an eddy, I thought it best to turn and

steam down; as the ship was turning, the tiller ropes parted. The ship was instantly stopped, and the engines reversed, but too late to avoid striking the bank. I endeavored to back her off the shore, but could not succeed. One of the river fleet, called the *Resolute*, had been run ashore early in the morning, just above where we were now lying, and had a white flag flying. I sent Lieut. Arnold, with ten men on board of her, with orders to haul down the white flag, and fight her guns as long as possible.

At 6:30 the enemy stood up the river — and as soon as our guns would no longer bear we ceased firing. At 7 a tow-boat came up from the forts, and hauled us off.[9]

Captain Beverley Kennon of the Louisiana State Navy, formerly of the United States Navy, commander of the wooden ram *Governor Moore*, gave his account of the desperate minutes under fire and the failure of the Confederates' River Defense Fleet rams:

The first gun fired brought my crew to their stations. We had steam within 3 minutes, it having been ordered by that hour; the cable was slipped, when we delayed a moment for Lieutenant Warley to spring the *Manassas*, then inside of us, across the channel. A little tugboat, the *Belle Algerine*, now fouled us— to her mortal injury. By the time we started, the space between the forts was filling up with the enemy's vessels, which fired upon us as they approached, giving us grape, canister, and shell.

My vessel being a large one, we had too little steam and elbow-room in the now limited and crowded space to gather sufficient headway to strike a mortal blow on ramming. So rather than "squeeze" my adversary, I made haste slowly by moving close under the east bank to reach the bend above, where I would be able to turn down-stream ready for work. I took this course also, to avoid being fired and run into by the Confederate rams moored above me; but the ground for this fear was soon removed, as, on getting near them, I saw that one had started for New Orleans, while the telegraph steamer *Star*, ram *Quitman*, and one other had been set afire at their berths on the right bank, and deserted before any of the enemy had reached them, and were burning brightly.

Another reason for leaving our berth directly under Fort St. Philip, where the *Louisiana*, *McRae*, and *Manassas* also lay, was to get clear of the cross-fire of the forts, and that of each ship of the enemy as they passed up close to us, for we sustained considerable damage and losses as we moved out into the stream.[10]

Kennon particularly found fault with the performance of the River Defense Fleet rams:

These six "rams" were an independent command, and recognized no outside authority unless it suited their convenience; and it was expected that this "fleet" and its branch in Memphis "would defend the upper and lower Mississippi, without aid from the regular navy." We lay at the head of the turn in the river just above the forts, the place of all ... the Confederate vessels to have been. Here they would have been less liable to be surprised; they would have been clear of the cross-fire from the forts and not exposed to the broadsides of the enemy when passing them, while both guns of each ram could have raked the enemy for over a mile as they approached; they would have been out of the smoke, and would have had extra time to raise steam, to prepare to fire and to ram; moreover, they would have been at a great advantage in ramming, since the advancing vessels would have had to incline to the eastward on reaching them. Not one of them to my knowledge, nor was it ever reported, availed itself of one of these advantages, for when they saw the enemy approaching, those having steam tried to escape, whilst others that did not have it were set afire where they lay, as I myself witnessed. Not one of them made the feeblest offensive or defensive movement, excepting in the case of the *Stonewall Jackson* nearly three hours after.... Had they done their duty simply in firing, what might they not have accomplished! Nearly every United States ship reports firing into them, but not a single one reports having been rammed or fired at by one of them, with the exception of the *Stonewall Jackson* and my ship.[11]

The *Stonewall Jackson* together with the *Governor Moore* rammed and sank the USS *Varuna*, one of the ships in Captain Bailey's division, after the *Varuna* had destroyed four Confederate vessels. The *Varuna*'s commander, Captain Charles Boggs, recounted the action:

> After passing the batteries with the Varuna, finding my vessel amid a nest of rebel steamers, I started ahead, delivering her fire, both starboard and port, at every one that she passed. The first vessel on her starboard beam that received her fire appeared to be crowded with troops. Her boiler was exploded, and she drifted to the shore. In like manner three other vessels, one of them a gun-boat, were driven ashore in flames, and afterward blew up.... The Varuna was attacked by the Morgan [actually the *Governor Moore*], iron-clad about the bow, commanded by Beverly [sic] Kennon, an ex-naval officer. This vessel raked us along the port gangway, killing four and wounding nine of the crew, butting the Varuna on the quarter and again on the starboard side. I managed to get three eight-inch shells into her abaft her armor, as also several shot from the after rifled gun, when she dropped out of action partially disabled.
>
> While still engaged with her, another rebel steamer [*Stonewall Jackson*], iron-clad, with a prow under water, struck us in the port gangway, doing considerable damage. Our shot glanced from her bow. She backed off for another blow, and struck again in the same place, crushing in our side; but, by going ahead fast, the concussion drew her bow around, and I was able with the port guns to give her, while close alongside, five eight-inch shells abaft her armor. This settled her, and drove her ashore in flames.
>
> Finding the Varuna sinking, I ran her into the bank, let go the anchor and tied up to the trees.
>
> During all this time our guns were actively at work crippling the Morgan [*Governor Moore*], which was making feeble efforts to get up steam....
>
> Thus, six of the enemy's fleet fell under the Varuna's fire before she sank, with colors flying, to the river's bed.[12]

Captain Kennon gave his own detailed account of the fight between the *Varuna* and the *Governor Moore*:

> Not wishing to avoid her [the *Varuna*'s] fire any longer, being quite near to her, we put our helm to port and received the fire from her pivot-gun and rifles in our port bow, but as her shot struck us, under the cover of the smoke, our helm was put hard to starboard — she not righting hers quickly enough — and before she could recover herself, we rammed her near the starboard gangway, receiving her starboard broadside and delivering our one shot as we struck her. Her engines stopped suddenly. We backed clear, gathered headway again, and rammed her a second time as near the same place as possible. Before separating, the two vessels dropped alongside each other for a couple of minutes and exchanged musket and pistol shots to some injury to their respective crews, but neither vessel fired a large gun. I expected to be boarded at this time and had had the after gun load with a light charge and three stand of canister, and pointed fore and aft ready for either gangway. It was an opportunity for the Varuna's two hundred men to make a second Paul Jones of their commander, but it was not embraced. As for ourselves, we had neither the men to board nor to repel boarders.
>
> The vessels soon parted, hostilities between them ceased, and the Varuna was beached to prevent her sinking in deep water.... Suddenly the ram *Stonewall Jackson*, having to pass the Varuna to reach New Orleans, rammed deep into the latter's port gangway. When close upon her, the Varuna delivered such of her port broadside guns as could be brought to bear. The *Stonewall Jackson* backed clear, steamed about four miles up the river, and was beached on the opposite bank, fired, and deserted....
>
> Soon after the *Stonewall Jackson* struck the *Varuna* the latter finished sinking, leaving her topgallant forecastle out of the water, and upon it her crew took refuge.[13]

"From the weighing of the anchors," Admiral Porter related, "one hour and ten minutes saw the vessels by the forts, and Farragut on his way to New Orleans, the prize staked upon the fierce game of war just ended."[14] Once the big vessels of Farragut's division — the *Hartford*, the *Brooklyn* and the *Richmond*— had passed the forts, the desperate mission was secure, the awful fight won by Farragut's fleet and the stalwart officers and men who manned it. Silence then came suddenly to the embattled river, as suddenly as the din of war had burst over it little more than an hour earlier.

Not all of Farragut's vessels had made it past the forts. The *Varuna* had been sunk, and the failure of three others was explained by Porter in his account of the battle:

> The "Itasca" [of Captain Bell's division, on the west side of the river] was much cut up, and having a shot through her boiler, was compelled to drop down the river, out of action, after which she was run ashore to prevent sinking. Fourteen shot and shell had passed through her hull, but the list of casualties was small.
>
> The "Kennebec" and "Winona," [both also of Captain Bell's division] being at the end of the line, had been left below the forts at daylight, and were there exposed to the fire of both works, with small ability to reply. Being slow vessels, with a rapid current against them, they were long exposed to the deliberate practice of the enemy and were obliged to haul out of action below.[15]

The *Manassas* was perhaps the last Confederate vessel to give up the fight. The ship's commander, Captain Alexander Warley, unwilling to concede defeat though the Union fleet had passed the forts, took off after Farragut's vessels as they steamed toward New Orleans. He described the final efforts of his ship:

> Day was getting broader, and with the first ray of the sun we saw the fleet above us; and a splendid sight it was, or rather would have been under other circumstances. Signals were being rapidly exchanged, and two men-of-war steamed down, one on either side of the river. The *Manassas* was helpless. She had nothing to fight with, and no speed to run with. I ordered her to be run into the bank on the Fort St. Philip side, her delivery-pipes to be cut, and the crew to be sent into the swamp through the elongated port forward, through which the gun had been used [destroyed]. The first officer, gallant Frank Harris, reported all the men on shore. We examined the vessel, found all orders had been obeyed, and we also took to the swamp....
>
> I soon heard heavy firing — some for our benefit, but most, I think, for the abandoned *Manassas*. I heard afterward that she was boarded, but, filling astern, floated off, on fire, and blew up somewhere below in the neighborhood of the mortar-fleet.[16]

Porter, too, detailed the demise of the *Manassas*, which he deemed the conclusion of the two navies' battle:

> As the [U.S.] fleet was approaching quarantine, some distance above the forts, the "Manassas," the most active and troublesome of the Confederate fleet, was seen, in the early daylight, coming up the river in chase. The Flag-Officer directed Commander Smith to leave the line with the "Mississippi," and run the ram down.
>
> The "Mississippi" turned instantly and started for the enemy at full speed. The "Manassas" had evidently practiced her parts before, for, shifting her helm quickly when but a short distance from the big vessel's bow, she dodged the blow, but in so doing ran ashore, where she was deserted by her crew.
>
> Commander Smith wished to preserve the "Manassas," but was obliged to recall the boats sent to secure her, on account of a burning wreck approaching him, The ram [*Manassas*] was therefore set on fire, and riddled with shot, after which she drifted away from the bank, and finally blew up below the forts.
>
> This ended the irregular fighting with the Confederate vessels.[17]

Before concluding his account of the *Manassas*'s actions, Warley made a point of telling just what kind of boat it was that he had captained in its bold challenges to the U.S. Navy's warships. Not unlike many other Confederate vessels, it was "a tow-boat *boarded* over with five-inch timber and armored with one thickness of flat railroad iron, with a complement of thirty-four persons and an armament of one light carronade and four double-barreled guns. She was very slow. I do not think she made at any time that night more than five miles an hour."[18]

Besides braving the fire of Farragut's vessels, the valiant *Manassas* also had contended with friendly fire in the confusion of the night's battle. "Captain Squires," Warley reported, "who commanded Fort St. Philip, informed me that his fort had fired seventy-five times at the *Manassas*, mistaking her for a disabled vessel of the enemy's floating down-stream." As luck would have it, however, the *Manassas*, Warley said, was not struck once by the guns of Fort St. Philip.[19]

An account of the fortunes of the thirteen Confederate vessels at the forts that night was compiled by J. Thomas Scharf, a Confederate naval officer who authored a history of the Confederate navy:

> The *Governor Moore*, disabled and aground, was burned by her commander, Beverley Kennon; the C.S.S. *Jackson* escaped to New Orleans; the *Manassas* disabled, was destroyed by Lieut. Commander Warley; the *Stonewall Jackson*, of the Montgomery flotilla [River Defense Fleet], escaped up the river and was destroyed by her officers, thirteen miles above the forts; the *Quitman* and the *Star* were abandoned at the very opening of the fight and burned; the *Warrior* was abandoned and burned on the Fort St. Philip side of the river; to the north of her, on the other side of the river, the *Breckinridge* (or *Defiance*) perished in the same ignoble manner—having taken no part in the fight except escaping from it.
>
> The *Louisiana*, the *McRae*, the *Resolute*, of the Montgomery flotilla (which was abandoned by her crew, and taken possession of by Lieut. Arnold and the men from the *McRae*, and brought back into the fight), with the *Burton* and the *Landis*, unarmed tenders, survived the fight, and for two days maintained their positions above the forts.[20]

The forts were passed, but not conquered. Around noon on April 25 Commander Porter, whom Farragut had left in charge at the forts, sent Lieutenant Commander John Guest aboard one of the Union gunboats to Fort Jackson under a flag of truce to seek the surrender of the forts. The forts' commander, General Duncan, declined to surrender before hearing from authorities in New Orleans. Upon receiving Guest's report of Duncan's refusal, Porter ordered, as he said, "a very rapid mortar-fire" on Fort Jackson.[21]

"The effect was such as to cause a mutiny among the garrison," Porter related, "who refused to longer undergo the probability of useless slaughter, and many deserted from the works and retreated up river out of range. The remainder refused to fight the guns, and reasoned that they had unflinchingly borne the terrible six days' bombardment, and had exposed themselves to the night ordeal of the fire of the passing fleet, it was time the fort should be surrendered without further loss of life."[22]

At midnight on April 28, General Duncan dispatched an officer to Porter aboard his flagship, the *Harriet Lane*, to inform him that he was ready to capitulate. The papers spelling out the terms of surrender were duly signed aboard the *Harriet Lane* on the 29th in a ceremony that was briefly interrupted when the hulking Confederate ironclad *Louisiana*, which had been set on fire and cut adrift by its commander, exploded in a fearsome blast that destroyed the boat, damaged Fort St. Philip, killed a soldier at the fort and rocked the *Harriet Lane* before the *Louisiana* reached the Union vessels anchored downstream of it.

Despite the six days of relentless bombardment by Porter's mortars and the intense shelling by the passing Union fleet, the two forts, on inspection by Major General Benjamin Butler's engineering officer, Lieutenant Godfrey Weitzel, remained as stout as ever in their structure and defensive capability. In his report to Butler, Weitzel concluded: "The navy passed the works, but did not reduce them. Fort St. Philip stands, with one or two slight exceptions, to-day without a scratch. Fort Jackson was subjected to a torrent of thirteen-inch and eleven-inch shells during a hundred and forty-four hours. To an inexperienced eye it seems as if this work were badly cut up. It is as strong to-day as when the first shell was fired at it."[23]

The forts' casualties were nearly as light as their damage. Fort Jackson suffered nine killed and thirty-three wounded. Fort St. Philip's casualties amounted to two killed and four wounded. The total number of Confederate naval casualties is not known for certain, but the records indicate that at least seventy-three were killed and seventy-three others were wounded. The *Governor Moore* alone suffered fifty-seven killed.[24] The U.S. Navy's casualties totaled thirty-seven killed and 147 wounded.[25]

As Porter sought to secure the forts, Flag Officer Farragut and his fleet continued to steam up the mighty river. When the first Union vessels reached the quarantine station, about seven miles above the forts, the Confederate gunboat *Jackson*, posted there to protect the station, sped off toward New Orleans. The *Hartford* and the other leading vessels of Farragut's fleet dropped anchor at the quarantine station, and Farragut waited to see how many of his fleet had made it past the forts. He at last counted thirteen, most of them showing signs of the battering they had taken from the rebel guns.

From the quarantine station Farragut sent a message to Porter saying that he was going to push on to New Orleans, now some sixty-five miles upriver. He left two of his gunboats at the quarantine station to guard it and then pushed on with his remaining eleven vessels, steaming past plantations with handsome houses, clusters of rustic slave cabins and expansive fields green with new crops of foot-high sugar cane stalks.

Not found were the batteries of artillery with which the banks of the river were said to be lined. At Point a la Hache, which the fleet reached about three o'clock in the afternoon, there was believed to be a formidable massing of big guns, but there turned out to be none. In a nearby field scores of slaves left their plows and crowded onto the riverbank to greet the ships, waving and shouting. In the growing darkness the fleet finally halted for the night around eight P.M., about eighteen river miles below New Orleans.

Around midnight alarms were sounded aboard the sleeping vessels. Three large, flaming objects were in the river ahead of them. They appeared to be fire rafts coming toward the fleet, drifting on the current. Steam was raised in the Union ships, and they began to maneuver in the river to avoid the floating fires. After about an hour it could be seen that the blazing objects were not moving, but were apparently moored in the river. The next morning, when Farragut's vessels were under way again, the fiery objects were discovered to be blockade runners freighted with cotton, apparently set ablaze to prevent their falling into Union hands.

Soon the fleet was approaching Chalmette, Louisiana, on the east side of the river, site of Andrew Jackson's historic defeat of the British invaders in the Battle of New Orleans during the War of 1812. There the Confederates had mounted two batteries of artillery, one on each side of the river, each with eight or so guns, which opened fire on the fleet as soon as it came into view. The lead vessels were under fire for some twenty minutes before they were in a position to return the fire, and when they were, several broadsides of shell and grape quickly forced the unprotected rebel gunners from their positions, abandoning their guns to seek shelter. The fleet suffered one casualty in the exchange.

At noon Farragut's vessels at last drew up to the storied city, its skies covered with threatening clouds and rising columns of dark smoke, as if presenting an ominous greeting to the invaders. The boisterous scene at the riverfront was captured in a contemporary account:

> Fires along the shore farther than the eye could reach; the river full of burning vessels; the levee lined with madmen, whose yells and defiant gestures showed plainly enough what kind of welcome awaited the new-comers. A faint cheer for the Union, it is said, rose from one part of the levee, answered by a volley of pistol-shots from the by-standers. As the fleet dropped anchor in the stream, a thunder-storm of tropical violence burst over the city, which dissolved large masses of the crowd, and probably reduced, in some degree, the frenzy of those who remained.[26]

By one o'clock all vessels of Farragut's fleet were anchored and stood menacingly before the defenseless but defiant city of New Orleans, which awaited the invaders' next move.

13. The Defiant City

The man the government in Richmond picked to defend the Confederate States' most important metropolis, the strategic city of New Orleans, was a seventy-one-year-old veteran of the Mexican War, the Seminole Wars, the Black Hawk War and the War of 1812. He was Major General David Emanuel Twiggs, who as a United States brigadier general at the outbreak of hostilities had commanded the U.S. Army's Department of Texas. Born in Richmond County, Georgia, and feeling intensely loyal to his native state, he had written to his commander, General Winfield Scott, in January 1861 and told him, "I am placed in a most embarrassing situation.... As soon as I know Georgia has separated from the Union I must, of course, follow her. I most respectfully ask to be relieved in the command of this department.... All I have is in the South."[1]

Twiggs was dismissed from the U.S. Army after he surrendered a 160-man garrison in San Antonio to a threatening thousand-man force of Texas rebels and handed over $1.6 million worth of U.S. government property to the Confederates in February 1861. He had earlier said that "If an old woman with a broomstick should come with full authority from the state of Texas to demand the public property, I would give it to her."[2] In appreciation of his spirit of Confederate cooperation the Texas secession convention commended him for his "patriotism and moral courage." In Washington his behavior was deemed appalling, and President Buchanan promptly ordered him dismissed in disgrace "for his treachery to the flag of his country." Twiggs took umbrage at the suggestion he had acted as a traitor and he wrote to Buchanan and threatened to come to Buchanan's home in Lancaster, Pennsylvania, and challenge him to a duel, a trip Twiggs never got around to making.

Within three months of his dismissal from the U.S. Army he was made a major general in the Confederate army, and on May 22 he was ordered to New Orleans to take command of the Confederacy's newly created military Department No. 1, which included south Alabama, south Mississippi and all of Louisiana. He arrived at his new post on May 31, 1861.

To the people of New Orleans, General Beauregard, a former engineering officer and a native Louisianan intimately familiar with the lower Mississippi River and the approaches to New Orleans, would have been a much better choice for the job of protecting the city. Braxton Bragg, another Confederate general familiar with the New Orleans area, owner of a plantation on Bayou Lafourche in south Louisiana, would also have been considered by New Orleanians as a good choice. They got neither.

In fact, they only got General Twiggs after Louisiana's governor, Thomas Moore, pleaded with the Richmond government to send someone to take charge of the defense of New Orleans. "The forts can be passed," Moore warned in a telegram to Secretary of War Leroy Walker on April 10, 1861. "We are disorganized, and have no general officer to command and direct." Moore also wired the Confederacy's then attorney general, Judah Benjamin of Louisiana, asking for help. Benjamin wired back to Moore that the fears of the people of New Orleans "are without cause."[3] Even so, Benjamin promised on April 9 that "an officer of high rank" would soon be sent to New Orleans.

Seven weeks later Twiggs showed up. It took him ten days to learn the sad state of the city's defenses. "This department," he reported to the secretary of war on June 10, "is very badly off for men and ammunition." Within another week the Confederate War Department, seeming either not to listen or not to care, virtually stripped the city of troops that could be used for its defense — the Sixth, Seventh and Eighth Louisiana regiments, the infantry battalion that would become known as the Louisiana Tigers, and the Washington Artillery were all sent from New Orleans to Virginia.[4]

As if to reassure a public that may have had doubts about the old general's ability to organize an effective defense of the city, the Common Council of the city of New Orleans issued a statement within days of Twiggs's arrival, citing his "integrity, sagacity, and nerve, so essential to a commandant." It also authorized a bond issue to raise $250,000 for the general to use to fortify the city. Twiggs, however, showed no sense of urgency to spend the money and begin building fortifications. It took him nearly a month to even bring up the subject of fortification to Secretary Walker. In a letter to Walker dated July 9, 1861, Twiggs claimed that he did not "feel authorized to expend money for such purposes without the special orders of the Secretary of War."

While the old general diddled, he acknowledged that the people of New Orleans were eager to get on with the task of fortifying the city. "The citizens," he told Walker, "are very desirous to have the defense of these approaches [to the city] attended to at once, and in this desire I participate."[5] But when the civil authorities took action to have defenses built, the New Orleans Common Council having adopted on July 2 a plan to encircle the city with fortifications, General Twiggs became a forbidding obstacle. "Concerning fortifications proposed by a committee of the City Council," he wrote to Governor Moore, "I would state that no plan of fortifications will be approved or sanctioned by me except such as may be prepared by or approved by the engineering officers of the Confederate army."[6]

Another month passed, and still no work on fortifications had begun. On August 9 the Common Council approved an appropriation of $100,000 to be used for fortifications as Twiggs saw fit. On August 20 Twiggs notified the council that "contracts covering the whole work are entered into, the lines of defence defined, and that Major M.L. Smith, the chief engineer of this department, is ready to commence operation so soon as the amount referred to is placed subject to draft."[7]

With Major Smith having been delegated by Twiggs to take charge of the project, contracts were let, and work on fortifications at last began on August 22. The *Picayune* crowed that "we shall soon be prepared to resist any force that the abolition despot, Lincoln, may send to invade our shores." Heavy guns were requisitioned from the Confederate government, and by late September ninety-five big artillery pieces had arrived from Norfolk. By the end of September the barrier chain supported by the line of hulks had been stretched across the Mississippi River at Fort Jackson.

Even so, dissatisfaction with General Twiggs grew. He completely lost the confidence of Governor Moore, who wrote to President Davis on September 20 and complained that Twiggs was decrepit and senile. What New Orleans needed, Moore told Davis, was an officer "who, with youth, energy and military ability, would infuse some activity in our preparations and some confidence in our people." A.B. Roman, a respected former governor of Louisiana, also wrote to Davis to complain about the apprehension among the people of New Orleans because of "the infirmities" of General Twiggs.

Reacting to the rising unease over the old general, President Davis attempted to dodge blame for having Twiggs in the job. It was the fault of the people in New Orleans who had urged Twiggs's selection, Davis protested. "They should sooner have informed me of the mistake they had made."[8] On September 25, Davis ordered Brigadier General Mansfield Lovell, a former U.S. Army officer and former deputy commissioner of streets in New York City, to New Orleans to take over from Twiggs. Choosing the smoothest way out, Twiggs ten days later gave up as readily as he had at San Antonio. He wrote to the new secretary of war, Judah Benjamin, saying, "My health will not permit me to take the field. I would like an active and efficient officer to be sent to relieve me."[9]

On Twiggs's resignation, Lovell was promoted to major general. He arrived in New Orleans on October 17, 1861, three days before his thirty-ninth birthday. Born in Washington, D.C., the son of the U.S. Army's surgeon general during the War of 1812, Lovell had entered West Point at age sixteen and had graduated in 1842, ranked ninth in his class. He had served as an artillery officer during the Mexican War and was wounded and later brevetted to captain in recognition of his "skill and distinguished gallantry." In 1854 he had resigned from the Army, and four years later his old friend and West Point classmate, Gustavus Smith, the commissioner of streets in New York City, hired him as his deputy. Although sympathetic to the South, as was Smith, Lovell waited till September 1861 to join its cause, selling his house in New York and traveling to Richmond with his wife and family. He had been recommended to President Davis by Major General Joseph Johnston, who thought he would make an effective division commander, and on September 25 Davis appointed Lovell a brigadier general.

Although New Orleans newspaper editorialists cheered Lovell's appointment, one of them lauding him as "a man of much promise ... remarkable for foresight, and exactly the general to calm the apprehensions and justify the hopes of the people," not everyone thought him the man for the job. The wife of General Bragg, for instance, Elise Ellis Bragg, wrote to tell her husband, who apparently shared her opinion, "Yesterday's paper informs us that Captain Lovell — Mansfield Lovell, never conspicuous that I am aware of, of doubtful attachment to our cause, certainly very slow in joining us, has been raised to the same rank as yourself & assumes this important command of two States! While you are still confined to the petty province of Pensacola...."[10]

What Twiggs took ten days to learn, Lovell discovered immediately. He quickly wrote to President Davis to advise him of the desperate conditions in New Orleans:

> I arrived yesterday, and assumed command at once. I find great confusion, irresolution and want of system in everything administrative. Such executive work as has been confided to Major Smith has been faithfully done so far as it lay in the power of one man to do it. It will be a mountain of labor to put things in shape. The city has been almost entirely stripped of everything available in the way of ordnance, stores, ammunition, clothing, medicines &c.... Our main want at present is powder, and as so much of our defense is to depend upon heavy artillery, it will require a large stock for guns which consume 8 to 10 lbs. for each discharge....
>
> Should you see in the New Orleans papers that we are well supplied with everything, you may regard it as a ruse. But every deficiency and want has been proclaimed from the housetops, until every boy in town knows just what we lack. This I may find it necessary to counteract by circulating contrary reports. You will always be advised of the true condition of affairs.[11]

Speedily taking on his responsibilities, Lovell toured the area of his command in the first two weeks after arriving in New Orleans. The tour revealed the inadequacies of the rebels' defense, including insufficient and poorly armed troops along the Mississippi gulf coast, deteriorating forts guarding the approaches to the city and unprotected entrances from the gulf into the heart of his area. At New Orleans he saw that the eight miles of fortifications were still under construction and discovered that the big guns sent from Norfolk, old U.S. Navy artillery, were virtually unusable. Lovell quickly set out to remedy those deficiencies as best and as soon as he could, working day and night to accomplish his huge and forbidding assignment.

When told by the Confederate army's chief of ordnance that there were no heavy artillery pieces that could be spared for New Orleans's defense, Lovell persuaded foundries in New Orleans to cast the needed big guns and the shot and shell they would fire. He furthermore established a factory for producing small-arms ammunition. He ordered barriers erected to block the streams that gave access to the city's approach routes and he reinforced the chain-and-hulk barrier across the river at Fort Jackson. He built a supplemental rail line to enable troops to be moved rapidly to the city's outer defenses. "Major General M. Lovell," the *Picayune* commented with satisfaction, "is indefatigable."

What lay beyond Lovell's ability to control or change, however, were the rebels' defenses, or more accurately, *potential* defenses, afloat on the Mississippi, ostensibly safeguarding New Orleans from the likeliest threat of all — an assault from the river. From the beginning of his assignment Lovell had asked for command of all Confederate forces — army and navy — in Department No. 1, but President Davis had curtly refused him any authority over naval forces and had prohibited him for communicating directly with naval officials. Not only did Davis's policy preclude a unified command in the effort to defend New Orleans and the lower Mississippi River, it also prevented Lovell from using his authority to press the Tift brothers to complete the *Mississippi*, which could have proved a powerful, perhaps decisive, weapon in combating Farragut's fleet but instead became a useless waste. The same could be said for the ineffectual, powerless *Louisiana* and its builder, E.C. Murray.

Davis had resisted all efforts to bolster the naval force at New Orleans. Confederate Navy Secretary Stephen Mallory had ordered the *Louisiana*, while still under construction, to be sent from its New Orleans shipyard to Memphis to aid the defense of the river there, and when Governor Moore wrote to Davis pleading that he countermand Mallory's order so that the *Louisiana* could be used to defend New Orleans and informing Davis that forts Jackson and St. Philip had already come under attack from Porter's mortars, Davis arrogantly refused, in effect telling Moore, a civilian politician, that *military* men, among whom he counted himself, knew best.

"The wooden vessels are below"; Davis wired Moore, "the iron gunboats are above. The forts should destroy the former if they attempt to ascend. The *Louisiana* may be indispensable to check the descent of the iron boats. The purpose is to defend the city and valley; the only question is as to the best mode of effecting the object. Military men must decide, and today their discretionary power has been enlarged."[12]

When military men on the scene, however, *did* decide that the vessels were needed at New Orleans, it was civilian Mallory who overruled them. Commander W.C. Whittle, the Confederate naval commander at New Orleans, had wired Flag Officer George Hollins, with the rebel fleet at Memphis, urging him to come down and help out, but when Hollins, eager to take on the Union fleet below New Orleans, asked Mallory for permission to do so, Mallory refused it. "Your proposition," Mallory told Hollins, "to quit the enemy and go to the mouth of the Mississippi cannot be entertained. You must oppose his descent of the river, and his movement of vessels and troops at every step."[13] The hodge-podge, amateur River Defense Fleet, under no authority but its own, had further failed to provide protection for the doomed city.

When the news reached New Orleans, before Farragut's sailors cut the telegraph line from the quarantine station, that the forts had been passed, the city's residents, already anxious, became openly panicky. At nine-thirty on the morning of Thursday, April 24, the bells of the churches that had been designated as the city's alarm givers— Christ Church on Canal Street, St. Patrick's on Camp Street and the First Presbyterian Church on Lafayette Square — tolled out twelve ominous strokes, repeated four times, the signal for all intended combatants to assemble at their headquarters and for the civilian public to rush to the nearest newspaper office to read the important news posted on the paper's bulletin board. The facts were scanty but worrisome. The assembling of the twenty-eight hundred Confederate troops posted in the city and the many more militia soldiers on hand, massed and impatiently awaiting the return of General Lovell from the forts, threw further concern into the minds of the citizens.

At two-thirty that afternoon the general, having raced back to the city on horseback, came galloping down from the levee with more complete and devastating information. The Union fleet had indeed managed to pass forts Jackson and St. Philip, had destroyed the Confederate gunboats and was steaming up the river to confront New Orleans. One account, written shortly after the event, described the public's reactions:

> Stores were hastily closed, and many were abandoned without closing. People left their houses forgetting to shut the front-door, and ran about the streets without apparent object. There was a fearful beating of drums, and a running together of soldiers. Women were seen bonnetless, with [a] pistol in each hand, crying, "Burn the city. Never mind us. Burn the city." Officers rode about impressing carts and drays to remove the cotton from storehouses to the levee for burning. Four millions of specie were carted from the banks to the railroad stations, and sent out of the city. The consulates filled with people, bringing their valuables to be stored under the protection of foreign flags....
>
> Only those who have seen a large city suddenly driven mad with apprehension and rage, can form an adequate conception of the confusion, the hurry, the bewilderment, the terror, the fury, that prevailed.[14]

In the atmosphere of terror and fury, Union sympathizers, the few individuals who showed any sign of joy in Farragut's success, became targets of irate mobs that roamed the streets. The eyes of one mob fell on a man who, someone said, looked like a spy, and the mob members swiftly put a rope around his neck and strung him up on a lamp post. He was, however, soon rescued by the so-called European Brigade, a military unit composed of Spanish, French, German, Italian, English and other foreign-born volunteers, the only armed force still in the city, Lovell's twenty-eight hundred Confederate troops and thousands of militiamen having taken flight by rail and road. In their absence the mayor of New Orleans had turned to the European Brigade and asked its commander, Brigadier General Paul Juge, to do his best to preserve a modicum of law and order. The brigade's efforts, heroically exerted, thwarted those who were intent on burning the city.

Along the city's waterfront pandemonium ruled. Looters jammed the streets leading to the wharves, and the poor of both races, white and black, ransacked warehouses to carry off in buckets, sacks or wheelbarrows quantities of sugar, rice, sweet potatoes, hams and other foodstuffs. Not all of the pillagers were from the city's throngs of poor. Opportunists seeking to turn a fast buck with looted goods drove up in wagons to haul off plunder. George Devol, one of the city's eminent riverboat gamblers, confessed his deeds in his memoir: "I hired a dray (for which I had to pay $10) and loaded it down to the guards. We put on a hogshead of sugar, twenty-five hams, a sack of coffee, box of tea, firkin of butter, barrel of potatoes, some hominy, canned fruits, etc. I would have put on more, but the dray wouldn't hold it."[15]

What wasn't carried off was burned. A contemporary account detailed the destruction: "Fifteen thousand bales of cotton on the levee; twelve or fifteen cotton ships, in the river; fifteen or twenty steamboats; an unfinished ram of great magnitude; the dry-docks; vast heaps of coal; vaster stores of steamboat wood; miles of steamboat wood; ship timber; board-yards; whatever was supposed to be of use to Yankees; all was set on fire, and the heavens were black with smoke."[16]

Wasting no time once the Union fleet had anchored before the city, and not waiting for either a change in the stormy weather or the mood of the threatening crowd at the riverfront, Flag Officer Farragut shortly after one o'clock in the afternoon of Friday, April 25, dispatched two of his officers, Captain Theodorus Bailey, captain of the *Cayuga*, and Lieutenant George Perkins, to demand surrender of the city. While they were being rowed to shore, the blazing hulk of the unfinished Confederate ironclad ram *Mississippi*, set afire by the rebels, came drifting past the anchored vessels of the U.S. fleet.

As Bailey and Perkins neared the dock, the crowd on shore was yelling, "Jeff Davis and the South!" Two or three men who cheered at the sight of the Stars and Stripes were instantly grabbed and hustled away. Seeming to ignore the threats and taunts of the crowd, Bailey and Perkins stepped ashore with apparent calm and announced that they had come to see the mayor. Perkins recounted the event in a letter to his family: "They were all shouting and hooting as we stepped on shore, but at last a man, who, I think, was a German, offered to show us the way to the council room, where we should find the mayor of the city. As we advanced, the mob followed us in a very excited state. They gave three cheers for Jeff Davis and Beauregard, and three groans for Lincoln. Then they began to throw things at us, and shout, 'Hang them! Hang them! Hang them!'"[17] That harangue continued for the entire distance of some ten blocks that Bailey and Perkins walked to City Hall.

A member of the crowd, New Orleans-born novelist George Washington Cable, then seventeen years old, later recalled the spectacle of the two Union officers facing the mass of tormentors as they "walked abreast, unguarded and alone, looking not to the right or left, never frowning, never flinching, while the mob screamed in their ears, shook cocked pistols in their faces, cursed and crowded, and gnashed upon them. So through the gates of death those two men walked to the City Hall to demand the town's surrender. It was one of the bravest deeds I ever saw done."[18]

At City Hall the building was surrounded by the crowd while the two officers entered and sought out the mayor, tall, slender John T. Monroe, who presented himself in the company of several city officials, including Pierre Soulé, a city councilman and a former U.S. senator with a gift of oratory. Following the obligatory salutations, courteously rendered, Captain Bailey got down to the business at hand. "I have been sent," he told the mayor, "by Captain Farragut, commanding the United States fleet, to demand the surrender of the city, and the elevation of the flag of the United States over the custom house, the mint, the post office and the city hall."[19]

The mayor swiftly replied, "I am not the military commander of the city. I have no authority to surrender it and would not do so if I had. There is a military commander now in the city. I will send for him to receive and reply to your demand."[20] The mayor had a point; the city was under martial law. He promptly dispatched a courier to find General Lovell, still in New Orleans although his troops had fled, and to summon him to City Hall.

To make conversation while they waited in Mayor Monroe's office for Lovell's arrival, Bailey and Perkins offered their flattering comments about the stout defense put up by the garrisons of Fort Jackson and Fort St. Philip and even went so far as to praise the vain efforts of the Confederate fleet to check the advance of the U.S. vessels. Bailey allowed as how he regretted the destruction of so much property and goods in New Orleans and said Captain Farragut deplored it as well. Mayor Monroe, his courteous conduct evidently having become too burdensome to sustain, replied that the property belonged to New Orleans people and its destruction did not concern outsiders. Bailey countered that the destruction looked very much like someone's biting off his nose to spite his face. The mayor said he took a different view of the matter. All the while, the mob outside yelled threats and insults.

Suddenly the shouts turned to cheers. Lovell had arrived. He entered the building and made his way to the mayor's office, where Bailey and Perkins were introduced to him.

"I am General Lovell," he announced himself, "of the army of the Confederate States, commanding this department." He then shook hands with Bailey and Perkins. Bailey repeated the demand from Farragut that New Orleans be surrendered to the Union force, and he further stated that he had been directed by Farragut to assure the people of the city that the U.S. presence was meant to protect private property and personal rights and that there was no intention to deprive individuals of their property, especially including slaves.

Lovell insisted he would not surrender the city. Neither would he allow it to be surrendered. He said he was overpowered by a superior naval force, but that his army would continue to fight on land. He said he had withdrawn his troops from New Orleans to prevent the city from being bombarded by the Union fleet, despite pleas from women of the city for him and his troops to stay and fight. If, however, Flag Officer Farragut decided to bombard the city anyway, despite the large number of women and children within it, there was nothing to stop him. He said he intended to leave New Orleans and allow city officials to do whatever they thought proper.

Bailey and Perkins then decided to return to the fleet, and Mayor Monroe promised that he would discuss with the council members what should be done next and that he would then report the council's decision to Flag Officer Farragut.

By now the mob outside City Hall had grown so large and threatening that Lovell instructed two of his officers to accompany Bailey and Perkins back to the waterfront. Then he went outside to speak to the crowd. Councilman Soulé also addressed it, urging moderation and dignity. In the meantime Bailey and Perkins were led out of the rear entrance of City Hall, ushered into a waiting carriage and hurriedly driven back to the waterfront, where the crewmen of their small boat were silently and anxiously enduring the harassment of another mob. The officers were speedily rowed back to the waiting vessels of the fleet.

Having said his speech to the crowd, General Lovell without delay decamped to where a train awaited him, on which he departed the city, leaving it to its own devices and uncertain fate.

That evening, as dark approached, from aboard the transport steamer *Mississippi*, moored near the wharf, came the stirring strains of "The Star Spangled Banner," loud and clear, played by a Navy band. Some in the crowd of onlookers still gathered at the riverfront cheered and waved their hats and handkerchiefs—a display of sentiment that was promptly subdued by a group of horsemen who came riding up and began firing indiscriminately into the crowd, which included women and children.

Aboard the vessels of the fleet there was calm, but no lack of concern, fearful as Flag Officer Farragut was for their safety. Some New Orleans newspapers had published notices appealing for a thousand volunteers to form boarding parties to assault the Union ships. As a precaution, he ordered that a revolver and cutlass be issued to every man in the fleet to ward off a nighttime attack by anyone attempting to board the vessels. Unaware of events at the forts, he further worried that his fleet might be trapped in the river if forts Jackson and St. Philip continued to hold out.

About six-thirty the next morning, Saturday, April 26, a small boat drew up to the *Hartford*, and from it climbed Mayor Monroe's secretary and the New Orleans chief of police to inform Farragut that the Common Council would be meeting at ten o'clock that morning to determine what the city's response to Farragut's demands would be and that its decision would be promptly passed on to Flag Officer Farragut.

In response to that notice from the mayor's emissaries, Farragut wrote a note addressed to Mayor Monroe: "I, therefore, demand of you, as its representative, the unqualified surrender of the city, and that the emblem of the sovereignty of the United States be hoisted over the City Hall, Mint and Custom-House, by meridian this day, and all flags and other emblems of sovereignty other than that of the United States be removed from all the public buildings by that hour."[21]

Farragut then dispatched Lieutenant Albert Kautz, with Midshipman John H. Read and a force of twenty Marines commanded by Lieutenant George Heisler, to deliver the note. "Farragut informed me," Kautz related, "that if a shot was fired at us by the mob, he would open fire from all ships and level the town."[22] Met by the angry mob, Kautz, heeding the plea of an officer of what he described as the City Guard, decided against having the Marines escort him to City Hall, thereby further antagonizing the mob. "As my object was to communicate with the mayor without unnecessary shedding of blood, I sent the marine guard back to the ship, retaining only one non-commissioned officer, with a musket. I tied my handkerchief on the bayonet, and with Midshipman Read and this man took up the march for the City Hall. We were cursed and jostled by the mob which filled the streets, but no actual violence was offered us."[23]

Kautz's mission to the mayor met with no more success than had Captain Bailey's the day before, and Farragut's representatives slipped out of City Hall and were driven back to the riverfront in a carriage to escape the crowd.

At the meeting of the city council that morning, Mayor Monroe briefed the council members on the meeting with Farragut's representatives at City Hall the day before and he let the council know what he thought about the situation. "My own opinion," he said, "is that as a civil magistrate, possessed of no military power, I am incompetent to perform a military act, such as the surrender of the city to a hostile force; that it would be proper to say, in reply to a demand of that character, that we are without military protection, that the troops have withdrawn from the city, that we are consequently incapable of making any resistance, and that, therefore, we can offer no obstruction to the occupation of the mint, the custom house and the post office; that we have no control over them; and that all acts involving a transfer of property must be performed by the invading force, by the enemy themselves; that we yield to physical force alone, and that we maintain our allegiance to the Confederate government."[24]

The council members responded by unanimously adopting a resolution that embraced the mayor's position and made it the city's official policy:

Whereas, the common council of the city of New Orleans, having been advised by the military authorities that the city is indefensible, declare that no resistance will be made to the forces of the United States;

Resolved, That the sentiments expressed in the message of his honor the mayor to the common council, are in perfect accordance with the sentiments entertained by the entire population of this metropolis; and that the mayor be respectfully requested to act in the spirit manifested by the message.[25]

On Sunday morning, April 27, Farragut received Mayor Monroe's promised reply to Farragut's demands:

I am no military man, and possess no authority beyond that of executing the municipal laws of the city of New Orleans. It would be presumptuous in me to attempt to lead an army to the field, if I had one at command; and I know still less how to surrender an undefended place, held, as this is, at the mercy of your gunners and your mortars. To surrender such a place were an idle and unmeaning ceremony. The city is yours by the power of brutal force, not by my choice or the consent of its inhabitants. It is for you to determine what will be the fate that awaits us here.

As to hoisting any flag not of our own adoption and allegiance, let me say to you that the man lives not in our midst whose hand and heart would not be paralyzed at the mere thought of such an act; nor could I find in my entire constituency so desperate and wretched a renegade as would dare to profane with his hand the sacred emblem of our aspirations.[26]

Farragut had misconceived the people's attitude in a city undefended and helpless before the guns of the United States fleet. He would soon see that he had also misconceived his power to impose his demands on the city. If the U.S. flag was going to be raised on any buildings, he now realized, his men would have to be the ones to raise it. Sometime before eight o'clock Sunday morning he ordered the captain of the *Pensacola*, moored off Esplanade Avenue, at the edge of the French Quarter, within sight of the mint, to send a party ashore and hoist the Stars and Stripes atop the building. By eight o'clock the mission had been accomplished, and Old Glory was once more wafting grandly over the defiant city of New Orleans.

The landing party that had raised the flag left no one to guard it, but the officer in charge of the party warned bystanders that the guns of the *Pensacola* were loaded with grapeshot and trained on the mint, ready to fire should anyone attempt to haul down the flag. At eleven o'clock that cloudy Sunday morning, the *Pensacola*'s crew, like the fleet's other crews, gathered on deck to hold a service that had been ordered "to render thanks to Almighty God for His great goodness and mercy in permitting us to pass through the events of the last two days with so little loss of life and blood." During the service the lookout atop the main mast fired a signal and sent the crewmen scrambling to their stations. From their positions they could see four men on the roof of the mint pulling down the U.S. flag, grabbing it and hurrying off with it.

Despite having no order to fire, the *Pensacola*'s gunners hastily snatched their guns' lanyards to give the building a broadside. However, with the skies threatening imminent rain, someone of the crew had removed the guns' firing wafers to avoid their getting wet and ruined by the rain. The guns would not fire without them. The daring rebels got away, but a disastrous slaughter had been prevented.

The four men, who dragged the flag through the muddy streets, paraded it about to accompaniment of a fife and drum and at last ripped it to shreds, were hailed as heroes by New Orleans newspapers. The *Picayune* discovered the names of the men and in the next morning's edition of the paper waxed eloquent in an editorial salute to them:

> The names of the party that distinguished themselves by gallantly tearing down the flag that had been surreptitiously hoisted, we learn, are W.B. Mumford, who cut it loose from the flag-staff amid the shower of grape, Lieutenant N. Holmes, Sergeant Burns and James Reed. They deserve great credit for their patriotic act. New Orleans, in this hour of adversity, by the calm dignity she displays in the presence of the enemy, by the proof she gives of her unflinching determination to sustain to the uttermost the righteous cause for which she has done so much and made such great sacrifices, by her serene endurance undismayed of the evil which afflicts her, and her abiding confidence in the not distant coming of better and brighter days— of speedy deliverance from the enemy's toils— is showing a bright example to her sister cities, and proving herself, in all respects, worthy of the proud position she has achieved. We glory in being a citizen of this great metropolis.[27]

Seeming impotent despite the power of his fleet, Farragut felt humiliated and frustrated. When Major General Benjamin Franklin Butler, without his troops, arrived later that Sunday, he was briefed on the events of the past two days and, joining Farragut in his feelings of exasperation, he advised Farragut to threaten the city with bombardment and to order that women and children be sent out of the city. Farragut, desperate enough to try almost anything, took the advice. He dashed off a letter to Mayor Monroe, warning him against further actions such as the one on Sunday morning and telling him that the city was in danger of drawing fire by the spontaneous reaction of the men of his fleet.

"The fire of this fleet may be drawn upon the city at any moment," Farragut wrote, "and in such an event the levee would ... in all probability, be cut by the shell, and an amount of distress ensue to the innocent population which I have heretofore endeavored to assure you that I desired by all means to avoid. The election ... is with you," Farragut told Monroe, "but it becomes my duty to notify you to remove the women and children from the city within forty-eight hours, if I have rightly understood your determination."[28]

The letter was delivered to Monroe at City Hall by Captain Henry H. Bell and Acting Master Herbert Tyson, who were forced to endure the same harassment from New Orleans mobs as had Farragut's other emissaries. When they left, they did as had the previous emissaries— through the rear entrance of City Hall and then by a speeding carriage back to the wharf where their small boat awaited.

Monroe turned to council members for their support of continued defiance, and they quickly authorized Pierre Soulé to draft a letter to Farragut for the mayor to sign. The letter disputed Farragut's right to place a U.S. flag on the mint (a United States mint turned into a Confederate mint by the rebels) and virtually challenged him to open fire on the city and its inhabitants:

> Sir, you can not but know that there is no possible exit from the city for a population which still exceeds 140,000 and you must therefore be aware of the utter inanity of such a notification. Our women and children can not escape your shells if it be your pleasure to murder them on a question of mere etiquette; but if they could, there are but few among them that would consent to desert their families and their homes and the graves of their relations in so awful a moment....
>
> You are not satisfied with the peaceable possession of an undefended city, opposing no resistance to your guns, because of its bearing its doom with something of manliness and

dignity; and you wish to humble and disgrace us by an act against which our nature rebels. This satisfaction you can not expect to obtain at our hands.

We will stand your bombardment, unarmed and undefended as we are. The civilized world will consign to indelible infamy the heart that will conceive the deed and the hand that will dare to consummate it.[29]

The letter was carried to the *Hartford* by Soulé and the mayor's secretary, Marion Baker, and delivered to Farragut in the early morning of Tuesday, April 29. While he had Farragut's ear, Soulé launched into an argument on international law, which Farragut ended by saying that he was not familiar with the fine points of international law, that he was just a sailor trying to do his duty as commander of a Navy fleet. The meeting concluded soon after.

Mayor Monroe and city officials in the meantime found a worthy ally in the commander of the French warship that had recently arrived at New Orleans, Captain Georges Charles Clouet. He wrote to Farragut, protesting Farragut's edict on the evacuation of the city. He was, he said, "sent by my government to protect the persons and property of its citizens, who are here to the number of thirty thousand.... I venture to observe to you that this short delay [forty-eight hours] is ridiculous; and, in the name of my government, I oppose it. If it is your resolution to bombard the city, do it; but I wish to state that you will have to account for the barbarous act to the power which I represent."[30]

On Monday, the 28th, while on his way down the river to direct his army's planned assault on forts Jackson and St. Philip, General Butler had received word that the forts had already surrendered. He had continued on to the forts, inspected them and ordered the Twenty-sixth Massachusetts regiment to garrison them. He then had ordered the rest of his army to proceed up the river to New Orleans on their transports—as fast as possible.

When Farragut learned of the forts' surrender, he immediately sent a message to Mayor Monroe telling him that since the forts had fallen, Monroe was the "sole representative of any supposed authority in the city" and informing him that he, Farragut, was going to raise the United States flag over the custom house and that Monroe was to use "all the civil power in the city" to see that the flag was respected.

At 11 o'clock on Tuesday morning, the 29th, Captain Bell and some one hundred Marines, with two pieces of artillery, went ashore, marched up Canal Street and raised the Stars and Stripes above the front of the custom house. Bell posted a guard at the building, then led his force of Marines through the crowd up the two blocks to St. Charles Street, did a column left and continued on to Lafayette Square. There in front of City Hall he formed the Marines into two lines and positioned the two howitzers to command the street below and above the building, keeping the huge throng of onlookers at bay. With Lieutenant Kautz and several others, Captain Bell then entered City Hall and confronted the mayor. "I have come," Bell quietly announced, "in obedience to orders to haul down the state flag from this building."

"Very well, sir," Monroe replied. "You can do it. But I wish to say that there is not in my entire constituency so wretched a renegade as would be willing to exchange places with you."[31]

While Boatswain's Mate George Russell made his way up to the roof to remove the state flag, Mayor Monroe left the building and made a show of standing in front of the muzzle of the howitzer that faced down St. Charles Street, toward Canal Street. The threatening crowd, overflowing Lafayette Square and filling the streets, moved so close to the formation of Marines as to feel the points of their bayonets. At 12:45 P.M. the flag of Louisiana came down. No United States flag was raised to replace it.

Minutes later Bell, Kautz and Russell descended the front steps of City Hall carrying the state flag. The Marine guard was ordered into column formation, and the entire force, with its two artillery pieces, marched back to the riverfront to embark in small boats and return to the fleet, all the while suffering the taunts and insults of the crowd.

By noon on Thursday — May 1— the U.S. Navy transport *Mississippi*, having steamed up from the forts in the company of Farragut's other transports, lay tied up to the wharf at New Orleans. Aboard it were fourteen hundred blue-coated Union troops. Also aboard was General Butler, with his wife, come to plant himself and the authority of the United States in the defiant, hostile city.

Butler, born in Deerfield, New Hampshire, the son of army Captain John Butler, who served with Andrew Jackson at the Battle of New Orleans, had made a name for himself as a trial lawyer in criminal cases in Massachusetts and also as a politician. He had served in the Massachusetts House of Representatives as well as the Massachusetts Senate. He had begun his military career as a lieutenant in the Massachusetts militia in 1839 and had advanced in rank as his political career had advanced. In 1855 he was appointed a brigadier general in the militia. Following a successful assignment to keep rail service open between Washington, D.C., and the Northeast, and his success in leading the Eighth Massachusetts and the Seventh New York infantry regiments to occupy the contested city of Baltimore, Butler was appointed a major general of volunteers by President Lincoln on May 16, 1861. Later that year he commanded a force that, in a combined operation with the Navy, captured Fort Hatteras and Fort Clark on the North Carolina coast.

In April 1862 he was forty-three years old, not tall but husky, stern-faced, with a drooping left eyelid, bald on the top of his head but with a fringe of hair that overhung his ears, beardless but with a mustache that curved down past the sides of his mouth.

To the defiant city of New Orleans General Butler was bringing a stubborn, forceful determination. Historian James Parton, Butler's earliest biographer, spent much time with the general, studied him and came to know him well. Marshaling his words carefully in his account, Parton meant to have his readers see into the mind of Butler and thus make them better judges of the man and his actions. General Butler, Parton pointed out, "had the peculiarity of feeling toward the rebellion that the rebel leaders felt toward the government they had betrayed. He *hated* it. He meant to do his part toward putting it down by the strong hand, not conciliating it by insincere palaver.... His was indeed a nobler devotion, but in mere warmth and entireness, it resembled the zeal of secessionists. He meant well to the people of Louisiana ... but it was his immovable resolve that the ruling power in Louisiana henceforth should be the UNITED STATES, which had bought, defended, protected, and enriched it."[32]

Like biographer Parton, the people of New Orleans would become acquainted with General Butler. They would not like him.

14. The Conquered City

The docking of the transport *Mississippi* at the New Orleans riverfront soon drew a crowd to the wharf. From the crowd, which included women and children, came shouts of "You'll never see home again!" and "Yellow Jack will have you before long!" and calls for General Butler to show himself and come ashore. While they shouted, Butler took a small boat over to the *Hartford* to confer with Farragut, who briefed him on recent events. Farragut also wrote a message to Mayor Monroe notifying him that General Butler was about to land his troops and that Farragut would no longer be in communication with city officials, that General Butler was assuming command of the situation in New Orleans. Once the conference with Farragut was over, Butler returned to the *Mississippi* and immediately began to disembark his troops.

About four P.M. a company of the Thirty-first Massachusetts Infantry Regiment went ashore, making their way onto the timbered loading dock, and quickly formed a tight line. At the point of their bayonets they forced back the taunting crowd to make room for the rest of the troops to disembark. When the remainder of the Thirty-first had gone ashore and moved from the loading dock onto the levee, the Fourth Wisconsin Infantry Regiment debarked and joined the Thirty-first in forming a column of march. Leading the procession was Lieutenant Henry Weigel, General Butler's aide, who was familiar with the city's streets. Behind him came the drum corps of the Thirty-first, followed by General Butler and his staff flanked by a file of troops of the Thirty-first on each side as they marched. Then came a battery of artillery, then the Fourth Wisconsin's regimental band, then Brigadier General Thomas Williams, the brigade commander, and his staff, followed by the men of the Fourth Wisconsin.

All had come ashore with strict orders issued by Butler. They were to march in silence, taking no notice of shouts from the crowd. If they were fired on from a house, they were to halt, arrest those inside the house and destroy the house. If they were fired on from the crowd, they were to arrest the person who had fired, if possible. They were not to fire into crowd unless absolutely necessary to defend themselves and even then were to wait for the order to do so.

At five o'clock the regimental bands struck up "The Star-Spangled Banner," and the column moved out as members of the crowd yelled taunts, cheered General Beauregard and shouted, "Go home, you damned Yankees!" The column proceeded along the levee to Poydras Street, marched up Poydras to St. Charles Street, then continued on to Canal Street, where it turned right and proceeded to the custom house, which it quickly surrounded. The door of the building had to be forced, since Captain Bell had locked it and kept the key. By six o'clock the building was occupied by troops of the Thirty-first, who turned the second floor into a barracks. General Butler and his staff then returned to the *Mississippi* to spend the night. In the meantime, the Twelfth Connecticut Infantry Regiment had come ashore and was bivouacked on the levee, protecting the fleet. Throughout the evening, however, all was calm.

At dawn of the next day, Friday, May 2, the debarkation of troops resumed. The Twelfth Connecticut moved to a position in Lafayette Square, across St. Charles Street from City Hall. Other regiments were posted around the downtown area, and one unit was sent across the river to establish a position in Algiers, on the west bank of the Mississippi, opposite New Orleans.

General Butler decided to set up his headquarters at the St. Charles Hotel, where General Lovell had had his command post, and sent a party of officers to make the arrangements. When they arrived and spoke with the son of one of the hotel's owners, he told them the owners were unavailable and that he couldn't turn over the hotel to General Butler without being shot by the hostile crowd. Major George Strong of Butler's staff replied that he need not worry about giving the hotel over to the U.S. Army, that they would simply take it, which they did. Butler came to the hotel later that morning — May 2 — and installed himself and his office in the ladies' parlor, turning the elegant hotel into a military headquarters.

One of his first items of business then was to dispatch the party of officers to City Hall to summon Mayor Monroe and city council members to a meeting at the newly established headquarters at two o'clock that afternoon. Monroe at first offered the officers impudence, saying that anyone who wished to talk with him could do so during regular hours at City Hall. Colonel Jonas French of the general's staff replied that that response was unlikely to satisfy the commanding general and that in view of the situation French hoped that the mayor would reconsider his answer and not try to make an issue of protocol. At two o'clock the mayor, along with a clutch of friends and supporters, including Pierre Soulé, showed up for the meeting at the St. Charles Hotel.

The meeting and Butler's commandeering of the hotel attracted a huge, boisterous throng, which stood threateningly outside the building. Guarding the hotel was a regiment of U.S. troops commanded by General Williams, who positioned an artillery piece at each corner of the building. The meeting had barely begun when General Williams's aide interrupted it with a message from Williams to General Butler: "General Williams' compliments, and he bids me say to the general commanding that the mob is getting unruly, and asks for orders as to what shall be done with them." Seemingly undisturbed by the report, Butler calmly replied to the aide, "Give my compliments to General Williams and tell him to clear the streets at once with his artillery." Monroe sprang from his chair to protest. "Don't, general. Don't give such an order as that."

"Why this emotion, gentlemen?" Butler returned. "The cannon are not going to shoot our way, and I have borne this noise and confusion as long as I choose to." Monroe proposed to speak to the crowd and try to calm them. "Very well," Butler responded. "So they do disperse, I do not care as to the means. Go out and try your hand at it."[1] The mayor and his friends quickly left the general's office and went out and addressed the crowd, which was temporarily pacified by the remarks and the threat of artillery fire.

The meeting then resumed in Butler's office, but before long was again interrupted. Lieutenant J.B. Kinsman, another member of Butler's staff, came in and asked to speak to him in private. Butler left the room and listened as Kinsman told him about the former city recorder, a man named Somers, who had declared his allegiance to the Union and had become an object of the crowd's vengeance. Somers had taken a hasty refuge on one of the Union warships and was now eager to return to the city, although extremely fearful of being overwhelmed by the angry crowd. Kinsman had managed to get Somers from the ship to the St. Charles Hotel in a carriage, the carriage driver being forced to move through the crowd at the point of the lieutenant's pistol. Somers, though, felt he was not safe at the hotel, fearing members of the mob would be able to get into the building and seize him. After hearing of his plight, General Butler turned to Somers and told him, "Well, then, there's the custom house over yonder. That will hold you. You can go there if you choose."

"But how can I get there?" Somers asked. "The mob will tear me to pieces." Butler paused several moments, then told Kinsman, "We may as well settle this question now as at any other time. Lieutenant Kinsman, take this man over to the custom house. Take what force you require. If anyone molests or threatens you, arrest him. If a rescue is attempted, fire." Butler then returned to his office.

Kinsman and Somers walked to a side entrance where Kinsman opened a door and looked out to see a company of the Thirty-first Massachusetts Regiment, some fifty soldiers, holding at bay an angry group of the crowd. Kinsman went out and ordered the company into a column of twos, the files about four feet apart, and he placed two men between the files at the head of the column and two men between the files at the rear of the column, forming a long, closed rectangle into which he and Somers entered as the crowd harassed them with shouted threats and the soldiers kept them back with bayonets fixed on their rifles. Kinsman gave the order, "Company! Forward! March!" and the column moved out, marching slowly through the crowd, at least some of whom in it recognized Somers and continuously harangued him.

Maj. Gen. Benjamin Franklin Butler. One of several political leaders whom President Lincoln appointed to high command in the U.S. Army, Butler commanded the troops that occupied New Orleans after its capture by Farragut. By a stern administration of martial law Butler forced the rebellious city into submission and became a controversial figure in doing so (Library of Congress).

One of the most vocal and abusive was a man sitting alone in a horse-drawn omnibus, yelling and urging the crowd on. Kinsman ordered the column to halt and sent a detail to the omnibus to arrest the man. Two soldiers grabbed him and hustled him out and forced him between the two files of the column as he continued to yell frantically. When Kinsman told him to shut up, he shouted back, "I won't! My tongue is my own!"

"Sergeant!" Lieutenant Kinsman ordered. "Lower your bayonet! If a sound comes out of that man's mouth, run him through!" The man suddenly fell silent.

Nearing the custom house, the column encountered another member of the mob who was more vociferous than the rest. This one was within reach of the column as it passed. Kinsman once more halted the column and ordered the man brought into the formation, pointing him out. As the man continued to incite the crowd, Kinsman ordered him bayoneted if he spoke again, causing a similar quieting effect.

When the company reached the custom house, Somers was safely escorted inside to his new refuge, and the two arrested rabble-rousers became prisoners in the fortresslike stone building. Lieutenant Kinsman then marched the company back to the hotel — through a crowd, as Kinsman reported it, "silent as a funeral."

The twice suspended meeting with the mayor and his supporters was adjourned until that evening, when it resumed following a modest dinner in the St. Charles's dining room. Butler especially wanted to take that occasion to read and explain to the mayor and the others the proclamation he had written, setting forth the rules by which he intended to govern the jurisdiction to which he had been assigned. The proclamation detailed the imposition of strict policies designed to suppress rebellion and restore order in New Orleans.

When he had finished reading it, the general commented, "The sum and substance of the whole is this: I wish to leave the municipal authority in the full exercise of its accustomed functions. I do not desire to interfere with the collection of taxes, the government of the police, the lighting and cleaning of the streets, the sanitary laws, or the administration of justice. I desire only to govern the military forces of the department, and to take cognizance only of offenses committed by or against them. Representing here the United States, it is my wish to confine myself solely to the business of sustaining the government of the United States against its enemies."

Pierre Soulé, the group's most facile speaker, was quick to reply. He told Butler that he did not believe tranquility could be maintained in the city so long as Butler's troops remained there. He urged the general to move his men to the outskirts, where they would not be constantly obvious to the people of New Orleans. "I know the feelings of the people so well," Soulé asserted, "that I am sure your soldiers can have no peace while they remain in our midst. Withdraw your troops, general, and leave the city government to manage its own affairs. If the troops remain, there will certainly be trouble." The people of New Orleans, he stated, had not been conquered and could not be expected to behave as a conquered people.

General Butler then cooly responded to Soulé's remarks. "I did not expect to hear from Mr. Soulé a threat on this occasion," he told the group. "I have been long accustomed to hear threats from Southern gentlemen in political conventions, but let me assure gentlemen present that the time for tactics of that nature has passed, never to return. New Orleans *is* a conquered city. If not, why are we here? How did we get here? Have you opened your arms and bid us welcome? Are we here by your consent? Would you or would you not expel us if you could?

"New Orleans has been conquered by the forces of the United States, and by the laws of all nations, lies subject to the will of the conquerors. Nevertheless, I have proposed to leave the municipal government to the free exercise of all its powers— and I am answered by a threat." Soulé hastily denied that he intended a threat, saying he merely meant to give his opinion of what would happen if the troops remained in the city. "Gladly," Butler rejoined, "will I take every man of the army out of New Orleans the very day, the very hour it is demonstrated to me that the city government can protect me from insult or danger if I choose to ride alone from one end of the city to the other.... I am aware that at this hour there is an organization here established for the purpose of assassinating my men by detail. But I warn you that if a shot is fired from any house, that house will never again cover a mortal's head. And if I can discover the perpetrator of the deed, the place that now knows him shall know him no more forever.

"I have the power to suppress this unruly element in your midst and I mean so to use it that in a very short period I shall be able to ride through the entire city, free from insult and danger, or else this metropolis of the South shall be a desert, from the plains of Chalmette to the outskirts of Carrollton."[2]

After another response from Soulé, defending the reputation of the people of New Orleans, Butler shifted the subject to food for the people of the city, particularly for the city's poor, and how he intended to cope with the problems. A lengthy discussion followed, which changed Butler's intentions not at all.

Mayor Monroe, apparently yielding to a surge of petulance, announced that effective immediately he was shutting down the operations of the city government and that General Butler could do whatever he wanted with the city. No sooner had the mayor got the words out his mouth than a member of the city council jumped up and told the group that the functioning of the city government was too important a matter to be summarily ended and that the matter should be considered and acted upon by the city's common council. The group, with both the mayor and General Butler assenting, then agreed to have the council meet and take up the matter the next morning, then report their decision to the general later the same day. The evening's session then concluded, the crowd outside by then having melted away.

The next morning, Saturday, May 3, while the city fathers were meeting, Butler's proclamation, printed as a handbill, was being distributed around the city, handed out to anyone who would take it. At the same time, Butler also announced his appointment of Major Joseph W. Bell to be provost judge and Colonel French to be provost marshal, two chief officials in Butler's administration of the army-occupied city of New Orleans. Colonel French then issued a handbill of his own, informing residents of his rules for carrying out the provisions of Butler's proclamation:

> Particularly does he [the commanding general] call attention to the prohibition against assemblages of persons; the sale of liquor to soldiers; the necessity for a license on the part of keepers of public houses, coffee-houses, and drinking saloons; to the posting of placards about the streets, giving information concerning the action or movements of rebel troops, and the publishing in the newspapers of notices or resolutions laudatory of the enemies of the United States.
>
> The soldiers of this command are subject, upon the part of some low-minded persons, to insult. This must stop. Repetition will lead to instant arrest and punishment. In the performance of his duties the undersigned will, in no degree, trench upon the regularly established police of the city, but will confine himself simply to the performance of such acts as were to be assumed by the military authorities of the United States; and, in such action, he hopes to meet with the ready co-operation of all who have the welfare of the city at heart.[3]

The deliberations of the council members having concluded, General Butler received a delegation that notified him the council had accepted his proposal concerning the operation of the city government, but requesting the general to withdraw the troops posted at City Hall, to avoid the appearance that City Hall was functioning under the direction of the U.S. Army. Butler granted the request and moved the troops to another location.

Within days of the imposition of Butler's brand of martial law, the effects became evident. The New Orleans *Bee* in an editorial published May 8 remarked: "The federal soldiers do not seem to interfere with the private property of the citizens, and have done nothing that we are aware of to provoke difficulty. The usual nightly reports of arrests for vagrancy, assaults, wounding and killing have unquestionably been diminished. The city is as tranquil and peaceable as in the most quiet times."[4]

Five days later Butler issued his General Order No. 27, indicating the city was not as peaceable as it seemed: "It having come to the knowledge of the commanding general that Friday next is proposed to be observed as a day of fasting and prayer, in obedience to some supposed proclamation of one Jefferson Davis, in the several churches of this city, it is ordered that no such observance be had. Churches and religious houses are to be kept open as in time of profound peace, but no religious exercises are to be had upon the supposed authority above mentioned."[5]

On May 15, two days later, Butler issued General Order No. 28, which set off a firestorm of outrage: "As the officers and soldiers of the United States have been subject to repeated insults from the women (calling themselves ladies) of New Orleans, in return for the most scrupulous and non-interference and courtesy on our part, it is ordered that hereafter when any female shall, by word, gesture, or movement, insult or show contempt for any officer or soldier of the United States, she shall be regarded and held liable to be treated as a woman of the town plying her avocation."[6]

What the general meant, according to the friendliest interpretation, was that such a woman would be liable to be arrested, confined in jail overnight, appear before a magistrate the next morning and fined five dollars. One of Butler's staff members, though, saw another possible interpretation and warned that an enormous scandal would result if only one man should act upon the order in the wrong way. "Let us, then," Butler responded, "have one case of aggression on our side. I shall know how to deal with that case, so that it will never be repeated. So far, all the aggression has been against us. Here we are, conquerors in a conquered city; we have respected every right, tried every means of conciliation, complied with every reasonable desire; and yet we cannot walk the streets without being outraged and spit upon by green girls. I do not fear the troops; but if aggression must be, let it not be all against *us*.[7]

The order drew a vehement reaction from Mayor Monroe, who wrote a letter to Butler saying, among other things, that he, Monroe, would "never undertake to be responsible for the peace of New Orleans while such an edict, which infuriates our citizens, remains in force."[8]

Butler dashed off a brief note in reply and gave it to the provost marshal to deliver to the mayor: "HEAD-QUARTERS, DEPARTMENT OF THE GULF, NEW ORLEANS, *May 16, 1862*. John T. Monroe, late mayor of the city of New Orleans, is relieved from all responsibility for the peace of the city, and is suspended from the exercise of any official functions, and committed to Fort Jackson until farther orders. B.F. Butler, *Major General Commanding*."

Monroe, appearing in person before the general, twice talked Butler out of jailing him, apologizing, then withdrawing the apology. After three visits to Butler's office, on the third of which the mayor was accompanied by a group of his supporters, the general once more reinstated his original order and sent not only Monroe but the chief of police and two others to be confined at Fort Jackson. Monroe was later transferred to Fort Pickens, near Pensacola, to be held in custody. He was promised release if he would take the oath of allegiance to the United States, but he refused after first saying he would take it.

Pierre Soulé, the veritable voice of rebellion in New Orleans, having at last breached the wall of Butler's tolerance, was also shipped out of the city into confinement. He was held in custody at Fort Warren, at the entrance to Boston harbor.

In early June General Butler settled one more outstanding account. William B. Mumford, the 42-year-old professional gambler who had gambled his life by tearing down the United States flag from the mint, who had desecrated the flag and had publicly boasted about his deed, was arrested, tried and sentenced to hang for his offenses. On the morning of June 7, despite pleas for mercy issued by Mumford's wife and others, Mumford was hanged on a scaffold near the mint as a huge crowd stood witness to the fulfillment of General Butler's promise to Flag Officer Farragut: "I will make an example of that fellow by hanging him."[9]

General Butler was becoming notorious and his rule increasingly controversial, but the defiant city in his charge was slowly becoming subdued.

15. The Ellet Fleet

Secretary of War Edwin Stanton was one of the few in Washington who thought Charles Ellet, Jr., was something other than a crank. A fifty-two-year-old civil engineer, Ellet had made a name for himself building bridges, including the nation's first suspension bridge, which spanned the Schuylkill River at Philadelphia. But as conflict between the states loomed, his interest turned from making bridges to making war.

He came up with an idea to rescue Fort Sumter, but couldn't get the government to accept it. He devised a plan to destroy communications in Virginia by taking over a train with a group of volunteers at Alexandria and driving it down through the state, burning all railroad bridges and stations as he went. That plan went nowhere. Other proposals followed. He doggedly called on administration and military officials seeking their support for his idea of the month, earning him a crank's reputation, which was reinforced by his published criticisms of the Navy Department and of General McClellan's management of the war.

Undeterred by the repeated rebuffs, Ellet returned to an idea he had first presented to the Navy Department in 1855, but which had been dismissed by the then secretary as unworthy of consideration, coming as it did from a landsman with little knowledge of ships or seas. His idea, renewed in 1862, was to turn riverboats into fighting rams by fitting them with iron prows that would stab giant holes in the hulls of wooden vessels. According to his plan, he would build the rams and command them in their operations against the enemy. Such a craft, he was convinced, would be an effective weapon against rebel vessels and would provide the Union's answer to the rams he believed the South was building. Lincoln's secretary of the Navy, Gideon Welles, however, supported a program to build more vessels like the iron-bound, floating artillery platform *Monitor* and he rejected Ellet's idea of fast, hard-hitting rams as the idea of someone "full of zeal to overflowing, not, however, a naval man."[1]

Secretary Stanton, on the other hand, had doubts about the *Monitor* program, and after the disaster wreaked on Union vessels by the Confederates' iron-encased ram *Virginia* (the former USS *Merrimack*)—most of the damage having been done by the ram's iron prow—in Hampton Roads on March 8, 1862, Stanton nearly panicked, imagining it to be unstoppable and an enormous threat to Washington and New York. His mood wasn't improved the next day when the *Monitor*, Welles's solution to the problem of the *Virginia*, proved ineffectual against it.

Ellet had predicted the menace the *Virginia* would present. In a pamphlet he wrote and published in February 1862 he informed Lincoln's administration that the Confederates were building steam rams and warned, "If the *Merrimac* [sic] is permitted to escape from Elizabeth River, she will be almost certain to commit great depredations on our armed vessels in Hampton Roads; and may even be expected to pass out under the guns of Fortress Monroe, and prey upon our commerce in Chesapeake Bay."[2] So far, Ellet's ideas and protestations had been ignored. Now Secretary Stanton at least was ready to hear more of what he had to say.

Stanton had known Ellet since 1849, when Stanton, as an attorney, had represented the commonwealth of Pennsylvania in its lawsuit seeking to block completion of the bridge that Ellet was building over the Ohio River at Wheeling, Virginia (now West Virginia). The suit had been instigated by Pittsburgh steamboat interests that alleged the bridge was an obstruction to navigation on the Ohio. The U.S. Supreme Court ruled in favor of Pennsylvania — and Stanton — but the bridge builders persuaded Congress and President Millard Fillmore to declare the bridge a part of the post road, necessary for the movement of mail, and it was therefore not subject to the decree of the Supreme Court. Ellet won; Stanton lost. But if there were adversarial hard feelings lingering in Stanton after thirteen years, as there probably were, they were not strong enough to affect his respect for Ellet, whom he knew to be a bright and creative thinker and engineer.

Six-foot-two, slight, thin-faced, with a long nose and dark hair that rose in a pile above his forehead and nearly covered his ears, Ellet, according to one account, "looked like a character out of a fairy story, one who would have fitted nicely into elf's clothes."[3] His wife, though, the former Elvira "Ellie" Daniel, thought, when she saw him for the first time, that he was the handsomest man she had ever seen. He was from Bucks County, Pennsylvania, the son of a shopkeeper turned farmer. He was largely self-taught, his brilliant mind overcoming whatever deficiencies he suffered in formal education. He had begun his career as a surveyor, at age seventeen, mapping out the North Branch of the Susquehanna River, and later worked on the construction of the Chesapeake and Ohio Canal, developing while at it a love for inland waterways and the western rivers, so strong that he named his eldest son Charles Rivers Ellet. In 1830, when he was twenty years old, he had traveled to Paris, taking with him a letter of introduction to the Marquis de Lafayette, who helped him gain admission to engineering lectures at the *École des Ponts et Chaussées*. It was there he was introduced to the technology that led to his bridge-building career — which in early 1862 he was eager to forsake for a role in the war.

Through public and official fright, the *Virginia/Merrimack* was going to help give him the role he sought. On March 14 Ellet received this note from the War Department: "Sir: The Secretary of War desires me to say that he would be pleased to see you at the War Department this afternoon at 5 o'clock. L. Thomas, The Adjutant General."[4]

At their meeting in Stanton's office, which lasted some four hours, Stanton praised Ellet's ability and patriotism and told him he would like to have his opinion on how to prevent the *Merrimack* from doing any further harm. Apparently unwilling to reply immediately, he waited until he could put his thoughts in writing. The advice he came up with was to use two or three steamers as rams, pounding them into the side of the *Merrimack*. "I doubt much," he told Stanton, "whether one fair hit in the waist will not open seams enough to disable her."[5]

Later that day, on a visit to Fort Monroe, at the entrance to Hampton Roads, where lay the wounded but still fearsome Confederate ironclad, Ellet was less than enthusiastically received by the commanding officers, Navy Captain John Marston and Major General John E. Wool, despite the letters of authority introduction Ellet bore from Washington. Marston let Ellet know that his help in combating the *Merrimack* was not needed. Ellet, however, did come away from the visit believing that, as he said, "the confidence in steam rams has suddenly become so great that no further effort of mine is needed to show their efficiency."⁶

Ellet met with Stanton, along with the secretary's advisors, a week later, on March 20. By then Stanton's concern over the threat presented by the *Merrimack* in eastern waters had diminished, and he had decided to let the U.S. naval forces at Hampton Roads handle the problem. (The problem was solved on May 11 when the Confederates, abandoning Norfolk, destroyed the ship to prevent its capture.) Stanton's attention at the moment was on the Mississippi River. He was thinking of more gunboats to aid the campaign to capture the river. Once Ellet had delivered his report and left, the subject of the meeting in Stanton's office shifted to gunboats on the Mississippi. The Army's quartermaster general, Brigadier General M.C. Meigs, suggested that Ellet might be helpful in getting the gunboats built.

"Perhaps he would be as good a man as we could get for the purpose," Stanton responded. "He has more ingenuity, more personal courage and more enterprise than anybody else I have even seen.... If I had a proposition that I desired to work out to some definite result, I do not know of anyone to whom I would entrust it so soon as Ellet."⁷

On March 25 Stanton received a message from General Halleck in St. Louis telling him that "the rebels are building one or more river boats at [New Orleans], clad in railroad iron, like the *Merrimack*."⁸ Worried that such vessels could steam up the Mississippi and play havoc with Flag Officer Foote's fleet of gunboats, and even defeat the Union's drive down the river, Halleck suggested that Stanton urge Secretary Welles to build more *Monitor*-type vessels to meet the threat of the new Confederate *Merrimack*s on the Mississippi. Stanton quickly replied that "the universal opinion among naval and military engineers in the East" was to attack an ironclad by ramming it. "Charles Ellet," Stanton told Halleck, "a distinguished engineer, has given the subject much attention. I will send him tomorrow to see and consult you, and with authority to act as you deem best. He is a man of courage and energy, and willing to risk his own life."⁹

On March 26, Stanton met again with his advisors and informed them, "I propose this day to send Mister Ellet to the West as the engineer of this department to construct, as speedily as possible, one or more rams at Pittsburgh, Cincinnati and New Albany. Is there any better person to whom I could commit that duty?"

"I do not believe there is," General Meigs replied. "He has genius and skill," the Army's adjutant general, Brigadier General Lorenzo Thomas, offered, "and I presume he can carry out the plan as soon as anybody."

The Army's chief engineer, Brigadier General Joseph G. Totten, wanted to know if Ellet had a clear idea of what he was going to do. "Yes," Stanton answered, showing he had paid attention when Ellet had explained his idea. "The plan is to take the largest and most powerful riverboats, remove the upper works, fill the bows with timber and furnish such protection as can be afforded. Each boat will require a crew of five men and a person to command. Mister Ellet is himself willing to risk it."

General Totten had another question, revealing how well the Army's administrators had come to know Ellet. "Do you make Ellet directly accountable to you?" Totten asked Stanton. "I make him directly accountable to me," Stanton said. "My inquiry," Totten told him, "turns upon a point of his personal character. He will be lord over all unless you make his path and wall him in." "He will be accountable to me," Stanton repeated. Totten seemed unconvinced and asked, "Is he to be subordinate to the commanding officer? What I fear is that he will not be tractable."

"Then," Stanton replied, "I will dismiss him. The building of the boats is all that I propose that he shall do. The boards of trade can select good river men to be captains. After their construction the boats will be placed under the command of the military officer in charge of the operations there. Ellet can go on any one of them if he chooses." "That will be ample security," Totten responded. "I do not propose to erect him into a military power," Stanton said.[10] The secretary also told his advisors that he had instructed Ellet to build the boats in twenty days. "That is the maximum," he said.

Stanton still had some things to learn about Ellet, things that Ellet's wife already knew and the secretary of war would soon find out. "It alarms me always," Ellie Ellet wrote in a letter to her nephew Edward in March 1862, "for Mr. Ellet to be placed in any position in which the views of other men may rule or conflict with his plans — He can never appear rightly, in any situation, unless he has full authority."[11]

On March 27 Ellet received Stanton's letter telling him to "proceed immediately to Pittsburgh, Cincinnati, and New Albany [Indiana], and take measures to provide steam-rams for defense against iron-clad vessels on the Western waters."[12] An Army quartermaster in each of those cities was to handle Ellet's purchases of the boats and pay for their refitting according to Ellet's specifications. Ellet was to be paid ten dollars a day plus ten cents a mile for travel expenses. He was still a civilian.

Ellet arrived in Pittsburgh on March 28 and from there sent a message to General Halleck, advising him that he was on the job and intended to work his way down the Ohio from Pittsburgh to Cincinnati to New Albany. He was ready to help Halleck, he said, but he let Old Brains know that he was taking his orders from the secretary of war. What he was looking for was fast wooden steamers that could be reinforced along the entire length of the boat, that could be fitted with an iron prow projecting from the bow just below the surface of the water. He did not want iron cladding for the boats, for that would slow them down. He further did not care if they were unarmed, since the weight of guns and ammunition could also impede their speed. Speed and maneuverability were the two major requisites. And because he expected to lose some in battle, they also had to be expendable.

In a letter to Foote, Ellet described the way he planned to strengthen the boats' structure against the shocks of ramming. The technique, he wrote, consisted

> simply in running three heavy solid timber bulk heads, from 12 to 16 inches thick, fore and aft, from stem to stern, placing the central one directly over the keelson; in bracing these bulk heads one against the other, and the outer ones against the hull of the boat, and all against the deck and floor timbers, and staying the hull from side to side by iron rods and screw bolts. In fact making the whole weight of the boat add its momentum to that of the central bulk head at the moment of collision. In addition the boilers and machinery are held in iron stays in all directions; the pilot-house protected against musketry, and the engines and boilers shielded by 2 feet thickness of oak timbers well bolted together.[13]

Ellet also had clear ideas about the crews he would recruit to command and man the boats. "I prefer daring and skillful river men," he wrote to Stanton in one of the daily reports that Stanton had requested, "if they can be got, to handle the boats; but will apply for naval officers if there is any difficulty in procuring the proper men ... which I do not expect."[14] Experienced civilian river captains, pilots, engineers and crewmen were what he was seeking. "The men must take service with a full knowledge of the dangerous nature of the duty," he told Stanton. He furthermore wanted them amply rewarded for their service. He asked that they be paid the going rate for riverboat officers and crewmen, plus hazardous-duty pay. "The crew is of great importance," he wrote. "I will give honorable reward and, also, prize money, for successful courage, in large and liberal measure."[15] Stanton turned down Ellet's proposal to award a bonus to a boat's crew for each fortified position it passed, but he did agree to pay something extra for each enemy vessel destroyed. The crewmen remained civilians, but signed a contract—a so-called "military obligation"—to remain on the job for six months.

To provide protection against the enemy Ellet was authorized to add to each boat's complement twelve to twenty armed Army volunteers, to be commanded by an officer Ellet would select. A further defensive measure would be provided by the hose connections Ellet would have installed on the boilers so that scalding water could be sprayed onto enemy troops attempting to board the vessels.

Stanton evidently changed his mind about making Ellet into a military figure, for he appointed him an Army colonel. Ellet told Stanton that he would prefer to remain a civilian, but if he were to be given an Army commission, he would like a rank higher than colonel. Stanton replied that colonel was the highest rank he could bestow without going through time-consuming confirmation proceedings in the U.S. Senate, which he wanted to avoid. When Ellet asked that his younger brother, Alfred, a captain in the Fifty-ninth Illinois Infantry Regiment, be named second-in-command of the operation and be given the job of selecting and commanding the soldiers who would join the flotilla, Stanton agreed. He promoted Alfred to lieutenant colonel, transferred him to Charles's command and allowed him to bring with him three first lieutenants—John H. Johnson, George E. Currie and Warren D. Crandall—and as many as a hundred volunteers from the Fifty-ninth Illinois. On May 2, Alfred reported to Charles in New Albany with not a hundred, but fifty-three volunteers, including Edward Ellet, Alfred's son, and John Ellet, Alfred and Charles's nephew.

With some help from Stanton, who contacted the boards of trade in Pittsburgh, Cincinnati and New Albany to enlist their aid and advice, Ellet moved ahead swiftly with the task of acquiring the steamers he had in mind. Stanton wisely anticipated attempts by boat owners to profiteer at the government's expense and wrote to the president of the Cincinnati board of trade that if Ellet encountered unreasonable prices, the government would seize the boats and let their owners go through the red tape of being compensated for them later. In Pittsburgh, Ellet bought three stern-wheel towboats—the *Lioness*, *Sampson* and *Mingo*—all for $20,000. In Cincinnati he bought the side-wheeler *Queen of the West* for $16,000 and at Madison, Indiana, he bought the side-wheeler *Switzerland* for $13,000. He also bought the *Monarch*, another large side-wheeler, for $14,000. After that, he bought the *Lancaster*, a small side-wheeler, and two small but fast stern-wheelers, the *Dick Fulton* and the *T.D. Horner*, which he intended to use as tenders and dispatch boats.

His fleet now numbered nine vessels, which he promptly sent downriver for their conversion into the rams he had conceived. He soon discovered that many of the boatyards along the Ohio were overloaded with Navy work and he asked Stanton for permission to use whatever boatyards were available to have the conversions done. Eager to put Ellet's rams into action, Stanton quickly agreed.

The first of the rams was ready for service by April 28, and on that date Stanton notified General Halleck that the ram fleet would be under the command of Colonel Charles Ellet, who would be assisted by his brother, Lieutenant Colonel Alfred Ellet. And to have Halleck understand the Ellets and their rams were not responsible to Halleck, he told Old Brains that the Ellets were subject to the order of Flag Officer Foote, which of course they were not. Two days earlier Stanton had assured Ellet that he would not be under the "direct control" of Foote, although at the same time telling Ellet to confer with the "Naval Commander on the Mississippi River" prior to taking any action. Stanton also said he would inform the

Navy that it was not to try to control the actions of the rams "unless they shall manifestly expose the general operations on the Mississippi to some unfavorable influence."[16]

The situation was entirely confusing to nearly everyone who was or might become involved, but Charles Ellet remained steadfast in his concentration on the mission he had chosen for himself. He thought so little of military protocol that until Alfred insisted that he should, he did not even bother to buy himself a uniform. And even after he bought one, he delayed wearing it until the end of May. That was when he learned, as he told his wife, "an eagle on the shoulder, and a military hat, are better passports than brains or character."[17]

What he did not tell Ellie was what he intended to do with the boats he had bought and was refitting. Suspecting the worst, on May 2 she wrote to him a tactful but pointed reproof:

Brig. Gen. Alfred W. Ellet. He was the younger brother of Charles Ellet, the engineer who talked Secretary of War Stanton into creating a fleet of rams to operate on the Mississippi, which Ellet would command. Alfred transferred out of an Illinois infantry regiment to become second in command of the Ellet fleet and became its commander following the death of Charles (Library of Congress).

> Never since we were married have I felt so little acquainted with the exact nature of your business, or your plans and expectations. While I thought that your whole time and attention were likely to be engaged in the superintendence of the work on your boats, I felt satisfied ... but I am now harassed by the fear that you may have determined to go down with your boats to the point where they may be used.
> Setting aside my own feelings in this matter it does seem to me that you are bound by ordinary intelligence and morality to avoid an unnecessary exposure of your health and life in performing services suited to men of more bodily strength and less intellect.[18]

Her suspicions were well justified. He planned to do exactly what she feared he might, although he never admitted it to her. Instead, on May 7 he wrote to tell her how well he felt: "I am ... pretty well all the time — stronger I think than I have been for years. I would be sure of it, indeed, but that there is a large looking glass in the hall, in which I see my image, as I approach at full stride, has lost the elastic step and energetic carriage of even a few years ago, when I was not so strong as I seem to be now."[19]

On May 10, Ellet was still in New Albany and still recruiting men for his fleet, taking on Army personnel when civilians were in short supply. One whose services he enlisted was Lieutenant David M. Dryden, then on sick leave from the First Kentucky Infantry Regiment owing to his wounds. At least one other was a former river boatman who had joined the Army and after later learning of Ellet's outfit, deserted his unit and signed on with the ram fleet. The commander of the boat to which he was assigned was confronted by an officer who came to arrest him, but he managed to talk the officer out of taking the deserter back to face a firing squad: "He's a good steamboatman, and we need him. He took service on the ram we're building to lick the Rebs with. What more do you want?" The officer yielded and told the boat's commander, "Well, I'm willing. He was a damn poor infantryman anyway."[20]

Also joining the fleet was Ellet's 18-year-old son Charlie — Charles Rivers Ellet — an Army medical cadet who was transferred into his father's command.

Pressured by Stanton to get his boats in action, Ellet at last assembled his officers and prepared them to enter the war being waged on the Mississippi. He explained a system of signals and procedures for coordinating the boats' actions during engagements. He also detailed a procedure for fending off would-be boarders. One of the vessels' greatest defenses, he told his officers, was their speed, which could reach twenty miles an hour when going with the current, and Ellet didn't think a rebel gunboat or even the rebels' guns on shore would be able to hit such a fast-moving target. And with grim candor he told the officers that their rams were meant to be expendable and that they should expect to lose some. He further ordered them to pass along his instructions to their crews.

He also chose one of the rams, the *Switzerland*, to be his flagship, one more indication he intended to participate in the fleet's action himself.

With five of the rams Alfred Ellet then set out for Cairo, steaming down the blue Ohio, along which clusters of onlookers watched and greeted the strange vessels as they passed. When the boats reached Cairo on May 16, Alfred was given messages that had come from Secretary Stanton. Alfred was told to draw three hundred pistols and three hundred carbines from the Navy's armory in Cairo. The men of the Ellet fleet would not be going into the fray unarmed. Alfred was also told that he was authorized to engage Doctor James Robards of Carbondale, Illinois, as the fleet surgeon.

After the arrival of a sixth ram in Cairo, Alfred moved the little fleet into the Mississippi and headed downriver to Fort Pillow. He expected to meet Flag Officer Foote and the Union gunboat fleet there, but when he arrived, he discovered that Foote, still suffering from the wound received at Fort Donelson, had been replaced by Captain Charles H. Davis.

Alfred also learned that he and Ellet's rams had arrived at the scene of battle one week too late. They had missed the biggest engagement of the Union gunboat fleet thus far, one in which the rams could have made a big difference in the outcome.

16. The Confederate Offensive

Captain James E. Montgomery, commanding the remaining eight ironclad rams of the River Defense Fleet, had at last decided to take the battle to the Union vessels that were assaulting Fort Pillow. On the night before his all-out attack was to be launched he held a council of war with the rams' captains to brief them on the planned operation, and at six o'clock the next morning, Saturday, May 10, 1862, the eight rams got up steam, cast off from their moorings under the protective guns of Fort Pillow and, intent on a fight, headed toward the fleet of eight Union gunboats and twelve mortar boats lying in the Mississippi about four miles above the fort.

Montgomery's boats were the *General Bragg*, the *General Sterling Price*, the *General Sumter*, the *General Van Dorn*, the *General M. Jeff Thompson*, the *Colonel Lovell*, the *General Beauregard* and the *Little Rebel*, Montgomery's flagship. The six other vessels of the River Defense Fleet, which had been assigned the task of protecting New Orleans, had been destroyed, either by Union forces or by the rebels themselves, during or shortly after Farragut's passing of Fort Jackson and Fort St. Philip on the night of April 24.

The Union fleet, under the command of Flag Officer Foote, had steamed down from New Madrid on April 12 and had posted three mortar boats along the Arkansas shore, about three and a half miles from the fort. On April 14 the mortar boats had commenced their bombardment of the rebel fort, firing, at times, at the rate of three shells every fifteen minutes. Standing by to guard the mortar boats from a rebel attack were Foote's seven ironclad gunboats and one wooden gunboat, vessels that only days before had valiantly overcome the forbidding rebel guns of Island No. 10.

Fort Pillow was an earthworks fortification the Confederates had begun building in June 1861 and which had been enlarged by General Pillow, for whom it was named, over a period of nine months. It extended along the top of the Chickasaw Bluff that overlooks the Mississippi some fifty river miles above Memphis, its perimeter measuring seven miles, its guns bristling along a half-mile front on the river. It was reported to have at least forty heavy guns, by Foote's estimate, mounted to repel an enemy force coming from upriver, and believed to be garrisoned by a force estimated at six thousand troops, but which was actually a little more than half that number, many of them having recently been withdrawn from Island No. 10.

Foote and General Pope, commanding twenty thousand troops that had come down the river on transport steamers following the fall of New Madrid and Island No. 10, had devised a plan to capture the fort by landing troops five miles above it and attacking it from the rear while Foote's gunboats and mortar boats kept the garrison busy with their artillery assault. After a reconnaissance, however, Pope decided that with the river being swollen by recent rains, there was no good place to put his troops ashore, and a new plan was hatched.

It called for Pope's troops to dig a canal on the Arkansas side of the river, allowing Foote's vessels to get around the fort and attack it from below. That plan was foiled when General Halleck on April 17 ordered Pope to turn around immediately and bring most of his army up the Tennessee River to Pittsburg Landing to join Halleck's forces already in the field there.

Now Foote was stymied. Fort Pillow had to be passed to maintain the Union drive down the Mississippi, but its guns were daunting, and the steady bombardment by Foote's mortar boats and gunboats had failed to quiet them. The two Army regiments that Pope had left behind were insufficient to take the fort and had no tools to dig the proposed canal. "I will do what I can," Foote wrote to Navy Secretary Welles, "but have little hope of doing much in the face of such forts."[1] Suffering increasingly from the effects of the wound he received in the battle for Fort Donelson and remembering the beating his vessels had taken from Confederate batteries in that battle, Foote, his spirit dampened, was unwilling to risk another Fort Donelson disaster. "A disaster," he told Welles in a letter dated April 19, "would place all that we have gained on this and other rivers at the mercy of the rebel fleet.... I therefore hesitate about a direct attack upon this place now."[2] On April 24 he confessed to Stanton the deteriorating state of his health: "I am very much prostrated by the continuous draft on my physique from my inflamed foot, which appears to be slowly but steadily getting worse, till I am confined mostly to my cabin with a swollen, painful leg, affecting my whole system.... I feel discouraged about it, and it has taken most of the energy out of me."[3]

By April 29, Foote was showing signs of despondency. "I am now but a comparatively weak officer," he wrote to Welles. "I am not what I have been even.... Our means render our position very embarrassing; but I look to Him who reigns in all worlds for wisdom and strength to do my duty."[4] On May 9 the demoralized and ailing Foote turned his responsibilities over to his assistant commander, Captain Charles H. Davis, writing this note:

> Sir — In consequence of the state of my health, the Secretary of the Navy has directed you to report to me for the purpose of performing such duties as the circumstances of the flotilla require.
>
> By authority of the Secretary of the Navy, and the advice of a board of surgeons, I leave the flotilla this day temporarily, for the purpose of recruiting my health at Cleveland, Ohio; and you will be pleased, during my absence, to perform all the duties of the flag-officer; and as such, and being hereby invested with flag-officer's authority, all officers and others attached to and connected with this flotilla will obey your orders and act under your instructions.
>
> I am, respectfully, your obedient servant,
> A.H. Foote, Flag-Officer[5]

Foote bade farewell to his officers and crew in a ceremony on his flagship, the *Benton*, on May 9, telling his shipmates, who crowded the boat's deck, "God bless you all, my brave companions. I know you will succeed in all you undertake, for such a cause, in such hands, cannot fail."[6] The ceremony concluded, Foote boarded a transport and steamed off toward Cairo.

In the early morning's light on May 10, Captain Montgomery's eight rebel vessels moved out into the current and formed up in a line, with the *Bragg* in the lead, followed by the *Sumter*, *Sterling Price*, *Van Dorn*, *Jeff Thompson*, *Lovell*, *Beauregard* and *Little Rebel*, then steamed briskly toward the unsuspecting Union fleet. About seven A.M. they rounded the salient known as Plum Point and in the distance, through the thin haze of a sunny morning, they could see the Union vessels resting in the river. Nearest to the advancing rebel fleet was the ironclad gunboat *Cincinnati*, apart from the others, standing guard over the mortar boat that it had towed into position two hours earlier. The rest of the gunboat flotilla lay farther upstream, three of the boats moored along the Tennessee shore and four along the Arkansas shore, all with their bows pointed downstream. As soon as the approaching rebel boats were spotted, the *Cincinnati*, captained by Commander Roger N. Stembel, turned and quickly headed toward the other Union gunboats. The *Bragg*, commanded by Captain W.H.H. Leonard, immediately chased after it.

A crewman aboard the *Cincinnati*, Elliot Callender, described the pursuit and the massive assault:

Adm. Charles H. Davis, who succeeded Flag Officer Andrew H. Foote as commander of the Union's Mississippi River fleet. Foote relinquished command after suffering wounds in his arm and foot during his gunboats' unsuccessful assault on Fort Donelson on February 14, 1862. Davis commanded the fleet at the Battle of Memphis (Library of Congress).

> On came the leader of the Confederate fleet, the "General Bragg," a powerful gulf steamer, built full in the bow and standing up twenty feet above the surface of the river. Her powerful engines were ploughing her along at a rate that raised a billow ten feet high at her bow. At a distance of not over fifty yards, she received our full starboard battery of thirty-two-pound guns. Cotton bales were seen to tumble, and splinters fly; but on she came, her great walking-beam engine driving her at a fearful rate.
>
> When less than fifty feet away the "Cincinnati's" bow was thrown around, and the two boats came together with a fearful crash. It was a glancing blow that the "General Bragg" gave us, and not the one she intended — a right-angle contact would have sunk us then and there; but glancing-blow as it was, it took a piece out of our midships six feet deep and twelve feet long, throwing the magazine open to the inflow of water, and knocking everything down from one end of the boat to the other.
>
> The force of the blow fastened the "Bragg's" ram temporarily into the "Cincinnati's" hull. "Give her another broadside, boys!" passed the word of command. The men sprang with a cheer to their guns, and the entire broadside was emptied into the "Bragg" at such close range that the guns could not be run out of the ports. This broadside settled the "Bragg," for she lay careened up against us so that it tore an immense hole in her from side to side. She slowly swung off from the "Cincinnati," and as the command to "Board the enemy!" was given, she lowered her flag.
>
> But it is doubtful how much "boarding" we could have done, for just at this moment the second Confederate ram, the "Sumter,"[7] reached the scene of action, and coming up under full head of steam, struck the "Cincinnati" in the fantail, cutting into her three feet, destroying her rudders and steering apparatus, and letting water pour into the hull of the boat.[8]

Callender was mistaken. The second hit suffered by the *Cincinnati* came from the *General Sterling Price*, which first opened fire on the nearest mortar boat, silencing its gun, then headed for the *Cincinnati*, catching it and bashing in its stern as Callender described. The *General Sumter* then also slammed into the stern of the stricken *Cincinnati*. By then the other Union gunboats had joined the battle, opening fire on the Confederate vessels from a distance of three miles while speeding to the aid of the *Cincinnati*. The *Cincinnati*'s flight toward the safety of the shoals at the river's edge, where the rebel rams could not follow, was ended when after receiving its third crushing blow, it sank in shallow water.

The purser aboard the *Sterling Price*, L.F. Delisdemier, recorded in the boat's log his account of the fight following the sinking of the *Cincinnati*:

> The *Van Dorn* in the meantime had come up. Those of the Federal fleet came down to the assistance of the *Cincinnati*, and surrounded the *Van Dorn*, who made a sudden dash at the *Mount* [Mound] *City*, striking her amidships, driving in her hull about six feet, causing her to leak badly; but as the Federal gunboats are all built in water-tight compartments, it was some time before she sank; she was able to make the bank.
>
> The U.S. gunboat *Pittsburg* was disabled, by getting between the fires of the two fleets. The firing of both fleets was rapid and heavy, and our boats were struck several times, doing some damage to the cabins, but only one was damaged in the hull, and that was the *General Price*, who received a shell (128 pounds) between wind and water, cutting off the supply pipes and causing her to leak.
>
> As the "Feds." had drawn off into shoal water, where we could not reach them, Commodore J.E. Montgomery signaled the fleet to retire, which was done in good order, all dropping down stream, below the guns of the fort. The total loss was two killed; but several firemen were wounded with splinters, and one man had his arm broken.[9]

Commander Henry Walke, the daring commander of the heroic U.S. gunboat *Carondelet*, the first to run past the guns of Island No. 10, gave his account of the battle:

> The *Carondelet* started immediately after the first verbal order; the others, for want of steam or some other cause, were not ready, except the *Mound City*, which put off soon after we were fairly on our way to the rescue of the *Cincinnati*. We had proceeded about a mile before our other gun-boats left their moorings. The rams were advancing rapidly, and we steered for the leading vessel, *General Bragg*, a brig-rigged, side-wheel steam ram, far in advance of the others, and apparently intent on striking the *Cincinnati*.
>
> When about three-quarters of a mile from the *General Bragg*, the *Carondelet* and *Mound City* fired on her with their bow-guns, until she struck the *Cincinnati* on the starboard quarter, making a great hole in the shell-room, through which the water poured with resistless force. The *Cincinnati* then retreated up the river and the *General Bragg* drifted down, evidently disabled.
>
> The *General Price*, following the example of her consort, also rammed the *Cincinnati*. We fired our bow-guns into the *General Price*, and she backed off, disabled also. The *Cincinnati* was again struck by one of the enemy's rams, the *General Sumter*.
>
> Having pushed on with all speed to the rescue of the *Cincinnati*, the *Carondelet* passed her in a sinking condition, and, rounding to, we fired our bow and starboard broadside guns into the retreating *General Bragg* and the advancing rams, *General Jeff. Thompson*, *General Beauregard*, and *General Lovell*. Heading up-stream, close to a shoal, the *Carondelet* brought her port broadside guns to bear on the *Sumter* and *Price*, which were dropping down-stream.
>
> At this crisis the *Van Dorn* and *Little Rebel* had run above the *Carondelet*; the *Bragg*, *Jeff. Thompson*, *Beauregard*, and *Lovell* were below her. The last three, coming up, fired into the *Carondelet*; she returned their fire with her stern-guns; and while in this position, I ordered the port rifled 50-pounder Dahlgren gun to be leveled and fired at the center of the *Sumter*.

The shot struck the vessel just forward of her wheel-house, and the steam instantly poured out from her ports and all parts of her casemates, and we saw her men running out of them and falling or lying down on her deck...

The smoke at this time was so dense that we could hardly distinguish the gun-boats above us. The upper deck of the *Carondelet* was swept with grape-shot and fragments of broken shell; some of the latter were picked up by one of the sharp-shooters, who told me they were obliged to lie down under shelter to save themselves from the grape and other shot of the *Pittsburgh* above us, and from the shot and broken shell of the enemy below us...

As the smoke rose we saw that the enemy was retreating rapidly and in great confusion. The *Carondelet* dropped down to within half a mile above Craighead's Point, and kept up a continual fire upon their vessels, which were very much huddled together. When they were nearly, if not quite, beyond gunshot, the *Benton*, having raised sufficient steam, came down and passed the *Carondelet*; the Confederates were under the protection of Fort Pillow before the *Benton* could reach them. Our fleet returned to Plum Point, except the *Carondelet*, which dropped her anchor on the battle-field, two miles or more below the point, and remained there two days on voluntary guard duty.

This engagement was sharp, but not decisive. From the first to the last shot fired by the *Carondelet*, one hour and ten minutes had elapsed.[10]

Captain Montgomery seemed pleased with the way his rams had performed. In his report to General Beauregard on May 11 he conceded that "our cannon were far inferior to theirs, both in number and size," and not wishing to exchange shots with them as the Union gunboats sought the safety of shoal water, he "signalled our boats to fall back, which was accomplished with a coolness that deserves the highest commendation," he wrote. He then told Beauregard:

> I am happy to inform you, while exposed to close quarters to a most terrific fire for thirty minutes, our boats, although struck repeatedly, sustained no serious injury.
> Our casualties were two killed and one wounded — arm broken.
> Gen. M. Jeff. Thompson was on board the *General Bragg*, his officers and men were divided among the boats. They were all at their posts ready to do good service should an occasion offer.
> To my officers and men I am highly indebted for their courage and promptness in executing all orders.
> On the 11th instant [May] I went, on the *Little Rebel*, in full view of the enemy's fleet. Saw the *Carondelet* [actually the *Cincinnati*] sunk near the shore, and the *Mound City* sunk on the bar.[11]

Captain Davis, the new commander of the Union fleet, had a somewhat different view of the battle, which he reported to Secretary Welles in a message dated May 10:

> The naval engagement for which the rebels have been preparing took place this morning. The rebel fleet, consisting of eight iron-clad gunboats, four of which were fitted with rams, came up handsomely. The action lasted one hour. Two of the rebel gunboats were blown up and one sunk, when the enemy retired precipitately under the guns of the fort. Only six vessels of my squadron were engaged. The *Cincinnati* sustained some injury from the rams, but will be in fighting condition to-morrow. Capt. Stembel distinguished himself. He is seriously wounded. The *Benton* is uninjured. Mortar boat No. 16, in charge of Second Master Gregory, behaved with great spirit.
> The rebel squadron is supposed to be commanded by Commodore Hollins.[12]

Commander Stembel had been hit in the mouth by a shot from a rebel sharpshooter aboard the *General Bragg*, and three others in the Union fleet had been wounded, the extent of Union casualties in the fight, which came to be called the Battle of Plum Point Bend.

U.S. Admiral David Dixon Porter, in *The Naval History of the Civil War*, which he authored, concluded that the rebel rams had indeed sunk two of the Union gunboats, in agreement with Confederate reports and in contradiction to Captain Davis's report to Welles: "The 'Cincinnati,' after proceeding some distance up the river, sunk near the Tennessee side. The 'Cairo' assisted the 'Mound City' to the first island above the scene of the action, where she [the *Mound City*] also sunk."[13]

Losing two boats, while the Confederates lost none, did not, in Porter's opinion, mean the Union Navy had lost the battle, the first fleet-against-fleet engagement of the war. "It is exceedingly difficult to give a correct account of this engagement," Porter wrote, "owing to the many conflicting versions which were published in the West at the time, but we know enough to be satisfied that victory remained with the Federal squadron.... Flag-officer Davis had the satisfaction of winning the first naval squadron fight."[14]

As J. Thomas Scharf observed in his *History of the Confederate States Navy*, "A little more of that kind of satisfaction would have left Commodore Davis without a vessel."[15]

Porter did not fail to find fault with the Union fleet, claiming that the action "would seem to indicate rather indifferent gunnery practice on the part of the Federals, who, with their heavy ordnance, ought to have swept the enemy from the face of the water, as his vessels were of wood and lightly built.... It appears that our gun-boats did not altogether act in concert, probably owing to their want of speed."[16] He had similar criticism for the Confederate fleet: "The Confederate Commander-in-chief was not accustomed to command vessels *en masse* and does not seem to have understood the necessity of concert of action. Each Confederate vessel seems to have been fighting on her 'own hook.'"[17]

The damaged Confederate rams were soon repaired in Memphis, and both the *Cincinnati* and the *Mound City* were refloated, towed upriver and repaired. Thus were both fleets restored. Captain Davis, now designated flag officer, made minor adjustments to his fleet's procedures, and continued the daily—and mostly futile—bombardment of Fort Pillow. The mortar boats were towed into position early each morning as usual, but now were watched over by *two* gunboats during the day and towed back upriver in the evening to spend the night in safety among the fleet's other vessels. Still waiting for something to happen that would allow them to pass Fort Pillow, Flag Officer Davis was unwilling as Foote to hazard his boats under the rebel guns.

On May 25, Colonel Ellet arrived with six of his rams, eager to put them in action against the rebel boats. Walke, the *Carondelet*'s captain, called them "a useful acquisition to our fleet," but Flag Officer Davis was unwilling to cooperate when Ellet proposed an attack on the Confederate boats. "The Commodore [Davis] intimates unwillingness to assume any risk at this time," Ellet complained to Secretary Stanton on May 26. On May 30 Ellet told Stanton, "To me, the risk is greater to lie here with my small squad and within an hour's march of a strong encampment of the enemy, than to run by the battery and to make the attack."[18]

As Ellet's annoyance with Davis was increasing, so was Davis's with Ellet. On June 2, Davis wrote Ellet a sharp note, saying, "I would thank you to inform me how far you consider yourself under my authority, and I shall esteem it a favor to receive from you a copy of the orders under which you are acting."[19]

The feisty Ellet was quick—and probably happy—to reply. He put together some of Secretary Stanton's letters and sent them to Davis, together with a note telling Davis, "While regretting sincerely your disposition [not] to cooperate in a movement against the enemy's fleet, lying within easy reach, I take great pleasure in giving you all the information you ask for. I do not consider myself under your authority."[20]

The letters' revelation of Ellet's direct connection to the secretary of war moderated Davis's attitude toward him, and after that, Davis became somewhat more cooperative, promising Ellet he would make him "acquainted with all the details" of future operations. Even so, on June 4, Ellet once more complained to Stanton: "Commodore Davis will not join me in a movement against them, nor contribute a gunboat to my expedition, nor allow any of his men to volunteer.... I shall therefore first weed out some bad material [in Ellet's fleet] and go without him."[21]

The "weeding out" began when a pilot on the *Monarch*, one of Ellet's rams, learning about the action Ellet was planning, asked for his pay and quit his job, saying that when he signed on, he didn't expect he would be exposed to the dangers of war. The captain of the *Queen of the West*, along with two of its pilots, its first mate and all of its engineers, also quit rather than face combat. They gathered up their baggage and took off on a barge going upstream. To replace the faint of heart Ellet called for volunteers, and among those who responded to the call were two soldiers from the Sixty-third Illinois Infantry Regiment who told him they were engineers. Ellet himself assumed command of the *Queen of the West*.

Acting without Davis's cooperation, Ellet took the *Queen* and the *Monarch* down the river to attack a Confederate vessel, pursuing it as far as Fort Pillow before giving up the chase. The two Ellet rams drew the fire from the fort's guns, but suffered no damage, the shots falling harmlessly into the river. From that action Ellet gained what he regarded as important intelligence: the rebel ram fleet was lying just below Fort Pillow, and the fort's guns were not very effective.

In the meantime, the river had fallen, and Davis and Colonel Graham N. Fitch, commander of the two regiments, some twelve hundred troops, still aboard the transports in Davis's boats, saw new possibilities for putting ashore the two regiments and making a successful assault on the fort following an intensified bombardment by Davis's fleet. The attack was planned for the morning of June 4, but was scrubbed after Alfred Ellet's ram suddenly and unexpectedly appeared down the river in pursuit of a rebel picket boat. Neither Ellet nor Davis had notified the other of his intended activity. The assault was rescheduled for seven o'clock the next morning, June 5. Davis again neglected to inform Ellet of the plan.

On the afternoon of June 4, Davis's planned attack was obviated. "Heavy clouds of smoke were observed rising from Fort Pillow," Lieutenant Walke reported, "followed by explosions, which continued through the night, the last of which, much greater than the others, lit up the heavens and the Chickasaw bluffs with a brilliant light, and convinced us that this was the parting salute of the Confederates before leaving for the lower Mississippi."[22]

At daybreak the following morning, June 5, the Union fleet set out for Fort Pillow and reaching it, discovered it wrecked and abandoned. "We found the casemates, magazines, and breastworks blown to atoms,"[23] Walke reported. They also found that the Stars and Stripes had already been raised above the scorched and smoking fort. Alfred Ellet had gotten there first. He described his actions:

> On the night of the 4th of June I crossed the timber point in front of the fort, and reported to the colonel commanding [his brother Charles] my conviction that the fort was being evacuated. About 2 o'clock in the morning I obtained permission, with many words of caution from Colonel Ellet, to run down opposite the fort in a yawl and, after lying off in

order to become assured that the place was abandoned, to land, with the assurance that the rams would follow in case my yawl did not return before daylight.

I landed with my little band, only to find the fort entirely deserted; and after planting the National colors upon the ruins of one of the magazines, we sat down to wait for the coming of daylight and the rams. They came, followed by the entire fleet, and after a short stop all proceeded down the river, the rams taking the lead, to Fort Randolph.[24]

Flag Officer Davis turned the fort over to Colonel Fitch, and he with a detachment of his soldiers was put ashore to take possession of it.

Having been defeated at Pittsburg Landing and having abandoned Corinth, exposing the flank and rear of every Confederate position west of Corinth, including Fort Pillow, General Beauregard, the Confederate army's commander in the West, had ordered the fort evacuated, and its commandant, Brigadier General John Bordenave Villepigue, and his garrison had hurriedly complied, destroying much of the fort before departing and allowing the rest, including the fort's forbidding guns, to fall into Union hands.

An enormous obstacle had been removed from the path of the Union fleet.

17. Showdown at Memphis

Captain Montgomery was feeling expansive on the evening of June 5. He was in Memphis at Gayoso House, the massive, four-story, brick hotel that stood a block from the busy riverfront, elegantly appointed with such amenities as marble tubs, silver faucets and flush toilets, all opulent symbols of the city's cotton prosperity. His confidence buoyed by the success of his eight rams at Plum Point Bend four weeks earlier, he stood to address an assembly of jittery Memphis residents, who after having heard the news of the abandonment of Fort Pillow were trying to decide if it was time for them to pack up their belongings and get out of town, before the Yankees arrived to ransack and burn their city.

"I have no intention of retreating any farther," Montgomery assured his audience. "I have come here that you may see Lincoln's gunboats sent to the bottom by the fleet which you built and manned."[1] He invited his listeners to come down to the riverfront at sunrise the next day and watch him sink the Union fleet.

Encouraged by Montgomery's words, the editor of the Memphis *Avalanche* composed an editorial for publication in the next morning's edition of his newspaper:

> The prospect is very good for a grand naval engagement which shall eclipse anything ever seen before. There are many who would like the engagement to occur, who do not much relish the prospect of its occurring very near the city. They think deeper water and scope and verge enough for such an encounter may be found farther up the river. All, however, are rejoiced to learn that Memphis will not fall till conclusions are first tried on water, and at the cannon's mouth.[2]

Earlier, on June 5, after raising the U.S. flag over Fort Pillow, Colonel Charles Ellet and three of his rams had pushed on to Fort Randolph, twelve miles below Fort Pillow, and Ellet himself had gone ashore, found the fort deserted, run up the Stars and Stripes there, then returned to Fort Pillow, passing Davis's fleet moving downstream while he proceeded up. Davis didn't bother to signal Ellet to ask what he had discovered below Fort Pillow and instead continued on to Island No. 45, about two miles above Memphis, where the fleet dropped anchor. Ellet meanwhile gathered up the rest of his rams and made his way back down the river, stopping for the night about twenty-five miles above Memphis. At first light on June 6 the rams were on the move again and by sunrise had reached the set of marshy islands known as Paddy's Hen and Chicks, where they came in sight of the Union gunboat fleet, standing in the river. Ellet signaled his ram commanders to tie up to the Arkansas shore.

Five of Davis's gunboats were in a line that extended across the breadth of the Mississippi, the *Benton* nearest the Tennessee shore, the *Carondelet* next to it, then the *Louisville*, *St. Louis* and *Cairo*, nearest the Arkansas shore. Two steam tugs that Davis used as dispatch boats, the *Jessie Benton* and the *Spitfire*, stood idling near the *Benton*, ready for immediate duty. The vessels had hoisted their anchors before sunrise and with steam up were holding their positions in the river, their big paddle wheels slowly churning in the current.

As the sun rose higher, the sky soon brightened. "Never was there a lovelier daybreak," the war correspondent aboard the *Benton* remarked. "The woods were full of song-birds. The air was balmy. A few light clouds, fringed with gold, lay along the eastern horizon."[3] Flag Officer Davis raised his hand and summoned the tug *Jessie Benton*, which quickly sidled up to the flagship. "Drop down towards the city," Davis shouted to the *Jessie Benton*'s captain, "and see if you can discover the rebel fleet."[4] The war correspondent, Charles Carleton Coffin, quickly leaped from the flagship onto the dispatch boat to join the expedition and later gave his report of the *Jessie Benton*'s reconnaissance:

> Below us was the city. The first rays of the sun were gilding the church-spires. A crowd of people stood upon the broad levee between the city and the river. They were coming from all the streets, on foot, on horseback, in carriages — men, women, and children — ten thousand, to see Lincoln's gunboats sent to the bottom. Above the court-house, and from flagstaffs, waved the flag of the Confederacy. A half-dozen river steamers lay at the landing, but the Rebel fleet was not in sight. At our right hand was the wide marsh on the tongue of land where Wolfe River empties into the Mississippi. Upon our left were the cotton-trees and button-woods, and the village of Hopedale at the terminus of the Little Rock and Memphis Railroad. We dropped slowly down the stream, the tug floating in the swift current, running deep and strong as it sweeps past the city.
>
> The crowd increased. The levee was black with the multitude. The windows were filled. The flat roofs of the warehouses were covered with the excited throng, which surged to and fro as we upon the tug came down into the bend, almost within talking distance.
>
> Suddenly a boat came out from the Arkansas shore, where it had been lying concealed from view behind the forest — another, another, eight of them. They formed in two lines, in front of the city.
>
> Nearest the city, in the front line, was the General Beauregard; next, the Little Rebel; then the General Price and the Sumter. In the second line, behind the Beauregard, was the General Lovell; behind the Little Rebel was the Jeff Thompson; behind the General Price was the General Bragg; and behind the Sumter was the Van Dorn....
>
> The Benton and St. Louis dropped down towards the city, to protect the tug. A signal brought us back, and the boats moved up-stream again, to the original position.
>
> There was another signal from the flag-ship, and then on board all the boats there was a shrill whistle. It was the boatswain piping all hands to quarters. The drummer beat his roll, and the marines seized their muskets. The sailors threw open the ports, ran out the guns, brought up shot and shells, stowed away furniture, took down rammers and sponges, seized their handspikes, stripped off their coats, rolled up their sleeves, loaded the cannon, and stood by their pieces. Cutlasses and boarding-pikes were distributed. Last words were said. They waited for orders.[5]

Soon an order came, but not one they were expecting. "Let the men have their breakfasts!" Flag Officer Davis wanted his crews fighting on full stomachs and took his time to feed them. Hot coffee, bread and beef were passed out to the men of his vessels while the rebel fleet waited, its crewmen wondering.

Aboard the *General Beauregard*, Captain J. Henry Hart, the boat's commander, who earlier had understood that the Confederate vessels would not make a stand, watched the Union fleet preparing to move against the rebel rams:

> After daylight, on the morning of the 6th, we could see by the movements of the enemy that they were making preparations to come down, for the heavens were one solid cloud of black smoke. In the meantime we were not idle in making preparations to back out in the

stream, which we did, one after another, until our whole fleet, eight in number, were drawn in line of battle. It was here we received the first intelligence that we were going to make a stand.

The enemy was now in full view, coming down in line of battle. The following boats were sent up to draw the Federal gunboats off of the bar: *General M. Jeff Thompson, Sumter, General Beauregard,* and *Colonel Lovell,* from the fact that they had sixty-four pound guns mounted on their bows. The fire was opened by the *Thompson,* but not until she had fired three rounds did the enemy make any reply. The fire on the Federal side was opened by the flag-ship *Benton.* The fight now became general. Brisk firing, from both sides was the order of the day....[6]

The sound of the *Thompson's* first shot carried up the river to where Ellet's fleet lay. Colonel Ellet's brother, Lieutenant Colonel Alfred Ellet, described the Union rams' response:

> Colonel Ellet was standing on the hurricane-deck of the *Queen of the West.* He immediately sprang forward, and, waving his hat to attract my attention, called out: "It is a gun from the enemy! Round out and follow me! Now is our chance!" Without a moment's delay, the *Queen* moved out gracefully, and the *Monarch* followed. By this time our gun-boats had opened their batteries, and the reports of guns on both sides were heavy and rapid.
>
> The morning was beautifully clear and perfectly still; a heavy wall of smoke was formed across the river, so that the position of our gun-boats could only be seen by the flashes of their guns. The *Queen* plunged forward, under a full head of steam, right into this wall of smoke and was lost sight of, her position being known only by her tall pipes which reached above the smoke. The *Monarch,* following, was greeted, while passing the gun-boats, with wild huzzas from our gallant tars. When freed from the smoke, those of us who were on the *Monarch* could see Colonel Ellet's tall and commanding form still standing on the hurricane-deck, waving his hat to show me which one of the enemy's vessels he desired the *Monarch* to attack — namely, the *General Price,* which was on the right wing of their advancing line. For himself he selected the *General* [sic] *Lovell* and directed the *Queen* straight for her, she being about the middle of the enemy's advancing line....[7]

Not until the *Queen of the West* and the *Monarch* burst through the black wall of smoke did the Confederates realize the Union fleet they had battled at Plum Point Bend had been reinforced and that they were now facing a more dangerous foe. Captain Hart of the rebel ram *General Beauregard* continued his account of the fight:

> It was while the battle was raging with intense fury, between our rams and the Federal gunboats, that their rams made their appearance; first came the *Queen of the West,* which made a bee-line for the *Colonel Lovell,* which tried to back out of the way, but in so doing got in such a position as to show her opponent a broadside, when she ran into her and sunk her immediately, in water to her hurricane deck, in the channel of the river. Life-boats were immediately dispatched from the *Little Rebel,* to assist her crew in getting ashore.
>
> Before the *Queen of the West* could regain her position, the Confederate ram *Sumter* struck her in midships, sending her ashore, during the balance of the engagement....[8]

Alfred Ellet reported the action as seen from the *Monarch:*

> As soon as the *Queen* was freed from the wreck of the sinking *Lovell,* and before she could recover headway, she was attacked on both sides by the enemy's vessels, the *Beauregard* on one side and the *Sumter* on the other. In the *melee* one of the wheels of the *Queen* was disabled so that she could not use it, and Colonel Ellet, while still standing on the hurricane-deck to view the effects of the encounter with the *General Lovell,* received a pistol-ball in his knee, and, lying prone on the deck, gave orders for the *Queen* to be run on her one remaining wheel to the Arkansas shore, whither she was soon followed by the *General Price*

in a sinking condition. Colonel Ellet sent an officer and squad of men to meet the *General Price* upon her making the shore, and received her entire crew as prisoners of war.

By this time consternation had seized upon the enemy's fleet, and all had turned to escape. The fight had drifted down the river, below the city....[9]

The *General Beauregard*'s captain went on with his account:

Next came the *Switzerland*, bearing down on the *Sumter*. The *Beauregard* next in turn singled out the *Switzerland* for her antagonist. The Federal ram, seeing her intention, drew off from the *Sumter* and headed down on the *Beauregard*; they struck head on, but glanced, placing the *Switzerland hors de combat*, knocking down her bridge-tree, when she had to go ashore, where she threw out her sharp-shooters as pickets. Next came the Federal ram *Monarch*, in chase of the *Jeff. Thompson*, she at the same time rounding to, head up stream, followed by the *Monarch*; here the *General Price* was put under a heavy head of steam, to overtake the *Monarch*, which she did, striking her a heavy blow on the starboard quarter, driving in her hull, and rounding her to, after which she stopped to back around and give her another blow; but, unfortunately, the *Beauregard* had made a dash at the *Monarch* and missed her object, and striking the *Price* on the port-side, completely disabling her. During this, with only one wheel left, she managed to get ashore, but too late for the crew to make their escape; disabled as she was, the enemy kept up a constant fire into her; for humanity's sake the "stars and bars" were hauled down.

It was about this time the *Beauregard* got headed up again to meet another of her adversaries, when a shell was shot into her hull and burst, damaging her boilers and hull; killed one engineer, and wounding three others, and scalding three firemen. She was unfit for duty, floated down the river about one-fourth of a mile, and sunk in twenty feet of water, face to the enemy, and colors flying.

It was about this [time] the *Little Rebel* made a dash at one of the rams; but before she could reach her received a shot in her boilers, when she kept her course into the shore, where all but three made their escape. In the meantime, the *Sumter* had been run ashore, and crew all escaped[10]; also the *Thompson* was run ashore, and burned to the water's edge.[11]

Commander Walke gave an account from his observations aboard the *Carondelet*:

The scene at this battle was rendered most sublime by the desperate nature of the engagement and the momentous consequences that followed very speedily after the first attack. Thousands of people crowded the high bluffs overlooking the river. The roar of the cannon and shell shook the houses on shore on either side for many miles. First wild yells, shrieks, and clamors, then loud, despairing murmurs, filled the affrighted city.

The screaming, plunging shell crashed into the boats, blowing some of them and their crews into fragments, and the rams rushed upon each other like wild beasts in deadly conflict. Blinding smoke hovered about the scene of all this confusion and horror; and, as the battle progressed and the Confederate fleet was destroyed, all the cheering voices on shore were silenced. When the last hope of the Confederates gave way, the lamentations which went up from the spectators were like cries of anguish.

Boats were put off from our vessels to save as many lives as possible. No serious injury was received by any one on board the United States fleet. Colonel Ellet received a pistol-shot in the leg; a shot struck the *Carondelet* in the bow, broke up her anchor and anchor-stock, and fragments were scattered over her deck among her officers and crew, wounding slightly Acting-Master Gibson and two or three others who were standing at the time on the forward deck with me.[12]

According to Captain Hart's account, not all the Confederate rams displayed courage when it was demanded. He singled out the *General Bragg* and the *General Van Dorn* as being diffident in the face of danger:

The *General Bragg* stood off and looked at the fight, likewise the *General Earl Van Dorn*; neither offering any assistance. The *Bragg*, in attempting to round to, to make good her retreat, was run into by one of the Federal rams, which drove in her side. The crew of the *Bragg* nearly all made their escape in yawls and life-boats. The *Van Dorn*, handling much better than the *Bragg*, was fortunate in making good her escape. Thus ended one of the hottest naval engagements ever fought in the Mississippi.[13]

Brigadier General M. Jeff. Thompson, who shared with Captain Montgomery the command of the Mississippi River defense efforts, offered his own version of the momentous battle. In a message to General Beauregard, his commander, dated June 7, Thompson wrote that after being given his responsibility for defending against the oncoming Union force in the early morning of June 6, he:

> immediately wrote a note to the Commodore [Montgomery], asking what I should do to co-operate with him. He requested two companies of artillery to be sent aboard at daybreak (all of my men were at the [Memphis] depot awaiting transportation to Grenada [Mississippi]). I at once ordered the companies to hold themselves in readiness. At the dawn of the day I was awakened with the information that the enemy were actually in sight of Memphis. I hurried on board to consult with Montgomery. He instructed me to hurry my men to Fort Pickering Landing, and sent a tug to bring them up to the gunboats, which were advancing to attack the enemy. I hastened my men to the place indicated, but before we reached it our boats had been either destroyed or driven below Fort Pickering, and I marched back to the depot to come to this place (Grenada) to await orders.
>
> I saw a large portion of the engagement from the river bank, and am sorry to say that in my opinion many of our men were handled badly, as the plan of battle was very faulty. The enemy's rams (Col. Ellet's fleet) did most of the execution, and were handled more adroitly than ours; I think, however, entirely owing to the fact that the guns and sharp-shooters of the enemy were constantly employed, while we were almost without either. The *Colonel Lovell* was so injured that she sank in the middle of the river; her captain, Jas. Delaney, and a number of others, swam ashore. The *Beauregard* and *Price* were running at the *Monarch* (Yankee) from opposite sides, when the *Monarch* passed from between them, and the *Beauregard* ran into the *Price*, knocking off her wheel-house, and entirely disabling her. Both were run to the Arkansas shore and abandoned. The *Little Rebel*, commodore's flag-boat, was run ashore and abandoned after she had been completely riddled, and I am satisfied the commodore was killed. The battle continued down the river, out of sight in Memphis, and it is reported that only two of our boats, the *Bragg* and the *Van Dorn*, escaped.[14]

Actually, only the *Van Dorn* escaped, swiftly fleeing to safety in the Yazoo River, just above Vicksburg. Captain Montgomery safely escaped on the Arkansas side of the river with most of the officers and crew of the abandoned *Little Rebel*. The pursuit of the Confederate vessels by Union gunboats and the *Monarch* continued to the foot of President's Island, as far as could be seen from the Memphis riverfront, "the gunboats rapidly firing as they went," as one Confederate eyewitness account had it, "a shot occasionally being returned from our fleet. In a short time two of the Federal iron-clad boats were observed steaming back, accompanied by the *Monarch*. The conclusion arrived at was that the remainder of our fleet had met the fate of the others."[15]

The war correspondent, Charles Carleton Coffin, who witnessed the battle from the deck of the *Jessie Benton*, summarized its results:

> The General Price, General Beauregard, Little Rebel, and General Lovell — one half of the Rebel fleet — were disposed of. The other vessels attempted to flee. The Union fleet had swept steadily on in an unbroken line. Amid all the appalling scenes of the hour there was

no lull in the cannonade. While saving those who had lost all power of resistance, there was no cessation of effort to crush those who still resisted.

A short distance below the Little Rebel, the Jeff Thompson, riddled by shot, and in flames, was run ashore. A little farther down-stream the General Bragg was abandoned, also in flames from the explosion of a nine-inch shell, thrown by the St. Louis. The crews leaped on shore, and fled to the woods. The Sumter went ashore, near the Little Rebel. The Van Dorn alone escaped. She was a swift steamer, and was soon beyond reach of the guns of the fleet.

The fight is over. The thunder of the morning dies away, and the birds renew their singing. The abandoned boats are picked up. The Jeff Thompson cannot be saved. The flames leap around the chimneys. The boilers are heated to redness. A pillar of fire springs upward, in long lances of light. The interior of the boat—boilers, beams of iron, burning planks, flaming timbers, cannon-shot, shells—is lifted five hundred feet in air, in an expanding, unfolding cloud, filled with loud explosions. The scattered fragments rain upon forest, field, and river, as if meteors of vast proportions had fallen from heaven to earth, taking fire in their descent. There is a shock which shakes all Memphis, and announces to the disappointed, terror-stricken, weeping, humiliated multitude that the drama which they have played so madly for a twelvemonth is over, that retribution for crime has come at last![16]

With satisfaction but some unsteadiness of syntax, Colonel Ellet filed this report to Secretary Stanton:

OPPOSITE MEMPHIS, June 6th, *via* Cairo, 8th.
Hon. Edwin M. Stanton, Secretary of War:
It is proper and due to the brave men on the *Queen* and the *Monarch* to say to you briefly that two of the rebel steamers were sunk outright and immediately by the shock of my two rams, one with a large amount of cotton, etc., on board was disabled by accidental collision with the *Queen*, and secured by her crew, after I was personally disabled.

Another, which was also hit by a shot from the gunboats, was sunk by the *Monarch*, and towed to shoal water by that boat. Still another, also injured by the fire of our gunboats, was pushed in to the shore and secured by the *Monarch*. Of the gunboats I can only say that they bore themselves, as our navy always does, bravely and well.
CHAS. ELLET, JR.
Col. Commanding Ram Fleet[17]

With General Thompson and his troops in the process of speedily departing the city by train once it was clear which way the battle would go—and the battle now having gone that way—Memphis was left defenseless. A report came to Colonel Ellet that white flags could be seen flying in the city, and never one to stand around waiting, the wounded colonel promptly dispatched a note to the mayor: "OPPOSITE MEMPHIS, June 6, 1862. "I understand that the City of Memphis has surrendered. I therefore send my son with two United States flags, with instructions to raise one upon the Custom-house and the other upon the Court-house, as evidence of the return or your city to the care and protection of the Constitution. CHARLES ELLET, JUN., Colonel Commanding."[18]

Ellet's nineteen-year-old son, Charlie, went ashore from the *Lioness* with three men — Lieutenant Warren Crandall, Colonel Ellet's assistant adjutant general, and two men of the Fifty-ninth Illinois Infantry Regiment, Sergeant William McDonald and Private Cyrus Lathrop — under a flag of truce and delivered the colonel's note to the mayor, after which young Ellet was handed the mayor's note of reply: "JUNE 6, 1862. SIR,—Your note of this date is received and the contents noted. The civil authorities of this city are not advised of its surrender to the forces of the United States Government, and our reply to you is simply to state respectfully that we have no forces to oppose the raising of the flags you have directed to be raised over the Custom-house and Post-office. Respectfully, JOHN PARK, Mayor."

With the mayor's reply in hand, young Ellet and his party proceeded to the post office, accompanied by the three-hundred-pound mayor, who had tried unsuccessfully to persuade them to wait till a detail of troops could escort them. A threatening crowd surrounded them, and someone in it snatched one of the flags and ripped it to shreds, leaving young Ellet with but one flag. At the post office Ellet and his party climbed to the roof of the four-story building and attached the Stars and Stripes to a makeshift flagstaff that they mounted at the front of the building, while some in the crowd below hurled stones and epithets at them and fired several shots at them, though no one was hurt.

While young Ellet and the others were still on the roof someone from the crowd closed the trap door that gave access to the roof and locked it, stranding the men atop the building as the crowd yelled at them and more shots were fired. Mayor Park, alarmed, forced his bulky body through the crowd and hurried to the riverfront to get help. He shouted to the soldiers aboard the *Lioness*, and Captain John Miller Shrodes, the boat's commander, who had served as an Army captain in the Mexican War, came ashore with all of the remaining soldiers from the *Lioness*, armed with carbines and hand grenades. The crowd followed them on their way to the post office, jeering them as they went. When an explosion went off in a downtown warehouse, many in the crowd ran off to investigate the newest excitement, and the detail from the *Lioness* continued on to the post office. Posting four men at the building's entrance, Shrodes sent the others up to rescue Ellet and his party.

Back out on the street, Crandall and Ellet led the detail of soldiers to the city square and hauled down Confederate flags from nearby buildings. With that work done, they marched back to the riverfront about three P.M., just in time to see the Union transport steamer *Henry Von Phul* drawing up to the landing with a boatload of Colonel Fitch's infantrymen, who came ashore and took possession of the surrendered city.

Confederate losses in the battle at Memphis were estimated at about one hundred killed or wounded and about 150 captured.[19] In addition to casualties, the Confederates lost a great amount of property. Commander Walke reported that Davis's force captured "six large Mississippi steamers, each marked 'C.S.A.' We also seized a large quantity of cotton in steamers and on shore, and the property at the Confederate Navy Yard, and caused the destruction of the *Tennessee*, a large steam-ram, on the stocks, which was to have been a sister ship to the renowned *Arkansas*."[20]

The Union casualties were four wounded, including Colonel Ellet, who died of apparent blood poisoning resulting from his wound on June 18, twelve days after the battle. He died while aboard a steamer near Cairo, on his way home with his wife, Ellie, and daughter Mary.[21] Ellie, in poor health herself, died several days later, and she and Colonel Ellet were buried in Philadelphia on June 25.

Alfred Ellet, on his brother's recommendation and with Secretary Stanton's concurrence, took over command of the Union ram fleet for the action that lay ahead.

18. Up from New Orleans

Flag Officer Farragut's orders were to push on from New Orleans and keep advancing northward until his fleet met up with Flag Officer Davis's fleet moving southward. "If the Mississippi expedition from Cairo shall not have descended the river," the Navy Department's instructions read, "you will take advantage of the [rebels'] panic to push a strong force up the river to take all their defences in the rear."[1] The Navy Department — and President Lincoln — were especially eager for Farragut to take Vicksburg and expected him to do so soon after taking New Orleans. When Captain Theodorus Bailey, who commanded the lead ship in Farragut's advance on New Orleans, arrived in Washington, D.C., to report the capture of New Orleans, he was immediately asked how many ships Farragut had sent up the river to Vicksburg. Bailey answered, "None," and Gustavus Fox, the assistant secretary of the Navy, in response, blurted out, "Impossible! Sending the fleet up to meet Commodore Davis was the most important part of the whole expedition. The instructions were positive!"[2]

The desk warriors in Washington failed to appreciate the problems. "The Department," Farragut wrote in response to a sharp letter from the Navy Department accusing him of forgetting his orders, "seems to have considered my fleet as having escaped all injury, and that when they arrived off New Orleans they were in condition to be pushed up the river. This was not the case; but, the moment the vessels could be gotten ready, the gunboats were all sent up under the command of Commander S.P. Lee, with directions to proceed to Vicksburg, take that place, and cut the railroad.... From all I could hear it was not considered proper, even with pilots, to risk the ships beyond Natchez."[3] Farragut's ships were not shallow-draft riverboats; they were ocean-going vessels with deep-V hulls, many of which required deep water, greater than the Mississippi River's usual depth above Natchez. Not all the ships that had blasted their way past Fort Jackson and Fort St. Philip would be able to ascend the river to Vicksburg.

Nevertheless Farragut got on with the business of moving up from New Orleans. He first ordered a flotilla of seven vessels commanded by Captain T.T. Craven to proceed up the river to Baton Rouge, then to Natchez and on toward Vicksburg. The *Richmond*, intended to compel the surrender of Baton Rouge, ran aground, its mission thwarted, but on May 7 the gunboat *Iroquois*, commanded by Commander James S. Palmer, another of the vessels of Craven's flotilla, drew up to the wharf at Baton Rouge, and Palmer sent an officer ashore to track down the mayor and demand the surrender of the city — from which state government officials had already fled to Opelousas, leaving behind some six thousand defenseless residents.

The officer found someone to direct him to city hall, where he met the mayor, Benjamin F. Bryan. Like the New Orleans mayor, Bryan replied to the demand for surrender by saying the city would not surrender, but that it was powerless to defend itself and that the Union forces could do as they pleased with the helpless city, which indeed they did.

Details of the Union forces' takeover of Baton Rouge, from a Southerner's perspective, were recorded in the diary of a twenty-year-old resident, Sarah Morgan, member of a prominent Baton Rouge family. On April 26 she wrote, "There is no word in the English language which can express the state in which we are all now, and have been for the past three days," since news of Farragut's passing of forts Jackson and St. Philip reached Baton Rouge. "We went this morning to see the cotton burning," she continued, "a sight which was never before presented to our view, and probably never will be again. Wagons and drays, and everything that could be driven, or rolled along were to be seen in every direction loaded with the bales, and taking them a few squares back, to burn on the commons.... Up and down the levee, as far as the eye could see, negroes were rolling it [cotton] down to the brink of the river, where they would them afire, and push them in to float burning down the tide."[4]

On May 5 she reported, "Vile old Yankee boats, four in number, passed up this morning without stopping! ... What in the world do they mean? The river was covered with burning cotton; perhaps they want to see where it came from."[5] On May 9 she wrote:

> Our lawful (?) owners have at last arrived. About sunset day before yesterday, the Iroquois anchored here, and a graceful young Federal stepped ashore, carrying a Yankee flag over his shoulder, and asked the way to the Mayor's office. I like the style! If we girls of B.R. had been at the landing instead of the men, that Yankee should never have insulted us by flying his flag in our faces! *We* would have opposed his landing except under a flag of truce; but the men let him alone, and he even found a poor Dutchman willing to show him the road!
>
> He did not accomplish much; said a formal demand would be made next day, and asked if it was safe for the men to come ashore and buy a few necessaries, when he was assured the air of B.R. was very unhealthy for Federal soldiers at night. He promised very magnanimously not [to] shell us out, if we did not molest him; but I notice none of them dare set their feet on terra-firma, except the officer who has now called three times on the Mayor, and who is said to tremble visibly as he walks the streets.
>
> Last evening came the demand: the town must [be] surrendered immediately; the federal flag Must be raised, they would grant us the same terms they granted to New Orleans. Jolly terms those were! The answer was worthy of a Southerner. It was "the town was defenseless, if we had cannon, there were not men enough to resist; but if forty vessels lay at the landing, — it was intimated that we were in their power, and more ships coming up — we would not surrender; if they wanted, they might come Take us; if they wished the Federal flag hoisted over the Arsenal, they might put it up for themselves, the town had no control over Government property." Glorious! What a pity they did not shell the town! But they are taking us at our word, and this morning they are landing at the Garrison, and presently the Bloody banner will be floating over our heads.[6]

The taking of Baton Rouge included the recapture of the federal arsenal that Confederate forces had seized sixteen months earlier. At that time a threatening rebel force of seven companies of militiamen had been positioned within a quarter of a mile of the arsenal, which was garrisoned by some sixty U.S. artillerymen and twenty soldiers of the Army Ordnance Corps. The arsenal's commandant was Brevet Major Joseph A. Haskins, who had lost an arm during service in the Mexican War. The Louisiana governor, Thomas Moore, dispatched rebel colonels Braxton Bragg and J.W. Taylor to deliver to Major Haskins a formal demand for the arsenal's surrender. To that demand Haskins replied: "I've lost one arm in the defense of my flag and I will lose the other or even my life if necessary, before I surrender to that lot of ragamuffins."[7]

His reply was more than bravado. Haskins had two artillery pieces positioned, manned and ready to open fire if there were an attempt to storm the arsenal. For those two very practical reasons the demand for the arsenal's surrender gave way to negotiations between Governor Moore and Major Haskins, and after Moore realized that Haskins would not yield his artillery post to an infantry force, the governor ordered the Washington Artillery in New Orleans to send a detachment to Baton Rouge to provide a force to which Major Haskins could honorably surrender. The major capitulated to the Louisiana artillerymen and marched his troops out of the arsenal and down to the riverfront to board a steamer.

Now looking past Baton Rouge, Farragut on May 13 ordered Commander S. Phillips Lee, commanding the gunboat *Oneida*, to move on Natchez and compel its surrender. Before the *Oneida* reached Natchez, however, it was overtaken by Commander Palmer's *Iroquois*, and Palmer put ashore a party to demand the city's surrender. As if following a pattern established in New Orleans and Baton Rouge, city officials in Natchez, replying to Palmer's demand, told him that since he came as a conqueror, he didn't need their cooperation in occupying the city.

Pushing on from Natchez, the gunboat flotilla that Farragut ordered to Vicksburg reached the city on May 18. There it ran into serious opposition. From atop the high bluff that overlooked the river, a large group of spectators, including Confederate soldiers, could see the Union boats approaching. One of the vessels drew up to the landing without incident, and from it an officer stepped ashore with a message from Flag Officer Farragut that demanded the surrender of the city. The message was delivered to Brigadier General Martin L. Smith, the military engineer assigned by General Lovell to strengthen Vicksburg's fortifications, and Lieutenant Colonel James L. Autrey, commander of Confederate forces at Vicksburg, which numbered thirty-six hundred troops, manning a formidable defensive position armed with eighteen big guns.

General Smith responded to the demand firmly but cordially. "I have to reply," he said, "that, having been ordered here to hold these defenses, my intention is to do so as long as it is in my power."[8] Colonel Autrey responded with defiance. "I have to state that Mississippians don't know, and refuse to learn, how to surrender to an enemy," he told the Yankee officer. "If Commodore Farragut or Brigadier General Butler can teach them, let them come and try."[9]

Commander Lee, who had landed the party, reacted to Autrey's haughty reply by instructing Vicksburg's mayor to evacuate the city's women and children, warning that when the Union vessels' shelling of the fortifications began, the city itself would be unable to avoid damage.

Farragut arrived at Vicksburg several days after that exchange of messages. With Farragut in transports were some fifteen hundred troops sent by General Butler, complying with orders from General McClellan,[10] which Butler had put under the command of Brigadier General Thomas Williams. Farragut promptly assessed the situation. He discovered that as many as ten of the rebels' columbiads atop the bluff could not be reached by his fleet's guns. The intelligence he received reported that the Confederate position was defended by ten thousand troops, a gross exaggeration, but the actual number still made a larger force than General Williams's fifteen hundred troops could be expected to overcome. Farragut furthermore had no idea where Flag Officer Davis and his fleet of ironclad gunboats were or whether they could be of any help in an attempt to take Vicksburg. Considering all that, and other problems, Farragut decided to withdraw and make another try later. It was a decision recommended by his gunboat captains and by General Williams. He explained it in a couple of letters. To his wife, he wrote: "I did not pass Vicksburg; not because it was too strongly fortified; not because we could not have passed it easily enough, but we would have been cut off from our supplies of coal and provisions. We would have been placed between two enemies (Vicksburg and Memphis), and so the captains advised me not to do it. I was very sick at the time, and yielded to their advice, which I think was good; but I doubt if I would have taken it had I been well."[11]

The second one, spelling out other problems, was a dispatch to the U.S. Navy Department:

> Fighting is nothing, to the evils of the river — getting on shore, running foul of one another, losing anchors, etc.... The army had been sent up early with a few days' rations, and I was compelled to supply them from the squadron, thereby reducing our own supplies, which were barely sufficient to bring the ships back to New Orleans, making allowance for probable delays. The river was now beginning to fall, and I apprehended great difficulty in getting down should I delay much longer. In the mean time coal vessels had been towed up the river just above Natchez (a hundred miles below Vicksburg), which vessels I was obliged to bring down and keep in company with the vessels of war, for fear of their being captured by the guerrilla bands which appear to infest almost the entire banks of the river wherever there are rapids and bluffs.[12]

Leaving several of his gunboats opposite Vicksburg to harass the rebel position, he steamed off for New Orleans on May 26, taking General Williams and his troops back with him.

On the way down Farragut stopped at Baton Rouge on May 28. Taking advantage of an opportunity to have his clothes washed while the fleet lay halted, the chief engineer of Farragut's flagship, James Kimball, climbed into a small boat with a bundle of laundry and four of the *Hartford*'s crewmen who would row him to shore to find a washerwoman. As the boat approached the shore, a group of guerrillas on horseback, at least some of them teenagers, appeared on the levee and fired on the boat, wounding Kimball and two of the sailors with buckshot.

Upon learning of the incident, Flag Officer Farragut swiftly ordered the *Hartford* and the *Kennebec* to shell the city. The Baton Rouge diarist, Sarah Morgan, wrote her account of the events she witnessed during the bombardment and her flight to Greenwell, a resort that included a hotel and several cottages, one of which the Morgans apparently owned or rented, seventeen miles east of Baton Rouge:

> I heard Lilly's [Sarah's sister] voice down stairs crying as she ran in — she had been out shopping — "Mr. Castle [eighteen-year-old guerrilla Henry Castle Jr., who was later arrested for the shooting] has killed a Federal officer on a ship, and they are going to shell —" Bang! went a cannon at the word, and that was all our warning.
>
> Mother had just come in, and was lying down, but sprang to her feet and added her screams to the general confusion. What awful screams! ... Charlie [Lilly's husband] had gone to Greenwell before daybreak ... so we four women, with all these children and servants, were left to save ourselves....
>
> Before we could leave, mother ... came to find us, with Tiche [a family slave]. All this time, they had been shelling, but there was quite a lull when she got there, and she commenced picking up father's papers, vowing all the time she would not leave. Every argument we could use, was of no avail, and we were desperate as to what course to pursue, when the shelling recommenced in a few minutes. Then mother recommenced her screams and was ready to fly any where, and holding her box of papers, with a faint idea of saving something, she picked up two dirty underskirts and an old cloak, and by dint of Miriam's vehement appeals, aided by a great deal of pulling, we got her down to the back door....

> As we stood in the door, four or five shells sailed over our heads at the same time, seeming to make a perfect corkscrew of the air—for it sounded as though it went in circles. Miriam cried never mind the door! Mother screamed anew, and I staid behind to lock the door.... We reached the back gate, that was on the street, when another shell passed us, and Miriam jumped behind the fence for protection. We had gone half a square when Dr Castleton begged of us to take another street, as they were firing up that one. We took his advice, but found our new street worse than the old, for the shells seemed to whistle their strange songs with redoubled vigor....
>
> We were alone on the road; all had run away before [us].... We passed the grave yard; we did not even stop, and about a mile and a half from home, when mother was perfectly exhausted with fatigue and unable to proceed farther, we met a gentleman in a buggy who kindly took charge of her and our bundles. We could have walked miles beyond, then, for as soon as she was safe we felt as though a load had been removed from our shoulders; and after exhorting her not to be uneasy about us, and reminding her we had a pistol and a dagger ... she drove off, and we trudged on alone, the only people in sight, on foot....
>
> We were two miles away when we sat down by the road to rest.... While we were yet resting, we saw a cart coming, and giving up all idea of our walking to Greenwell, called the people to stop. To our great delight, it proved to be a cart loaded with Mrs Brunots affairs, driven by two of her negroes, who kindly took us up with them, on the top of their baggage, and we drove off in state, as much pleased at riding in that novel place, as though we were accustomed to ride in wheelbarrows....
>
> Three miles from town we began to overtake the fugitives. Hundreds of women and children were walking along, some bare headed, and in all costumes. Little girls of twelve and fourteen years were wandering on alone. I called to one I knew, and asked where her mother was; she didn't know; she would walk until she found out. It seems her mother lost a nursing baby, too, which was not found until ten that night. White and black were all mixed together, and were as confidential as though related....
>
> The negroes deserve the greatest praise for their conduct. Hundreds were walking with babies, or bundles; ask them what they had saved, it was invariably "My mistress's clothes, or silver, or baby." Ask what they had for themselves, it was "Bless your heart, honey, I was glad to get away with mistress things; I didn't think 'bout mine."
>
> It was a heart-rending scene. Women searching for their babies along the road, where they had been lost, others sitting in the dust crying and wringing their hands, for by this time, we had not an idea but what Baton Rouge was either in ashes, or being plundered, and we had saved nothing.[13]

The guns of the two ships finally ceased fire, and when they did, three Baton Rouge citizens rowed out to the *Hartford* and apologized for the shooting by the guerrillas, saying the people of Baton Rouge had no control over them. Farragut promised he would not fire on the city again unless his men were again fired on and that, if possible, he would give warning before commencing fire. Sarah Morgan, returning home after the ceasefire, wrote her comments:

> It seems the only thing that saved the town, was two gentlemen who rowed out to the ships, and informed the illustrious commander that there were no men to be hurt, and he was only killing women and children. The answer was "he was sorry he had hurt them; he thought of course the town had been evacuated before the men were fools enough to fire on them, and had only shelled the principal streets to intimidate the people!" Those streets, were the very ones crowded with flying women, which they must have seen with their own eyes....
>
> As to the firing, four guerillas were rash enough to fire on a yawl which was about to land, with out a flag of truce, killing one, wounding three, one of whom afterwards died. They were the only ones in town, there was not a cannon in our hands, even if a dozen

men could be collected, and this cannonading was kept up in return for half a dozen shots from as many rifles, with out even a show of resistance after!

So ended the momentous shelling of Baton Rouge, during which the valiant Faragut killed one whole woman, wounded three, struck some twenty houses several times a piece, and indirectly caused the death of two little children who were drowned in their flight, one poor little baby that was born in the woods, and several case[s] of the same kind, besides those who will yet die from the fatigue, as Mrs W.D. Phillips who had not left her room since January, who was carried out in her night gown, and is now supposed to be in a dying condition.... There were many similar cases. Hurrah for the illustrious Farragut, the "Woman Killer!!!"[15]

The fire from the Union vessels left many of the houses along the river pecked or pierced by shot. Among the most heavily damaged structures were the Catholic church and the castlelike state capitol.

On May 29, the morning after the shelling, the transports bearing the troops of General Williams arrived, and Farragut ordered Williams to put them ashore with several pieces of artillery to ward off a possible attack on the city by guerrillas. That done, Farragut posted two of his gunboats opposite Baton Rouge to support General Williams and then left for New Orleans with the remainder of his fleet. Williams instituted strict regulations to keep Baton Rouge under control, requiring residents to be issued a pass before they could leave the city and granting passes only to those who sought to bring home family members who had fled the bombardment. Guards were posted at every corner of the city, and daily patrols searched nearby areas for guerrillas.

When Farragut returned to New Orleans on May 30, he found orders from Washington, three copies of them, sent on three different ships, awaiting him. Assistant Secretary of the Navy Fox told him that President Lincoln had given the capture of Vicksburg the highest priority and that he, Farragut, was to make it his urgent business to take Vicksburg and open the Mississippi, as the president desired. Clearly exasperated, Farragut expressed his feelings in another letter home:

> They will keep us in this river until the vessels break down and all the little reputation we have made has evaporated. The Government appears to think that we can do anything. They expect me to navigate the Mississippi nine hundred miles in the face of batteries, ironclad rams, etc., and yet with all the ironclad vessels they have North they could not get to Norfolk or Richmond.... Well, I will do my duty to the best of my ability, and let the rest take care of itself.... They can not deprive me and my officers of the historical fact that we took New Orleans. Now they expect impossibilities.[16]

As for Assistant Secretary of the Navy Fox, he was telling Flag Officer Farragut, "The only anxiety we feel is to know if you have followed up your instructions and pushed a strong force up the river to meet the Western flotilla,"[17] meaning Flag Officer Davis's force, which at that time had not yet taken Memphis. In his reply to Fox, Farragut showed something of his feelings about the difficulties, but ended up saying he would do what he could to accomplish the objective:

> I had no conception that the Department ever contemplated that the ships of this squadron were to attempt to go to Memphis, above which the Western flotilla then was; nor did I believe it was practicable for them to do so, unless under the most favorable circumstances, in time of peace, when their supplies could be obtained along the river. The gunboats are nearly all so damaged that they are certainly not in condition to contend with ironclad rams coming down upon them with the current....
>
> I arrived in New Orleans with five or six days' provisions and one anchor, and am now

trying to procure others. As soon as provisions and anchors are obtained we will take our departure for up the river, and endeavor to carry out, as far as practicable, the orders conveyed in your different dispatches.[18]

General Butler offered more troops to storm Vicksburg's heights, provided Commander David Porter brought up his mortar boats to soften up the fortifications and knock out the guns that were beyond the reach of Farragut's gunboats. The mortar boats were then at Pensacola, and it took till June 9 for them to reach New Orleans. Then it took till June 20 for them to be towed upriver and positioned to commence their bombardment. The next day, June 21, the sixteen mortar boats opened fire with their mammoth artillery, raining shells down on the rebel batteries atop the bluff. Porter described the assault and the Confederates' nearly impregnable position:

> The [Confederate] soldiers in the hill forts refused to stay shelled out, and when the mortars stopped playing on them they would come back from the fields and again open fire. It was not here as at Fort Jackson, where the besieged were cooped up in casemates with bricks and mortar all around, where a shell in falling would displace huge masses of masonry, dealing death and destruction to the garrison. The fortifications of Vicksburg were scattered over the hills in groups, the guns fifty yards apart, and concealed from view. The heavy shells would whistle over the ships, throwing up the water in spouts and occasionally crashing through the vessels' timbers....
>
> The whole power of the Confederacy had been set to work to save this Gibraltar of the Mississippi, the railroads poured in troops and guns without stint, enabling it to bid defiance to Farragut's ships and the mortar flotilla.
>
> There was an area of twenty-eight square miles within which the Federals might throw all the shot and shells they pleased. The Confederates did not mind it much, even when the shots fell in the city. This was their last ditch, so far as the Mississippi was concerned, and here they were determined to make a final stand.
>
> Farragut could only obey his orders and effect a junction with Flag-officer Davis above the city, and they pummeled away to their hearts' content with shells and mortars for many days, with little effect....
>
> It was evident enough that Vicksburg could only be taken after a long siege by the combined operations of a large military and naval force.[19]

Farragut's fleet had been standing in the river since June 25, waiting to make the move past Vicksburg's fortifications. The vessels included the transports that were carrying three thousand troops under the command of General Williams, who had left a token security force in Baton Rouge and, reinforced by more of Butler's troops from New Orleans, had joined the Vicksburg expedition. The troops' first mission had been to dig a canal, with substantial help from slave labor, across the salient created by the Mississippi River's hairpin turn at De Soto Point, above Vicksburg, aiming to divert the flow of the river into the shortcut channel, which would transform Vicksburg into an inland city and its fortifications into relics. That mission failed when the river fell so low that its waters could not be diverted into the newly dug canal.

By June 28, Farragut knew that Lieutenant Colonel Alfred Ellet and three of his rams had reached De Soto Point, above Vicksburg. Ellet had been in communication with him, messages being carried across the narrow tongue of land that separated them, now occupied by Williams's troops. Farragut by then had also learned that the Ellet rams and Davis's gunboats had destroyed the Confederate ram fleet at Memphis and had taken that city on June 6. The linking with the fleet from the upper Mississippi, so urgently sought by Washington, lay just around that hairpin turn above Vicksburg, and Farragut now determined he would run past the rebel guns and effect a meeting.

In the early-morning darkness of June 28, at two A.M., signal lights aboard the flagship were hoisted on its mast, and ten warships of Farragut's fleet — the *Hartford*, *Richmond* and *Brooklyn*, the big ships, and the gunboats *Iroquois*, *Oneida*, *Wissahickon*, *Sciota*, *Winona*, *Pionola* and *Kennebec*—formed into two columns to begin moving upstream in their pre-arranged order, later joined by the gunboat *Katahdin*.

At four A.M., once Farragut's vessels had passed the mortar boats' position, Porter's mortars resumed fire, and the vessels that had towed the mortar boats opened with their guns, blasting the rebel fortification with a hellish bombardment. The rebel guns, now numbering twenty-nine, quickly responded, opening up against the slowly moving targets, shadowy shapes trudging against the current, through the darkness and the clouds of gunsmoke, firing steadily as they went. Bonfires were lighted by the Confederates to illuminate the river, muzzle flashes and brilliant shell bursts providing the only other brightness in the night.

The Union vessels were struck repeatedly by the rebels' fire, but many of the fortification's shells merely crashed into the vessels' rigging or fell harmlessly into the river, the result of too much or too little elevation of the rebel guns. None of the vessels were sunk or seriously damaged. Palmer, commander of the *Iroquois*, leading the formation, described the onslaught of fire: "We so fought our way up, running close into the town, having a raking fire from the fort above and a plunging fire from the batteries on the hill, together with broadsides from the cannon planted in the streets, and, what is strange, through all this heavy concentrated fire, with the exception of the cutting away both our mainstays, and some other immaterial damage to the rigging, we escaped without injury."[20]

Richard Wainwright, commander of the *Hartford*, reported, "We were under fire about one hour and a half, receiving it on the broadside, and being raked ahead and astern.... We are much cut up, both in hull and rigging."[21] The commander of the *Wissahickon*, Commander John DeCamp, reported, "The action continued for one hour, during which the "Wissahickon" received four shots. Our port main rigging was shot away, and an eight-inch shell struck the vessel at the water line, entering the berth-deck, where it killed one man and wounded all the men stationed to pass shot and powder on that deck."[22]

Except for the *Brooklyn*, the *Kennebec* and the *Katahdin*, all of Farragut's vessels had passed the fortifications by six A.M. and had anchored above Vicksburg, and at that hour Farragut was meeting with Colonel Ellet. The passing had taken the lives of seven of Farragut's men and had wounded thirty. Porter's vessels suffered two killed and six wounded. Announcing his dubious success, Farragut wired Secretary Welles:

> Sir — I passed up the river this morning, but to no purpose; the enemy leave their guns for the moment, but return as soon as we have passed, and rake us. Our loss, as far as ascertained, is not very great. Commander Porter shelled them two days to get his ranges, and all his vessels entered into the attack with great spirit, and did excellent service. The fire of the ships was tremendous. The "Brooklyn," "Kennebec," and "Katahdin" did not get past the batteries. I do not know why.[23]
>
> I am satisfied it is not possible for us to take Vicksbug without an army force of 12,000 or 15,000 men. General Van Dorn's division is here, and lies safely behind the hills. The water is too low for me to go over twelve or fifteen miles above Vicksburg.
> Very respectfully, your obedient servant,
> D.G. Farragut,
> *Commanding Western Gulf Squadron*[24]

Seven days later Farragut sent Welles a more detailed report, which repeated his contention that Vicksburg could only be taken by the deployment of a sizeable army:

Sir — In obedience to the orders of the department and the command of the President, I proceeded back to Vicksburg with the "Brooklyn," "Richmond" and "Hartford," with the determination to carry out my instructions to the best of my ability....

The Department will perceive from this (my) report that the forts can be passed, and we have done it, and can do it again as often as may be required of us. It will not, however, be an easy matter for us to do more than silence the batteries for a time, as long as the enemy has a large force behind the hills to prevent our landing and holding the place....

It gives me great pleasure to say that General Williams, Colonel Ellet, and the army officers of the division generally, have uniformly shown a great anxiety to do everything in their power to assist us; but their force is too small to attack the town, or for any other purpose than a momentary assault to spike guns, should such an opportunity offer.[25]

Colonel Ellet offered to have one of his rams take to Memphis any messages that Flag Officer Farragut would like dispatched, and Farragut quickly accepted the offer. He sent a note to General Halleck, who had recently occupied Corinth, Mississippi, and asked him for troops for an assault on Vicksburg. He also sent a note to Flag Officer Davis, asking him to bring his gunboats to Vicksburg. Halleck answered on July 3: "The scattered and weakened condition of my forces renders it impossible for me, at the present, to detach any troops to co-operate with you on Vicksburg. Probably I shall be able to do so as soon as I can get my troops more concentrated; this may delay the clearing of the river, but its accomplishment will be certain in a few weeks. Allow me to congratulate you on your great success."

Davis, however, swiftly complied with Farragut's request, leaving for Vicksburg at once. On July 1, as Farragut's vessels still lay in the river on the west side of De Soto Point, Davis arrived with all available vessels of his fleet, including four mortar boats. He had suffered the loss of the gunboat *Mound City* in an attack on a Confederate battery at St. Charles, Arkansas, on the White River. A shell had exploded the vessel's boiler, and 103 of the officers and crew were killed or missing, and thirty-eight were wounded, one of the heaviest losses incurred by a Navy vessel during the war.[26]

Ellet's rams had also been busy since their battle at Memphis. Ellet had been probing the Yazoo River, which enters the Mississippi about four miles above Vicksburg, hunting for the Confederate ironclad ram *Arkansas*, reported to be under construction at Yazoo City and nearing completion. Hence Ellet was already in the vicinity of Vicksburg, within the sound of the guns, when Farragut's vessels ran past the fortifications.

Now, as Farragut's and Porter's vessels continued to pound away at the rebel position, a task at which they were joined by Davis's newly arrived mortars, came the first sign that in Washington, the reports from Farragut and Porter and others having been read and absorbed, the urgency of taking Vicksburg had slackened. On July 6 Secretary Welles wired Farragut with orders to send Porter and twelve of his sixteen mortar boats to Hampton Roads right away. More important than Vicksburg at the moment was General McClellan's peninsula campaign to capture Richmond, which suddenly had taken a frightening turn for the worse, since General Robert E. Lee had assumed command of the Confederate forces. Porter's mortars were apparently needed immediately to help stave off a disaster.

The Union campaign to capture the Mississippi, after so many early, quick successes, had stalled. Vicksburg would have to wait.

19. The Arkansas vs. the U.S. Navy

The two fleet commanders, Flag Officer Farragut and Flag Officer Davis, were having a hard time believing the Confederates were capable of building and putting into action the sort of ship the *Arkansas* was rumored to be, and so on the night of July 14 they listened doubtfully as two Confederate deserters, who had managed to make their way to the U.S. gunboat *Essex,* told them that the *Arkansas* was for real and that it was on its way down the Yazoo River, headed for Vicksburg, despite the presence of the Union fleets.

On the chance that the deserters' reports might be true, Farragut decided to send three boats up the Yazoo at dawn the next day. At daybreak on July 15 the hunt for the dread *Arkansas*, begun by Colonel Ellet days earlier, resumed. The wooden gunboat *Tyler*, the unarmed Ellet ram *Queen of the West* and the Eads ironclad *Carondelet* cast off from their moorings in the Mississippi and, leaving the rest of the fleets lying idle above Vicksburg, warily began steaming up the Yazoo on a mission, according to their orders, "to procure correct information concerning the obstructions and defences of the river, and ascertain if possible the whereabouts of the ram *Arkansas*."[1]

The Confederate navy had started building the *Arkansas* and its twin sister ship, the *Tennessee*, at a shipyard in Memphis in October 1861. The rebels' shortage of materials and of skilled labor had forced the builder to concentrate his efforts on one of the two vessels, and he had chosen to complete the *Arkansas* first. Even so, the work lagged because of the shortages, and construction soon fell impossibly far behind the schedule that called for completion by Christmas Eve of 1861. After Columbus and Island No. 10 fell and the River Defense Fleet was facing a last-ditch confrontation at Memphis, the Confederates had hastily burned the embryonic *Tennessee* and towed the unfinished *Arkansas* down the Mississippi and up the Yazoo, hoping to hide and protect it until it could fight for itself. They took it as far as Greenwood, Mississippi, more than 200 miles from where the Yazoo empties into the Mississippi above Vicksburg. There it sat more or less neglected, with little work done and practically no one to do the work, until late May 1862, when Confederate navy Commander Isaac N. Brown, a former U.S. Navy officer, was given the task of rushing completion of the vessel, which he would then command. He had it towed downriver to Yazoo City and put 200 workers, conscripted from nearby rebel army units, on the job of making it serviceable.

Now, six weeks later, according to the two deserters, the *Arkansas* was all but finished and was headed toward the assembled Union river fleets. A fearsome rebel weapon, the *Arkansas* was a 165-foot-long ironclad ram mounting ten guns of various sizes, three on each broadside, two at the bow and two at the stern, all enclosed in an iron-plated casemate, with a menacing iron ram fixed to its prow. It was powered by two low-pressure steam engines mounted deep in the hull, below the water line, to protect them from enemy fire, each driving one of the vessel's two screw propellers. It was capable of a speed of eight miles an hour in still water and about half that when running against the current. It was manned by a complement of officers and men that numbered about two hundred, many of whom had served on other Confederate vessels. From later information about the *Arkansas*, Commander (later Admiral) David Porter pronounced it "superior to all the *Carondelet* class of gun-boats put together."[2]

Days before the deserters gave their report, the Yazoo had begun falling, and the *Arkansas*, which drew thirteen feet of water, faced being stranded if it were not soon moved. Assured that if he acted quickly, while the river was still deep enough, he could get the vessel over or through the obstructions the rebels had placed in the river below Yazoo City to bar Union vessels from ascending the Yazoo, Commander Brown dispatched one of his officers, Lieutenant Charles W. Read, by horseback to Vicksburg to ask instructions from Major General Earl Van Dorn, then commanding the forces at Vicksburg to which President Jefferson Davis had assigned the *Arkansas*. Riding some fifty miles through the night, Read reached Van Dorn's command post about eight o'clock on the morning of July 10. Van Dorn responded by writing a letter to Brown, instructing him to descend the Yazoo, come into the Mississippi, make his way past the Union fleet above Vicksburg and proceed to the fortification, where the *Arkansas* would find protection beneath the fortification's guns. Van Dorn told Brown there were thirty-seven Union vessels within sight from Vicksburg and "plenty more up the river," but, he said in his letter, he believed that the *Arkansas* could run past them all.[3] Lieutenant Read galloped off with the general's orders. On July 11 they were in Commander Brown's hands.

On Saturday, July 12, Brown sent his carpenters and machinists ashore and took aboard the men who had transferred out of the ranks of General Thompson's artillery units to serve the guns of the *Arkansas*. Before cheering onlookers who crowded the river's edge, the *Arkansas* cast off its lines and pulled away from the dock at Yazoo City, gliding out into midstream, its Stars and Bars flying from the mast above the after end of its iron-bound casemate.

It reached the barricade the rebels had strung across the river, removed enough of the barrier to slip through it, then continued a short distance to Satartia Bar, where it tied up for the night. Commander Brown and the *Arkansas* were now less than sixty river miles from where the Union fleets lay in the Mississippi. The next day Brown had his executive officer, Lieutenant Henry K. Stevens, drill the crew so that each man knew what he was to do when the *Arkansas* engaged the enemy.

On Monday morning, July 14, as the *Arkansas* reached the spot where the Sunflower River joins the Yazoo, the first bad news came. Steam escaping from an engine and boiler had seeped into the forward magazine and dampened the store of gunpowder there, rendering it unusable. "We were just opposite the site of an old saw-mill," Brown related in his account, "where the opening in the forest, dense everywhere else, admitted the sun's rays. The day was clear and very hot; we made fast to the bank, head downstream, landed our wet powder (expecting the enemy to heave in sight every moment), spread tarpaulins over the old saw-dust and our powder over these. By constant shaking and turning we got it back to the point of ignition before the sun sank below the trees, when, gathering it up, we crowded all that we could of it into the after magazine and resumed our way, guns cast loose and men at quarters, expecting every moment to meet the enemy."[4]

To make up the time lost drying the gunpowder, the *Arkansas* continued its descent of the river into the night, not stopping till midnight, when Brown at last ordered a halt and had the boat tied up to the landing at Haines's (or Haynes's) Bluff, about eight miles from the mouth of the Yazoo. At first light the vessel was once more on the move. One of its officers, Lieutenant George W. Gift, described the scene aboard the *Arkansas* that morning:

> Many of the men had stripped off their shirts and were bare to the waists, with handkerchiefs bound round their heads, and some of the officers had removed their coats and stood in their undershirts. The decks had been thoroughly sanded to prevent slipping after the blood should become plentiful. Tourniquets were served out to division officers by the surgeons, with directions for use. The division tubs were filled with water to drink; fire buckets were in place; cutlasses and pistols strapped on; rifles loaded and bayonets fixed; spare breechings for the guns, and other implements made ready. The magazines and shell-rooms forward and aft were open, and the men inspected in their places. Before getting underway, coffee (or an apology thereof) had been served to the crew, and daylight found us a grim, determined set of fellows, grouped about our guns, anxiously waiting to get sight of the enemy.[5]

Standing with Lieutenant Stevens atop the forward end of the casemate, between the low pilothouse and the smokestack, Commander Brown, squinting, could see ahead in the bright sunlight three black plumes of smoke rising into the air a few miles in the distance. He could make out three steamers, abreast of each other, headed toward the *Arkansas*.

The *Carondelet*, in the center of the formation, with the *Queen of the West* and the *Tyler* flanking it, had arrived. They had found the great rebel ram and were steaming toward it.

Brown now called his officers together, and they huddled around him as he spoke final words in anticipation of the impending engagement: "Gentlemen, in seeking the combat as we now do, we must win or perish. Should I fall, whoever succeeds to this command will do so with the resolution to go through the enemy's fleet, or go to the bottom. Should they carry us by boarding, the *Arkansas* must be blown up. On no account must she fall into the hands of the enemy." He then dismissed them with the command, "Go to your guns!"[6]

Brown's orders were for the gunners not to fire the bow guns, lest the boat's speed be diminished by the effects. Brown was, he said, "relying for the moment upon our broadside guns to keep the ram and the *Tyler* from gaining our quarter, which they seemed eager to do."[7] He ordered the pilot, John Hodges, to aim the *Arkansas* straight at the ironclad *Carondelet*, which was captained by Commander Henry Walke, with whom Brown had been friends in what Brown called "the old navy." The two officers had been messmates on a voyage around the world. Brown had decided now to try to ram the *Carondelet* as it steadily approached, but when the distance between the two vessels closed to about half a mile, the *Carondelet* fired one round from its bow gun, a shot that came nowhere close to its target, then backed around and hurried downriver, bow first, a burst of speed immediately lengthening the distance between it and the *Arkansas*.

The *Queen of the West* promptly followed *Carondelet*'s maneuver, turning about and hastening downstream. The *Tyler*, commanded by Lieutenant William Gwin, reversed its engines and began backing downstream, firing its bow guns as it retreated, but when Gwin saw that the *Arkansas* was rapidly gaining on him, he turned the *Tyler* about and fled bow first. The *Tyler* took a position on the *Carondelet*'s port bow, Lieutenant Gwinn reported, "about one hundred yards distant, keeping up a continuous fire on the ram from our stern gun, and an occasional fire from our broadside battery, the *Carondelet* having already opened on the ram with her stern guns."[8]

Gradually the *Arkansas* gained on the *Carondelet*, even while zig-zagging to spoil the aim of the *Tyler*'s guns. "While our shot seemed always to hit his stern and disappear," Brown reported, "his missiles, striking our inclined shield, were deflected over my head and lost in air. I received a severe contusion on the head, but this gave me no concern after I had failed to find any brains mixed with the handful of clotted blood which I drew from the wound and examined."[9]

Moments later a shot from the *Tyler* landed near Brown's feet, pierced the pilothouse, took off the top half of the boat's wheel, mortally wounded the chief pilot and severely wounded the vessel's Yazoo River pilot, J.H. Shacklett. The pilothouse debris was quickly cleared away, and James Brady, a Mississippi River pilot whom Brown called "a Missourian of nerve and equal to the duty," grabbed the fractured wheel and followed Brown's order, "Keep the ironclad ahead!"[10]

"All was going well," Brown recounted, "with a near prospect of carrying out my first intention of using the ram, this time at a great advantage, for the stern of the *Carondelet* was now the objective point, and she seemed to be going slow and unsteady. Unfortunately the *Tyler* also slowed, so as to keep near his friend, and this brought us within easy range of his small-arms."[11] The *Tyler* had aboard a detachment of sharpshooters from the Fourth Wisconsin Infantry Regiment, and they opened up with a volley from their rifles. "I was near the hatchway at the moment when a minie-ball, striking over my left temple, tumbled me down among the guns," Brown recalled. "I awoke as if from sleep, to find kind hands helping me to a place among the killed and wounded. I soon regained my place on the shield [the armored casemate]."[12]

Back atop the casemate, Brown could see that the *Arkansas* had drawn closer to the *Carondelet*. At a one-hundred-yard distance, Lieutenant Gift, at the *Arkansas*'s bow guns, could see a gunner loading a gun at the stern port on the *Carondelet*. "I pointed the Columbiad for that port and pulled the lock-string. I have seen nothing of the man or gun since."[13] Both vessels were nearing the shoals where willow trees grew up from a bar near the shore on the *Arkansas*'s port side, and Brown grew wary. "To have run into the mud, we drawing 13 feet (the *Carondelet* only 6)," he commented, "would have ended the matter with the *Arkansas*."[14] He correctly guessed that the *Carondelet* had gone that close to shore because it had suffered disabling damage to its steering apparatus, rendering it *hors de combat*.

"Our wheel ropes were cut off for a third time," the *Carondelet*'s commander reported, "and we had to run the boat into shore. As she swung round, we gave the rebel vigorous discharges from our bow and starboard guns.... We had now received severe damages in our hull and machinery, more than twenty shots having entered the boat.... We had some thirty killed, wounded and missing."[15]

Off the *Arkansas*'s starboard bow, in the river's deep water, Commander Brown could see the *Tyler* and *Queen of the West* seemingly waiting to discover whether the *Arkansas* would run aground. Brown disappointed them. Disengaging from the *Carondelet*, he fired one last salvo at it before pursuing the two other vessels. "Hard a-port, and depress port guns!" he shouted, and moments later the *Arkansas* let loose a point-blank broadside, blasting the crippled *Carondelet* and rocking it so severely that the port side of its deck dipped underwater as the boat heeled over, then righted itself.

It was then about seven-thirty A.M., some thirty minutes since the three Union vessels had first discovered the *Arkansas*. Now the rebel ram turned away from the *Carondelet* and headed for the *Tyler*, about two hundred yards away.

"We then stood down the river at all speed," the *Tyler*'s log reads, "and managed to keep the ram from two hundred to three hundred yards distant from us, keeping up a rapid fire from our stern gun and an occasional discharge from our broadside batteries as we could bring them to bear, receiving the fire of her two bow guns, and occasional discharges from her broadside batteries."[16]

As the chase proceeded and the firing continued, a crewman aboard the *Arkansas*, curious to see what was happening, stuck his head out of a broadside gun port just as a shot from the *Tyler*, missing the ram's shield by inches, whistled past the port, decapitating the crewman. Lieutenant Stevens, standing nearby, feared that the gruesome sight of the headless, bloody corpse might demoralize the gun crew at that station. He rushed forward to lift the body and throw it out the port and asked the man nearest to him to help him. "I can't do it, sir!" the crewman replied. "It's my brother!" The body was thrown overboard nevertheless.[17]

Unable to close the distance between it and the fleeing Union boats, the *Arkansas* fell about thirty minutes behind the *Tyler* as the pursuit took all three vessels to the mouth of the Yazoo and into the broad Mississippi. Not long after entering the big river, Commander Brown discovered a serious new problem, which he described:

> On gaining the Mississippi, we saw no vessels but the two we had driven before us. While following these in the direction of Vicksburg I had the opportunity of inspecting engine and fire rooms, where I found engineers and firemen had been suffering under a temperature of 120 degrees to 130 degrees. The executive officer, while attending to every other duty during the recent firing, had organized a relief party from the men at the guns, who went down into the fire-room every fifteen minutes, the others coming up or being, in many instances, hauled up, exhausted in that time; in this way, by great care, steam was kept to service guage.... The connection between the furnaces and smoke-stack (technically called the breechings) were in this second conflict shot away, destroying the draught and letting the flames come out into the shield, raising the temperature there to 120, while it had already risen to 130 in the fire-room.... We went into action ... with 120 pounds of steam, and though every effort was made to keep it up, we came out with but 20 pounds, hardly enough to turn the engines.[18]

The *Queen of the West* and the *Tyler* came within sight of the moored fleets about eight-thirty, and fifteen minutes later *Tyler* rounded to under the stern of the *Essex*. From that position it delivered a broadside at the *Arkansas* as it ran the gantlet between the lines of Union warships, which opened streams of fire on the rebel ram. Commander Brown described the perilous run through the fleets of Farragut and Davis:

> Aided by the current of the Mississippi, we soon approached the Federal fleet — a forest of masts and smoke-stacks — ships, rams, iron-clads, and other gun-boats on the left side, and ordinary river steamers and bomb-vessels along the right.... We were not yet in sight of Vicksburg, but in every direction, except astern, our eyes rested on enemies.... It seemed at a glance as if a whole navy had come to keep me away from the heroic city.... The rams seemed to have been held in reserve, to come out between the intervals. Seeing this, as we neared the head of the line I said to our pilot, "Brady, shave that line of men-of-war as close as you can, so that the rams will not have room to gather head-way in coming out to strike us."
>
> As we neared the head of the line our bow guns, trained on the *Hartford*, began this second fight of the morning (we were yet to have a third one before the day closed), and within a few minutes, as the enemy was brought in range, every gun of the *Arkansas* was at its work.... As we advanced, the line of fire seemed to grow into a circle constantly closing. The shock of missiles striking our sides was literally continuous, and as we were now sur-

rounded, without room for anything but pushing ahead, and shrapnel shot were coming on our shield deck, twelve pounds at a time, I went below to see how our Missouri backwoodsmen [his gunners] were handling their 100-pounder Columbiads. At this moment I had the most lively realization of having steamed into a real volcano, the *Arkansas* from its center firing rapidly to every point of the circumference, without the fear of hitting a friend or missing an enemy.

I got below in time to see [Lieutenant] Read and [Midshipman] Scales with their rifled guns blow off the feeble attack of a ram on our stern. Another ram was across our way ahead. As I gave the order, "Go through him, Brady!" his steam went into the air, and his crew into the river. A shot from one of our bow guns had gone through his boiler and saved the collision....

I sought a cooler atmosphere on the shield, to find, close ahead and across our way, a large iron-clad displaying the square flag of an admiral [Davis's flagship, the *Benton*]. Though we had but little head-way, his beam was exposed, and I ordered the pilot to strike him amidships. He avoided this by steaming ahead, and, passing under his stern, nearly touching, we gave him our starboard broadside, which probably went through him from rudder to prow. This was our last shot, and we received none in return.

We were now at the end of what had seemed the interminable line.... I now called the officers up to take a look at what we had just come through and to get fresh air; and as the little group of heroes closed around me with their friendly words of congratulation, a heavy rifle-shot passed close over our heads; it was the parting salutation, and if aimed two feet lower would have been to us the most injurious of the battle. We were not yet in sight of Vicksburg, but if any of the fleet followed us farther on our way I did not perceive it.[19]

When the *Arkansas* came into view of the Union vessels lying below the fortification, sudden panic broke out. Vessels scurried to get out of the way of the seemingly invincible rebel ram. A mortar boat that had run aground was set aflame to avoid capture, and Union troops encamped near the river bank piled up their supplies and set fire to them, then boarded transports that quickly bore them away, fleeing downstream (only to return later when it became obvious the rebel ram was not going to attack them then).

At eight-fifty A.M. the embattled *Arkansas* at last reached the Vicksburg wharf and tied up. Its successful run past the Union fleets had come at a price, paid in both blood and heroism, some of which was described by Lieutenant Gift:

Some one called out that the colors had been shot away. It reached the ear of Midshipman Dabney M. Scales, and in an instant the glorious fellow scrambled up the ladder which was being swept by a hurricane of shot and shell, deliberately bent on the colors again, knotted the halyards and hoisted them up, and when they were again knocked away would have replaced them had not he been forbidden by the captain.

Midshipman Clarence Tyler, aide to the captain, was wounded at his post alongside the captain. We were passing one of the large sloops-of-war when a heavy shot struck the side abreast of my bow-gun, the concussion knocking over a man who was engaged in taking a shot from the rack. He rubbed his hip, which had been hurt, and said they would "hardly strike twice in a place." He was mistaken, poor fellow, for immediately a shell entered the breach made by the shot, and bedding itself in the cotton-bale lining on the inside of the bulwark proper, exploded with terrible effect. I found myself standing in a dense, suffocating smoke, with my cap gone and hair and beard singed. The smoke soon cleared away, and I found but one man (Quartermaster Curtis) left. Sixteen were killed and wounded by that shell, and the ship set on fire. Stevens, ever cool and thoughtful, ran to the engine-room hatch, seized the hose and dragged it to the aperture. In a few moments the fire was extinguished....

We got through, hammered and battered, though. Our smoke-stack resembled an immense nutmeg-grater, so often had it been peppered. A shot had broken our cast-iron ram. Another had demolished a hawse-pipe. Our boats were shot away and dragging....

A great heap of mangled and ghastly slain lay on the gun-deck, with rivulets of blood running away from them. There was a poor fellow torn asunder, another mashed flat, whilst in the "slaughter-house" brains, hair and blood were all about. Down below fifty or sixty wounded were groaning and complaining, or courageously bearing their ills without a murmur.[20]

Concluding his report of the *Arkansas*'s terrible success, Gift depicted the scene at the close of the drama: "All the army stood on the hills to see us round the point. The flag had been set up on a temporary pole, and we went out to return the cheers the soldiers gave us as we passed. The generals came on board to embrace our captain, bloody, yet game."[21]

On that same day, July 15, when all was done, Commander Brown wired a succinct report to the Confederate navy secretary, Stephen Mallory:

VICKSBURG, MISS., July 15, 1862.

To Hon. S.R. Mallory:

We engaged to-day from 6 to 8 A.M. with the enemy's fleet above Vicksburg, consisting of four or more iron-clad vessels, two heavy sloops-of-war, four gunboats, and seven or eight rams. We drove one iron-clad vessel ashore, with colors down and disabled, blew up a ram, burned one vessel, and damaged several others. Our smoke-stack was so shot to pieces that we lost steam, and could not use our vessel as a ram. We were otherwise cut up, as we engaged at close quarters. Loss, ten killed, fifteen wounded, and others with slight wounds.

ISAAC N. BROWN,
Lieut.-Commanding[22]

When the New York *Herald* published its report of the engagement, it included this table showing the losses of the Union fleets and the shots received from the *Arkansas*[23]:

	Killed	Wounded	Shots Received
Carondelet	5	20	20
Tyler	8	16	14
Lancaster	18	10	1
Benton	1	3	6
Sumter	0	0	12
Champion	0	0	3
Dickey	0	0	3
Great Western	0	0	1
Farragut's Fleet	10	20	13

From Flag Officer Farragut the news of the *Arkansas*'s nearly unbelievable feat was reported to the U.S. Navy Department "with deep mortification." According to one account, Farragut proposed launching an immediate, all-out attack to sink or capture the *Arkansas* where it lay beneath the fortification's guns. Davis talked him out of that, pointing out the dangers of approaching the fortification in daylight, and Farragut, consulting with his chief officers, agreed to a nighttime assault, to be executed on the evening of the 15th.[24] An eyewitness Union account records the *Arkansas*'s third battle with vessels of the Union fleet that day:

> The fleet of Commodore Davis accordingly took up a station at about dark, and opened on the batteries to draw their fire. They succeeded admirably, and at an unexpected moment the fleet of large vessels struck into the channel and descended the river. As each boat arrived opposite the *Arkansas* she slackened and poured her broadside into her. She answered as well as she could in such a storm of missiles, and put one or two balls into our

vessels, but her main occupation was to be still and take it. Upwards of a hundred guns, some of them throwing ten-inch shots, poured their deadly charges into her....

The roar of guns was like an earthquake, and nothing more terrific ever was conceived than this grand artillery duel by night. It lasted an hour, and then our vessels passed below and took up their old anchorage.

In the morning messengers were despatched to see what damage the *Arkansas* had sustained. By going up the opposite bank of the river, she could be plainly seen. Two battles, such as no boat in the world ever went through before, had failed to demolish her.[25]

Lieutenant Gift then reported what the Union observers could not see from the outside:

The *Hartford* stood close in to the bank, and as we spit out our broadside at her, she thundered back with an immense salvo. Our bad luck had not left us. An eleven-inch shot pierced our side a few inches above the water-line, and passed through the engine-room, killing two men outright (cutting them both in two) and wounding six or eight others. The medicines of the ship were dashed into the engine-room, and the debris from the bulkheads and splinters from the side enveloped the machinery....

The great ships with their towering spars came sweeping by, pouring out broadside after broadside, whilst the batteries from the hills, the mortars from above and below, and the iron-clads, kept the air alive with hurtling missiles....

We had more dead and wounded, another hole through our armor and heaps of splinters and rubbish. Three separate battles had been fought, and we retired to anything but easy repose. One of our messmates in the ward-room (a pilot) had asserted at supper that he would not again pass through the ordeal of the morning for the whole world. His mangled body, collected in pieces was now on the gun-deck; another had been sent away to the hospital with a mortal hurt. The steerage mess was about four or five members, whilst on the berth-deck many poor fellows would never again range themselves about the mess-cloth.[26]

When the morning sun revealed that the *Arkansas* was still afloat, relatively uninjured and with its steam up, the Union mortar boats below and above the fortification diverted their massive artillery from the bluffs and city of Vicksburg to the impudent rebel ram, blasting from their monstrous maws thirteen-inch, two-hundred-pound shells that they could hurl two and a half miles.

Commander Brown frequently shifted the *Arkansas*'s mooring below the fortification to keep the mortars' gun crews repeatedly replotting their target's range. "For seven days and nights," Brown reported, "the huge shells were lobbed toward the ironclad, but in time, we became accustomed to this shelling, but not to the idea that it was without danger; and I know of no more effective way of curing a man of the weakness of thinking that he is without the feeling of fear, than for him, on a dark night, to watch two or three of these double-fused descending shells, all near each other, and seeming as though they would strike him between the eyes."[27]

Unwilling to passively endure the bombardment, the *Arkansas*'s commander on July 18 ordered its mooring lines cast off and took the limping vessel upriver to answer the mortar boats with fire from its own guns. Although the mortar boats were protected by Flag Officer Davis's ironclads, each with armament superior to that of the *Arkansas*, the mortar boats were swiftly taken in tow and hustled farther up the river when the rebel ram was seen approaching at a distance. One of the *Arkansas*'s engines then failed, which caused the vessel to veer to one side and make a complete circle in the middle of the river before it could, with the aid of the Mississippi's current, hobble back to its moorings, the chase of its quarry abandoned.

None of the mortar rounds struck the *Arkansas*. On July 21, after all attempts to hammer it to pieces with mortar fire had proved futile, and while repairs were continuing and the *Arkansas*'s officers and crew were healing from wounds and a rash of illnesses, Farragut met with Flag Officer Davis and Commander William D. Porter, commander of the gunboat *Essex* (and brother of Commander David Porter), in a council of war to plot a new assault on the intrepid rebel ram. They devised a plan and on the morning of July 22 put it into action.

Davis's fleet got under way at four A.M. and when within range, began to bombard the fortification's upper batteries. At the same time, following the plan, the vessels below the fortification, under Farragut's command, moved out and attacked the lower batteries. The *Essex* then pushed ahead on the east side of the river, aiming to strike the rebel ram and blast it with cannon fire, then drop down the river to where the lower fleet lay. Behind the *Essex* was the *Queen of the West*, the two vessels fast approaching the *Arkansas* in a concerted attack. Lieutenant Gift, who was aboard the *Arkansas*, waiting with his gun crew as the two Union boats came at them, later recounted the engagement:

> On the morning of the 22d of July, a week after our arrival, as we awakened early in the morning by the drum calling us to quarters, great commotion was observed in the fleet above. Everything seemed under way again, and it was evident that we were soon to have another brush. On our decks were not men enough to man two guns, and not firemen enough to keep steam up if we were forced into the stream! ... We were moored to the bank, head up the river, as a matter of course. The fires under the boilers were hastened, and every possible preparation made for resistance.
>
> In a few minutes we observed the iron-clad steamer *Essex* ... steaming around the point and steering for us. The upper battery [of the fortification] opened, but she did not reply. Grimball unloosed his Columbiad, but she did not stop. I followed, hitting her fair, but still she persevered in sullen silence. Her plan was to run into and shove us aground, when her consort, the *Queen of the West*, was to follow and butt a hole in us.... On she came like a mad bull, nothing daunted or overawed. As soon as Capt. Brown got a fair view of her, followed at a distance by the *Queen*, he divined her intent, and seeing that she was as square across the bow as flat boat or scow, and we were as sharp as a wedge, he determined at once to foil her tactics.
>
> Slacking off the hawser which held our head to the bank, he went ahead on the starboard screw, and thus our sharp prow was turned directly to her to hit against. This disconcerted the enemy and destroyed his plan. A collision would surely cut him down and leave us uninjured....
>
> The two Columbiads had been ringing on his front and piercing him every shot; to which he did not reply until he found that the shoving game was out of the question; then, and when not more than fifty yards distant, he triced up his three port bow shutters and poured out his fire. A nine-inch shot struck our armor a few inches forward of the unlucky forward port, and crawling along the side entered. Seven men were killed outright and six wounded. Splinters flew in all directions.
>
> In an instant the enemy was alongside, and his momentum was so great that he ran aground a short distance astern of us. As he passed we poured out our port broadside, and as soon as the stern rifles could be cleared of the splinters and broken stanchions and wood-work, which had been driven the whole length of the gun box, we went ahead on our port screw and turned our stern guns on him, every man — we had but seventeen left — and officer went to them. As he passed he did not fire; nor did he whilst we were riddling him close aboard. His only effort was to get away from us. He backed hard on his engines and finally got off; but getting a shot in his machinery just as he got afloat, he was compelled to float down stream and join the lower fleet, which he accomplished without damage from batteries on the hills.

He fired only the three shots mentioned. But *our* troubles were not over. We had scarcely shook this fellow off before we were called to the other end of the ship — we ran from one gun to another to get ready for a second attack. The *Queen* was now close to us, evidently determined to ram us. The guns had been fired and were now empty and inboard. Somehow we got them loaded and run out, and by the time she commenced to round to, I am not sure, but I think we struck her with the Columbiads as she came down, but at all events the broadside was ready.

Capt. Brown adopted the plan of turning his head to her also, and thus received her blow glancing. She came into us going at an enormous speed, probably fifteen miles an hour, and I felt pretty sure that our hour had come. I had hoped to blow her up with the thirty-two pounder as she passed, but the gun being an old one, with an enlarged vent, the primer drew out without igniting the charge. One of the men — we had no regular gun's crews then, every man was expected to do ten men's duty — replaced it and struck it with a compressing lever ... and the shot went through his cylinder timbers without disabling him.

His blow, though glancing, was a heavy one. His prow, or beak, made a hole through our side and caused the ship to careen, and roll heavily; but we all knew in an instant that no serious damage had been done, and we redoubled our efforts to cripple him so that he could not again attempt the experiment. As did the *Essex*, so he ran into the bank astern of us, and got the contents of the stern battery; but being more nimble than she, was sooner off into deep water. Returning up stream he got our broadside guns again, and we saw that he had no disposition to engage us further....

Beating off these two vessels, under the circumstances, was the best achievement of the *Arkansas*.... We were left to our fate, and if we had been lost it would have been no unusual or unexpected thing.[28]

While the *Essex*, as Gift reported it, "was drifting down stream unmanageable," the *Queen of the West*, having survived the barrages of the *Arkansas*, was racing to safety upstream while absorbing the fire of the rebels' shore guns. When it arrived to rejoin the fleet, it was a far different boat than when it had set out on its mission. A correspondent for the New York *Tribune* described it:

The *Queen* presents a most dismantled and forlorn appearance, and is as nearly shot to pieces, for any vessel that will float, as can well be imagined. The many who have visited her since her terrible experience are with difficulty persuaded that not one of her crew was killed or dangerously wounded. She has the semblance of a complete wreck, and it will be necessary to send her North at once for repairs, though some think her injury too great for remedy — that she is not worth the mending.

Shells exploded in her cabin, shivering her furniture, crockery, and state-rooms to pieces. The wardrobe of the crew was converted into rags, and hardly a whole garment or a pair of boots or shoes can be found on the boat. She is dented and damaged, and blackened and splintered, and singed and shattered, as if she had passed through a score of the fiercest battles, and presents as good an example of the amount of injury that may be done to a boat without absolutely destroying her as it would be convenient to present, or easy to discover in twelve months' service on the flotilla.[29]

Thwarted by Butler's and Halleck's refusals to send more troops to take Vicksburg, frustrated in his attempts to destroy or capture the dangerous *Arkansas,* his fleet now running low on fuel and burdened with mounting numbers of malaria-stricken and ailing crewmen, Farragut on July 24 called off his siege of both Vicksburg and the redoubtable rebel ram, and he and his fleet shoved off toward New Orleans, leaving but one gunboat, the *Essex*, behind to patrol the nearly two hundred miles of river between Vicksburg and Baton Rouge. With Farragut's fleet went General Williams and his troops, many of them suffering from malaria, aboard their transports. A week later, on July 31, Davis and his fleet, its crewmen ailing as well, also abandoned the fight, turning upstream and heading back toward Memphis and Cairo.

The *Arkansas* remained resting beneath the guns of Vicksburg, its men and machinery trying to recuperate.

20. A Battle Too Far

John Cabell Breckinridge had been a political comer. He had the looks—tall, husky and handsome. He had a strong voice and the gift of oratory. His manner was courtly, his personality genial, and he had a knack for remembering people's names and faces. He had graduated from Centre College in Danville, Kentucky, attended the College of New Jersey (later Princeton University) and studied law at Transylvania University in Lexington, Kentucky. His father, who died when John was a child, was a politician; his grandfather, the first John Breckinridge, served in the Virginia militia during the Revolutionary War, was appointed attorney general of Kentucky, served as a United States senator from Kentucky and later became U.S. attorney general in the cabinet of President Thomas Jefferson.

During the Mexican War Breckinridge served as a major in the Third Kentucky Volunteer Regiment and in 1849, winning his first election, he became a representative in the Kentucky legislature at age twenty-eight. By then he had established a law practice in Lexington, where he and his wife, the former Mary Burch of Georgetown, Kentucky, made their home, near the Breckinridge family estate where he was born. One of his friends was the Illinois lawyer who had married his cousin—Abraham Lincoln.

In 1851, as a Democrat, Breckinridge scored a huge upset victory over his Whig opponent and won a seat in the U.S. House of Representatives, a feat that brought him to the attention of leaders in the national Democratic party. In 1856, having gained a place on the Democratic ticket with James Buchanan, he was elected vice president and at age thirty-six he became the youngest vice president in the nation's history.

Then his Southern and pro-slavery sentiments took control of his promising political career. He agreed to be the breakaway Southern Democrats' candidate for president in 1860, running against the national Democrats' candidate, Stephen A. Douglas, the Constitutional Union party's candidate, John Bell, and the Republican candidate, Abraham Lincoln. He finished third in the four-man race. He then became a U.S. senator from Kentucky, serving from March 4, 1861, until December 4, 1861, when, after he had volunteered for duty in the Confederate army, the Senate unanimously voted to expel him as a traitor who had joined the enemies of his country.

Commissioned a Confederate brigadier general, then soon promoted to major general, he served under Albert Sidney Johnston and Beauregard, commanding a corps at Shiloh. After Major General Earl Van Dorn was placed in charge of the District of the Trans-Mississippi, Department No. 2, Breckinridge and his troops were assigned to Van Dorn's command, whose mission it was, as General Beauregard pronounced it, to "hold the line of the Mississippi."[1]

There wasn't much in Van Dorn's record, though, to indicate he could do so. He was a West Pointer, a native of Mississippi who had been appointed to the academy by his great-uncle, Andrew Jackson. He graduated in 1842, in time to see action in the Mexican War, during which he served valiantly and was five times wounded. Although a bold and able leader of units up to brigade size, he had not done well with the larger commands given him in the Confederate army, commands that required talents greater than the personal courage and energy in which he abounded. He suffered two conspicuous defeats, one at Pea Ridge and one at Corinth, the latter resulting in an investigation by a court of inquiry, which ended up exonerating him of misconduct. The former he denied was a defeat. "I was not defeated," he claimed in his report to Richmond, "but only foiled in my intentions."[2] His intentions had been to make a triumphal march to St. Louis, capture it and, along with it, all the glory to be derived from a spectacular victory.

Besides his glory-seeking, he had another noticeable and troublesome weakness. Not tall—he was five-foot-five—but trim of build, dark-complexioned and elegant appearing, his wavy, black hair cut long, a dark mustache drooping beneath high cheekbones, and projecting, at age forty-one, an aura of glamour and daring, he had become something of a ladies' man, despite being married. His amorous pursuits, which some of his fellow officers considered a distraction to him, would eventually prove fatal. He was killed by a suspicious husband who gunned him down in his headquarters in Spring Hill, Tennessee, on May 7, 1863.

In the meantime, he leaped to a new opportunity for glory as soon as Farragut and Williams pulled away from Vicksburg. The seeming invincibility of the floating iron fortress, the *Arkansas*, was presenting previously unseen possibilities. Grasping for them, Van Dorn wired President Jefferson Davis, who had given him the Trans-Mississippi command: "Smokestack riddled; otherwise not materially damaged. Soon to be repaired and then, Ho! for New Orleans."[3]

The first big step in that direction, Van Dorn decided, was to Baton Rouge. Using the *Arkansas* to sweep Union gunboats from the river on the west of the city and with its guns support a ground force moving in from the east, the Confederates could smash or take prisoner General Williams's occupation army and recapture the Louisiana capital. That accomplishment would give the Confederacy domination of the Mississippi from Baton Rouge to Vicksburg, allowing the free movement of needed supplies and provisions across and up and down the river and safeguarding access from the Red River into the Mississippi—*and* it would provide a base for an assault on New Orleans by land and water.

What was more, a vigorous attack on Baton Rouge would permit Van Dorn to break out of the stagnant defensive position he had been doggedly maintaining at Vicksburg since late June. It was offense, not defense, that excited him and ignited his imagination.

Nearly as quickly as he had been issued his marching orders by Van Dorn, General Breckinridge began executing them. He loaded some four thousand troops—regiments and parts of regiments from Alabama, Tennessee, Kentucky, Mississippi and Louisiana—onto a few railroad cars at Vicksburg on July 27 and with them traveled by train to recently constructed Camp Moore, near the community of Tangipahoa, Louisiana, on the New Orleans, Jackson and Great Northern Railroad line, about seventy-five miles north of New Orleans, beyond sprawling Lake Pontchartrain, and about fifty miles northeast of Baton Rouge. The troops reached Camp Moore in the evening on July 28. There they waited for Breckinridge to receive word that the *Arkansas* was ready to join them in the attack. The wait lasted several days, while the idle troops suffered from the heat and rain and a shortage of food; and as sickness spread throughout the camp the fighting force was reduced by as many as a thousand men.

At last Breckinridge received a message saying the *Arkansas* was on its way, and he then ordered his men to begin a two-day march to a position on the Comite River at Greenwell Springs, a community about twelve miles northeast of Baton Rouge. As many as a third of the men had no boots or shoes and had to walk the sandy roads barefoot. Weakened by heat, hunger, thirst and chronic dysentery, many fell out along the way. "We had nothing to eat but roasting ears," one Kentucky soldier reported, "and these we ate raw because we had not time to stop long enough to roast them. Our command, with the horses, consumed forty acres of green corn one evening."[4] The survivors finally reached the Comite River on the afternoon of Monday, August 4, and Breckinridge let them rest, bathe and cool off in and beside the river. While they were doing so, a messenger came that evening with the news that the *Arkansas* would be in position before Baton Rouge early the next morning, ready to support Breckinridge's assault.

Commander Isaac Brown, the *Arkansas*'s captain, wounded and weary from sixty straight days of toil and trouble, had taken advantage of the break in the hostilities and the timeout for the necessary repairs to his vessel. He had requested a four-day rest-and-recreation leave in Grenada, Mississippi, which the Navy Department in Richmond granted, and with Van Dorn's permission, he had given temporary command of the *Arkansas* to Lieutenant Henry Stevens and left by train for Grenada. Almost immediately after arriving in Grenada, he was stricken by a malady that made him violently ill.

"While in bed," he recounted, "unable, as I supposed, to rise, I received a dispatch from Lieutenant Stevens saying that Van Dorn required him to steam at once down to Baton Rouge to aid in a land attack of our forces upon the Union garrison holding that place."[5] Instantly alarmed, Brown wired a quick reply to Stevens ordering him to stay at Vicksburg until Brown could get back there. He then managed to have himself taken to the Grenada train station, where, he said, "I threw myself on the mail-bags of the first passing train, unable to sit up, and did not change my position until reaching Jackson, 130 miles distant."[6]

At Jackson, while hastily making arrangements for a special train to take him to Vicksburg, some sixty miles away, he learned that he was too late. The *Arkansas* had steamed off for Baton Rouge four hours earlier. With scorn and sarcasm Brown described how the vessel's untimely departure had occurred:

> Van Dorn had been persistent beyond all reason in his demand, and Stevens, undecided, had referred the question to a senior officer of the Confederate navy, who was at Jackson, Miss., with horses and carriages, furnished by Government in place of a flag-ship, thus commanding in chief for the Confederacy on the Mississippi, sixty miles from its nearest waters.
>
> This officer, whose war record was yet in abeyance, had attained scientific celebrity by dabbling in the waters of the Dead Sea, at a time when I was engaged in the siege of Vera Cruz and in the general operations of the Mexican war. Ignorant or regardless of the condition of the *Arkansas*, fresh from Richmond on his mission of bother, not communicating with or informing me on the subject, he ordered Stevens to obey Van Dorn without any regard to my orders to the contrary.[7]

Making matters worse, the *Arkansas*'s chief engineer, George W. City, was not aboard. Exhausted and running a high fever, he was being treated in a Vicksburg hospital. Lieutenant Gift explained the significance of his absence: "His care and nursing had kept the machinery in order up to the time of leaving. We soon began to feel his loss. The engineer in charge, a volunteer from the army, had recently joined us, and though a young man of pluck and gallantry, and possessed of great will and determination to make the engines work, yet he was unequal to the task."[8] The consequences of Van Dorn's rush to action and the ineptness of Confederate navy Captain William F. Lynch — the officer derided by Brown — would soon show themselves.

On the banks of the Comite River, the ragged, tired, hungry, decimated army of General Breckinridge, now down to twenty-six hundred effectives, awaited orders. At eleven P.M. they came. The move on Baton Rouge was begun.

Marching warily through the darkness along the Greenwell Springs road, which entered Baton Rouge from the east, Breckinridge's men reached the city's eastern outskirts about four o'clock in the morning on Tuesday, August 5. A two-hundred-man troop of irregular cavalry, the Louisiana Partisan Rangers, led by Colonel Francis Pond, Jr., which had attached itself to Breckinridge's command, was assigned to scout out the roads leading into the city. As they probed, they suddenly came upon Union pickets at the outer edge of the garrison's perimeter and drew their fire, which dropped several of the rangers from their saddles. The rangers briefly returned the fire, then wheeled and raced back toward the Confederate line.

That line stretched north and south across the Greenwell Springs Road. Breckinridge had divided his force into two divisions. The First Division, commanded by Brigadier General Charles Clark, was positioned on the north side of the road to form the right side of the Confederate line. The Second Division, commanded by Brigadier General Daniel Ruggles, was placed on the south side of the road to form the left side. Clark's division comprised a brigade led by Brigadier General Benjamin Hardin Helm (brother-in-law of President Lincoln's wife) and a brigade led by Colonel T.B. Smith. Ruggles's division was composed of a brigade under Colonel A.P. Thompson and a brigade under Colonel Henry Watkins Allen. Each division included an artillery battery, positioned between the two brigades. A squadron of cavalry, led by Captain Augustus Scott, was placed on the far left to anchor the line and protect it from a flanking movement by the Union force. Two regiments and two field pieces were held in reserve, one for each of the two divisions.

At daybreak, through the wet early-morning fog, the rebel troops began moving forward on both sides of the Greenwell Springs Road. Near Ward's Creek they could hear the sound of horses thudding toward them, galloping up the dirt road. As hazy, mounted figures approached them in the fog, pounding across the Ward's Creek bridge, the Kentuckians of General Helm's units opened fire from cover behind trees and along the shoulder of the road. The horsemen were Pond's rangers, hurrying back to the Confederate line, but in the fog and dim light of dawn they went unrecognized by the advancing Kentuckians. Among the casualties of the Kentuckians' fire was twenty-three-year-old Lieutenant Alexander H. Todd, half-brother of President Lincoln's wife, who died of his wound two weeks later.

While Flag Officer Farragut had continued on to New Orleans following the Union withdrawal from the vicinity of Vicksburg, General Williams had stopped at Baton Rouge and disembarked his troops on July 26. The voyage down the river had not been uneventful. A rebel battery at Grand Gulf, Mississippi, just below Vicksburg, had fired about sixty shots at the transports, killing a private and wounding a captain, and the wooden gunboat *Kineo* had retaliated by shelling the town, after which General Williams had sent ashore four companies of the Fourth Wisconsin to break up the nearby rebel camp. In that clash one of Williams's aides was mortally wounded.

The arrival of the troops from Vicksburg had increased the Union strength at Baton Rouge to about three thousand, but about half that number were on the sick list, ailing from malaria, scurvy or exhaustion. Of the thirty-two hundred men who had gone up to Vicksburg in late June, barely eight hundred had come back fit for duty.[9]

Williams had known about the planned rebel attack since July 28, when he received a report that Breckinridge's troops had left Vicksburg bound first for Camp Moore and ultimately for Baton Rouge. He had also been noticing the movement of the city's civilian population. Many of the women and children were leaving town; others were moving into the state asylum for the deaf, near the center of the city, to seek refuge. Around two o'clock in the afternoon on August 4 he learned from several black residents of the area that the attack was imminent — Confederates were approaching in force along the Greenwell Springs road. Acting on that news, Williams put his men on alert. At three-thirty the next morning, August 5, he ordered reveille beat to call the troops into formation, then marched them to the positions where they would meet the impending rebel attack.

He had already scouted out the city and knew where he would put his troops, some of whom were already in place, living in tents. Baton Rouge was a rectangle, with its two long sides on the north and south, one short side facing east and the other short side facing the river on the west. Unsure from which direction, or directions, the rebel attackers would come, he had decided to defend all of the three sides approachable by land, leaving the river side to Farragut's gunboats to defend. Near the city's northwest corner, on the north bank of Bayou Grasse, which flowed west into the Mississippi, he put two artillery pieces of Captain Charles Manning's battery, their field of fire covering the north side of the city. Farther east and about three hundred yards south he positioned the Fourth Wisconsin Regiment and beside it, slightly to the east, he put the other guns of Manning's battery. Just east and about a hundred yards south, on the other side of Manning's guns, he placed the Ninth Connecticut.

In the northeast he positioned the Fourteenth Maine Regiment, its rear at the north side of the Greenwell Springs road. Just south and west of the Fourteenth Maine, across the road, he positioned Captain Charles Everett's artillery battery, and he placed the Twenty-first Indiana nearby but farther south, behind the gravestones of Magnolia Cemetery, and he positioned the Seventh Vermont some two hundred yards behind the Indiana regiment. Captain Ormand Nims's artillery battery was positioned to the right of Twenty-first Indiana, on the south end of the cemetery. Still farther south, where Perkins Road entered the city, west of the race track, he posted the Sixth Michigan. The Thirtieth Massachusetts, to be held in reserve, was positioned just north of the center city, near the capitol. Another battery was placed on the eastern edge of the city, on the south side of the Greenwell Springs road, and an additional battery was held in reserve. The army's main installation was the barracks in the northwest corner of the city, facing the river. The arsenal was near the river and the capitol in the city's southwest corner.

In the river, supporting the Union left flank, were the gunboats *Essex*, *Sumter* (captured from the rebels' River Defense Fleet at Memphis) and the *Cayuga*. Below them, supporting the Union right flank, were the gunboats *Kineo* and *Katahdin*.

First to move out from the Confederate formation to engage General Williams's defense was a detail led by Lieutenant Colonel Thomas Shields of the Thirtieth Louisiana Regiment. His orders were to take two companies of infantry, a company of dismounted partisan rangers and two guns from Captain Oliver Semmes's battery around to the right side of the Confederate line and, on the sound of rifle fire to his left, he was to attack the Union artillery battery believed positioned there. Shields and his men marched through the pre-dawn darkness to get into position and when they heard the rifle fire, they rushed to the supposed

Union gun emplacement. They found no guns, only the abandoned equipment of pickets who had speedily withdrawn at the sounds of firing.

The first fighting, according to one contemporary report, was between two Mississippi regiments and the Twenty-first Indiana Regiment, whose pickets were driven in by the advancing Confederates:

> As soon as the firing was heard, General Williams sent the other companies of the Twenty-first Indiana to the support of the pickets. On reaching the scene of action, they found that the enemy was in too great force to contend with successfully, upon which they fell back to the front of their tents, followed by the enemy. There they made a stand and engaged the entire brigade of General Clarke [*sic*].... The fighting at that place was very severe. The Indiana boys performed prodigies of valor and kept the enemy in check for a considerable time. General Williams, finding however, that they were too far advanced to receive support from the other regiments, ordered them to fall back, which was done to the distance of from 200 to 250 yards.[10]

Colonel Shields, meanwhile, turned his attention toward the camp of the Fourteenth Maine, whose tents he could see a few hundred yards away to the left. Taking his two artillery pieces with him, he moved cautiously down the street that led to the encamped Maine regiment, which suddenly appeared, coming forward to meet the rebel force and blocking their advance. The guns of Semmes's battery were wheeled into position and opened fire, driving the Maine troops back toward their camp. The volleys from the Maine regiment wounded four of Semmes's artillery horses, and the others balked at continuing forward, thereby stopping Shields's detachment some two hundred and fifty feet from the Maine encampment. In the face of the Maine regiment's superior numbers, Shields's men

Battle of Baton Rouge. A Confederate force led by Maj. Gen. John C. Breckinridge, a former U.S. vice president, on August 5, 1862, attempted to recapture Baton Rouge from the occupying Union garrison. In the battle, which ended in a draw, the half-brother of President Lincoln's wife, a young Confederate officer, was mortally wounded (Library of Congress).

fell back. As they did, they were mistaken for Union troops, and General Clark's regiments, advancing on the right side of the Confederate front, opened fire on them, doing but little harm, however. When the mistake was realized, Clark assigned Shields's force, including the two artillery pieces, a position at the city's northeast corner, near the road that led to Clinton, Louisiana.

Clark's main body continued its push forward, overwhelming the Fourteenth Maine and forcing it out of its encampment, driving it southwestward into the camp of the Twenty-first Indiana, on the south side of the Greenwell Springs road.

On the left side of the Confederate line General Ruggles's troops advanced through an open field, climbing over or under fences, at times forcing their way through underbrush, and ran into a line of skirmishers from the Twenty-first Indiana. From the Union line came the fire of rifles and the artillery of Captain Nims's battery. Ruggles ordered Semmes's Louisiana battery to move up and respond, which they swiftly did, firing rapid rounds of grape and canister shot against the Union guns and chasing off the Indiana skirmishers. A contemporary account offers a description of the fierce action from the Union perspective:

> Just about this time the right wing of the Union army was engaged by Colonel Allen's brigade. This wing consisted of the Sixth Michigan and Nims's battery. Simultaneous with this movement our left was attacked by Ruggles' brigade. Attached to the left wing was the Fourteenth Maine and Everett's battery.
>
> The fighting at this point was excessively severe, and the roar of battle was heard all along the line from left to right. This lasted for about twenty minutes, during which time the rebels kept their troops masked under the cover of the woods as much as possible, while the Union soldiers were exposed to their fire in the open field. Considerable inconvenience was experienced by our troops, too, in consequence of their facing to the east, which caused the looming sun to shine in their faces, rendering their operations exceedingly difficult. Still our brave troops flinched not, but manfully bore the shock of overwhelming numbers in the face of every difficulty.[11]

Colonel Thompson's brigade, of General Ruggles' division, was advancing through the cemetery when it encountered heavy fire coming from a wooded area, which stalled its movement. To its right troops from General Clark's division suddenly started falling back, and a report was spread that an order had been given for the whole rebel line to fall back. Acting on that report, Thompson ordered his men to fall back a short distance. When the troops of the Twenty-first Indiana saw some of Thompson's brigade withdrawing, they let out a raucous cheer and took off in pursuit, which so enraged the men of the Thirty-fifth Alabama and Sixth Kentucky regiments that they rushed into the path of the pursuing Indiana troops and halted their advance. In the fierce exchange of gunfire, Colonel Thompson, on his horse at the head of his troops, was severely wounded and had to be carried from the field.

Farther to the Confederate right the troops of Colonel Hunt's brigade pushed through the camp of the Fourteenth Maine, forced the Fourteenth Maine out of its fall-back position, and drove it past the position of the Seventh Vermont and into a ravine. Colonel Hunt, struck by a shot in his thigh, fell from his mount and was carried away from the action, whereupon Captain John A. Buckner took over command of the brigade and was ordered by General Clark to continue the attack on the Fourteenth Maine, which had surged forward during the lull that followed the loss of Colonel Hunt. As the rebels renewed the attack, General Clark was severely wounded, and General Breckinridge rode up to rally the troops, who let out a series of yells and turned back the charge of the Fourteenth Maine.

In the center of the two lines, where the fighting was the most furious, as the Indiana troops fell back, they came under heavy fire from their comrades in the Seventh Vermont, who mistook them for advancing Confederates. Realizing their mistake and demoralized by it, the Vermonters started retreating but were soon halted by General Williams, who berated them and ordered them forward to support the Twenty-first Indiana. Williams also directed the Thirtieth Massachusetts and two units of Nims's artillery battery to support the Sixth Michigan on the Union's far right, and the Ninth Connecticut and Fourth Wisconsin were ordered to reinforce the harassed Twenty-first Indiana. In the continuing fury of the engagement, General Williams was shot in the chest and instantly killed. Colonel G.T. Roberts of the Seventh Vermont was critically wounded in the neck. On the death of General Williams, Colonel N.A.M. Dudley assumed command of the entire Union force.

In the early hours of fighting, the Union troops' efforts were supported by fire from Farragut's gunboats; then, as the two sides drew closer to each other, the gunboats ceased firing, later resuming as the fight grew more desperate. Those early sounds of the U.S. Navy's guns were General Breckinridge's first notice that something had happened to the *Arkansas*, whose help he had counted on. The correspondent covering the battle from the Union side reported the action of the gunboats, free from the *Arkansas*'s menace:

> When the long [drum] roll was beaten, the gunboats Essex, Sumter, Kineo and Katahdin took up their positions, the two former to protect our left and the two latter our right flank. The Essex and the Sumter opened fire in the woods, their shells screaming through the trees, tearing them into shreds and scattering an iron hail around. Signal-officer Davis, of the Kineo, stationed himself on the tower of the State House, from which elevation he had an excellent view of the field, and could signal to the vessels where to throw in their shells. After the battle had raged for some time the Union troops began to fall back on the Penitentiary, when several well-directed shots from the 11-inch guns of the boats kept the rebels in check. Shortly after this the firing ceased.
>
> At half past three P.M. firing was reopened, the gun-boats Kineo and Katahdin shelling the woods in different directions where the enemy were doing great execution. It has been stated that one shell from the Kineo killed from forty to sixty rebels. Toward evening the firing again ceased; but the gunboats continued to send in a shell every half hour in different parts of the woods during the whole night, with the view of keeping the rebels at bay.[12]

The battle for Baton Rouge by mid-afternoon had degenerated into a stalemate, the hostilities reduced to artillery barrages and scattered rifle fire, both sides having worn themselves out, neither able to overcome the other, neither willing to make another try. The rebels' last remaining act of war was to burn and destroy the camps, equipment and stores of the Union regiments, whose men had abandoned them to seek refuge at the river's edge, protected by the guns of the U.S. Navy.

The thirsty, hungry, sleep-deprived, heat-stricken, battle-weary troops of General Breckinridge were exhausted. He pulled them back out of the city, withdrawing to the east, whence they had come, where they found water in Ward's Creek and the cisterns of nearby farms. Near the creek they rested for the remainder of the day, many of the wounded being taken in and cared for by residents along the Greenwell Springs road.

At four P.M. General Breckinridge at last got the news of the ill-fated *Arkansas*. The vessel's woeful end was described by its resentful and absent captain, Commander Brown:

> Under the double orders of two commanders-in-chief to be at Baton Rouge at a certain date and hour, Stevens could not use that tender care which his engines required, and before they completed their desperate run of three hundred miles against time, the starboard one suddenly broke down, throwing the vessel inextricably ashore. This misfortune,

for which there was no present remedy, happened when the vessel was within sight of Baton Rouge. Very soon after, the *Essex* was seen approaching under full steam. Stevens, as humane as he was true and brave, finding that he could not bring a single gun to bear upon the coming foe, sent all his people over the bows ashore, remaining alone to set fire to his vessel; this he did so effectually that he had to jump from the stern into the river and save himself by swimming; and with colors flying, the gallant *Arkansas*, whose decks had never been pressed by the foot of an enemy, was blown into the air.[13]

Sarah Morgan, the young Baton Rouge diary keeper, had sought safety with her family at the nearby plantation of friends, and on the morning of August 5 she had intended to take a walk along the levee with several companions to see what they could of the battle. She was at first deterred by her mother, but then:

Phillie, Lilly, and I jumped in the carriage that was still waiting, and ran after the others to bring them back before they got in danger; but when we reached the end of the long lane, we saw them standing on the high levee, wringing their hands and crying. We sprang out and joined them, and there, way at the bend, lay the Arkansas on fire!

All except myself burst into tears and lamentations, and prayed aloud between their sobs. I had no words or tears; I could only look at our sole hope burning, going, and pray silently. O it was so sad! Think it was our sole dependence! And we five girls looked at her as the smoke rolled over her, watched the flames burst from her decks, and the shells as they exploded one by one beneath the water, coming up in jets of steam. And we watched until down the road we saw crowds of men toiling along towards us. Then we knew they were those who had escaped, and the girls sent up a shriek of pity.

On they came, dirty, half dressed, some with only their guns, a few with bundles and knapsacks on their backs, grimy and tired, but still laughing. We called to the first, and asked if the boat were really afire; they shouted yes, and went on, talking still. Presently one ran up and told us the story.... Several of the crew were around us then, and up and down the road they were scattered still in crowds.... Then Miriam came down, and talked to him, and then we went to the top of the levee where the rest were, and watched the poor Arkansas burn....

They all talked over their loss cheerfully, as far as the loss of money, watches, clothes, were concerned; but they were disheartened about their boat....

After a while the men were ordered to march up the lane, to some resting spot it is best not to mention here, and straggled off; but there was many sick among them, one wounded at Vicksburg, and we instantly voted to walk the mile and three quarters home, and give them the carriage and buggy. But long after they left, we stood with our new friends on the levee watching the last of the Arkansas, and saw the Essex, and two gunboats crowded with men, cautiously turn the point, and watch her burn.... We saw them go back as cautiously, and I was furious, knowing the accounts they would publish of what we ourselves had destroyed.... But we had to leave her a mere wreck, still burning, and started off on our long walk.[14]

The battle was over, and all thoughts of renewal had vanished. The Union losses were eighty-four killed, 266 wounded and thirty-three captured or missing. The Confederates lost eighty-four killed, 315 wounded and fifty-seven captured or missing. What was more devastating to the rebel cause, the Confederates had also lost, wasted through haste, their most effective weapon, the fearsome *Arkansas*.

In the sultry stillness of the day after the battle, Negro workers were given the job of digging mass graves for the fallen while the troops of the occupation force put their shovels, picks and axes to the task of constructing breastworks and rifle pits to fend off any possible future assaults on the city. Trenches were dug, and additional artillery emplacements built. Magnificent old oaks, giant magnolias and other trees that shaded the streets and gardens of residential Baton Rouge were felled and dropped across the city's roadways to provide barriers and allow clear fields of fire for the protective Union gunboats the next time the rebel army threatened the Union occupation of the city.

Those preparations were soon abandoned when in New Orleans, General Butler abruptly changed his mind about defending Baton Rouge. He decided instead to recall the Baton Rouge garrison and concentrate his forces at New Orleans, which he feared would be the next rebel objective. On August 21 the troops at Baton Rouge, after gathering up their equipment, stores, artillery and everything of value that they had looted from the homes of Baton Rouge before burning them, boarded their transports and steamed away to New Orleans, leaving the smashed, charred, ransacked Louisiana capital city in their wake, undefended except for two gunboats stationed at the riverfront to ward off any new rebel incursion.

Once rested, the troops of General Breckinridge were marched off to Port Hudson, Louisiana, above Baton Rouge, to give additional strength to another rebel bastion on the bluffs of the Mississippi, one that still guaranteed the Confederates continued access to the Red River. On August 19, traveling with a contingent of his troops, Breckinridge departed Port Hudson, bound for Jackson, Mississippi. Left behind him was the embattled river. Its next bloody struggles were for others to wage.

21. New Attempts at Vicksburg

In the maze of the U.S. Navy Department's bureaucracy someone decided that Commander David Dixon Porter, one of the most activist officers in the Navy, could best be used as a production supervisor, overseeing the construction of ironclads in St. Louis. Refusing to accept that assignment, he was on the verge of resigning from the Navy to captain a commercial vessel, but while he was on a visit to Washington his intentions became known in high places, and his orders were suddenly changed. In new orders dated October 9 he was appointed to command all U.S. naval forces on the Mississippi, relieving Flag Officer Charles Davis. He was also promoted to rear admiral, which passed him over more than eighty officers more senior than he. His favorite axiom had proved true: "There is a divinity that shapes our ends, rough-hew them how we will."

Once the *Arkansas* had been destroyed there was no Confederate navy left to be engaged on the Mississippi, and the Union's river fleet, which Porter now commanded, was reduced to serving as floating artillery in support of the Army and patrolling the river to suppress rebel guerrillas.

"In October, 1862," Porter wrote in *The Naval History of the Civil War*, "the guerillas were exceedingly troublesome all along the rivers, firing at every unarmed steamer which passed. Large quantities of goods were shipped from St. Louis to points along the river professedly Union, which ultimately reached the Confederates. All this was stopped, and the guerillas, when captured, were summarily dealt with, and the houses where they were harbored laid in ashes.

"No commerce was allowed on the Mississippi except with Memphis, and the river looked almost as deserted as in the early days of its discovery, its silence being seldom disturbed except by gun-boats and army transports, and the sharp report of the howitzers as they sent the shrapnel shells into the dense wood or over the high banks where it might be supposed guerillas were lying in wait to fire on the transports. This was slow work compared to the active warfare the iron-clads had been engaged in."[1]

Further changes were occurring in the Navy on the Mississippi. Control of the Union gunboats, which had been in the hands of the Army, was transferred to the Navy Department in October, and on November 7 the ram fleet of the Ellets was also transferred from the War Department to the Navy Department.

The Army was making changes, too. On October 25, General Grant was placed in command of the Department of the Tennessee, which put Vicksburg within his area of responsibility. It was then to Vicksburg that he immediately turned his attention. He quickly developed a plan that called for him to move down from Jackson, Tennessee, to Holly Springs, Mississippi, on the Mississippi Central Rail Road line, where he would establish a supply base, then proceed with some sixty thousand troops farther south to Grenada, Mississippi, forcing Vicksburg's defenders, now led by Lieutenant General John C. Pemberton, who had replaced General Van Dorn, to try to stop Grant's army before it reached Vicksburg. In response to Grant's threat, Pemberton established a line of defense that straddled the Mississippi Central Rail Road line at Grenada, on the south side of the Yalabusha River, and he tore up the rail line leading to Grenada from the north.

In a dispatch dated November 2, Grant informed the Army's general in chief: "I have commenced a movement on Grand Junction [Tennessee], with three divisions from Corinth and two from Bolivar [Tennessee]. Will leave here [Jackson, Tennessee] to-morrow, and take command in person. If found practicable, I will go to Holly Springs, and, may be, Grenada, completing [repairs of] railroad and telegraph as I go."[2]

Meanwhile, a thorn had been placed in Grant's side. Major General John A. McClernand — President Lincoln's fellow lawyer and friend from Springfield, another of the war's politically appointed generals, believed to have political ambitions that he could further by making a name for himself in the war — had sold Lincoln on his idea of raising an army of new recruits in Illinois and elsewhere in the Midwest, organizing it apart from Grant's army, and taking it down the Mississippi to capture Vicksburg.

One of the first to learn about McClernand's assignment was Porter, to whom the president somewhat gleefully reported it just before Porter left Washington to take command at Cairo. According to one account, Lincoln asked Porter who should be the general to lead the Army in a joint Army-Navy operation to capture Vicksburg. "General Grant, sir," Porter answered. "Vicksburg is within his department, but I presume he will send Sherman there, who is equal to any occasion."

Lincoln surprised Porter by replying, "Well, admiral, I have in mind a better general than either of them. That is McClernand, an old and intimate friend of mine."[3] And from there the president went on to give McClernand credit for the victory at Shiloh. The president handed Porter a note of introduction to McClernand, who was also then in Washington, and suggested Porter go see him and discuss the Vicksburg operation. Porter did go to see McClernand at his hotel — and, having met him, decided McClernand was a pompous ass.

Evidently alarmed by the prospect of having to cooperate with McClernand, and by the possibility that McClernand may be superseding General Grant, Porter wrote Grant to tell him of Lincoln's plans for McClernand and to inform Grant that he, Porter, was taking command of the Mississippi River fleet.

Grant's reaction to the news about McClernand was expectable. "At this stage of the campaign against Vicksburg," Grant wrote candidly in his memoir, "I was very much disturbed by newspaper rumors that General McClernand was to have a separate and independent command within mine, to operate against Vicksburg by way of the Mississippi River. Two commanders on the same field are always one too many, and in this case I did not think the general selected had either the experience or the qualifications to fit him for so important a position. I feared for the safety of the troops intrusted to him, especially as he was to raise new levies, raw troops, to execute so important a trust."[4]

General Old Brains Halleck, the Army's new general in chief, agreed. Halleck wasn't keen on McClernand's idea or on McClernand himself, whose military ability he, like Grant, distrusted. Halleck apparently worked it out with the president and then wrote Grant to reassure him. "On the 12th [of November]," Grant reported, "I received a dispatch from General Halleck saying that I had command of all the troops sent to my department and authorizing me to fight the enemy where I pleased."[5]

Grant continued about his business of conducting the campaign against Vicksburg. On November 13 his cavalry was in Holly Springs, and from Holly Springs he and his troops advanced as far as Oxford, Mississippi, pursuing a confrontation with Pemberton's army. At Oxford, however, Grant's drive was stalled by the forbiddingly high water in the Tallahatchie River, by the broken bridge across the river and by the rail line that had been torn up by the rebels. The bridge and the rail line had to be restored to secure the flow of supplies coming by rail from Grant's depot at Columbus, Kentucky. At Oxford, Grant waited while the time-consuming repairs were made.

While he waited, he learned that some sort of expedition down the Mississippi was, as he said, inevitable, the pressure rising from Washington for immediate action to capture Vicksburg. To make certain there was a competent general in command of that inevitable expedition, Grant ordered General Sherman to return to Memphis from his position just north of Oxford and upon his arrival in Memphis he was to "assume command of all the troops there ... and organize them into brigades and divisions in your own army. As soon as possible move with them down the river to the vicinity of Vicksburg, and with the cooperation of the gunboat fleet under command of Flag Officer Porter proceed to the reduction of that place in such a manner as circumstances, and your own judgment, may dictate."[6] Grant confessed that "my object in sending Sherman back was expedited by a desire to get him in command of the forces separated from my direct supervision. I feared that delay might bring McClernand, who was his senior and who had authority from the President and Secretary of War to exercise that particular command, — and independently. I doubted McClernand's fitness; and I had good reason to believe that in forestalling him I was by no means giving offence to those whose authority to command was above both him and me."[7]

Grant had earlier left his command post to meet Porter, for the first time, at Cairo to discuss a joint operation. The two officers eyed each other wonderingly despite their warm reciprocal greetings. "While I was looking earnestly at Grant, trying to find out how much of a man there was under the plain exterior," Porter recalled, "Grant was regarding me to see what amount of work there was under the gilt buttons and gold lace with which the Department had bedizened my coat."[8] The meeting lasted only half an hour, but Grant was evidently sufficiently impressed, believing Porter had the nerve and judgment to do whatever was required of him. Porter was likewise impressed with the disheveled General Grant, who came to the meeting dressed in a worn brown coat and dusty gray pants.

At Memphis, Sherman, too, met Porter for the first time. The two of them, kindred spirits, men of action and determination, hit it off immediately, and cooperation in a joint effort against Vicksburg, which they discussed, promised to present no problem for either officer. Grant's plan was for Sherman to take a force by transport steamers, escorted by gunboats, to the Yazoo, and there at a suitable site Sherman would land his troops to move against Vicksburg on its defenders' right, or northern, flank while Grant engaged Pemberton's army on the east. With Vicksburg's defenders thus divided, Grant hoped the city could be taken.

The destruction of the *Arkansas* had left Confederate Commander Isaac Brown without a boat, but not idle. He was supervising construction of more ironclads at the boatyard in Yazoo City. And while in the area, he had met a forty-two-year-old millwright from Glasgow, Kentucky, Zere McDaniel, who had developed some expertise about torpedoes, a subject that arrested Brown's interest. Without the *Arkansas* standing guard, the Yazoo River, including Yazoo City and the Confederate boatyard, were vulnerable to Union vessels coming up from the Mississippi. McDaniel's torpedoes, planted in the river, might be exactly what was needed, Brown had decided, to thwart an enemy ascent of the Yazoo. And so he had taken it upon himself, acting for the Confederate Navy Department, to send McDaniel and McDaniel's associate, Francis Ewing, up the Yazoo to conduct experiments with various devices designed to explode powder charges under water. He had advised Secretary Mallory of the project, and Mallory in late August had obligingly written a note of instruction to Captain Lynch, the Confederate navy commander who no longer had a navy to command:

> Mr. F.M. Ewing and Z. McDaniel have been strongly recommended to the Department for perilous service, [and] I have given their appointments as Acting Masters to report to you privately for secret service. They will detail their plans for using submarine batteries and you will grant them such aid as your judgment may approve in executing their plans. They propose nothing expensive, but think they can float secure alongside of an [enemy's] vessel and place and explode a torpedo to sink it. I deem it proper to afford such adventurous spirits the opportunity to test their skill and judgment, and you will please aid them accordingly by and approve their necessary bills, to be paid by your disbursement officer at Jackson.[9]

The torpedo design finally settled on by McDaniel and Ewing employed a five-gallon glass bottle, or demijohn, filled with black powder that was exploded by an artillery friction primer encased within the gunpowder. The primer was attached to a wire threaded through a wooden tube that protruded from the narrow neck of the bottle and was made watertight by a mixture of beeswax, beef tallow, gummy gutta percha and lead carbonate. The bottle was attached to a log or other large piece of driftwood, which acted as a buoy, and was anchored to the riverbed with a rope that could be taken in or let out to position the bottle at an appropriate depth in the water. Two of the bottle torpedoes were connected by a length of rope that was also connected to the primer wire. When a boat snagged that rope between the two torpedoes, it would draw both torpedoes to its sides, and when the slack was pulled out of the rope as the vessel continued forward, the primer wire would be jerked and the black powder ignited, causing a huge explosion.

McDaniel and Ewing planted a number of their torpedoes in the Yazoo, about three miles below Haynes's Bluff. There, unseen and menacing, the crude but deadly devices awaited the vessels of the enemy.

Before Sherman's troops were scheduled to arrive at the Yazoo, Admiral Porter ordered a gunboat flotilla to scout out the river and discover whatever difficulties might be encountered on Sherman's mission. Porter described that reconnaissance:

> The expedition from Memphis got away early in December, 1862, Commander Walke, in the "Carondelet," being sent ahead with the "Cairo," "Baron DeKalb," [formerly the *St. Louis*] and "Pittsburg," (iron-clads) and the "Signal" and "Marmora" ("tin-clads") to clear the Yazoo River of torpedoes and cover the landing of Sherman's Army when it should arrive. This arduous and perilous service was well performed. On the 11th of December, Commander Walke dispatched the two "tin-clads" on a reconnoisance up the Yazoo.
>
> They ascended some twenty miles, when they were apprized of the presence of torpedoes by a great number of small boats along the channel of the river and an explosion near the "Signal." Another torpedo was exploded from the "Marmora" by firing into it with a musket as it appeared just below the surface. The commanding officers of these two vessels reported that with the assistance of two iron-clads to keep down the sharpshooters, they could clear the river of torpedoes, but not otherwise, as there were rifle-pits all along the left [south] bank of the Yazoo, and the enemy were supplied with light artillery.
>
> At Lieutenant-Commander Selfridge's request he was sent on this duty in the "Cairo," with the "Pittsburg," Lieut.-Commanding Hoel, and the ram "Queen of the West," Colonel

Charles Ellet, Jr., [Charlie] commanding. These officers were cautioned to be particularly careful and run no risks.

On the 12th of December the vessels proceeded on the duty assigned them under a shower of bullets from the rifle-pits, which was only checked by the gun-boats dropping close into the left bank and enfilading the rifle-pits with shrapnel. This cleared the enemy out, and the boats from the vessels were enabled to drag for the infernal machines and haul them to the shore, where they were destroyed by firing volleys of musketry into them.

After this work had been prosecuted for some time Lieut.-Comr. Selfridge proceeded ahead in the "Cairo" to cover the "Marmora," which was thought to be sorely beset by the enemy's sharpshooters. The "Cairo" encountered a floating torpedo. Two explosions in quick succession occurred, which seemed almost to lift the vessel out of the water. Everything was done to keep the "Cairo" afloat, but without avail, and she sank in twelve minutes after the explosion, in six fathoms of water, with nothing but the tops of her chimneys showing above the surface.[10]

Of the many torpedoes planted in the river, it was McDaniel and Ewing's device that sank the *Cairo*, the first of the Eads ironclad gunboats to be destroyed. Commander Brown, with satisfaction, claimed credit for the device he had championed. "Soon after it was put in position," Brown reported, "the iron-clad *Cairo* came up the river, and, keeping the middle of the stream, hit the demijohn, and within twelve minutes went to the bottom in thirty feet of water. In this way a belligerent vessel was 'neutralized' by an enemy's torpedo."[11]

Remarkably, no one on the *Cairo* was killed, and only two men were injured, neither seriously. All were quickly taken aboard the *Queen of the West*. Although reports of the incident tended to show the *Cairo*'s captain, Lieutenant Commander Thomas Selfridge, had acted rashly in recklessly steaming ahead in water known to be infested with torpedoes, Admiral Porter declined to find fault with him. "It was an accident liable to occur to any gallant officer whose zeal carries him to the post of danger," Porter wrote, "and who is loath to let others do what he thinks he ought to do himself."[12] Instead of issuing a reprimand, Porter, who arrived on the scene a day or two after the occurrence, gave Selfridge the *Conestoga* to command, and at the same time put the entire gunboat squadron to work clearing the Yazoo of torpedoes as far up the river as the vicinity of Haynes's Bluff.

General Sherman's troops, meanwhile, were boarding transports at Memphis to be taken to their intended landing site on the Yazoo. Sherman described the movement:

> Meantime a large fleet of steamboats was assembling from St. Louis and Cairo, and Admiral Porter dropped down to Memphis with his whole gunboat fleet, ready to cooperate in the movement. The preparations were necessarily hasty in the extreme, but this was the essence of the whole plan, viz., to reach Vicksburg as it were by surprise, while General Grant held in check Pemberton's army about Grenada, leaving me to contend only with the smaller garrison of Vicksburg and its well-known strong batteries and defenses. On the 19th [of December] the Memphis troops were embarked, and steamed down to Helena, where on the 21st General Steele's division was also embarked; and on the 22d we were all rendezvoused at Friar's Point....
>
> The Mississippi boats were admirably calculated for handling troops, horses, guns, stores, etc., easy of embarkation and disembarkation, and supplies of all kinds were abundant, except fuel. For this we had to rely on wood, but most of the wood-yards, so common on the river before the war, had been exhausted, so that we had to use fence-rails, old dead timber, the logs of houses, etc. Having abundance of men and plenty of axes, each boat could daily procure a supply.
>
> In proceeding down the river, one or more of Admiral Porter's gunboats took the lead; others were distributed throughout the column, and some brought up the rear. We manoeuvered by divisions and brigades when in motion, and it was a magnificent sight as

we thus steamed down the river. What few inhabitants remained at the plantations on the river-bank were unfriendly, except the slaves; some few guerrilla-parties infested the banks, but did not dare to molest so strong a force as I then commanded.[13]

The day after Christmas, Sherman's transports reached the mouth of the Yazoo and proceeded thirteen miles up the river to Johnson's plantation, where the troops disembarked. The division commanded by Brigadier General Frederick Steele was posted above the mouth of Chickasaw Bayou, which emptied into the Yazoo; the division of Brigadier General G.W. Morgan was posted at the burned-out Johnson plantation house (burned earlier by Porter's gunboats); and the division of Brigadier General Morgan L. Smith was posted just below the Johnson house. Brigadier General A.J. Smith's division arrived the following evening and was posted below Morgan Smith's division. The troops were spread out on a large island, separated by a broad, shallow bayou from the high bluff known as Walnut Hills, on which the town of Vicksburg stands. To their right as they faced Vicksburg was another broad bayou, called Old River; and on their left was a narrower but deeper stream called Chickasaw Bayou, too deep to be forded. Behind them was the Yazoo River.

"All the island was densely wooded," Sherman wrote, "except Johnson's plantation, immediately on the bank of the Yazoo, and a series of old cotton-fields along the Chickasaw Bayou. There was a road from Johnson's plantation directly to Vicksburg, but it crossed numerous bayous and deep swamps by bridges, which had been destroyed; and this road debouched on level ground at the foot of the Vicksburg bluff, opposite strong forts, well prepared and defended by heavy artillery."[14] From that island Sherman would launch his attack.

Aboard the gunboats officers and crew were spending their Christmas slightly less uncomfortably than were Sherman's troops. From the gunboat *Tyler* twenty-five-year-old Ensign Symmes Browne of Cincinnati wrote to his fiancée on December 26:

On going up the Yazoo, we did not see a man, woman or child, nor hear a sound save that made by the boats until we were 15 miles from the mouth, where we came near the boats that came up in the morning ... and then we heard heavy firing. On nearing the boats from below, we heard musketry and then we knew that the guerrillas were firing on the boats, and the boats were shelling the banks. We continued to advance with the "Benton" ahead until we got [to within a] mile of where the "Cairo" [was blown] up by a torpedo, so we stopped and sent the small boats ahead with grappling hooks and drags to pick up the torpedoes....

Only one torpedo was found, however; and as it was exposing our men too much to the fire of the enemy, the boats were called in, and we dropped down the river a mile or so and anchored for the night.

The 24th and 25th (Xmas) were spent about the same way, and I sometimes thought: If the folks at home and my dear one could see how we were celebrating Xmas, they would think we were having a good time generally. As the enemy had nothing but muskets and squirrel rifles, they were only playthings for us, and during the whole expedition only one negro was killed and three or four men wounded, all on other boats....

But I did not tell you how I spent Christmas Eve. About 7 P.M. Capt. Pritchett invited all the officers in the cabin to take a glass of champagne with him, and as it was the birthday of our surgeon ... as well as my own, thought I might at least take a glass of wine to commemorate the day and drink to the health of the "dear ones at home." Oh dearest, how very often I thought of you and thought how happy you all were, enjoying the evening, and how you would all be on the alert at daylight to catch each a "Merry Xmas." We were enjoying it in a different style and fired lots of salutes. I guess there are some of the rebels that will long remember that Christmas....

Dearest, I must close as it is getting quite late, and I come on watch at midnight.

Symmes[15]

Having to drive off Confederate skirmishers as they went about their task, it took two days for Sherman and his generals to reconnoiter the island and for his four divisions to get into position to storm across the bayou that separated them from the hills and bluffs defended by the Confederates. The reconnaissance revealed to Sherman that because of the position of rebel guns on the heights, the bayou could be crossed at only two points, one near Chickasaw Bayou, in front of General Morgan's division, and the other about a mile lower, in front of General Morgan Smith's division. During the reconnaissance on the 28th General Morgan Smith suffered a disabling wound in his hip and had to be sent back to his transport. Brigadier General D. Stuart took over for him.

On the morning of December 29 all was in readiness for the attack. "The first step," Sherman explained,

> was to make a lodgment on the foothills and bluffs abreast of our position, while diversions were made by the navy toward Haynes's Bluff, and by the first division directly toward Vicksburg. I estimated the enemy's forces, then strung from Vicksburg to Haynes's Bluff, at fifteen thousand men, commanded by rebel Generals Martin Luther Smith and Stephen D. Lee. Aiming to reach firm ground beyond this bayou, and to leave as little time for our enemy to reenforce as possible, I determined to make a show of attack along the whole front, but to break across the bayou at the two points named, and gave general orders accordingly....
>
> The front was very narrow, and immediately opposite, at the base of the hills about three hundred yards from the bayou, was a rebel battery, supported by an infantry force posted on the spurs of the hill behind. To draw attention from this, the real point of attack, I gave instructions to commence the attack at the flanks.[16]

Unknown to Sherman as he stood poised to launch the assault, events affecting General Grant's army had already blighted Sherman's mission. On December 20, General Van Dorn, commanding Pemberton's cavalry, had swept into Holly Springs, Grant's forward supply base, and captured the entire garrison of fifteen hundred men and destroyed all of Grant's supply of munitions and provisions. At the same time a rebel cavalry force led by Brigadier General Nathan Bedford Forrest had torn up sections of the railroad between Jackson, Tennessee, and Columbus, Kentucky, cutting off Grant's line of communication. Grant had sent his cavalry to force Van Dorn out of Holly Springs, but the damage had already been done. "This cut me off from all communication with the north for more than a week," Grant wrote, "and it was more than two weeks before rations or forage could be issued from stores obtained in the regular way. This demonstrated the impossibility of maintaining so long a line of [rail] road over which to draw supplies for an army moving in an enemy's country. I determined, therefore, to abandon my campaign into the interior with Columbus as a base, and returned to LaGrange [Tennessee] and Grand Junction [Tennessee], destroying the [rail] road to my front and repairing the [rail] road to Memphis, making the Mississippi River the line over which to draw supplies."[17]

As Grant withdrew, General Pemberton did also—back to Vicksburg, in time to bring massive reinforcements to defend against Sherman's attack. Vicksburg's defenders were no longer divided. Not only were Pemberton's forces united but Sherman now could not count on Grant to follow Pemberton, as Grant had promised, "even to the gates of Vicksburg."[18] Sherman, though, did not yet know that.

At about noon on the 29th Sherman's artillery opened a furious bombardment along the whole Union line, signaling the start of the attack. The Confederate batteries immediately commenced firing in response. The artillery exchange was soon followed by small-arms fire as Sherman's infantry moved forward. One brigade of General Morgan's division made it safely across the bayou, but took cover behind the bank of the stream and could not move ahead under the heavy fire. A brigade of General Steele's division also crossed the bayou and continued on across the stretch of level ground to the base of the hills and there came under a murderous artillery crossfire. It was stopped and gradually fell back, leaving behind about five hundred men, including its wounded, all of whom became prisoners. Another of Steele's brigades took a wrong turn while still on the island and did not even make it to the bayou.

The Sixth Missouri Infantry Regiment crossed the bayou farther downstream, taking severe losses as it did so, and was stalled at the bank, which at that spot was too steep for the men to climb. Sharpshooters from the Thirteenth U.S. Infantry, firing from cover behind logs, stumps and trees, attempted to suppress the rebels' fire into the Sixth Missouri, but succeeded only partly. The Missouri troops, desperate to avoid the hailstorm of lead, clawed crevices in the bank, into which they squeezed themselves while the rebels above them reached over their parapet and fired vertically down onto them. "So critical was the position," Sherman wrote, "that we could not recall the men till dark, and then one at a time."[19]

Sherman's assault on the rebels' fortress had failed. Union losses were heavy, and little harm had been inflicted on the rebels. Sherman put his casualties at 175 killed, 930 wounded and 743 captured. Rebel losses were estimated to be sixty-three killed, 134 wounded and ten captured. Nothing had been accomplished. Sherman's first thought was to order another assault, but he decided against it, realizing that the Confederates now knew where the Union crossings were to occur and would concentrate their fire there, causing even greater losses. He thought a landing somewhere below Haynes's Bluff, presenting a second front, might work. He conferred with Admiral Porter that night — December 29 — and Porter agreed to cover the landing with his gunboats. The transports that were to carry the troops were selected the next day, December 30, but their captains and pilots were so reluctant to hazard enemy gunfire that Sherman had to place guards with loaded muskets on the boats to prevent the captains and pilots from fleeing their vessels.

Under cover of darkness General Steele's division and a brigade from General Morgan Smith's (now General Stuart's) division were pulled out of the line and quietly loaded aboard the transports waiting for them in the river. "The night of December 30th," General Sherman related, "was appointed for this force, under the command of General Fred Steele, to proceed up the Yazoo just below Haines's [sic] Bluff, there to disembark about daylight, and make a dash for the hills. Meantime we had strengthened our positions near Chickasaw Bayou, had all our guns in good position with parapets, and had every thing ready to renew our attack as soon as we heard the sound of battle above."[20]

The sound of battle never came. Shortly after daybreak Sherman received a note from General Steele saying that before the boats had even raised steam, a thick, impenetrable, blinding fog had settled over the Yazoo, making it impossible for the boats to move. The landing was canceled.

As the morning slowly advanced at Sherman's campsite, more torrential rain came with it. On the trees around his command post he could see high-water marks that were ten feet above his head, and growing alarmed over the prospect of sudden flooding, he became convinced that, as he said, "the part of wisdom was to withdraw."[21] He ordered all stores and equipment to be loaded back onto the transport steamers and all his troops then to re-embark.

The entire operation was ended.

Part III: 1863

22. The Tributaries and Distributaries

Throughout New Year's day General Sherman and his troops, preparing to leave their encampment, could hear in the distance the whistles of trains arriving in Vicksburg and could at times see Confederate troops marching toward Haynes's Bluff, some units pulling out of the line of march to take positions opposite what had been the Union front. Heavy reinforcements were pouring in to strengthen Vicksburg's defenses; whether from General Pemberton's army at Grenada or from General Bragg's in Tennessee, Sherman couldn't tell. They made no move against Sherman's army, though, not even as his rear guard was withdrawing.

The next morning, January 2, his troops having embarked on their transports during the night, Sherman and his army, more than thirty thousand men, stood ready to steam away. The rebels then decided to give them a parting shot. Two Confederate regiments let loose with their field pieces on four Union vessels at the rear of the convoy as it started to move downriver. The vessels were not transports, as the rebels apparently supposed, but were the gunboats *Lexington* and *Marmora* and the recently armed Ellet rams *Monarch* and *Queen of the West*. Before the Confederates could get off a second round, the four Union boats opened on them with shrapnel, grape and canister, biting into the rebel formation, dropping some of the attackers and scattering the rest.

As the convoy got under way, Admiral Porter met with General Sherman and informed him that General McClernand had arrived at the mouth of the Yazoo aboard the steamer *Tigress* and the scuttlebutt was that he had come to take command of Sherman's army. On that news Sherman promptly boarded a tugboat, left the convoy and sped down the river to find McClernand. Reporting to him, Sherman learned that McClernand carried orders from the War Department, endorsed by President Lincoln, to command the forces on the Mississippi. Sherman, as Grant had feared, had been superseded by the president's friend.

"I explained what had been done," Sherman recounted in his memoir, "and what was the actual state of facts; that the heavy reenforcements pouring into Vicksburg must be Pemberton's, and that General Grant must be near at hand."[1]

McClernand, who was up to date on the fortunes of Grant's campaign, then informed Sherman that Grant was not coming, that his supply base at Holly Springs had been overrun, that he had fallen back to LaGrange and that one of his divisions was already at Memphis getting supplies when McClernand stopped there days earlier. Grant had notified Sherman of those events, but his dispatches had been routed to Memphis, and Sherman had not yet received them.

"This then fully explained how Vicksburg was being reenforced," Sherman related. "I saw that any attempt on the place from the Yazoo was hopeless."[2] And so the convoy carrying his thwarted army continued down the Yazoo, with no thought of returning to it.

On January 3 the Union commanders and their troops rendezvoused at Milliken's Bend, Louisiana, about ten miles up the Mississippi River from Vicksburg, while Admiral Porter and his gunboats remained at the Yazoo. On January 4, McClernand issued his general order No. 1, stating that he was assuming command of the Army of the Mississippi (until then that army had been called the right wing of General Grant's Thirteenth Army Corps and numbered about thirty thousand men) and that his army would be divided into two corps. One corps would be composed of the divisions of General Morgan and General A.J. Smith and would be commanded by Morgan. The other corps would comprise the divisions of General Steele and General Stuart (formerly General Morgan Smith's division) and would be commanded by General Sherman.

While at Milliken's Bend, Sherman learned that two weeks earlier the Union steamer *Blue Wing* had left Memphis carrying arms and ammunition and towing coal barges, bound for the Yazoo, and had been captured by a Confederate vessel that steamed out of the Arkansas River and fell on the unescorted *Blue Wing*. The captured vessel had been taken up the Arkansas to Fort Hindman, a strong, earthworks fortification the Confederates had erected at Arkansas Post, a community built around an Indian trading post that the French had founded nearly two centuries earlier.

Sherman was familiar with the fort. "We had reports from this fort," he wrote in his memoir, "usually called the 'Post of Arkansas,' about forty miles above the mouth, that it was held by about five thousand rebels, was an inclosed work, commanding the passage of the [Arkansas] river, but supposed to be easy of capture from the rear."[3]

Admiral Porter described it in detail:

Arkansas Post was a large, well constructed fort built with the best engineering skill. It mounted thirteen guns: two ten-inch Columbiads, one nine-inch Dahlgren, and ten rifled guns of various calibres. The Columbiads were mounted in casemates covered in with four layers of heavy railroad iron, neatly fitted together to offer a smooth surface, and slanting iron roof to make the shot glance off. These were simply after the plan of the iron-clads afloat and were formidable structures.

The nine-inch gun was mounted in an embrasure protected by sand-bags, as were the ten rifled guns. All the guns except one bore down the river and on the vessels coming abreast of the forts. The fort itself was built close to the river; the front not being more than twenty yards from the bank. There was nothing known to the military art that had been neglected in constructing these works."[4]

Like many politicians, McClernand had a way of speaking in platitudes and generalities, without offering specifics. "He spoke in general terms of opening the navigation of the Mississippi," Sherman wrote, "'cutting his way to the sea,' etc., etc., but the *modus operandi* was not so clear."[5] Sherman, on the other hand, had definite ideas about waging the campaign to capture the Mississippi. Believing that as long as Fort Hindman provided a convenient base from which rebel vessels could attack unescorted Union shipping on the Mississippi it would remain an impediment to the campaign to take Vicksburg, Sherman decided it would be a good idea to capture the fort and eliminate it as a Confederate haven. He proposed to McClernand that they launch an attack on it with the army they now had aboard their transports. McClernand had objections to an attack, but eventually agreed to go with Sherman to ask Porter for his opinion.

On the night of January 4, Sherman, on his headquarters boat, the *Forest Queen*, stopped to pick up McClernand from his command vessel, the *Tigress*, and together they called on Admiral Porter aboard his recently acquired, well-appointed flagship, the *Black*

Hawk. "It must have been near midnight," Sherman recounted, "and Admiral Porter was in *deshabille*. We were seated in his cabin and I explained my views about Arkansas Post, and asked his cooperation." During the conversation Sherman noticed that Porter's manner toward McClernand was curt, so much so that Sherman took him to task. "I invited him out into a forward-cabin where he had his charts, and asked him what he meant by it. He said that 'he did not like him;' that in Washington, before coming West, he had been introduced to him by President Lincoln, and he had taken a strong prejudice against him. I begged him, for the sake of harmony, to waive that, which he promised to do."[6] They then rejoined McClernand and resumed the discussion, which included the generals' offer to tow Porter's gunboats up the river to save their coal, then in short supply.

As the three officers conferred, Lieutenant William Gwin, commander of the gunboat *Benton*, lay dying in a nearby stateroom on the *Black Hawk*, victim of a massive wound suffered when he was struck by a shell that tore away his right arm and breast while the *Benton* was attempting to clear torpedoes from the Yazoo River. He died two days later. He was one of Porter's best officers, Sherman wrote. "We of the army deplored his loss quite as much as his fellows of the navy, for he had been intimately associated with us in our previous operations on the Tennessee River, at Shiloh and above, and we had come to regard him as one of us."[7] The gloom of his imminent death may have contributed to Porter's poor mood that night.

According to his own account of the meeting, Porter refused to have anything to do with the proposed attack on Fort Hindman unless Sherman went as commander. "To this McClernand agreed," Porter reported, "only stipulating that he [McClernand] should accompany the expedition. So the matter was arranged, and the expedition started."[8]

The entire army of more thirty thousand men, on their transports, convoyed by a flotilla of Porter's gunboats, including the *Black Hawk*, steamed up the Mississippi to the mouth of the White River, which they reached on January 8, then continued up the White to its confluence with the Arkansas and proceeded up the Arkansas to Notrib's farm, a site just below Fort Hindman, beyond the range of the fort's guns, arriving there in the evening of January 9. The troops began disembarking early the next morning.

As General Stuart's division moved up along the river bank to within about four miles of the fort, it encountered the rebels entrenched behind an earthworks line that extended from the river on the rebels' right to the swamp on their left. Behind the line were dense woods. Sherman, meanwhile, marched General Steele's division around the Confederates' far left, using a road that passed through the swamp and debouched onto firm ground at the rear of the fort. While they were proceeding up that road, they were overtaken by a message from General McClernand, reporting that the Confederates had abandoned their line and had withdrawn toward the fort and ordering Sherman to turn around and march back to where General Stuart's division was now advancing through the woods, continuing toward the fort.

The early darkness of the short winter day came on as the Union troops neared the fort, and after a bright moon rose, Sherman's patrols reconnoitered the approaches to the fort, observing some abandoned huts and discovering that the whole force of defenders had fallen back into and around the fort. "Personally," Sherman related, "I crept up to a stump so close that I could hear the enemy hard at work, pulling down houses, cutting with axes, and building intrenchments. I could almost hear their words, and I was thus listening when, about 4 A.M. the bugler in the rebel camp sounded as pretty a reveille as I ever listened to."[9]

At dawn, in the growing daylight, the Union forces could see that the Confederates had erected a new parapet straight across the peninsula formed by the curve of the river, stretching from the fort, beside the river, to an impassable swamp, the edge of which stood about a mile to the rear of the fort. "This peninsula," Sherman explained, "was divided into two nearly equal parts by a road. My command had the ground to the right of the road, and Morgan's corps that to the left. McClernand had his quarters still on the *Tigress*, back at Notrib's farm, but moved forward that morning (January 11th) to a place in the woods to our rear, where he had a man up a tree, to observe and report the movements. There was a general understanding with Admiral Porter that he was to attack the fort with his three ironclad gunboats directly by its water-front, while we assaulted by land in the rear."[10]

Porter had begun pounding the fort, seeking to silence its guns, on the day before. He described his flotilla's opening action, on January 10:

> The Confederates supposed the gun-boats would attack the works from a distance of 1200 yards, and range buoys had been placed at that distance by which to regulate the enemy's fire, and they had been practicing at that distance on the targets so that the gunners would become expert. But all these calculations were upset by the "DeKalb" leading, and the "Cincinnati" and "Louisville" close behind her, running up and taking position close to the fort where the current was slack and the vessels could maintain their places without any difficulty; while the other vessels could take such positions in the river as best suited and throw in shrapnel from their small shell guns.
>
> The fort opened on the iron-clads as soon as they reached the range buoys—made some good shots, and then lost their range, during which time the gun-boats were within 150 yards of them and firing accurately and steadily through their iron casemates, and committing sad havoc in the rear amongst the soldiers. It was evident from the first that this fort was doomed to fall, under the fire of the gun-boats. The superiority of their fire over that of the guns in the fort was such that the latter were silenced in the space of an hour, and the gun-boats ceased firing. As darkness was coming on and the smoke hung densely over the river, the gun-boats dropped down and tied up to the bank.[11]

About ten-thirty on the morning of the 11th, while the troops of Sherman and Morgan stood within six hundred yards of the fort, poised to launch their assault, awaiting the sound of the Navy's guns, Porter's ironclads opened up on the fort once more. "The battle commenced and soon became very hot," Porter reported. "The tin-clads ... were ordered by the admiral to force their way through the obstructions above the forts, reach the ferry and cut off the enemy's retreat. In a short time all the guns in the works were silenced and the flag-ship 'Black Hawk' was run to the bank alongside the fort to board it with her crew; at the same time a messenger was sent to General Sherman informing him of the condition of affairs, and that if he would send a storming party from the rear, the Navy would board from the water side."[12]

From the upper deck of the *Black Hawk*, as it drew up beside the fort, Admiral Porter could see down into Fort Hindman. "A dreadful scene of killed and wounded," he called it. "A large number of artillery horses had been kept in the fort for some reason, and the shells and shrapnel had made sad havoc with the dead and dying men, mixed up with the killed and wounded animals. It was a scene ever to be remembered."[13]

From his vantage point on the field behind the fort General Sherman could see the flags of Porter's gunboats wafting above the fort's parapets as the vessels drew up to the fort. Shortly after he noticed them, someone on the rebels' new line suddenly stood up waving a large white flag, and smaller white flags then began popping up all along the line. Sherman immediately shouted, "Cease firing!" and ordered one of his aides, Colonel Dayton, to mount his horse and ride straight to the large white flag. Sherman and the rest of his staff followed him. "All firing had ceased, except an occasional shot away to the right," Sherman related. "On entering the line, I saw that our muskets and guns had done good execution; for there was a horse-battery, and every horse lay dead in the traces. The fresh-made parapet had been knocked down in many places, and dead men lay around very thick."[14]

Sherman ordered the Confederate officer commanding that section of the line, Colonel Garland, to have his men stack their arms and wait for further orders. "I inquired of Colonel Garland who commanded in chief," Sherman recounted, "and he said that General Churchill did, and that he was inside the fort. I then rode into the fort.... I found it full of soldiers and sailors, its parapets toward the river well battered in, and Porter's gunboats in the river, close against the fort, with their bows on shore. I soon found General Churchill, in conversation with Admiral Porter and General A. J. Smith."[15]

The *Black Hawk*'s officers and crewmen had entered the fort from the river side, and General Churchill and his officers had come forward to give their swords to Admiral Porter and surrender. Many of Fort Hindman's garrison were members of the Confederate navy and had deliberately surrendered to a U.S. naval officer — Admiral Porter — rather than surrender to an officer of the Army. General McClernand, however, was in charge of the U.S. forces, and by messenger sent from his command post he ordered General Sherman to leave General Smith in charge of the fort and Sherman and his troops, who had captured two of the fort's three brigades of defenders and held the ground outside the fort, to withdraw. Miffed by the order, Sherman went to see McClernand.

"I found General McClernand on the *Tigress* in high spirits," Sherman recalled. "He said repeatedly: 'Glorious! Glorious! My star is ever in the ascendant!' He spoke complimentarily of the troops, but was extremely jealous of the navy.... He very kindly ordered something [to eat] be brought, and explained to me that by his 'orders' he did not wish to interfere with the actual state of facts; that General A.J. Smith would occupy 'Fort Hindman,' which his troops had first entered, and I could hold the lines outside, and go on securing the prisoners and stores as I had begun."[16]

Sherman returned to the area where Colonel Garland had surrendered and after ordering the disarmed prisoners to be marched into two deep gullies and held there, he took over a nearby house that had been used as a hospital. With Colonel Garland as his guest he moved in and started looking for something to eat. "A cavalry-soldier lent me his battered coffee-pot with some coffee and scraps of hard bread out of his nose-bag," Sherman recounted. "Garland and I made some coffee, ate our bread together, and talked politics by the fire till quite late at night, when we lay down on straw that was saturated with the blood of dead or wounded men."[17]

The next day, January 12, Sherman ordered the Confederate prisoners herded onto transports that would take them to St. Louis. "We then proceeded to dismantle and level the forts, destroy or remove the stores," Sherman related, "and we found in the magazine the very ammunition which had been sent for us in the *Blue Wing*, which was secured and afterward used in our twenty-pound Parrott guns."[18] He also went about the grim business of counting casualties. Union losses totaled 1,047, including 134 killed. In Sherman's corps alone four officers and seventy-five men were killed, and thirty-four officers and 406 men wounded. "The number of rebel dead," Sherman reported, "must have been nearly one hundred and fifty; of prisoners, by actual count, we secured four thousand seven hundred and ninety-one."[19]

"General McClernand," Admiral Porter recounted, "assumed all the direction of affairs on the surrender of the fort and the Confederate troops, and wrote the report of this affair, in which he gave fair credit to the Navy; but he actually had nothing to do with the management of the Army, and was down four miles below the forts during all operations. Sherman was virtually the military commander."[20]

Two days later, on January 13, the Union troops re-embarked on their transports and steamed down the Arkansas through a heavy snowstorm to the mouth of the river at Napoleon, Arkansas. There McClernand informed Sherman that he had received a letter from General Grant, dispatched from Memphis, expressing his disapproval of the Arkansas Post expedition. Grant later changed his mind, though, as Sherman suspected he would after the results were known. "I was at first disposed to disapprove of this move as an unnecessary side movement having no especial bearing upon the work before us," Grant recalled. "But when the result was understood I regarded it as very important. Five thousand Confederate troops left in the rear might have caused us much trouble and loss of property while navigating the Mississippi."[21]

Besides reports of their success at Fort Hindman, Sherman and Porter sent other, more pressing, messages to Grant. "I received messages from both Sherman and Admiral Porter," Grant reported, "urging me to come and take command in person, and expressing their distrust of McClernand's ability and fitness for so important and intricate an expedition [as the capture of Vicksburg]."[22]

Heeding their appeal, Grant took a steamer down to Napoleon and visited with McClernand on January 17. Grant then drew his own conclusions:

> It was here [at Napoleon] made evident to me that both the army and navy were so distrustful of McClernand's fitness to command that, while they would do all they could to insure success, this distrust was an element of weakness. It would have been criminal to send troops under these circumstances into such danger. By this time I had received authority to relieve McClernand, or to assign any person else to the command of the river expedition, or to assume command in person. I felt great embarrassment about McClernand. He was the senior major-general after myself within the department. It would not do, with his rank and ambition, to assign a junior over him. Nothing was left, therefore, but to assume the command myself. I would have been glad to put Sherman in command, to give him an opportunity to accomplish what he had failed in the December before; but there seemed no other way out of the difficulty, for he was junior to McClernand.[23]

Grant's authority to relieve McClernand of his duties had come from General Halleck, to whom Grant had earlier reported that McClernand, forsaking his mission to capture Vicksburg, had "gone off on a wild goose chase to the Post of Arkansas."

On January 20, General Grant ordered McClernand and his entire command to Young's Point and Milliken's Bend, neighboring towns in Louisiana, on the west bank of the Mississippi, above the mouth of the Yazoo. Both were occupied by Union forces and together they provided bases for the Army as well as the Navy. Returning to his headquarters in Memphis, Grant made preparations for an indefinite absence and placed Major General Stephen A. Hurlbut, another politician-general and friend of President Lincoln, in charge while he was gone.

On January 29, Grant arrived at Young's Point and took command of the Army of the Mississippi the next day. McClernand, who had recently married and had brought his bride with him on his expedition to conquer Vicksburg, did not relinquish his command — or his dream of glory and political fortune — without protest. "His correspondence with me on the subject was more in the nature of a reprimand than a protest," Grant recalled. "It was highly insubordinate, but I overlooked it, as I believed, for the good of the service."[24] In his memoir Grant gave his reasons for tolerating McClernand's objectionable reaction:

> General McClernand was a politician of very considerable prominence in his State [Illinois]; he was a member of Congress when the secession war broke out; he belonged to that political party [Democrat] which furnished all the opposition there was to a vigorous prosecution of the war for saving the Union; [yet] there was no delay in his declaring himself for the Union at all hazards, and there was no uncertain sound in his declaration of where he stood in the contest before the country. He also gave up his seat in Congress to take the field in defence of the principles he had proclaimed.[25]

By now Grant had seen the hopelessness in attempting to take Vicksburg by an assault from either the north or the east, where the terrain and Confederate arms remained insurmountable, impenetrable barriers. "North of the Yazoo was all a marsh, heavily timbered, cut up with bayous, and much overflowed. A front attack was therefore impossible," Grant wrote, "and was never contemplated; certainly not by me. The problem then became, how to secure a landing on high ground east of the Mississippi."[26]

His army, Grant decided, should make a landing below Vicksburg and attack the city from the south. But to get below Vicksburg, his troops had to move past the rebel guns that stood menacingly on Vicksburg's heights, barring vessels bearing enemy troops from doing exactly what Grant knew had to be done. It could be done, of course. Farragut had run by Vicksburg's guns twice without losing a vessel, once going up and once going down the river. But Grant was looking for a way that was less risky. An alternative would be to march his troops down the west side of the river, then ferry them across the river at a point below Vicksburg's fortifications. The problem with that option was that Grant would have to get his transports below Vicksburg to ferry the troops across, and the transports would have to get past Vicksburg's forbidding guns to reach the ferrying point. Also, the roads and fields on the far side of the west bank's levee were largely inundated from many days of rain, and marching an army over those flooded roads and fields was a near impossibility.

While he was deciding how and when to move them, his troops, encamped in tents on the levee on the west bank, were avoiding idleness by resuming work on the canal that General Williams had started months earlier to allow boats to avoid the Mississippi on the way past Vicksburg. When Williams abandoned the canal, it was a ditch ten to twelve feet wide and about as deep as it was wide, and about a mile long, but it had failed to divert the river's flow as it was intended to do.

"Mr. Lincoln," Grant related, "had navigated the Mississippi in his younger days and understood well its tendency to change its channel, in places, from time to time. He set much store accordingly by this canal. General McClernand had been, therefore, directed before I went to Young's Point to push the work of widening and deepening the canal. After my arrival the work was diligently pushed with about 4,000 men — as many as could be used to advantage."[27]

Grant had no confidence in the project, believing that even if it were made into a navigable channel, it would not avoid Vicksburg's guns. "It runs in a direction almost perpendicular to the line of bluffs on the opposite side, or east bank, of the river. As soon as the enemy discovered what we were doing he established a battery commanding the canal throughout its length. This battery soon drove out our dredges, two in number, which were doing the work of thousands of men."[28] Yet he resumed the work on the canal, knowing that the president favored the idea.

Grant at the same time had ideas of his own. One was to cut a breach in the levee at

Lake Providence, which is part of a former course of the Mississippi, in the northeast corner of Louisiana, and divert the Mississippi from there into a chain of connected bayous and rivers, the last of which is the Red River, which joins the Mississippi above Baton Rouge, near Port Hudson, about four hundred river miles below Vicksburg. On the day after he arrived at Young's Point, Grant ordered Major General James B. McPherson, who had been positioned with his corps at Lake Providence, to cut the levee there. He then waited to see if that diversion would work. While waiting, Grant was pursuing another scheme, this one involving a former course on the east side of the river.

Admiral Porter, meanwhile, most of his fleet also waiting, decided to harass the rebels operating on the west side of the Mississippi. Rebel vessels coming down the Red River, through the interior of Louisiana, continued to bring to Vicksburg and Port Hudson provisions and supplies that not only fed and supported Vicksburg but were transported by rail from Vicksburg to the Confederate army in the field elsewhere. Porter ordered one of his boats to run past Vicksburg's guns and proceed down the Mississippi and then up the Red River, attacking rebel vessels as it went.

Curiously, the vessel he selected for that challenging mission was the Ellet ram *Queen of the West*, now armed with light guns. Its commander was nineteen-year-old Charles R. Ellet, the youngest colonel in the U.S. Army, whose experience at naval warfare had begun at the Battle of Memphis, seven months earlier. Speculation has it that Porter chose the *Queen of the West* over more substantial vessels of his fleet—and young Ellet over more experienced, better trained commanders—because the *Queen* was faster than the gunboats, especially going against the current. There seems no other possible explanation.

"Ellet was a gallant young fellow," Porter related, "full of dash and of enterprise, and was delighted with this opportunity to distinguish himself; and, although his vessel was a very frail one for such an enterprise, he did not hesitate to accept the risk when this duty was proposed to him."[29] The first indication that young Ellet's judgment may have been less than expected of a boat commander occurred within hours after beginning his mission. Porter had intended the *Queen* to run past the Vicksburg guns in darkness, starting around midnight, but the vessel was delayed by a mechanical problem. Porter recounted the event, which occurred on the morning of February 2:

> It was nearly daylight when he reached the first [Vicksburg] battery, which he passed at full speed. The alarm gun was fired from the fort and in an instant the gunners of the lower batteries were at their posts, and when the "Queen" arrived abreast of the city, battery after battery opened upon her. As it was supposed that Colonel Ellet would pass during the night-time, he had been ordered to ram a large steamer (the "Vicksburg") lying at the levee, and also to throw lighted tow balls on board of her to set her on fire. This could have been easily done at night, but it was almost certain destruction to attempt it in day-time, but the gallant young fellow determined to carry out his orders at all hazards, rammed the vessel as directed and endeavored to set her on fire, but by this time the enemy's shot were rattling about him, and the current carrying him past the steamer, he was obliged to speed on.... The "Queen" was struck twelve times, twice just above the water line.[30]

Some success and more misfortune followed. The *Queen* made it down to the mouth of the Red River, where Ellet and his crew captured and destroyed three rebel vessels loaded with stores intended for Vicksburg's garrison. Ellet then ventured up the Red River and advanced about ten miles, sending several rebel transports fleeing farther up the river. Running low on coal, Ellet turned the *Queen* about and headed toward Warrenton, Mississippi, about five miles below Vicksburg, to replenish his fuel supply from a coal barge near there.

By February 10 that was done, and taking a small, captured steamer, the *De Soto*, with him, he steamed down the Mississippi again, probing the Old River and the Atchafalaya, returning the fire of rebel snipers on shore, before heading back toward the Red River. A *New York Tribune* correspondent aboard the *Queen of the West* recorded the voyage:

> The air was as balmy as June in our Northern climate, the trees were decking themselves with green, men were walking about the hurricane deck in their shirt sleeves, as we entered the Red. We could not help commiserating poor Northerners, shivering before coal fires.... Late Friday night we anchored at the mouth of Black River, as before, the De Soto thrown out as our advance picket.
>
> Saturday morning at daylight we raised anchor and proceeded up the [Red] river.... At 10 o'clock the lookout reported a steamer descending the river, and shortly after[,] the *Era No. 5* hove in sight. She saw us as quickly as we discovered her, and was half turned around as if attempting to escape, when Col. Ellet ordered a shot to be sent after her. This took effect in her stern, passing through the cook-room, demolishing a stove, and slightly wounding the negro cook. The officers and passengers then came on deck and hoisted white sheets and waved white handkerchiefs in token of surrender. The *Queen* ran alongside and took possession. The *Era No. 5* is a fine boat of 150 tons burden, belonging to the Red River Packet Company, and heretofore engaged in transporting supplies for the Confederate army. At that time she was laden with 4,500 bushels of corn intended for the Quartermaster's Department at Little Rock.
>
> The citizens on board were set on shore without parole, the soldiers were set on shore with parole, and the officers were retained.... Our prisoners being thus disposed of, the fleet, now numbering three steamers, moved toward Gordon's Landing. Four miles from the landing in a direct line across the country but fifteen miles as the river runs, we left the *Era*, with three or four men to guard the boat and the prisoners.
>
> We reached the vicinity of Gordon's Landing just at sundown, and moved cautiously around the bend near the point, 400 yards beyond which the fort [the Confederates' Fort Taylor] and batteries are situated.
>
> The Red River is here extremely tortuous, so much so that at a point four miles below the fort by river, we were only a mile from it by land. The batteries are entirely concealed from sight by dense forests until we approach within 400 yards of them, or until the nose of the steamer begins to show around the point upon which the negro cabins are built.[31]

It was here that the trouble began for Ellet and the *Queen of the West*. As they moved slowly up the river, chasing away a steamer some distance ahead of them, negotiating a bend in the river with difficulty, the *Queen* suddenly ran aground, making it a sitting duck for the guns of Fort Taylor, less than four hundred yards away. Whether the grounding was by accident, negligence or treachery was uncertain. In his account Admiral Porter called the pilot treacherous. In any event, the rebels quickly opened fire on the grounded *Queen* with four thirty-two-pounders and with deadly accuracy.

"The air was filled with fragments of exploding shells, which flew before, behind, and all about us," the *Tribune* correspondent wrote. "Still another [shot], and the steam chest was fractured. The whole boat shook with the rush of the escaping steam, which penetrated every nook and cranny.... Men crowded to the afterpart of the vessel. Some tumbled cotton-bales [which had protected the boat against solid shot] into the river, and getting astride of them, sought to reach the *De Soto*, a mile below."[32]

The *De Soto* managed to rescue a number of the survivors, including Ellet and the *Herald* correspondent, but many others fell into the hands of the Confederates and became prisoners. The *De Soto* also became a victim, losing its rudders and becoming unmanageable, drifting downriver until it met the *Era No. 5* coming up the river. The survivors then boarded the *Era*, and after the crippled *De Soto* was set afire to avoid recapture, the *Era* turned around and steamed toward the Mississippi. On the way, it, too, ran aground, ten feet from shore, while the same pilot who had grounded the *Queen* was again on duty. Ellet ordered the suspect pilot placed under arrest, and after four hours, the crew finally managed to spar the vessel free, letting it resume its voyage to reach the Mississippi.

On the morning of February 16, about ten miles below Natchez, the *Era No. 5* was met by the U.S. ironclad gunboat *Indianola*, which Porter had sent to support Ellet. After some discussion between Ellet and the *Indianola*'s captain, Lieutenant Commander George Brown, it was decided that Ellet would continue on to Vicksburg in the unarmed *Era* and the *Indianola* would proceed up the Red River on its search-and-destroy mission. The two vessels parted on February 18.

By then the Confederates had repaired the *Queen of the West*, and it had joined the rebel gunboat *William H. Webb* and four Confederate cotton-clad rams to form a flotilla bent on guarding against further incursions by Union gunboats. About nine-thirty on the night of February 24 four vessels of the flotilla confronted the *Indianola* near Grand Gulf, Mississippi. The unfortunate Commander Brown described the one-sided engagement:

> The sixth blow we received was from the "Webb," which crushed in the starboard wheel, disabled the starboard rudder and started a number of leaks abaft the shaft.... I continued the fight until after we received the seventh blow, which was given us by the "Webb."
>
> She struck us fair in the stern and started the timbers and starboard rudder-box so that the water poured in in large volume. At this time I knew the "Indianola" could be of no more service to us, and my desire was to render her useless to the enemy, which I did by keeping her in deep water, until there was two and a half feet of water over the floor, and the leaks were increasing rapidly as we settled, so as to bring the opening made by the "Webb" under water....
>
> As further resistance could only result in a great loss of life on our part, without a corresponding result on the part of the enemy, I surrendered the "Indianola," a partially sunken vessel, fast filling with water, to a force of four vessels, mounting ten guns and manned by over one thousand men.[33]

Before the Confederates could begin to salvage the *Indianola*, which they managed to tow to the east bank of the Mississippi, a fearsome-looking shape was spotted up the river, headed downstream, striking fear in the breast of Confederate Major Joseph L. Brent, commander of the rebel flotilla. Having heard the gunfire from the *Indianola*'s battle and suspecting his gunboat had run into trouble, Admiral Porter, unwilling to risk another ironclad, had ordered a dummy gunboat hastily put together and sent it down the river in hopes of bluffing the rebels. It was a creation of the carpenters of Porter's fleet, who had taken a three-hundred-foot barge and built a superstructure on it, with fake wheelhousings, fake chimneys and fake guns, all made from logs and lumber, painted the creation, fired up two smudge pots to give off pillars of black smoke, put an American flag on the dummy boat and shoved it into the current. The "Yankee ruse," as Porter called it, worked. Brent mistook the dummy for a real gunboat and not wishing to have his battered flotilla take it on, ordered his boats to retreat downriver, which they did, after setting fire to the partly submerged *Indianola*.

Disappointed over the failure of the Union vessels to accomplish more than a temporary halt in commerce on the rebel-held rivers and regretting the loss of two of his gunboats, Admiral Porter reported to Secretary Welles, "My plans were well laid, only badly executed. I can give orders, but I can not give officers good judgement."[34]

A dummy Union gunboat bluffs the rebels. Unwilling to risk one of his gunboats against Vicksburg's guns, Adm. David Porter ordered a dummy vessel built on a 300-foot barge and then set it adrift in the Mississippi's swift current to frighten Confederate boats away from their attack on the USS *Indianola* below Vicksburg. The ruse worked (Library of Congress).

General Grant's efforts were not going well either. He had put in motion a plan to carve out a new route from the Mississippi River through the swamps and lowlands north of Vicksburg and enter the Yazoo River above Haynes's Bluff, thereby flanking Vicksburg's defensive line along the lower Yazoo. On the opposite side of the Mississippi from, and about six miles below, Helena, Arkansas, near the place where some believe that Spanish explorer Hernando de Soto first saw the Mississippi River and crossed it in 1539, reposes Moon Lake, described by a *Harper's Weekly* correspondent in 1863 as "a beautiful sheet of clear water in the midst of forest trees." From Moon Lake ran a narrow, crooked, rapid stream called Yazoo Pass, which flowed into the Coldwater River, which, the *Harper's* correspondent reported, after a tortuous course of about forty miles, empties into the Tallahatchie River, which in turn merges with the Yalobusha River to form the Yazoo River some fifty miles farther south, at Greenwood. On February 3 Grant's engineers blasted a wide breach in the levee at Moon Lake. The breach let the rain-swollen Mississippi flow, as it once had, into the lake, into Yazoo Pass and into the pass's connecting streams, remaking a navigable waterway as it flushed through the lowlands above the Yazoo River.

It took weeks for the river water to fill the lowlands to the river's level, and once it did, the forty-five hundred men of Brigadier General Leonard F. Ross's division embarked onto the fourteen transports that would take them up the flooded stream. Escorting them were two ironclad gunboats, six thinclads and a ram, the entire naval force being commanded by Lieutenant Commander Watson Smith. On the morning of March 2 the convoy cleared Yazoo Pass and entered Coldwater River. Porter gives his account of the expedition's travails in *The Naval History of the Civil War*:

> To describe the difficulties which attended this expedition would be impossible and they could only be realized by those who saw them. The pass had been closed for many years and trees had grown up in the middle of the channel which had become dry after the levee was built across its mouth. Great rafts were left in this dry channel as the water ran off and bushes and vines now grew thickly around them and tied them together as with withes. Overhanging trees joined together over the channel — and their branches were so low that steamers could not pass without having their smoke-pipes knocked down and all their boats and upper-works swept away.
>
> The current was running swiftly, for the vessels entered the cut before the water had reached its level. On the first day, not more than six miles was made, and this was only accomplished by all hands going to work and sawing or cutting away the obstructions....
>
> On the second day, the vessels were so torn to pieces that no more harm could be done to them — they had hulls and engines left and that had to suffice. The officers and men performed a great deal of manual labor, but no one found fault, and their jolly songs echoed through the woods as they worked, frightening the birds out of their quiet retreats, where they had rested undisturbed for a quarter of a century.[35]

After four days of hacking and plowing their way, the task force reached the Tallahatchie River and started down it, with the gunboats *Chillicothe*, one of the new ironclads, and the *Baron DeKalb* in the lead. About ten o'clock in the morning on Wednesday, March 11, it encountered an obstacle it could neither pass nor remove.

General Pemberton had received intelligence informing him of Grant's move into Yazoo Pass, and Pemberton had immediately responded by ordering Major General William Wing Loring to take his division from its position on the Yalobusha River and hurry to the Tallahatchie to block the Union force's advance. After scouting the Tallahatchie and Yazoo for a hundred miles above Yazoo City, Loring and his engineering officer, Major Minor Meriwether, chose a site near Greenwood, just above the confluence of the two rivers. He erected a line of works, named Fort Pemberton, built of cotton bales and mud and extending up from the Yazoo to the Tallahatchie. A hastily constructed raft was placed in the river as a barrier, and a steamer the Confederates had captured, the *Star of the West*, which as a U.S. vessel had attempted to relieve Fort Sumter two years earlier, was scuttled and sunk immediately behind the raft as a further deterrent to the task force's passage downriver.

The official report of General Loring summarizes the engagement between the fort and the task force:

> At 10 A.M. [Wednesday, March 11] the formidable iron-clad *Chillicothe* steamed around the bend of the river in our front, as though it was intended to rush upon the raft and destroy it. A well-directed shell from our 32-pounder fell upon her turret, and she sensibly diminished her speed. This was followed by a solid shot from an 18-pounder rifle, which also struck, and the *Chillicothe* backed up stream until her hull was hidden around the bend, save her bow and that portion of her which contained the 11-inch guns. She then opened fire, and cannonading was kept up for an hour, when the gunboat withdrew, having been struck several times by three of our guns.
>
> Thursday (the 12th), the enemy was engaged in erecting a battery upon a point in front, thickly wooded, which we could not prevent in consequence of the scarcity of ammunition.
>
> On Friday morning, at 10 o'clock, the enemy again opened upon our works from two gunboats abreast, their land batteries, and a 13-inch mortar. We promptly responded with every gun we had in position, and the fight raged furiously the entire day, night putting an end to it....
>
> In this day's [Friday's] engagement we experienced our only loss. A shell exploded over ... our guns, wounding 3 of the gunners, one of whom died in a few hours.... Saturday was

quiet until 4 P.M., when we were engaged by their land batteries and a gunboat spiritedly for about half an hour. Sunday was occupied by the enemy and ourselves in adding strength to our respective works. Monday, as we afterward discovered, was fixed by the enemy for a grand assault with their entire force upon our works. Accordingly, the gunboat *Chillicothe* (the other ironclad [*Baron DeKalb*] having been disabled in Friday's engagement) got into position, bow on, at 1,200 yards range, and with their land batteries and sharpshooters the day's work began. In about twenty minutes after the engagement commenced, a shot from one of our heavy guns penetrated the *Chillicothe* and so badly injured her that the proposed assault was abandoned and she withdrew, leaving the land batteries and sharpshooters to keep up the fight until sunset.

Our loss during the engagement was 1 killed and 4 wounded, and 16 severely burned or injured by the explosion of our magazine. Total of casualties, 21.

A significant silence characterized their movements the three following days, although we could see them plainly at their batteries.

On Friday [March 20], before day, they abandoned their breastwork and commenced a rapid retreat up the river. Thus was conducted the battle of the Tallahatchee.[36]

Admiral Porter found fault with both his naval commander and with the Army in the engagement. "The only way this fort could be taken was by siege guns brought up close to the works," Porter wrote. "But this was not done. The general commanding the military contingent did not consider himself strong enough to attempt anything of consequence, and after a delay of thirteen days, in which neither side did anything, the Federal forces withdrew."[37]

The failure of the Union attack was a tribute not only to the skill of the Confederate gunners but especially to the wisdom of General Loring and Major Meriwether in locating Fort Pemberton on a site virtually surrounded by water and marsh, which made an assault by land impracticable. Except in establishing shore batteries—which actually proved ineffectual against the rebels' cotton-and-mud entrenchments—General Ross's troops, thwarted by the terrain, were useless. As the Union convoy withdrew back the way it had come it was joined in retreat by transports bearing the two additional divisions that General Grant on March 7 had sent up Yazoo Pass to reinforce Ross's command. All returned to him defeated.

While that expedition was ending, another, with the same purpose of flanking Vicksburg's northern defenses, was starting. "Lieutenant McLeod Murphy," Admiral Porter reported, "discovered a pass through the woods some ten miles above the mouth of the Yazoo, by which it was thought the gunboats could reach the valley of Deer Creek, and, perhaps get into the Yazoo River by the Sunflower and Yallabusha [Yalobusha], thereby reaching the rear of Vicksburg. The water in the Mississippi had risen remarkably, so much so that land usually dry for miles in the interior, now had seventeen feet of water over it. The question was, could the gun-boats get through the woods and thick underbrush which abounded in that locality."[38]

To find the answer to that question, an expedition including five gunboats, two mortar boats and four tugs was launched on March 14. Two days later that flotilla was followed by two transports carrying General Sherman's troops, all vessels beginning their mission at Steele's Bayou and proceeding through Black Bayou to Deer Creek and from there taking any course the vessels could find to lead them into the Yazoo River. Their purpose, as General Grant explained in his order to Sherman, was to determine "the feasibility of getting an army through that route to the east bank of that river, and at a point from which they can act advantageously against Vicksburg."[39]

The expedition ended in near disaster. The vessels were forcing their way through not a water course but a flooded jungle, and the major stream that the gunboats were exploring became more and more narrow and constricting, and rebel harassment from its banks grew more and more deadly. At last the gunboats were stopped by a barricade of trees the rebels had felled into the stream, and Admiral Porter, who had gone along on the expedition, so promising had he believed it to be, feared being boarded by the Confederates operating in the surrounding woods. He quickly made plans to have his men burn the boats and flee into the swampy wilds around them. He and his boats were saved at the last minute by the arrival of Sherman and his troops, who scattered the menacing Confederates. The expedition's mission was then ended, and the vessels laboriously made their way back to the Mississippi. The answer sought by Porter and Grant was "no." Getting an army behind Vicksburg by that route was not feasible.

"I reported the facts to General Grant," Sherman wrote, "who was sadly disappointed at the failure of the fleet to get through to the Yazoo above Haines's Bluff, and ordered us to resume our camps at Young's Point. We accordingly steamed down, and regained our camps on the 27th [of March]."[40]

A flanking movement via Yazoo Pass or Steele's Bayou now eliminated as an option, Grant would have to try something else in his campaign to conquer Vicksburg.

23. New Directions

His misdeeds in the administration of New Orleans's government having been exposed Major General Benjamin Franklin Butler had been relieved of command of the U.S. Army's Department of the Gulf in November 1862, and to replace him Secretary Stanton (or the president) had chosen Major General Nathaniel Prentice Banks, another, like Butler, on the long list of politicians made generals by the commander in chief, President Lincoln.

Born in Waltham, Massachusetts, forty-seven years old in 1863, Banks was a lawyer, a former speaker of the U.S. House of Representatives, first elected to the House as a Democrat and re-elected as a Republican. He was governor of Massachusetts from January 1858 to January 1861 and was briefly a Republican candidate for president in 1860. Lincoln appointed him a major general in May 1861, one of the first to be made a major general. And although he had no military experience or training, he outranked even General Grant. His service in the field, mostly in Virginia, during his first Army assignments was undistinguished. A contemporary photograph, however, shows him looking prepossessingly smart in his tailored uniform with its tasseled epaulets and knee-length frock coat, his hand resting on his sword. His only military success had come as a recruiter. Asked in November 1862 to form a force of thirty thousand new recruits from New England and New York, he used his political contacts to enlist the help of the governors of those states and succeeded in that recruitment drive.

In December 1862 he sailed off to his new assignment in New Orleans. At the end of his voyage down the Atlantic coast, into the gulf and up the Mississippi, past the captured forts, he arrived in New Orleans on December 14. On December 16 he and his staff met with General Butler and Butler's staff at Butler's headquarters in the mausoleumlike New Orleans Custom House near the river, and there Butler formally handed over command of the Department of the Gulf. During the next several days Butler briefed his replacement on both the civil and military aspects of his new and vast responsibilities. Banks would be not only commander of an army but a military governor, with a special charge given him by the president to overhaul Louisiana's secessionist civil government.

According to one account, Banks quickly made his presence felt in New Orleans society as well as in the city's business and civil affairs and in the city at large: "The Bankses, with their fashionable clothes, bodyguards, servants, and stylish airs, were comparable to royalty. Mrs. Banks had her weekly receptions at the St. Charles [Hotel] and all the 'best ladies appeared there in lace and diamonds.' Many of the confirmed Confederate ladies whose husbands were given jobs by the new commander seemed to be won back to the Union."[1]

Banks's Job No. 1, in the mind of the Army's general in chief, General Halleck, was to lend his efforts to the capture of the Mississippi. "The first military operations which will engage your attention on your arrival at New Orleans will be the opening of the Mississippi

River," Halleck wrote to Banks. "The President regards the opening of the Mississippi River as the first and most important of all our military and naval operations, and it is hoped that you will not lose a moment in accomplishing it.... The opening of the Mississippi River is now the great and primary object of your expedition."[2] Halleck had his doubts about Banks, but he relentlessly urged him on anyway.

In the meantime, Admiral Farragut had quit Pensacola and returned to New Orleans in response to Porter's reports that the Confederates were strengthening their fortification at Port Hudson and turning it into another Vicksburg. In November 1862, turning over his gulf blockading duties to a subordinate, he had returned to the Mississippi, eager to have another go at extinguishing all rebel control of the big river. In December 1862 he had promised General Banks his cooperation in pursuing the capture of the river and in turn he hoped to receive from Banks the necessary troops to accomplish the mission, troops that he had failed to receive from Butler.

In the Department of the Gulf, which embraced southeastern Louisiana and coastal parts of Texas, Mississippi and Florida, General Banks had some forty-two thousand troops, nearly forty thousand of whom were posted in Louisiana, the rest being stationed at Pensacola. Many of those who had come with him to New Orleans were the raw, nine-month volunteers he had recently recruited. Altogether his troops comprised the U.S. Nineteenth Army Corps, also known as the Army of the Gulf, and was divided into four divisions. The first division was commanded by Brigadier General Cuvier Grover, the second by Brigadier General William Hemsley Emory, the third by Major General Christopher Columbus Augur, and the fourth by Brigadier General Thomas West Sherman. All four division commanders were West Point graduates. Each division was composed of three brigades and three field artillery batteries. Also included in Banks's command were six troops of cavalry, numbering about seven hundred effectives, and a regiment of heavy artillery.

Banks immediately took up the burdens of his office, revising some of Butler's harsh policies and trying to win over the people of New Orleans. One of his first actions, taken at Farragut's urging, was to order the re-occupation of Baton Rouge. "I have recommended to General Banks the occupation of Baton Rouge," Farragut wrote to the Department of the Navy. "It is only twelve or fifteen miles from Port Hudson, and is therefore a fine base of operations. He has approved the move, and ordered his transports to proceed directly to that point. I ordered Commander James Alden, in the *Richmond*, with two gunboats, to accompany them and cover the landing."[3] On December 17, following a brief naval bombardment that drove off the five hundred or so Confederates who were garrisoning the town, General Grover and the troops of the first division disembarked from their transport steamers and marched into the wasted and woebegone state capital. There they remained.

Until he reached New Orleans, Banks didn't know that Vicksburg was not the only remaining major obstacle to U.S. control of the Mississippi. In Washington there were apparently others who lacked that same knowledge. Yet Port Hudson, 135 miles above New Orleans, stood like Vicksburg, fortified on a commanding bluff, brazenly defying any Union vessel to ascend the river beyond Baton Rouge. Despite his orders, Banks could not give Grant much help at Vicksburg so long as he had to run past the guns of Port Hudson to do so. He couldn't even communicate directly with Grant.

Lieutenant Colonel Richard B. Irwin, assistant adjutant general in Banks's army, explained Banks's predicament: "The Confederate occupation of Port Hudson had completely changed the nature of the problem confided to General Banks for solution, for he had now to choose among three courses, each involving an impossibility: to carry by assault a strong line of works [at Port Hudson], three miles long, impregnable on either flank and defended by 16,000 good troops; to lay siege to the place, with the certainty that it would be relieved from Mississippi and the prospect of losing his siege train in the venture; [or] to leave Port Hudson in his rear and go against Vicksburg, thus sacrificing his communications, putting New Orleans in peril, and courting irreparable disaster as the price of the remote chance of achieving a great success."[4]

Banks first considered the first option. He had been informed that Port Hudson was garrisoned by 12,000 men, a strength that tempted him, but then, on December 18, 1862, he heard that reinforcements had increased that number to 23,000 and that more reinforcements were on the way. On December 31, 1862, Banks had 31,253 officers and men present for duty, about 10,000 of whom were occupying Baton Rouge.[5] Believing his force insufficient in numbers and in preparation, Banks ruled out the first option.

He then decided to try a variant of Option No. 3 and developed a plan to implement it. The idea for the operation he proposed had come from Brigadier General Godfrey Weitzel, commander of the Union brigade posted at Brashear City (now Morgan City), Louisiana, about seventy miles southwest of New Orleans, on the east bank of the Atchafalaya River, who from his position could see how Port Hudson could be bypassed. The plan called for Banks to take his troops across the Mississippi, proceed west by rail to the Atchafalaya River, cross it, then march up beside Bayou Teche, paralleling the Atchafalaya, all the way to the Red River at Alexandria, Louisiana, then, assuming steamers could be obtained, one way or another, he would move down the Red River to its mouth on the Mississippi, where he could either turn upstream to join Grant at Vicksburg or downstream to attack Port Hudson. It seemed to Banks a good plan, temporarily satisfying Washington, which was pushing him to move on Vicksburg, and at the same time delaying a confrontation at Port Hudson. On January 15 Banks wrote to General Halleck to inform him and to justify the move, telling Halleck the operation would give Banks's army "control of the water communications and approaches to the Red River, which will become of great importance to us as soon as we are prepared to move against Port Hudson."[6]

In the meantime Admiral Farragut, restless from inactivity, was pursuing a plan of his own. Greatly disturbed by the news of the capture of the *Queen of the West* and the loss of the *Indianola*—and the consequent lost ability of the U.S. Navy to control the mouth of the Red River, from which the Confederate army at Vicksburg and Port Hudson was being supplied—Farragut, in his "damn the torpedoes" fighting spirit, decided to take a squadron of his warships past Port Hudson's menacing guns and resume the blockade of the Red River. Although Admiral Porter commanded the Navy's Mississippi River fleet, Farragut had been given the responsibility for bottling up rebel shipping on the Red River. On October 2, 1862, Secretary Welles had issued to Farragut the following orders: "While the Mississippi River continues to be blockaded at Vicksburg, and until you learn from Commander D. D. Porter, who will be in command of the Mississippi squadron, that he has, in conjunction with the army, opened the river, it will be necessary for you to guard the lower part of that river, especially where it is joined by the Red River, the source of many of the supplies of the enemy."[7]

To better his chance of successfully passing Port Hudson, he asked General Banks to cooperate by having a force make a demonstration on the land side of the fortifications, drawing the attention and fire of Port Hudson's gunners away from the river while Farragut's vessels attempt to steal past under cover of darkness.

Banks agreed to do so. He saw the possibility that Farragut's choking off supplies to

Port Hudson could lead to its surrender, gaining for Banks a bloodless victory and an opened door to Vicksburg. He and Farragut set the date and time for the demonstration by Banks's troops.

On March 12 the seven warships Farragut selected for the mission had come up from New Orleans and were at Baton Rouge. Two days later they anchored at Profit Island, seven miles below Port Hudson, where they were arranged for their perilous run past the rebel guns. All but one of the seven vessels were screw propelled, three of them large warships, heavily armed, and three were smaller. Farragut had them lashed together in pairs, one large and one smaller, the larger one to starboard of the smaller one as they would move northward up the river. The advantages of pairing them that way were (1) the vessels would present fewer targets than if they were strung out in single file, (2) each vessel would have, in effect, an auxiliary engine to propel the pair in the event one was hit and lost power, and (3) the larger, stouter, more heavily armed vessels would be the ones more exposed to enemy fire and whose more numerous guns would bear on the rebel fortification. The flagship, *Hartford*, was paired with the *Albatross*, and they would be the lead ships. Next would come the *Richmond*, paired with the *Genesee*. Then would come the *Monongahela*, paired with the *Kineo*. Last would come the frigate *Mississippi*, the only side-wheeler, its wheel housings and guards making pairing impractical. It would proceed without a partner. Supporting the seven vessels with suppressing fire would be the gunboats *Essex* and *Sachem* and five mortar schooners, positioned along the east bank of the river just below the fortification.

Farragut's squadron waited at Profit Island for several hours, till darkness covered them, then shortly before ten P.M. the vessels shoved off, headed into the night, stealthily making their way toward the rebel fortification. Farragut's nineteenth-century biographer, Captain A.T. Mahan, described the endangering event that came next:

> Just as they were fairly starting, a steamer was seen approaching from down the river, flaring lights and making the loud puffing of the high-pressure engines. The flag-ship slowed down, and the new arrival came alongside with a message from the general [Banks] that the army was then encamped about five miles in rear of the Port Hudson batteries. Irritated by a delay which served only to attract the enemy's attention and to assure himself that no diversion was to be expected from the army, the admiral was heard to mutter: "He [Banks] had as well be in New Orleans or at Baton Rouge for all the good he is doing us." At the same moment the east bank of the river was lit up, and on the opposite point huge bonfires kindled to illumine the scene.[8]

General Banks's messenger boat had given away the squadron's approach as clearly as if it had sounded an alarm for the Confederate gunners. And it had done so to deliver a worthless message: General Banks and twelve thousand of his troops, on whom Farragut was depending for a diversion that would perhaps save him ships and lives, would not be participating after all. They had taken too long to march the two dozen miles from Baton Rouge and had missed their crucial appointment. And so they had simply bedded down for the night, far from the action, leaving Farragut on his own.

The attempt at passage was a disaster. Farragut's vessels ran the Confederate gantlet of heavy guns for a mile and a half, and only two of the seven — the *Hartford* and its partner, the *Albatross* — made it to the other end. The *Richmond* had reached the 90-degree turn in the river near the end of the line of fortifications when a plunging shot struck the engine's safety valves, releasing so much steam that the ship lost power, and the captain, believing the *Genesee* was not powerful enough to move both vessels against the current, turned about and headed the *Richmond* back downstream, taking the *Genesee* with it. The *Monongahela* grounded in the shoals opposite the town of Port Hudson, hitting the river bottom with such force that the *Kineo*'s lashings were sundered. For twenty-five minutes, under constant fire, both vessels struggled to pull the *Monongahela* free, at which they finally succeeded, only to have the *Monongahela*'s overheated engine break down and stop as the two vessels tried to resume their run past the rebel guns. Crippled and unmanageable, the *Monongahela*, with the *Kineo* again bound to it and having lost six killed and twenty-one wounded, drifted helplessly downriver. The *Mississippi* ran aground near the turn of the river and after its crew labored for thirty-five minutes to free it, enduring enemy fire the entire time, its captain ordered it set on fire and abandoned. The three small boats on it that could still float took the crew, including the wounded, to shore on the west bank. The abandoned ship burned until three o'clock in the morning, then floated free and drifted downstream till it exploded about two hours later. Its losses included twenty-five killed, thirty-nine missing and thirty-seven taken prisoner. Altogether Farragut's flotilla had lost some seventy-five men killed or wounded.

The *Hartford* had been thrown off course by the current at the turn in the river and had nearly run aground and become another victim, but had been saved by the additional power of the *Albatross*, which reversed its engine and managed to swing the larger vessel sharply away from shore.

Although a disaster in its losses of ships and men, Farragut's run past Port Hudson was to prove a success in hindering the Confederates' war effort. The *Hartford* and *Albatross* would not be able to patrol and command the entire two-hundred-mile stretch of river between Port Hudson and Vicksburg, as Farragut had intended, but they would substantially curtail the Confederates' use of the Red River to supply Vicksburg and Port Hudson. "Your services at Red River," Porter wrote to Farragut when he heard Farragut had passed Port Hudson, "will be a godsend; it is worth to us the loss of the 'Mississippi,' and is at this moment the severest blow that could be struck at the South. They obtain all their supplies and ammunition in that way.... The great object is to cut off supplies. For that reason I sent down the 'Queen of the West' and the 'Indianola.' I regret that the loss of the 'Indianola' should have been the cause of your present position."[9]

On March 20, a week after Farragut's passage, General Pemberton reported to his superiors in Richmond that "The Mississippi is again cut off. Neither subsistence nor ordnance can come or go."[10] Pemberton also wrote to Confederate Major General Richard Taylor in Louisiana to have him understand the seriousness of the new situation, "Port Hudson depends almost entirely for supplies upon the other side of the river."[11]

After passing Port Hudson, Farragut slowly proceeded on to Vicksburg, destroying on his way quantities of provisions the rebels had placed on the levees to await shipment up or down the river. Near Vicksburg he anchored and sent a message to General Grant, offering whatever help the two vessels could provide, but also asking for a supply of coal for them. Grant responded by cutting adrift a barge loaded with four hundred tons of coal, which in the dark of night floated down to where Farragut's vessels were anchored and were intercepted by small boats sent out from the *Hartford*. Grant also lent his support to Farragut's blockade of the Red River, proposing in a message to Farragut that the Navy should patrol the entire Mississippi between Vicksburg and the Red River. "I will have a consultation with Admiral Porter on this subject," Grant wrote to Farragut. "I am happy to say the admiral and myself have never yet disagreed upon any policy."[12]

Porter was then on the misadventurous mission up Steele's Bayou and out of touch, but in Porter's absence the ever eager, young Colonel Ellet volunteered two of his rams, then moored in the Mississippi above Vicksburg, to aid Farragut's blockade. Near dawn on March 25 the *Lancaster* and the *Switzerland* set out to join Farragut, anchored below Vicksburg. The sun came up as the rams were attempting to slip past Vicksburg's guns, which opened fire as soon as the boats were spotted. The *Lancaster* was struck by a shell that exploded in its boilers, shattering and sinking it. The *Switzerland* was also hit by a shell in its boilers, but stayed afloat, drifted powerless down to the *Hartford*, where it was hauled to safety, then repaired by Farragut's engineers and restored to service.

On March 28, Farragut and his three-vessel flotilla left the anchorage below Vicksburg and headed back toward the Red River. Before he left the vicinity of Vicksburg, though, Farragut sent to Porter his teen-age son, Loyall, his only child, who had been aboard the *Hartford* with his father serving as a cabin boy ever since they left Pensacola. Farragut earlier had written his wife, "I am trying to make up my mind to part with Loyall and to let him go home by way of Cairo. I am too devoted a father to have my son with me in troubles of this kind. The anxieties of a father should not be added to those of the commander."[13]

On April 1 the three vessels dropped anchor near the mouth of the Red River. Shortly after arriving Farragut sent a message to General Banks, still below Port Hudson, via a courier aboard a skiff disguised as a tree, which floated past the rebel guns unmolested. The message was that Grant planned to send General McPherson's Seventeenth Corps down from Lake Providence through the newly devised waterway to the Red River, and McPherson would then steam down the Red River to Bayou Sara, Louisiana, a community on the Mississippi just above Port Hudson. From that site McPherson would be able to cooperate with Banks in a campaign against Port Hudson.

Banks doubtlessly welcomed the message, but hounded by General Halleck to move against Port Hudson, he was desperate to take some sort of action immediately. "Nothing but absolute necessity will excuse any further delay on your part," Halleck told him in one dispatch, and then warned him that there was "much dissatisfaction here at the delay" in attacking Port Hudson. The president apparently was expressing to Halleck his displeasure over the lame efforts of his political general. And so Banks acted, launching his campaign into the heart of Louisiana as General Weitzel had suggested. As March ended, he ferried two divisions—General Grover's and General Emory's—across to the west side of the Mississippi at and above New Orleans, leaving behind General Thomas Sherman's division and a contingent of General Augur's division to defend New Orleans and Baton Rouge.

Grover's and Emory's divisions, moving southwestward, converged on Brashear City. The entire force, numbering some sixteen thousand men, including Weitzel's brigade, with Banks himself in command, crossed the Atchafalaya on April 11 and prepared to turn northwestward on the west bank of nearby Bayou Teche, an ancient former course of the Mississippi, as muddy brown as the big river itself, lined by gnarled, Spanish-moss-draped oaks as it flows southeastward through Cajun country to the Atchafalaya River.

Contesting Banks's advance was a three-thousand man force commanded by Louisianan Major General Richard Taylor. Hearing of Banks's approach, Taylor raised a line of mud breastworks, named Fort Bisland, that extended on both sides of the Teche about four miles north of Pattersonville (now Patterson), west of Brashear City. Banks overwhelmed the outnumbered Confederates, attacking with Emory's artillery on their front beginning April 12 while sending Grover's division around Taylor's left flank, using transport steamers to carry Grover's troops across Grand Lake, east of Bayou Teche. Once he learned the enemy was in his rear, Taylor abandoned Fort Bisland in the middle of the night and hastily withdrew northwestward, his retreating troops on April 14 desperately fighting their way past Grover's force at a bow in Bayou Teche called Irish Bend. Each side suffered some six hundred casualties in the April 12–14 engagements.

Taylor continued to retreat to the northwest along the west side of the Teche, and Banks stayed right behind him, skirmishers from the two forces intermittently engaging each other and Taylor's army gradually losing strength as deserters dropped out of the march and headed for home, intending to defend their families from the Yankee invaders. On April 17 Banks's army reached Vermillionville (now Lafayette) and on April 20 it arrived at Opelousas, from which Louisiana's government officials had recently fled to seek new refuge in Shreveport.

At Opelousas the pursuit abruptly halted, Banks leaving his troops for two weeks while he hurried back to New Orleans and tended to some mysteriously urgent business there. He rejoined his army on May 4, and it resumed its march toward Alexandria. Seeing the Union army rushing toward them and unable to stop it, the Confederates evacuated Alexandria, Taylor's diminishing force retreating toward Shreveport and the troops of Major General Edmund Kirby Smith, which had occupied Alexandria, hurriedly moving west to Texas, many civilians joining the rebel troops in their flight, the slaveholders among them taking their slaves with them to avoid their confiscation.

While the U.S. Army was moving through Louisiana, the U.S. Navy, Admiral Farragut cooperating with General Banks, was also making an incursion. Four gunboats under the command of Lieutenant Commander Augustus P. Cooke steamed up the Atchafalaya in support of Banks's army, and on April 13 three of them — the *Estrella*, the *Arizona* and the *Calhoun*— were lying at anchor in Grand Lake, a broad, lakelike expanse of the river, when three Confederate vessels, the captured ram *Queen of the West* and two river steamers, were spotted coming toward them, the rising plumes of dark smoke from the rebel vessels betraying them from a distance. Third Assistant Engineer George W. Baird was standing watch on the *Calhoun* at the time and recorded the remarkable events:

> April 14, 1863.—I had the midwatch; the fires were banked. I was on deck now and then. About 2 o'clock I saw two lights as if on boats, up the lake, and they were moving. Somehow I thought they were on vessels and told the officer of the deck (Sargeant), but he was a phlegmatic old fellow and was not enthused. He noted it and later reported it. The light came nearer and nearer, but very slowly. At 4 I was relieved and I turned in, thinking I had overrated the importance of those lights. At 5:10 I was awakened by "All hands to quarters!" for we had no drum, nor fife, nor bugle; it was the call by the boatswain's mate. I was so sleepy I waited a moment to see if there was any excitement; I heard the cable slipped and then a gun fired; then I got out in a hurry. The engine was going ahead slowly; day was breaking. There were three vessels, and one of them had opened fire on us. They were the rebel ram *Queen of the West* and the rebel transports *Grand Duke* and *Mary T.* I did not go to the engine room, but joined Jordan, Bostwick, Brown, and Dr. Whitehead, who stood together on the hurricane deck. We were steaming away from the enemy. The *Arizona* and the *Estrella* were headed toward the enemy, and I could see the *Arizona*'s beam working. Brown and Dr. Whitehead began to remark about our leaving; then one of them said, "Why, even the *Estrella* is headed toward the enemy." Jordan then put the helm down and we headed up....
>
> This was a remarkable battle.... [As] soon as the Parrott would bear, it was fired at extreme elevation, for the vessels were nearly 3 miles away. Brown and Dr. Whitehead who stood over the gun, both said they saw the shot as it left the gun and traced its trajectory and saw it strike the *Queen*. I did not see the shot, but I heard it fired, heard its flight, and its landing on the *Queen*, its explosion and the rush of steam that followed. The *Queen* had

been cotton-clad above [and] armored around her machinery ... but she had no armor on her upper deck. So the shell we fired, being a percussion shell, had struck on her roof, exploded, cut a steam pipe, and set fire to the cotton. The engineers were driven from the casemate and no pump could be started; in a few moments the *Queen of the West* was in a blaze; 26 of her people were scalded or burned to death. The boats of our fleet took off her crew, and in about two hours (7:40) her magazine exploded and she was no more.[14]

The checkered career of Charles Ellet's prized *Queen of the West*, oft victorious, twice defeated, had come to an inglorious end.

On Monday, April 20, while Banks's troops were moving into Opelousas, the Union gunboats captured the rebel fort at Butte a la Rose (now Butte La Rose) on the Atchafalaya, roughly halfway between Baton Rouge and Lafayette. The fourth vessel of Commander Cooke's flotilla, the *Clifton*, led the attack and after a short but furious exchange of fire drove off the crews of the fort's two guns and forced the fort's surrender, taking about two hundred Confederate prisoners. Aboard the *Clifton* one man was killed and one wounded. "Some cotton, sugar and molasses has fallen into our hands," a Marine aboard the *Clifton* reported in his journal, "and undoubtedly some prize money will be due us from this affair."[15] The *Clifton* was so severely damaged in the battle that it had to return to Brashear City for repairs.

On May 1, the gunboats *Estrella* and *Arizona* reached the confluence of the Atchafalaya and Red rivers, east of Alexandria, and proceeded down the Red to the Mississippi, joining the *Hartford*, *Albatross* and *Switzerland* there. Commander Cooke, reporting to Farragut, happily announced that the Atchafalaya River was now open from one end to the other, all the way to the Gulf of Mexico. Port Hudson could now be circumnavigated.

On May 4, Admiral Porter, having run past Vicksburg with several ironclad gunboats, arrived at the mouth of the Red River, where he conferred with Farragut, and the next day steamed up the Red River, headed for Alexandria. Seeing that his presence was no longer needed, Farragut on May 6 turned over command of his little squadron to Commander James S. Palmer and, taking advantage of the newly reopened Atchafalaya River, steamed off to New Orleans, where he could give closer attention to his gulf blockading duties.

General Banks and his army marched triumphantly into Alexandria on May 7. Well pleased with himself for having registered his first successful military campaign, Banks wrote to his wife, "Our success has been splendid. All say it is the cleanest, the best conceived and best executed campaign of the war."[16] The "all," one might guess, were all members of his staff.

Banks at last stood able to cooperate with General Grant in the campaign to take Port Hudson and Vicksburg, the objective toward which General Halleck had been ceaselessly pressing him. Even in his note congratulating him on his Louisiana campaign, Halleck urged Banks to join Grant as quickly as possible and finally free the Mississippi.

On entering Alexandria, Banks discovered Porter's ironclads tied up in the Red River, with Porter awaiting him. Porter had brought not only congratulations for Banks but also surprising news. Grant and his army, including the troops of General McPherson's Seventeenth Corps, which Grant had promised would assist Banks in the campaign against Port Hudson, had crossed to the east side of the Mississippi on the night of April 30 and were marching on Vicksburg.

Grant had left Banks on his own — and left him wondering what he should do now.

24. The Other Side of the River

General Grant tried one last time to build a detour to avoid Vicksburg's batteries. On March 31 work began on a canal that would connect Duckport Landing, on the west side of the Mississippi above Vicksburg, with Walnut Bayou and a thirty-five-mile-long chain of streams that ultimately debouched back into the Mississippi at New Carthage, Louisiana, below Vicksburg. New Carthage was the place Grant had been eyeing as a staging area for ferrying his troops across to the east side of the river. After much digging, by the troops with picks and shovels gouging out the canal and by dredges clearing the lower waterway, the project was finally forsaken after the swollen Mississippi River on April 25 fell five and a half feet, leaving but six inches of water in the canal where it entered Walnut Bayou and stranding two dredges and twenty work barges deep in the swampy wilds until a new winter would bring more rain.

Grant also made one last stab at choosing the Yazoo as the route for his assault on Vicksburg. In early April he made a personal reconnaissance up the Yazoo on an ironclad gunboat, intent on seeing for himself whether another attack against the fortified heights at Haynes's Bluff and Walnut Hills might be successful. He came away pessimistic about his chances. "After the reconnaissance of yesterday," he wrote Porter, "I am satisfied that an attack upon Haynes' Bluff would be attended with immense loss of life, if not with defeat. This, then, closes out the last hope of turning the enemy by the left."[1]

Only days before that reconnaissance, Grant had ordered General McClernand to take his Thirteenth Corps down the west side of the Mississippi, marching southward from Milliken's Bend to New Carthage. Grant had second-guessed himself with new thoughts of launching an assault from the Yazoo, but now he had confirmed that his earlier decision to move down the west side of the river and attack Vicksburg from the south was the correct one. The advance units of McClernand's corps, men of Brigadier General Peter J. Osterhaus's division, reached New Carthage on April 11, and more were laboriously pushing their way southward, following the west-bank levee, overcoming the obstacles of the terrain and the harassing rebel infantry and cavalry.

Grant had already contacted Admiral Porter about having ironclad gunboats support the proposed crossing and landing, and Porter had agreed to provide them, but he wanted to wait until Grant's troops had established their base at New Carthage before he attempted the run past Vicksburg, so that the boats would have a friendly port to put into once they had withstood Vicksburg's guns. On April 11, though, Porter received orders from Secretary Welles to "occupy," as he said, the Mississippi below Vicksburg, taking over that stretch of the river from Farragut, so that Farragut could get back to his gulf blockading assignment. Porter now would have to make the run past Vicksburg sooner than he had expected or wanted to. He notified Grant of the sudden move and knowing that Grant was eager to get

Grant's transport steamers run past Vicksburg's guns. Repeatedly thwarted in his attempts to find a way to avoid the Confederate fortifications at Vicksburg, Grant, on the night of April 16, 1863, sent three transport steamers, loaded with freight only, in a convoy of Union gunboats to pass Vicksburg in defiance of the rebel guns (Library of Congress).

his transports down to New Carthage as soon as possible, Porter asked him if the transports were ready to go and how many would be going.

Grant answered that he was ready to go whenever the Navy was. The run was then tentatively scheduled for the night of April 14 or 15, but when a windstorm suddenly blew into the area, the run was postponed to the night of the 16th. Three transport steamers, carrying only stores, no passengers, and twelve loaded barges, escorted by seven gunboats—the *Benton* (Porter's flagship), the *Lafayette*, *Louisville*, *Mound City*, *Pittsburg*, *Carondelet* and *Tuscumbia*—would attempt to pass the rebel batteries. Barges loaded with coal were lashed to the port side of the gunboats, both as protection from the rebel fire and as a future fuel supply. Barges freighted with equipment for the troops were tied to the starboard side of five of the gunboats. The *Benton* had the tug *Ivy* lashed to its starboard side, and the *Lafayette* had the former Confederate ram *General Sterling Price* tied to its starboard side. The transports were insulated from enemy gunfire by bales of cotton and water-soaked hay stacked around their boilers and decks.

The convoy shoved off from its anchorage on the east side of the Mississippi above the mouth of the Yazoo at 9:15 P.M., skirting the west bank of the river. The plan was to try to avoid drawing the fire of the Confederate guns, slipping silently past the fortification, a muffling contrivance having been installed on the steamers to abate the noise of their engines. But if the convoy was detected and fired on, the boats were to shift over to the east side of the river to make it more difficult for the rebel guns to be depressed sufficiently to fire on them. The barge bearing ammunition was cut adrift as the convoy started, allowing it to float downriver on its own, lest it be struck and explode, destroying any vessel that was towing it. Down the river the convoy steamed in single file, the *Benton* in the lead, followed by five of the gunboats, then the transports, then the *Tuscumbia* in the rear.

The Confederates had posted pickets in yawls in the river off De Soto Point, and as the convoy approached, at about eleven P.M., gliding menacingly through the darkness, the pickets spied them and quickly rowed for shore, the pickets in one yawl heading for the east bank to warn the Confederate gunners, the others rowing hard to the west bank to light up the night by setting fire to tar barrels and a number of buildings in the village of De Soto, opposite the guns.

Fierce fusillades immediately opened, the gunboats returning the fire as they ran before the rebel batteries, billows of smoke from the guns mingling with thick black smoke from the burning buildings and barrels of tar along the shore. A Confederate shell blasted a hole in the side of the coal barge being towed by the *Lafayette*, and the barge had to be cut loose and left adrift. The *General Price* was struck twice and run into by the *Louisville* in the smoky confusion, then cut itself free from the *Lafayette* and sped away on its own. The *Louisville* lost its coal barge when it sideswiped the transport *Silver Wave*. Both the *Louisville* and the *Mound City* were struck repeatedly by rebel guns, as was the *Pittsburg*. The *Benton* was hit six times, wounding six crewmen but suffering only minor damage to the boat. The *Carondelet* was hit twice, wounding four sailors. The *Tuscumbia*, repeatedly hit, ran aground, but managed to free itself and take in tow the steamer *Forest Queen*, which had taken a disabling hit. Lost was the steamer *Henry Clay*, which was struck in the stern by a shell that exploded and set the vessel afire. Soon the entire river seemed ablaze as the wrecked steamer and flaming bales of cotton streamed southward.

General Sherman had ordered Colonel Charles Abbott, commander of the Thirtieth Iowa Infantry Regiment, which was posted on the west bank just below the Confederate batteries, to put men in yawls and have them wait in the river for any survivors of stricken vessels who were swimming or floating downstream on pieces of wreckage. At least one man was saved by Sherman's forethought — the pilot of the ruined *Henry Clay* was plucked from the river while clinging to a plank.

Then suddenly the noise of battle ended, and from the silence General Grant, aboard his headquarters steamer, the *Henry von Phul*, with his wife and young children, positioned a safe distance above Vicksburg, concluded that the flotilla of gunboats and transports had by then either passed the rebel guns or been destroyed by them.

The battered flotilla had survived not only the guns of Vicksburg but those of Warrenton, the fortified community below Vicksburg on the east bank. By three A.M. all seven gunboats as well as the tug *Ivy* and the transport *Silver Wave* had anchored near Diamond Island, about twelve miles above New Carthage. All were damaged, but none so severely that they could no longer serve. Twelve crewmen were wounded.

The transport *Forest Queen*, which the *Tuscumbia* had had to cut loose and leave behind on the west bank, by April 19 had been repaired and rejoined the flotilla at New Carthage.

Only one transport, the *Henry Clay*, had failed to make it past the dreaded rebel guns, and when General Grant received that news, he was elated and eager to do it again. This time the gantlet would be run by six transports and twelve barges, two barges lashed to the sides of each of the transports. The transports would be making the run without gunboats and thus without guns of their own. To enhance their chances of success, a detachment from Colonel Abbott's Thirtieth Iowa Infantry Regiment was ordered to move into the village of De Soto and set fire to the remaining buildings there, leaving the Confederates with nothing to burn on the night of the attempted passage. That plan was thwarted, however, by the rebels' strong defense of the village, and Abbott's troops were twice turned back without entering it.

A new problem soon developed for the expedition. The transports were manned by civilians, and most of them balked at risking their lives under Vicksburg's guns. Only two boat captains and only one of the boats' crews agreed to make the run. A call for volunteers was issued to the troops, and the response — largely by men from Missouri and southern Illinois who had experience on river steamers— produced more hands than were needed to man the deserted vessels.

At nine o'clock on the night of April 22 the six transports—*Tigress, Anglo-Saxon, J.W. Cheeseman, Moderator, Horizon* and *Empire City*—cast off at Milliken's Bend, then rendezvoused at the mouth of the Yazoo and arranged themselves in single file, the *Tigress* taking its place at the head of the valiant little convoy. As soon as the moon slid below the treetops along the shore and the darkness deepened, the vessels shoved off toward the hazards of Vicksburg's guns.

Shortly before the boats reached the tip of De Soto Point the *Empire City* unintentionally passed the *Tigress* in the darkness, and when the *Empire City* rounded the turn at the point, it was spotted by the Confederate lookouts, who fired an alarm shot to alert all rebel gunners and signal the illuminating fires to be lighted. Within minutes the darkness disappeared in the glow of flames, and the rebel guns opened on the Union transports, which now sped downriver as fast as their engines could carry them. The *Tigress* was hit repeatedly and began veering toward the Vicksburg shoreline despite all efforts by the pilot to keep it headed downriver. As a last resort, the barge on its port side was cut away, and the transport was able to swing away from shore while taking a heavy pounding.

The *Moderator*'s upper structure was battered by shot, its engines disabled and several of its crew wounded, but managed to make it past the batteries as the smoke of the rebel fires, hanging low on the river, began to obscure the Union vessels. The *J.W. Cheeseman*, concealed by the dense smoke, made it through almost unscathed, although it had paused long enough to take aboard the crew of the *Tigress* before it sank. The *Anglo-Saxon* was struck by a shot in its bow and veered toward the Louisiana shore, where it grounded. The vessel's crew of volunteers cut its barge loose, and *Anglo-Saxon* was then able to back away and free itself. Once freed, it was hit twice; one shot disabled its engine and the vessel drifted downriver. The *Horizon* was hit fifteen times, but maintained its speed and course.

By noon of the next day, April 23, all of the transports except the sunken *Tigress* had arrived at New Carthage, battered and broken but not beyond repair. Porter estimated that all five of the surviving vessels would be back in service within two days. Six of the twelve barges had also made it through the murderous gantlet, their cargoes intact. The boats' casualties totaled two crewmen mortally wounded and six others slightly wounded.

General Grant now had his transports where he wanted them, soon able to carry his troops to the enemy's shore, with Admiral Porter's gunboats to cover the critical crossing. As soon as the bulk of his army was in place at New Carthage, Grant had thought, the all-out land war against Vicksburg would be ready to commence. However, the limited dry areas of New Carthage's sodden soil were soon crowded by the troops of McClernand's four divisions and two divisions of General McPherson's Seventeenth Corps. General Sherman's Fifteenth Corps was yet to arrive. Grant could see when he visited the site on April 18 that a larger staging area for the crossing was urgently needed.

On April 19, McClernand's troops marched southward in two parallel columns a short distance apart, moving toward Somerset, Louisiana, a river landing about eight miles below

New Carthage. Somerset proved inadequate also. McClernand's men slogged farther south to Hard Times, Louisiana, the next landing, which, McClernand's reconnaissance patrol had discovered, offered enough high, dry ground to marshal Grant's vast army for the crossing.

About thirty land miles below Vicksburg, on the east side of the Mississippi, where the Big Black River flows into the Mississippi, stands the town of Grand Gulf, much of which Farragut's warships had blasted into charred ruins after his vessels were fired on from the town. Unaffected, though, were the roads leading out of Grand Gulf, roads that could provide an invading army access to the interior of Mississippi. Moreover, Grand Gulf was situated nearly opposite Hard Times, which would make the crossing of the river by Grant's troops a short, quick boat ride. Grand Gulf was just the place, Grant decided, to land his army for the attack on Vicksburg.

While his troops were still gathering at Hard Times, Grant asked Sherman to stage a demonstration above Vicksburg to divert General Pemberton's attention from the troops massing blow Vicksburg. Sherman sent two divisions under Brigadier General Frank Blair up the Yazoo to Haynes's Bluff aboard ten transport steamers, regimental bands blaring from the decks and the boats' steam whistles screaming so the Confederates would be sure to notice their coming. The troops went ashore and skirmished for two days in front of the rebel fortifications at Haynes's Bluff and Walnut Hills, then re-embarked on the transports and steamed quietly away, returning to Young's Point to begin their march to join the rest of Grant's army at Hard Times.

Pemberton may not have been fooled by the brief, showy demonstration, but he was apparently deceived by other movements. When Grant sent several of his transports back up the river from Vicksburg, returning them to the Union's transport pool, spies informed Pemberton of their move, and Pemberton, thinking wishfully, concluded that Grant, frustrated by his failure to launch an assault via Yazoo Pass, had given up and was abandoning the fight. From his new headquarters in Jackson, Pemberton on April 11 reported to General Samuel Cooper, the Confederate army's adjutant general, and General Joseph E. Johnston, Pemberton's commander, "I think most of Grant's forces are being withdrawn to Memphis."[2]

Pemberton furthermore had to divine what the cavalry raids of Union Colonel Benjamin Grierson meant. On April 17, Grierson — leading 1,700 cavalrymen from Grant's Seventeenth Corps, based at Memphis and commanded by General Hurlbut — had set out from La Grange, Tennessee, east of Memphis, to disrupt the Confederates' railroad communication line. The raiders plunged south through a gap in the rebels' lines and rampaged to Newton Station, Mississippi, sixty-five miles east of Jackson, which they reached on April 24, having ripped up train tracks and torn down telegraph lines as they penetrated the heart of Mississippi. It turned out that Grierson's mischief had not meant anything substantial in Grant's plans for attacking Vicksburg, but Pemberton had to wrestle with the possibilities nevertheless.

Not very good at assessing significance in his adversary's movements, Pemberton had dismissed a warning that units of Grant's army were assembling at New Carthage. The Confederate commander at Grand Gulf, Brigadier General John S. Bowen, a West Pointer, had taken alarmed notice of the arrival of Union forces at New Carthage, fifteen miles above his position at Grand Gulf, and had sent three regiments across to the west side of the Mississippi to discover what was going on. The commander of that reconnaissance mission, Colonel Francis Cockrell, after a week of intelligence gathering, reported to Bowen that

Union forces were streaming down the west side of the river in force, presaging a large operation. Bowen speedily relayed the report to Pemberton. Pemberton's official response, made to the Confederate War Department in Richmond on April 9: "Much doubt it."[3]

So convinced was Pemberton that the immediate threat from Grant's army was ended that he even pulled units out of Port Hudson and Vicksburg to assist Confederate efforts elsewhere. On April 15 he wired Major General Simon Buckner, commander of the Confederates' Department of the Gulf, telling him, "I am sending troops to General Johnston, being satisfied that a large portion of Grant's army is re-enforcing [General] Rosecrans [in Tennessee]."[4]

Later that same day, April 15, Pemberton discovered how mistaken he had been. Reports began coming into his headquarters from various locations, all confirming Bowen's warning of a massive troop movement threatening Vicksburg from the south. Pemberton quickly wired the Confederate commander at Vicksburg, Major General Carter Stevenson: "Information just received that the travelers out of Memphis say the impression amounts almost to certainty that the retrograde movement from Vicksburg a ruse, and an attack expected soon. You must be on the look-out."[5]

Two days later, on April 17, Pemberton telegraphed General Johnston in Tennessee asking him to return the troops Pemberton had sent him. On April 18 Pemberton asked President Davis for more artillery. Thoroughly alarmed now, he also hurriedly reinforced Bowen's garrison at Grand Gulf, increasing its strength to 4,200 men.

By April 23 Pemberton had at last discerned design in the Union troop movements and the repeated passage of Vicksburg's guns by Porter's gunboats and Grant's store-laden transports and barges. He sent a message to General Stevenson at Vicksburg: "Indications now are that the attack will not be made on your front [from the Mississippi] or right [from the Yazoo], and that all the troops not absolutely necessary to hold the works [at Vicksburg] should be held as a movable force, either for Warrenton or Grand Gulf."[6]

Grant, meanwhile, was planning an assault on Grand Gulf. He would have Admiral Porter's gunboats pound to pieces the town's riverfront fortifications, as Porter's boats had done at the Post of Arkansas, and then he would disembark an overwhelming Union force into the shattered town. "Accordingly," Grant wrote of the planned operation, "on the morning of the 29th [of April] McClernand was directed to embark all the troops from his corps that our transports and barges could carry. About 10,000 men were so embarked. The plan was to have the navy silence the guns at Grand Gulf, and to have as many men as possible ready to debark in the shortest possible time under cover of the fire of the navy and carry the works by storm."[7]

On the morning of the 29th the troops were embarked aboard the transports as planned, and the transports pulled out from the Hard Times landing. They then stopped behind a peninsula called Coffee Point, waiting for the gunboats to blast away the threatening rebel defenses at Grand Gulf. Admiral Porter described the defenses, which consisted mainly of two earthworks fortifications, one above Grand Gulf and one below it:

> Grand Gulf was by nature as strong as Vicksburg, the Confederates in their pride called it "the little Gibraltar." The principal work called Bald Head, was on a bold bluff promontory at a bend in the river commanding a view for miles up and down the Mississippi. The current of the river, which ran here five miles an hour with innumerable eddies, had cut away the shore until beneath the fort was a perpendicular wall more than eighty feet in height, while in the rear[,] hills rising three hundred and fifty feet above the river were dotted with field works to protect the flanks of Bald Head, which fort mounted four heavy guns,

Brooke rifles and 8-inch Columbiads. In front of this the river formed a large circular bay or gulf from which the place took its name. Black River emptied into the gulf and the approach to it was commanded by two 8-inch Columbiads.

The lower forts were half a mile below Bald Head, and were connected with the latter by intrenchments by which troops could pass under cover from one fort to another. The lower batteries mounted nine heavy guns situated on the brow of a hill eight hundred yards from the river and one hundred and fifty above it.[8]

While Grant watched from aboard the tug *Ivy* in mid-stream, the seven ironclad gunboats moved into position and shortly before eight A.M. opened fire on the rebel works. The *Pittsburg, Louisville, Carondelet* and *Mound City* attacked the lower fort, hammering it into silence after three hours, then struggled against the current to join the assault on Bald Head, which the *Benton* (Porter's flagship), the *Lafayette* and the *Tuscumbia* had begun about eight-thirty. The tough ironclads blasted away at the rebel fortification, which answered with unrelenting ferocity until twelve-fifty, when the Confederates ceased firing, their ammunition now running low. Porter then moved upstream to the *Ivy* to confer with Grant. Grant told Porter that, having seen the strength of the Confederate defenses, he had decided Grand Gulf was too hazardous to land his troops there and that he would try an alternate plan. The assault was halted, the troops disembarked from the transports, and Porter's vessels were drawn back to the west bank to assess their damage and count their losses.

The *Benton* had been hit seventy times, including by a shell that exploded and set the vessel afire. Nine men were killed, and nineteen were wounded. The *Pittsburg* was struck in the hull thirty-five times. It had six killed and thirteen wounded. The *Tuscumbia* took eighty-one hits and was "completely riddled," as Porter said, having an engine disabled and suffering the loss of six men killed and twenty-four wounded, some of them mortally so. The *Lafayette* was struck forty-five times. One of its officers was wounded.

"The other vessels," Porter reported, "although considerably cut up, were not materially damaged, and all reported 'ready for service' half an hour after the action, when the gunboats tied up to the bank at Hard Times. Then came the melancholy duty of burying the dead, who were followed mournfully to their graves by their messmates and friends."[9]

Grant's twelve-year-old son, Fred, was accompanying his father on the Vicksburg expedition, and when the *Benton* returned to the dock at Hard Times, the boy boarded the vessel and witnessed the damage inflicted on it. He later wrote about the experience. He was, he said,

> sickened with the scenes of carnage. Admiral Porter had been struck on the back of the head with a fragment of shell, and his face showed the agony he was suffering, but he planned a renewal of the conflict for that night, in order to permit our transports to run past the Confederate batteries. During this inteview with the Admiral he asked me if I wanted to stay with him, and suggested that I might fill the place of a gunner he had lost. The scene around me dampened my enthusiasm for naval glory, so I replied, "I do not believe that papa will allow me to serve in the navy."[10]

While both sides waited in expectation of a renewal of the bombardment, General Bowen assessed his losses and the damage to the Grand Gulf fortifications. The Union gunboats had fired an estimated 2,500 rounds of shot and shell into the rebel works, but the damage they inflicted was reported as "not extensive." The rebels quickly repaired breaks in the parapets, and guns that had been dismounted were restored to their mounts. Telegraph lines were also restored. Casualties totaled three killed and nineteen wounded. The survival of the Confederates and their fortifications under hours of bombardment was remarkable and believed to be owed to the rebels' highly elevated position above the guns of the warships.

Not to be outdone, though, General Grant made a new move that evening as Porter's gunboats shoved off from the Hard Times landing at seven-forty-five and resumed their assault on Grand Gulf, covering the movement of the empty transports as they slipped untouched past the fortifications in the darkness. The transports and barges continued downriver, and after those vessels had passed Grand Gulf, the gunboats ceased firing and followed them to the Disharoon plantation landing on the Louisiana side of the river about four miles below Grand Gulf and about seven miles below Hard Times.

Grant now had his eye on Rodney, Mississippi, a town about fifteen miles below Grand Gulf, intending to march his troops down along the levee on the west side of the river and effect a crossing from a point opposite Rodney. From Rodney a road led to Port Gibson, Mississippi, an important road junction that Grant planned to capture and use as the point of departure for his march on Vicksburg. He directed McClernand and McPherson to move their two corps from Hard Times that evening, April 29, marching them southward through the darkness. Around midnight they reached Disharoon plantation, where the transports and gunboats were waiting.

Earlier in the day Grant had ordered a cavalry reconnaissance along the Louisiana shore in the area above Rodney. The cavalrymen questioned a number of residents of the area, seeking intelligence on the roads and conditions across the river. One of those who were questioned was a slave who claimed to be familiar with western Claiborne County, Mississippi, on the other side of the river. He said there was a good road that led to Port Gibson from Bruinsburg, Mississippi, on the river about ten miles above Rodney and six miles below Disharoon plantation.

When Grant got that report, he quickly and enthusiastically changed his plans. Bruinsburg, not Rodney, would be the site of his army's landing on the Mississippi's east bank. He immediately notified Porter, who that night, aboard the *Benton*, wrote to Navy Secretary Welles informing him of the day's action at Grand Gulf and advising him of what lay ahead on the morrow. "We land the army in the morning on the other side," he told Welles, "and march on to Vicksburg."[11]

By eight o'clock the next morning, April 30, the invading troops were loaded on the transport steamers, and on a signal from the flagship *Benton*, the little armada of gunboats and transports shoved off from Disharoon and headed downstream. From the *Benton*'s pilothouse the eyes of General Grant and Admiral Porter searched the east bank of the Mississippi looking for Confederate soldiers as Porter's crews stood ready at their battle stations. The search revealed no enemy.

At a point opposite Bruinsburg, the flagship signaled "prepare to land" and then slowly rounded to, headed for the riverbank. As soon as the prow of the boat touched shore, troops of the Twenty-fourth and Forty-sixth Indiana infantry regiments leaped from the boat's deck and rushed up the riverbank, the first ashore. They met no opposition, encountering only one person at the landing. He was taken aboard the *Benton* and detained to prevent his spreading the news of the Union troops' arrival. By noon most of McClernand's Thirteenth Corps—some seventeen thousand men—was ashore and Bruinsburg had been secured as a Union bridgehead.

"When this was effected," Grant later reflected, "I felt a degree of relief scarcely ever equalled since. Vicksburg was not yet taken it is true, nor were its defenders demoralized by any of our previous moves. I was now in the enemy's country, with a vast river and the stronghold of Vicksburg between me and my base of supplies. But I was on dry ground on the same side of the river with the enemy. All the campaigns, labors, hardships and exposures from the month of December previous to this time that had been made and endured, were for the accomplishment of this one object."[12]

25. Vicksburg at Last

Once the crossing had been made and his troops were ashore at Bruinsburg, Grant's thoughts were of his next step toward Vicksburg: the capture of Grand Gulf to use as a base. Between Bruinsburg and Grand Gulf flows Bayou Pierre, a navigable stream that empties into the Mississippi just north of Bruinsburg, presenting to Grant's army a formidable natural barrier that was then running high and fast. To capture Grand Gulf, Grant would have to get his troops across the bayou. The nearest bridge spanning it was at Port Gibson, about thirteen miles northeast of Bruinsburg. Anticipating an attempt by General Bowen to block his advance on Grand Gulf, Grant immediately sent McClernand's corps toward Port Gibson to seize the bluffs east of Bruinsburg, thus denying the rebels the high ground behind Bruinsburg, and then to push on to Port Gibson to capture the bridge before Bowen could get to it and cross or destroy it.

McClernand reached the bluffs about an hour before sunset and kept going. The advance was described by a member of the 99th Illinois regiment, Sergeant Charles A. Hobbs:

> At 9 o'clock ... we start away and climbing the steep hill push on toward Port Gibson. As we pass along[,] an old darkey gives us his blessings, but fears there will be few of us ever to return. The moon is shining above us and the road is romantic in the extreme. The artillery wagons rattle forward and the heavy tramp of many men gives a dull but impressive sound.
>
> In many places the road seems to end abruptly, but [when] we come to the place we find it turning at right angles, passing through narrow valleys, sometimes through hills, and presenting the best opportunity to the Rebels for defense if they had but known our purpose.[1]

About five miles west of Port Gibson, McClernand's point unit, a sixteen-man patrol from the Twenty-first Iowa Infantry Regiment, being guided along the Rodney–Port Gibson road by a local black man, ran into the rebel defenders. Late in the afternoon of the Union troops' landing at Bruinsburg, April 30, Confederate General Bowen had ridden out from Grand Gulf to Port Gibson and conferred with Brigadier General Martin Green, whom Bowen the day before had ordered to assemble a five-hundred-man brigade and patrol the roads leading to Port Gibson from Natchez and Rodney, the two places where Bowen was evidently expecting Grant to land. Green's command would be reinforced, Bowen told him, and Green was then ordered to position two companies on the Bruinsburg–Port Gibson road and put the rest of his men on the Rodney–Port Gibson road. On receiving the promised reinforcements, Green posted the bulk of his brigade on the Rodney road, their mission being to hamper the Union troops' movement toward Port Gibson.

The sixteen-man Union patrol, backed up by four companies of the Twenty-first Iowa, moved up a ridge rising from a ford on Widow's Creek and as they passed a clearing in which there was a vegetable garden, a shot came at them from the trees at the northeast corner of the garden. In the dim moonlight they instantly turned their weapons toward those trees, fired off a volley and then scurried for cover behind trees and a fence. Brigadier General Stone, the Twenty-first Iowa's brigade commander, was accompanying the patrol's advance, and upon the exchange of gunfire he quickly ordered his men to deploy as skirmishers and had them cautiously move ahead, probing both sides of the road. He also dispatched a runner to hurry to the rear to urge the commander of the Twenty-first Iowa, Colonel Samuel Merrill, to rush forward with the regiment's six other companies.

After the skirmishers had advanced eastward about a hundred yards, hearing only a few scattered shots, Stone concluded that they had merely encountered a roaming mounted patrol or perhaps pickets posted far in front of some distant rebel position.

Meanwhile, the rebel line established earlier by General Green was waiting silently in the darkness on a ridge east of Magnolia Church on the Rodney Road. "We could hear the enemy forming," Confederate Lieutenant John S. Bell of the Twelfth Arkansas Sharpshooter Battalion reported, "and it was so still we could hear every command given. Our men had orders not to fire until word was given. Soon we could see their line of skirmishers coming down the road and could hear them say there was no one here, it was only a cavalry scout. When they were within 50 yards the word 'fire' was given."[2]

The sudden gunfire shortly after midnight sent the Union skirmishers rushing for cover, quickly positioning themselves to return the rebels' fire, and at the same time the sounds of gunfire set off an unmistakable alarm to McClernand's regiments still moving up on the Rodney road. Union artillery swiftly wheeled into position at the head of the advancing regiments, unlimbered their guns and blasted away at shadowy targets to their front as hundreds of infantrymen deployed on both sides of the narrow dirt road. At last, around three o'clock in the morning, May 1, the firing tapered off and stopped.

At daylight the fight resumed. General Grant described the action:

> Near the point selected by Bowen to defend, the road to Port Gibson divides, taking two ridges which do not diverge more than a mile or two at the widest point. These roads unite just outside the town. This made it necessary for McClernand to divide his force. It was not only divided, but it was separated by a deep ravine.... One flank could not reinforce the other except by marching back to the junction of the roads.
>
> McClernand put the divisions of [Brigadier General Alvin] Hovey, [Brigadier General Eugene] Carr and [Brigadier General] A.J. Smith upon the right-hand branch and Osterhaus on the left. I was on the field by ten A.M., and inspected both flanks in person. On the right the enemy, if not being pressed back, was at least not repulsing our advance. On the left, however, Osterhaus was not faring so well. He had been repulsed with some loss.
>
> As soon as the road could be cleared of McClernand's troops I ordered up McPherson, who was close upon the rear of the 13th [McClernand's] corps, with two brigades of [Major General John A.] Logan's division. This was about noon. I ordered him to send one brigade (General John E. Smith's was selected) to support Osterhaus, and to move to the left and flank the enemy out of position. This movement carried the brigade over a deep ravine to a third ridge and, when Smith's troops were seen well through the ravine, Osterhaus was directed to renew his front attack. It was successful and unattended by heavy loss. The enemy was sent in full retreat on their right, and their left followed before sunset.... We followed up our victory until night overtook us about two miles from Port Gibson; then the troops went into bivouac for the night.[3]

The Confederates took advantage of the darkness to withdraw to Port Gibson and then back across Bayou Pierre. The Battle of Port Gibson was over. The rebels had abandoned the field. From a force of fewer than eight thousand men, they had lost sixty killed, 340 wounded and 387 missing. From the Union force of some eighteen thousand troops Grant had lost 131 killed, 719 wounded and twenty-five missing.

As soon as the rising sun gave enough light for the Union troops to see the road, they started again for Port Gibson. On reaching the town they discovered the bridge that spanned the south fork of Bayou Pierre had been burned and they promptly set about building what General Grant called a raft bridge, hastily constructed from boards and timbers removed from fences, barns, stables and other wooden buildings. Colonel J.H. Wilson, a member of Grant's staff, supervised the construction. The raft bridge was completed that same day, May 2, and the troops crossed it and marched eight miles to Bayou Pierre's north fork, where they encountered another burned bridge, plus a Confederate artillery battery and infantry detachment posted on the north side of the fork to prevent Grant's troops from repairing the bridge.

Grant sent two brigades up the bayou to find another crossing site, where a bridge could be built without the threat of artillery fire. When the rebels learned the Union troops were building a new bridge upstream of the battery's position, they withdrew, leaving the burned bridge for Grant's troops to repair and cross. "During the night of the 2d of May the bridge over the North Fork was repaired, and the troops commenced crossing at five the next morning [May 3]," Grant reported. "Before the leading brigade was over, it was fired upon by the enemy from a commanding position; but they were soon driven off. It was evident that the enemy was covering a retreat from Grand Gulf to Vicksburg."[4]

After skirmishing with Confederate troops that had been posted along the road to delay the Union troops' advance, Grant's men reached the road from Grand Gulf to Vicksburg before nightfall. Leaving General Logan in charge at that intersection, Grant rode into Grand Gulf with a twenty-man cavalry escort and saw that General Bowen had evacuated the town and abandoned the heavy guns that had prevented Grant's attacking Grand Gulf from the Mississippi. The silence of those now abandoned guns had been duly noticed by Admiral Porter, who had already landed his gunboat fleet at the town and was on hand to greet General Grant when he arrived.

"When I reached Grand Gulf on May 3d," Grant wrote with appealing candor, "I had not been with my baggage since the 27th of April and consequently had had no change of underclothing, no meal except such as I could pick up sometimes at other headquarters, and no tent to cover me. The first thing I did was to get a bath, borrow some fresh underclothing from one of the naval officers and get a good meal on the flag-ship."[5]

When all that was done, he read his messages, wrote his reports, issued orders for his corps commanders and around midnight set off to rejoin his troops. He caught up with them at Hankinson's Ferry, where the Port Gibson–Vicksburg road crossed the Big Black River, which he reached before dawn. By then he had revised his plans:

> While at Grand Gulf I heard from [General] Banks, who was on the Red River, and who said that he could not be at Port Hudson before the 10th of May and then with only 15,000 men. Up to this time my intention had been to secure Grand Gulf, as a base of supplies, detach McClernand's corps to Banks, and co-operate with him in the reduction of Port Hudson.
>
> The news from Banks forced upon me a different plan of campaign from the one intended. To wait for his co-operation would have detained me at least a month. The reinforcements [from Banks] would not have reached ten thousand men after deducting casualties and necessary river guards at all high points close to the river for over three hundred miles. The enemy would have strengthened his position and been reinforced by more men

than Banks could have brought. I therefore determined to move independently of Banks, cut loose from my base, destroy the rebel force in rear of Vicksburg and invest or capture the city.

Grand Gulf was accordingly given up as a base and the authorities at Washington were notified. I knew well that [General] Halleck's caution would lead him to disapprove of this course; but it was the only one that gave any chance of success. The time it would take to communicate with Washington and get a reply would be so great that I could not be interfered with until it was demonstrated whether my plan was practicable.[6]

Grant's plan now was to apply the lesson he had learned after he had prematurely terminated his drive in north Mississippi because rebel cavalrymen had cut the railroad from Columbus, Kentucky, and had overrun his supply base at Holly Springs. In a land of abundance, he had decided, an army can live off the land, a principle he soon proved true. "Beef, mutton, poultry and forage were found in abundance," Grant reported. "Quite a quantity of bacon and molasses was also secured from the country, but bread and coffee could not be obtained in quantity sufficient for all the men. Every plantation, however, had a run of stone, propelled by mule power, to grind corn for the owners and their slaves. All these were kept running while we were stopping, day and night, and when we were marching, during the night, at all plantations covered by the troops."[7] Ammunition and equipment, of course, would still have to come first by boat and then by wagon over the area's roads.

Grant was taking a grave risk in changing the plan. Not only was he acting contrary to Halleck's orders, which directed him to cooperate with Banks in an attempt to capture Port Hudson, but also contrary to the wishes of President Lincoln, who expected him to join Banks once Grand Gulf and Port Gibson had been taken. Success with the new plan would excuse Grant's disobedience; failure would likely end his career.

The new plan that Grant had devised relieved his troops of the necessity of struggling northward from Grand Gulf toward Vicksburg, traversing deep, nightmarish ravines thick with underbrush, ideal for resistance by an outnumbered but stubborn defensive force, costly in men and time for an attacking force. So instead of crossing the Big Black River above Grand Gulf and trudging up beside the Mississippi for an attack from the south side of Vicksburg, Grant decided to advance his army northeastward toward Jackson, using the Big Black River as a shield against Pemberton's force. He planned to capture the Jackson-to-Vicksburg road and rail line, then execute a huge column left and turn westward to launch his assault on Vicksburg from the east. He intended to move quickly, not allowing the Confederates time to receive substantial reinforcements or form strong defensive positions. He also planned on deception, ordering McClernand and McPherson to make reconnaissances that would lead rebel commanders to believe he intended to cross the Big Black and move on Vicksburg immediately.

On May 6, Sherman arrived at Grand Gulf, having marched the troops of his Fifteenth Corps down the west side of the Mississippi to Hard Times. His men crossed to Grand Gulf behind him that night and the next day, May 7. That same day he was ordered to move his troops toward Jackson to become part of a three-pronged advance. Grant had put McClernand's corps on the left of the massive movement, nearest Pemberton's army, and had put McPherson's corps on the right. Sherman's corps would be positioned in the center and rear, where it could quickly support either McClernand or McPherson.

On the night of May 6, while Sherman's troops were still crossing the Mississippi, McClernand and McPherson were both at Rocky Springs, ten miles from Hankinson's Ferry. McClernand moved out on the 7th while McPherson waited there through May 8, when

Sherman's force, marching from Grand Gulf, arrived at Hankinson's Ferry. By May 11, McClernand, advancing with his left flank skirting Big Black River, was at Five Mile Creek, Sherman was at Auburn, and McPherson was five miles outside Utica, headed for Raymond.

Meanwhile Pemberton, who had shifted his headquarters back to Vicksburg, had drawn conclusions from the reports reaching him concerning the movements of Grant's army. Consulting his map, he decided Grant was aiming for the Southern Railroad line between Jackson and Vicksburg, which lay directly north of the advancing Union army. Pemberton had moved the bulk of his Vicksburg garrison out from there, and now he marched them northeastward along the west (or north) side of the Big Black, as if stalking McClernand's force as it moved northeastward on the east (or south) side of the diagonally flowing river. He also ordered Brigadier General John Gregg, who was in Jackson, to march his brigade to Raymond, southwest of Jackson, and be ready to attack the right flank or rear of Grant's army as it wheeled westward to strike along the railroad. (Historians William L. Shea and Terrence J. Winschel critically comment, "It is worth noting that while Pemberton called on Gregg to attack Grant with a single brigade of three thousand men, he remained firmly on the defensive behind the Big Black with his main body, about thirty-eight thousand strong."[8])

On the morning of May 12, as McPherson's corps resumed its march from Utica toward Raymond, a brigade from Major General John A. Logan's division in the lead, the Union troops descended a ridge and began moving into the valley through which ran Fourteenmile Creek, about two miles southwest of Raymond. Suddenly muskets and artillery opened on Logan's men from the line of trees along the creek, bringing them to an abrupt halt. The Confederates then came out from their cover behind the trees and advanced on the Union infantrymen. Logan deployed his men and managed to have them hold their positions while additional Union troops came running up from the rear, bursting through clouds of smoke and dust to join the battle. By early afternoon the rebel advance had stalled as McPherson's troops continued to pour down the ridge to confront them in a thickening line of battle on both sides of the road and Union artillery rolled up and began pounding the rebel position.

General Gregg now could see he had taken on more than he could handle. His right flank collapsed, and he ordered a retreat, speedily withdrawing back to Raymond, then rushing through the town's streets, where townspeople had set up tables of food for what they had thought would be a victorious rebel army. Not stopping to enjoy the town's hospitality, Gregg's troops hurried past the food and exited the town, leaving the food for hungry Union soldiers to devour instead. While the invaders took time to eat, the Confederates escaped toward Jackson, which they reached the next day.

In the battle McPherson lost sixty-six killed, 339 wounded and thirty-seven missing, most of the casualties being suffered by Logan's division. The Confederates lost 100 killed, 305 wounded and 415 taken prisoner.[9] In his account of the battle Grant singled out General Logan and Brigadier General Marcellus Crocker, another of McPherson's division commanders, for special praise. Both were capable of higher command, he wrote. "Crocker, however, was dying of consumption when he volunteered. His weak condition never put him on the sick report when there was a battle in prospect, as long as he could keep on his feet. He died not long after the close of the rebellion."[10]

McPherson apparently exaggerated the number of Confederate troops his corps had faced in what came to be known as the Battle of Raymond, and in so doing he caused Grant to alter his plan once more. He had intended to turn north and attack the rail line before reaching Jackson. But now, thinking he must not leave a substantial rebel force in his rear, he decided to continue on to Jackson and capture it. He ordered Sherman to move his column up and hit Jackson's defenders on the southwest corner of the city while McPherson's column attacked the northwest side.

Gregg apparently considered McPherson's advance the Union's major thrust at the city and so concentrated his defenses at the northwest. About nine o'clock on the morning of May 14, as the forward elements of McPherson's army advanced to the edge of the city under skies still clouded from a rainstorm that soaked the area the night before, Gregg's artillery opened fire. In response, McPherson formed his troops for an attack on the rebel position. The attackers waited until a passing rain shower ended, then dashed forward and forced the Confederates to withdraw to their fortifications in the city, about a mile to their rear. On a second charge, made after a pause to regroup, McPherson's troops found their enemy had vanished, their position abandoned.

On the city's southwest side, Sherman's troops also discovered Jackson's defenders gone, their earthworks fortification left empty but for a rear-guard detail manning a number of field pieces to hold off the Union advance as long as possible before being overrun.

The two Union armies then proceeded to take over Jackson, its residents as well as it defenders having yielded Mississippi's capital city to Grant's forces, and the state government having fled for refuge to Enterprise, a community about ninety miles east of Jackson, near the Alabama line. Jackson's capture had cost McPherson thirty-seven men killed and 228 missing. Sherman lost four killed and twenty-one wounded or missing. Confederate casualties were put at 845, including killed, wounded and captured.

General Grant rode into the city later that day and at four P.M. called Sherman and McPherson together to give them new instructions. "Sherman," Grant recorded, "was to remain in Jackson until he destroyed that place as a railroad centre, and manufacturing city of military supplies."[11] Perhaps afflicted with a degree of pyromania — on his own initiative he had already burned plantation buildings along his path from Young's Point to Hard Times, though he was yet to make his reputation as a ravager — Sherman diligently took up the task of hellish destruction. "He did the work most effectually," Grant reported.[12]

General Pemberton could see that the end — at least the end of the status quo — was near, and he made a desperate attempt to rally his troops against the imminent Yankee threat. On May 12, two days before the fall of Jackson, he issued a dramatic call to arms in hopes of stirring the troops to greater effort, and in which he asserted his devotion to the common cause, which some believed he lacked because of his Northern birth and background. Eschewing a personal appearance — and thereby avoiding the oratory required by a speech — he had his words printed and distributed to his men as a flyer:

> Headquarters Department Mississippi and East Louisiana.
> Vicksburg, May 12th, 1863.
> **Soldiers of the Army, In and Around Vicksburg:**
>
> The hour of trial has come! The enemy who has so long threatened Vicksburg in front, has, at last, effected a landing in this department; and his march into the interior of Mississippi has been marked by the devastation of one of the fairest portions of the State! He seeks to break the communications between the members of the Confederacy and to control the navigation of the Mississippi River! The issue involves everything endeared to a free people! The enemy fights for the privilege of plunder and oppression! You fight for your country, homes, wives, children, and the birth-rights of freemen! Your Commanding

General, believing in the truth and sacredness of this cause, has cast his lot with you, and stands ready to peril his life, and all he holds dear, for the triumph of the right! God, who rules in the affairs of men and nations, loves justice and hates wickedness. He will not allow a cause so just, to be trampled in the dust. In the day of conflict, let each man appealing to Him for strength, strike home for victory, and our triumph is at once assured. A grateful country will hail us as deliverers, and cherish the memory of those who may fall as martyrs in her defence.

Soldiers! be vigilant, brave and active; let there be no cowards or laggards, nor stragglers from the ranks—and the God of battle will certainly crown our efforts with success.

J. C. PEMBERTON,
Lt. Gen. Comd'g.[13]

The day after publication of the flyer, May 13, units of Pemberton's army at last crossed the Big Black, moving to Grant's side of the river, headed east toward Edwards, about halfway between Vicksburg and Jackson. On May 14, while marching through Bovina, about eight miles west of Edwards, Pemberton received distasteful orders from General Johnston, who was on the Jackson-Canton road, running from the Union troops who were then threatening Jackson. The message containing the orders had been written the night of the 13th and had been dispatched to Pemberton by courier, since McPherson's troops, on the way to Jackson, had cut the telegraph lines west of Jackson. To ensure the message's delivery to Pemberton, Johnston had sent it in triplicate, one copy carried by each of three couriers: "I have lately arrived, and learn that Major-General Sherman is between us with four divisions at Clinton. It is important to establish communication, that you may be reinforced. If practicable, come up in his rear at once. To beat such a detachment would be of immense value. All the troops you can quickly assemble should be brought. Time is all-important."[14]

One of the couriers happened to be a Union loyalist, and instead of taking his copy of the orders to Pemberton, he took it to General McPherson, who passed it on to General Grant. "Receiving this dispatch on the 14th," Grant related, "I ordered McPherson to move promptly in the morning [of May 15] back to Bolton, the nearest point where Johnston could reach the [Jackson-Vicksburg] road. Bolton is about twenty miles west of Jackson."[15] Grant also sent orders to McClernand, telling him to move all his forces to Bolton immediately, using the shortest, quickest route to get there.

In the meantime, Johnston issued new orders to Pemberton, written on the night of May 14, after the Union

Lt. Gen. John C. Pemberton, commander of the Confederate forces defending Vicksburg. As Grant's army closed in on the embattled city, Pemberton issued a printed statement to his troops, urging them to pray for strength (Library of Congress).

forces captured Jackson: "As soon as the reinforcements are all up, they must be united to the rest of the army. I am anxious to see a force assembled that may be able to inflict a heavy blow upon the enemy...."[16]

Many among Pemberton's troops were eager to inflict that heavy blow. With a passionate mixture of religious fervor and boiling outrage over imagined wrongs, Lieutenant Calvin Smith of the Thirty-first Tennessee Infantry Regiment, whose feelings were perhaps representative of the feelings of others in the rebel army, wrote in his journal as he awaited the impending action:

> It will ... appear that we won't lack men to fight or compete with the enemy that might oppose us here.... I should say that not less than 20,000 have passed [our camp] since we stopped [at Edwards]....
>
> These are effective men, men that are fighting for their properties of their families for their rights.... Such men can't be subjugated, unconquerable with too much hatred to even wish for peace, all joyful and full of glee marching perhaps into the jaw of death. Ah, will the GOD of battles give this splendid army to Lincoln's hordes who have robbed the defenseless women and children of the staff of life.... No, the GOD of battle [will give] us victory in answer to the thousands of prayers that go up every day and night in and out of the Army.[17]

Pemberton's chief officers were impatient to take the offensive. Pemberton, however, was anything but eager to meet Grant's army head-on, preferring to defend from a prepared position. After much indecision and several councils of war, Pemberton agreed to go along with his generals. The plan was not what Johnston had in mind, though. Pemberton was firm in his opposition to the idea of trying to join forces with Johnston at Clinton, which was occupied by McPherson's troops, and make a major attack against the Union force. He believed that plan to be extremely hazardous. Instead, he would follow the plan proposed by Major General William Loring, his senior division commander. It would have Pemberton's army move southeast toward Raymond and interdict what the Confederate commanders mistakenly thought was Grant's line of communications, thereby forcing Grant, they reasoned, to pull back from the Jackson-Vicksburg road and attack Pemberton's army at a place of the rebels' choosing, where they would hold the advantage.

Grant narrated the events that immediately followed the Confederates' agreement to move against his army:

> On the 15th Pemberton had actually marched south from Edward's [sic] station, but the rains had swollen Baker's Creek, which he had to cross, so much that he could not ford it, and the bridges were washed away. This brought him back to the Jackson road, on which there was a good bridge over Baker's Creek. Some of his troops were marching until midnight to get there. Receiving here early on the 16th a repetition of his order to join Johnston at Clinton, he concluded to obey, and sent a dispatch to his chief, informing him of the route by which he might be expected.
>
> About five o'clock in the morning (16th) two men, who had been employed on the Jackson and Vicksburg railroad, were brought to me. They reported that they had passed through Pemberton's army in the night, and that it was still marching east [toward Grant's position]. They reported him to have eighty regiments of infantry and ten batteries; in all, about twenty-five thousand men.[18]

The report of the railroaders, whose train was inexplicably headed for Jackson and had been stopped by Union troops in Clinton, was nearly accurate. Pemberton's force consisted of forty-nine infantry regiments and fifteen artillery batteries, totaling some twenty-three thousand officers and men.[19] Grant reacted swiftly to this new intelligence. He sent orders to Sherman, who was still in Jackson burning buildings, to move to Bolton on the Jackson-Vicksburg road. Sherman's corps would be positioned on the Union's right as Grant's army did an about face to confront its enemy on the west instead of the east. Grant ordered General Blair, then near Auburn, to move his division, part of Sherman's Fifteenth Corps, quickly to Edwards, also on the Jackson-Vicksburg Road, west of Bolton. Grant further ordered McPherson to clear the roads of his supply wagons to make way for the advancing troops, and he ordered McClernand to begin an advance on the rebel position via the Raymond road.

By midmorning on the 16th Grant's army was moving toward what was to Grant a long-sought showdown with Pemberton's Vicksburg defenders. Union skirmishers, advancing in front of the forward units, were already exchanging fire with rebel pickets, and Union artillery had opened up on the rebel positions.

General Pemberton had set up his headquarters at the plantation home of Sarah Ellison on the road to Raymond, toward which Pemberton's army was advancing, following General Loring's plan. On the morning of the 16th, with the sound of distant artillery in his ears, he received the startling report of Colonel Wirt Adams, who had ridden at horse-race speed to tell Pemberton that a Union column, which he had just witnessed, was advancing toward them along the Raymond road and that the Confederates' roadblock was then under attack. While Pemberton was mulling over that bad news, a weary courier came galloping up to the Ellison house bearing a new message from General Johnston.

The message, dated May 15, informed Pemberton that Jackson had been evacuated and repeated the instruction for Pemberton to bring his Vicksburg defenders north of the Vicksburg-Jackson railroad line to meet up with Johnston and his force. Now, with Grant's army approaching his rear, Pemberton decided he would obey Johnston's order after all. He dashed off a note to Johnston telling him he was coming, then he issued orders to his commanders to begin a countermarch northward. The army was to recross Baker's Creek, go back to Edwards, turn northeast toward Brownsville and march to a meeting with Johnston.

By late morning those instructions had to be scrapped. A meeting with Johnston's force had become impossible for the time being. Responding to General Loring's urging, Pemberton began looking for a likely location on which he would establish a line of defense against Grant's rapidly approaching columns. About three-fourths of a mile west of Ellison's plantation, Pemberton noticed, lay a ridge, the highest point of which was called Champion Hill. There Pemberton ordered the defensive line to be laid.

Grant thought it was a site well selected, "whether taken by accident or design," he commented. "It is one of the highest points in that section, and commanded all the ground in range. On the east side of the ridge, which is quite precipitous, is a ravine running first north, then westerly, terminating at Baker's Creek. It was grown up thickly with large trees and undergrowth, making it difficult to penetrate with troops, even when not defended.... On the west side the slope of the ridge is gradual and is cultivated from near the summit to the creek."[20]

At that ridge Grant hurled his blue-clad army. He put McPherson in tactical control of the assault, and at ten-thirty in the morning of May 16, McPherson gave the signal that sent the divisions of Brigadier General Alvin Hovey and Major General John A. Logan, some ten thousand men, storming forward, yelling and cheering, and by early afternoon, after fierce fighting, the bluecoats had swept across the crest of Champion Hill, driving the Confederates before them in scattered disarray. Facing disaster, Pemberton ordered a counterattack, which burst against the surprised Union troops at the crossroads south of Champion Hill and drove them back over the hill. Union reinforcements, however, the divisions of generals Osterhaus and Carr of McClernand's corps, struck the flank of the outnumbered Confederates and forced a withdrawal that turned into a rout as rebel soldiers dropped their weapons and ran pell-mell through the woods to escape; others suffered the storm of Union fire as they dashed back to the crossroads with the Union troops on their heels.

Apprised of the desperate situation, Pemberton sent word to his commanders to fall back northwestward to Edwards, and he ordered Brigadier General Lloyd Tilghman to have his brigade hold the Baker's Creek bridge at all costs until the retreating rebel army had crossed it — a mission Tilghman accomplished, but at the cost of his life.

In hot pursuit of the retreating Confederates, Grant's troops crossed Baker's Creek late in the afternoon and continued on toward Edwards, reaching there about eight o'clock that evening and finding the community blazing with the supplies and equipment the rebels had set afire before swiftly moving farther westward. At Edwards, Grant called it a day for his worn and weary troops, and they bivouacked for the night.

Grant's success at Champion Hill had driven Pemberton's army from the field and was forcing it into the confines of the walled fortress that Vicksburg had become. Both sides had paid a stiff price for the results at Champion Hill, especially the Confederates, who from a force of twenty-two thousand men had lost 381 killed, 1,018 wounded and 2,441 missing, a total of 3,840 casualties. From a Union force of thirty-two thousand Grant had lost 410 killed, 1,844 wounded and 187 missing, a total of 2,441 casualties.

The night brought no rest for the fleeing rebels. Through the darkness they plodded westward on the road to Vicksburg, streaming across the two vital bridges over the Big Black River, one of which, a railroad bridge, where Grant intended to cross the Big Black, was protected on the east side by fortifications constructed of cotton bales covered with dirt. At three-thirty the next morning, Sunday, May 17, the Union force resumed its pursuit of the rebels and about six miles from where they had spent the night they came upon the fortifications. Quickly preparing to assault the rebel position, General Carr deployed his men to the right of the road, and General Osterhaus deployed to the left. McPherson's column was on the road to the rear, ready to throw itself into battle as needed.

While the troops were deploying, an officer from General Banks's staff rode up and handed Grant a letter from General Halleck dated May 11. It had been sent to Banks by way of New Orleans, to be forwarded to Grant. "It ordered me to return to Grand Gulf," Grant related, "and to co-operate from there with Banks against Port Hudson and then return with our combined forces to besiege Vicksburg." Grant refused that bit of Washington management. "I told the officer that the order came too late, and that Halleck would not give it now if he knew our position. The bearer of the dispatch insisted that I ought to obey the order and was giving arguments to support his position when I heard great cheering to the right of our line and, looking in that direction, saw [General] Lawler in his shirt sleeves leading a charge upon the enemy. I immediately mounted my horse and rode in the direction of the charge and saw no more of the officer who delivered the dispatch."[21]

Seeing the Union assault carrying the rebel position on the east side of the river, the Confederate troops on the west side set fire to the bridge, stranding their comrades on the east side between the swarming Union troops and the river. Many of the trapped rebel soldiers plunged into the river to escape. Some succeeded; others drowned. By nine A.M. the Confederate position had been captured. Also captured were 1,751 Confederate soldiers and eighteen rebel guns. Grant's losses were thirty-nine killed and 237 wounded.

The destruction of the bridge temporarily stalled the Union pursuit of Pemberton's army, and Grant's force had to wait until new bridges—three of them—could be built by his engineers, using felled trees and lumber taken from buildings in the vicinity. By eight o'clock in the morning of Monday, May 18, the new bridges had been completed and the Union troops were marching across them, bound for Vicksburg.

In Vicksburg the streets were filling with the returning troops of Pemberton's weary army. A resident described the scene in her diary: "I hope never to witness again such a scene as the return of our routed army! From twelve o'clock [on the 17th] until late in the night the streets and roads were jammed with wagons, cannons, horses, men, mules, stock, sheep, everything you can imagine that appertains to an army being brought hurriedly within the intrenchment. Nothing like order prevailed, of course, as divisions, brigades and regiments were broken and separated."[22] The scene in the city became even more congested and confused after Pemberton ordered the troops brought in from the outposts at Haynes's Bluff, Walnut Hills and Warrenton.

The dispirited rebel troops were soon organized by their officers and put to work preparing for the arrival of their pursuers, some details repairing the earthworks that had been damaged by the recent heavy rains, and many others laboriously cutting down trees in nearby woods to erect a lengthy abatis outside the perimeter of the earthworks. By the morning of the 19th Vicksburg and its defenders stood ready to face the coming Union assault.

General Sherman and his troops, having missed the battle of Champion Hill, finally caught up with Grant's two other corps to become part of the forty-thousand-man force marching toward Vicksburg. Remembering the march, Sherman later described a stop along the way:

> Just beyond Bolton there was a small hewn-log house, standing back in a yard, in which was a well; at this some of our soldiers were drawing water. I rode in to get a drink, and, seeing a book on the ground, asked some soldier to hand it to me. It was a volume of the Constitution of the United States, and on the title-page was written the name of Jefferson Davis. On inquiry of a negro, I learned that the place belonged to the then President of the Southern Confederation. His brother Joe Davis's plantation was not far off; one of my staff officers went there with a few soldiers.... He found Joe Davis at home, an old man, attended by a young and affectionate niece; but they were overwhelmed with grief to see their country overrun and swarming with Federal troops.[23]

At another stop along the way, after desultory fighting had broken out as Grant's army neared the city on the evening of the 18th, Sherman sat with Grant by the side of the road watching Brigadier General Frederick Steele's men troop past them, and while they did, a Union soldier standing beside them was hit and killed by a gunshot.

The road on which Sherman's corps was advancing from the northeast forked about two miles outside Vicksburg, the left leading to the main Jackson road, and the right, called the Graveyard Road, entering the city near a large cemetery. Grant instructed Sherman to take the Graveyard Road. Eager to follow up the staggering blow he had struck at Champion Hill, Grant ordered an attack on Vicksburg the day after his army had reached its approaches, many of his troops having arrived during the night of the 18th.

At ten o'clock on the morning of May 19, Grant's artillery commenced a bombardment of the Confederates' earthworks with shot and shell, continuing the thunderous assault until two in the afternoon. As the smoke began to clear, the Union infantry advanced on the rebel entrenchments. Sherman described the action from the perspective of his troops astride the Graveyard Road:

My corps (the Fifteenth) had the right of the line of investment; McPherson's (the Seventeenth) the centre; and McClernand's (the Thirteenth) the left, reaching from the [Mississippi] river above to the railroad below. Our lines connected, and invested about three-quarters of the land-front of the fortifications at Vicksburg. On the supposition that the garrison of Vicksburg was demoralized by the defeats at Champion Hills [sic] and at the railroad crossing of the Big Black, General Grant ordered an assault at our respective fronts on the 19th. My troops reached the top of the [rebels'] parapet, but could not cross over. The rebel parapets were strongly manned, and the enemy fought hard and well. My loss was pretty heavy, falling chiefly on the Thirteenth Regulars, whose commanding officer, Captain [Edward] Washington, was killed, and several other regiments were pretty badly cut up. We, however, held the ground up to the ditch till night, and then drew back only a short distance, and began to counter-trench. On the graveyard road, our parapet was within less than fifty yards of the rebel ditch.[24]

Grant seemed unfazed by the failure of the assault, which resulted in 942 casualties (including killed, wounded and missing) in Sherman's corps. Executing some glaring spin on the failure, in his memoirs he implies that the failed attack was in fact a tactical success, claiming that "it resulted in securing more advanced positions for all our troops where they were fully covered from the fire of the enemy."[25] He offered no details and no other comment.

At the day's end, General Pemberton, apparently satisfied that his twice-defeated troops had held the line this time, dispatched a stealthy courier to President Davis with a message, saying: "We are occupying the trenches around Vicksburg. The enemy is investing it, and will probably attempt an assault. Our men have considerably recovered their morale, but unless a large force is sent at once to relieve it, Vicksburg before long must fall. I have used every effort to prevent all this, but in vain."[26]

On the morning after the repulsed attack, Pemberton sent a courier to General Johnston, in Canton, reporting his desperate situation and pleading for help:

The enemy assaulted our intrenched lines yesterday at two points (center and left), and was repulsed with heavy loss. Our loss small. I cannot estimate the enemy's force now engaged around Vicksburg at less than 60,000; it is probably more. [It was considerably less.] At this hour (8:30 A.M.) He is briskly cannonading with long-range guns. That we may save ammunition, his fire is rarely returned. At present our main necessity is musket-caps. Can you send them to me by hands of couriers or citizens? An army will be necessary to relieve Vicksburg, and that quickly. Will it not be sent? Please let me hear from you, if possible.[27]

Johnston had no idea of relieving Vicksburg or its embattled defenders. He had already given up on saving the city. On May 17 he had written to Pemberton: "Your dispatch of to-day by Captain Henderson was received. If Haynes' Bluff is untenable, Vicksburg is of no value and cannot be held. If, therefore, you are invested in Vicksburg, you must ultimately surrender. Under such circumstances, instead of losing both troops and the place, we must, if possible, save the troops. If it is not too late, evacuate Vicksburg and its dependencies, and march to the northeast." Pemberton received that message on May 18, and by then, of course, it was too late.

On May 20, the day after the rebels had thwarted his hurried attempt to take Vicksburg, General Grant called his three corps commanders together for a critique of the failed effort. "We compared notes," Sherman related, "and agreed that the assault of the day before had failed, by reason of the natural strength of the position, and because we were forced by the nature of the ground to limit our attacks to the strongest parts of the enemy's line, viz., where the three principal roads entered the city."[28] The discussion concluded with Grant issuing orders for a new assault to be made simultaneously by all three corps at 10 A.M. on May 22.

Sherman summarized the action of the 22nd:

> All our field batteries were put in position, and were covered by good epaulements; the troops were brought forward, in easy support, concealed by the shape of the ground; and to the minute, viz., 10 A.M. of May 22d, the troops sprang to the assault.... The rebel line, concealed by the parapet, showed no sign of unusual activity, but as our troops came in fair view, the enemy rose behind their parapet and poured a furious fire upon our lines; and for about two hours, we had a severe and bloody battle, but at every point we were repulsed....
>
> After our men had been fairly beaten back from off the parapet, and had got cover behind the spurs of ground close up to the rebel works, General Grant came to where I was, on foot, having left his horse some distance to the rear. I pointed out to him the rebel works, admitted that my assault had failed, and he said the result with McPherson and McClernand was about the same.[29]

Grant's new assault on Vicksburg's defenses had cost his army 3,199 casualties, including killed, wounded and missing. The field before the rebel parapet was littered with the bodies of Union dead and dying, the wounded crying out for help as sunlight faded into darkness on the bloodied ground. Confederate losses were estimated at fewer than five hundred. Not until May 25 did Grant agree, at Pemberton's urging, to a two-and-a-half-hour ceasefire to allow the rapidly rotting corpses of the dead to be collected for burial, and the wounded, those still holding on to life after such a long wait for assistance, to be carried to the rear for treatment. At the end of the two and a half hours, the white flags came down, and the troops of both sides, who had intermingled in friendly exchanges during the lull, ran for cover.

Grant then decided he would make no more bloody assaults, but would resort to formularized siege tactics. "I now determined upon a regular siege," he wrote, "to 'out-camp the enemy,' as it were, and to incur no more losses. The experience of the 22d convinced officers and men that this was best, and they went to work on the defences and approaches with a will. With the navy holding the river, the investment of Vicksburg was complete. As long as we could hold our position the enemy was limited in supplies of food, men and munitions of war to what they had on hand. These could not last always."[30]

There was, however, a lingering danger to his forces, now spread out in a huge horseshoe-shaped line around the north, east and south sides of the city. By early June reinforcements had increased Johnston's army, idling in the vicinity of Jackson, to some thirty-two thousand men, a force strong enough to threaten Grant's siege line from the rear. Grant's own call for reinforcements was quickly answered by Washington, which sent him troops from several distant points, including the veteran Ninth Corps, commanded by Major General John G. Parke, marching from Kentucky, and the division of Major General Francis Herron, arriving from northwest Arkansas. Grant used most of those new arrivals to protect him from the possibility of an attack by Johnston's forces, having them build and fortify a long, twisting line of trenches outside his siege line. While his interior line faced Vicksburg, the new, exterior line, manned by thirty-four thousand blue-jacketed troops and studded with seventy-two artillery pieces, faced whatever enemy force might approach from outside Vicksburg. Grant put Sherman in charge of that exterior line.

Johnston, however, lacking the heart for a fight, had no intention of moving on Grant's

The siege of Vicksburg begins. After two failed and costly attempts to take the rebel fortifications by storm, Grant decided against any further bloody assaults (Library of Congress).

army. He repeatedly pleaded a lack of sufficient men, artillery, wagons, horses and whatever else he could think of. Yet in Vicksburg, among the residents and the troops, a vain hope remained that he would come to the rescue.

The efforts of Grant's engineers and troops, working under the direction of Captain Frederick Prime, Grant's chief engineer, were resulting in the creation of thirteen saps, zigzag trenches that reached toward the enemy's fortification and tunneled under it to allow explosives to be placed and set off beneath the enemy's works. With every passing day the saps extended closer and more threateningly toward Vicksburg's fortifications. On June 15 Pemberton wrote in desperation to Johnston: "The enemy has placed several very heavy guns in position against our works, and is approaching them very nearly by sap. His fire is almost continuous. Our men have no relief; are becoming much fatigued, but are still in pretty good spirits. I think your movement should be made as soon as possible. The enemy is receiving reenforcements. We are living on greatly reduced rations, but I think sufficient for twenty days yet."[31]

The bombardment by the artillery of Grant's army and the guns of Admiral Porter's gunboats in the Mississippi River reached every part of Vicksburg, presenting a constant roar and a rain of metal and debris, taking more lives every day. Terrified civilians hired black workers to dig caves for them in the cliffs around the city and there many took refuge from the unceasing cannonades.

The greatest danger that loomed, though, was starvation. "A new general has arrived," the wags in Vicksburg remarked sardonically. "General Starvation." Rations for the troops were cut to not much more than a handful of peas and rice a day. Hungry civilians were offered skinned rats at the markets. To avoid having to feed livestock, the army's horses and mules were turned out of the city to graze in fields beyond the rebel line — where they were speedily captured by Union soldiers. Water, too, was in short supply, and rationing limited residents to a cup a day. The city's water came from streams that originated outside the city, and Union soldiers dumped animal carcasses into the streams to render the water unpalatable. Union guns firing from De Soto Point discouraged residents from going to the river for water. Under such conditions disease became rife, particularly dysentery. Desertions from the rebel ranks became increasingly frequent as famished soldiers quit their posts during the night and fled to the Union lines seeking food and water.

Stymied by General Johnston's refusal to attempt to relieve the beleaguered city, officials in Richmond called for army commanders elsewhere to do what they could to support Vicksburg's defenders. Confederate units in Louisiana and Arkansas answered the appeal by staging attacks on the minor Union posts at Milliken's Bend, Young's Point and Lake Providence in hopes of drawing some of Grant's troops from Vicksburg to defend those outposts, which they failed to do. A larger assault was planned for the important Union supply depot at Helena, which was garrisoned by a substantial force of some four thousand men commanded by Major General Benjamin Prentiss. A Confederate force of more than seventy-five hundred men commanded by Lieutenant General Theophilus Holmes left Little Rock in late June, beginning a long march eastward, planning to strike Helena in early July.

Meanwhile the rebels' situation at Vicksburg was deteriorating rapidly. By July 1 Pemberton had decided that no relieving army was coming to save them and that he had only

The surrender of Vicksburg. Starving troops of the besieged garrison wrote a letter to their commander, Lt. Gen. John Pemberton, telling him he should surrender. Pemberton decided to surrender on July 4, 1863, hoping to gain more lenient terms by capitulating on Independence Day (Library of Congress).

two options remaining—either try to break through the Union lines and run from the city or surrender. His generals dismissed the possibility of breaking through Grant's lines and advised him to begin negotiations for surrender. His troops, in a letter sent to him signed, "Many soldiers," bluntly told Pemberton, "If you can't feed us, you had better surrender us, horrible as the idea is, than suffer this noble army to disgrace themselves by desertion."[32]

The die was cast, and Pemberton announced to his generals that he would surrender on July 4, hoping to gain more lenient terms by capitulating on Independence Day. On the morning of July 3 white flags went up along a section of the Confederate works, and guns fell silent over that part of the opposing lines. At mid-morning General Bowen and Lieutenant Colonel Louis Montgomery, one of Pemberton's aides, rode out from the rebel line and across the Union line to deliver to General Grant a letter from General Pemberton. The letter read:

> I have the honor to propose an armistice for ___ hours, with the view to arranging terms for the capitulation of Vicksburg. To this end, if agreeable with you, I will appoint three commissioners, to meet a like number to be named by yourself, at such place and hour today as you may find convenient. I make this proposition to save the further effusion of blood, which must otherwise be shed to a frightful extent, feeling myself fully able to maintain my position for a yet indefinite period. This communication will be handed you under a flag of truce, by Major-General John S. Bowen.[33]

Bowen was one of Grant's neighbors when he lived in Missouri, and Grant knew him, as Grant said, "well and favorably." Nevertheless, Grant refused the request for a ceasefire to negotiate a surrender. His reason was stated in the note he wrote in reply to Pemberton:

> Your note of this date is just received, proposing an armistice for several hours, for the purpose of arranging terms of capitulation through commissioners, to be appointed, etc. The useless effusion of blood you propose stopping by this course can be ended at any time you may choose, by the unconditional surrender of the city and garrison. Men who have shown so much endurance and courage as those now in Vicksburg, will always challenge the respect of an adversary, and I can assure you will be treated with all the respect due to prisoners of war. I do not favor the proposition of appointing commissioners to arrange the terms of capitulation, because I have no terms other than those indicated above.[34]

Bowen, unwilling to let that be Grant's final word, then suggested that Grant meet with Pemberton, and Grant told him that if Pemberton desired a meeting, Grant would meet with him at three o'clock that afternoon at the section of the Union line where McPherson's corps was posted.

At three o'clock, Pemberton, along with Bowen and Montgomery, showed up for the meeting. Grant was there with generals McPherson, Logan and A.J. Smith and with Major General Edward Ord, who had succeeded McClernand as commander of the Thirteenth Corps.[35] Grant recounted: "Pemberton and I had served in the same division during part of the Mexican War. I knew him very well, and greeted him as an old acquaintance. He soon asked what terms I proposed to give his army if it surrendered. My answer was the same as proposed in my reply to his letter. Pemberton then said, rather snappishly, 'The conference might as well end,' and turned abruptly as if to leave. I said, 'Very well.'"[36]

General Bowen, however, determined to have the surrender occur, quickly stepped in to avoid a hasty departure by Pemberton. He suggested that he and one of Grant's generals be given a chance to talk while Pemberton and Grant waited elsewhere. "I had no objection to this," Grant related, "as nothing could be made binding upon me that they might propose."[37] And so while Grant and Pemberton withdrew and held a friendly conversation about times gone by, Bowen and Smith conferred. After awhile, Grant and Pemberton returned to hear what Bowen and Smith had discussed. According to Grant's account, Bowen suggested that Pemberton's troops be permitted to march out of their position "with the honors of war, carrying their small arms and field artillery." Grant summarily rejected that proposal, ending the meeting. Before the Confederate officers left, though, Grant promised to send Pemberton a letter stating his final terms by ten o'clock that night.

After conferring with his corps and division commanders, Grant sent the promised letter to Pemberton. In it he offered parole for Pemberton's officers and men (rather than take them prisoner and have to feed and transport some thirty thousand soldiers to prison camps) and he spelled out other details of the surrender process. To that letter Pemberton replied in a letter of his own, which Grant received after midnight:

> I have the honor to acknowledge the receipt of your communication of this date, proposing terms of capitulation for this garrison and post. In the main your terms are accepted; but, in justice both to the honor and spirit of my troops, manifested in the defence of Vicksburg, I have to submit the following amendments, which, if acceded to by you, will perfect the agreement between us. At ten o'clock A.M. tomorrow, I propose to evacuate the works in and around Vicksburg, and to surrender the city and garrison under my command, by marching out with my colors and arms, stacking them in front of my present lines. After which you will take possession. Officers to retain their side-arms and personal property, and the rights and property of citizens to be respected.[38]

Grant okayed most of Pemberton's proposals, made some changes and wrote a new note to Pemberton telling him, "Should no notification be received of your acceptance of my terms by nine o'clock A.M. I shall regard them as having been rejected, and shall act accordingly. Should these terms be accepted, white flags should be displayed along your lines to prevent such of my troops as may not have been notified, from firing upon your men."[39] Pemberton promptly accepted those terms.

Grant's narrative of the struggle for Vicksburg described the moving, final scene of the drama:

> At the appointed hour the garrison of Vicksburg marched out of their works and formed line in front, stacked arms and marched back in good order. Our whole army present witnessed this scene without cheering. Logan's division, which had approached nearest the rebel works, was the first to march in; and the flag of one of the regiments of his division was soon floating over the court-house. Our soldiers were no sooner inside the lines than the two armies began to fraternize. Our men had had full rations from the time the siege commenced, to the close. The enemy had been suffering, particularly towards the last. I myself saw our men taking bread from their haversacks and giving it to the enemy they had so recently been engaged in starving out. It was accepted with avidity and with thanks.[40]

With the end of hostilities, Vicksburg, on the Fourth of July, had become a United States city again.

26. Finale at Port Hudson

To the men of the rebel garrison at Port Hudson, Major General Franklin Gardner seemed to be the commanding officer their threatened post needed. Although born in New York, the son of a U.S. Army colonel who had served in the War of 1812, his heart and interests were in the Deep South. His mother was from Louisiana, the daughter of a plantation-owning family, and he had married into a prominent Louisiana family, the Moutons. Alexandre Mouton, his father-in-law, was a former governor of Louisiana and former U.S. senator, and his brother-in-law, Alfred Mouton, was a Confederate brigadier general.

Gardner was a career army officer, having graduated from West Point in the same 1843 class as Grant. He finished seventeenth in the class. Grant finished twenty-first. He served in the Mexican War, starting as a second lieutenant. In recognition of his bravery in the battle at Monterey he was brevetted to first lieutenant and then brevetted again to the rank of captain for bravery displayed at the siege of Vera Cruz and Molino del Rey. Without resigning from the U.S. Army he entered the Confederate army as a lieutenant colonel in March 1861, a month before the assault on Fort Sumter, and commanded a cavalry brigade at the Battle of Shiloh, after which he was promoted to brigadier general. In December 1862 he was promoted to major general and days later was given command of the Confederate army's Third District, which included Port Hudson.

A tall, pleasant-faced man with a high forehead, a drooping mustache and a dark, bushy beard, he had made a favorable first impression on the troops at Port Hudson. When he arrived there by train on December 27, 1862, there was no one at the station to meet him—a serious breach of courtesy. He unassumingly asked for directions to the headquarters of the garrison's commandant, Brigadier General William N.B. Beall, and with no fuss, modestly made his way to it on foot.

Taking over, he immediately set out to strengthen Port Hudson's defenses, which had come under the threat of attack as soon as Union troops had occupied Baton Rouge. He repositioned the fortification's heavy guns for maximum coverage of the river approaches and he ordered the construction of new packed-earth parapets for the guns and had access routes built to enable the guns to be supplied with ammunition more efficiently and safely. He promptly asked Richmond for more heavy guns and ammunition. He put his troops and hired black laborers to work strengthening the breastworks. He ordered medical and other supplies to be stored closer to the fortification for quicker access. He sent reconnaissance patrols across the river to discover whatever Union movements were occurring on the west side. He further issued orders that would keep the otherwise idle garrison troops busy, working them as stevedores, laborers, cattle herders, hospital attendants and at a multitude of other tasks. And when they were not working during their duty hours, they drilled.

Meanwhile, in Alexandria, Union General Banks, having considered his options after receiving the news of Grant's crossing to the east side of the Mississippi below Vicksburg, had decided he could not catch up with Grant's army. "It is out of human power to do this," he wrote to Washington, "and I am left to move against Port Hudson."[1] In search of reinforcements for his Army of the Gulf, which casualties, sickness, service term expirations and other losses had reduced to about ten thousand men, Banks took a steamer to New Orleans via the Atchafalaya River and after arriving, he learned that General Gardner's garrison at Port Hudson had also diminished.

On Pemberton's orders, Gardner had sent three brigades, about five thousand men, to join Johnston's forces at Jackson, and on May 19, with orders to hold Port Hudson to the last, Gardner had fewer than six thousand troops manning the guns and fortifications there. To make Gardner's job more difficult, General Johnston, in contradiction to President Davis's wishes and General Pemberton's orders, on May 19 ordered Gardner to "evacuate Port Hudson forthwith."[2] Gardner received Johnston's order on May 21. By then events had overtaken the order. Gardner fired back a message to Johnston, letting him know that evacuation was not feasible and telling him, "A large force ... is moving down to cross [the Mississippi River] at Bayou Sara against this place. His whole force from Baton Rouge is in my front. I am very weak and should be rapidly re-enforced."[3]

Banks's drive against the rebel stronghold had begun. On May 14, Banks's Army of the Gulf had begun a march from Alexandria southeast to Simmesport, crossed the Atchafalaya River and continued on to Bayou Sara, on the west bank of the Mississippi. During the night of May 23 Banks's troops crossed the Mississippi and moved to the rear of Port Hudson. There they linked up with two brigades commanded by General Augur that had come up from Baton Rouge, and two brigades from New Orleans that were commanded by Brigadier General Thomas Sherman. Augur's troops had had to fight their way up to their position, overcoming a Confederate force in what became known as the Battle of Plains Store, fought May 21 near a two-story building at a crossroads east of Port Hudson.

Altogether Banks now had a force estimated at around twenty-five thousand men. Morale was high among his troops, having so recently marched through central Louisiana with a string of victories in the Bayou Teche campaign, and they were eager to take on the rebels again at Port Hudson. General Banks was also eager to get on with the confrontation. By May 26 his troops had fully invested the Confederate fortifications, and he chafed at the thought they would have to remain there for a prolonged siege before the garrison was starved out. He worried about the possibility of a rebel attack on New Orleans, now occupied by a shrunken Union force, and about the oncoming summer that would bring yellow fever and malaria, and about the imminent end of his nine-month volunteers' term of service, which could cut his army in half. On the day the investment was completed, May 26, he called his commanders together for a council of war and proposed to them an immediate, all-out assault on the Confederate defenses. Not all of his commanders thought it was a good idea, but Banks was insistent and ordered a general assault to be made the next morning, May 27.

General Gardner was braced and prepared for the coming assault. He placed one of his brigades, about two thousand men from Alabama, Arkansas and Mississippi, commanded by Colonel Isaiah Steedman, on the left of his line, facing north and northwest. On the right side of the line, facing southeast, he placed some eleven hundred Louisiana troops commanded by Colonel William Miles, and in the center of his line, facing east and northeast, he put the twenty-three hundred men, mostly from Arkansas, of General Beall's command. The rest of the garrison was assigned to the big guns facing the Mississippi River on the west side.

26. Finale at Port Hudson

Union assaults on Port Hudson, Louisiana. Neither Farragut's fleet nor an assault by the army of Maj. Gen. Nathaniel Banks was able to overcome the garrison of the rebel works that were the last remaining obstacle blocking the passage of Union vessels on the Mississippi. Union forces suffered heavy losses in the failed attempt to storm the works on May 27, 1863 (Library of Congress).

Lieutenant Colonel Richard B. Irwin, assistant adjutant general for Banks's army, described the battlefield and the opening action:

> Early in the morning [General] Weitzel, who commanded the right wing on this day, moved to the attack in two lines, [Brigadier General William] Dwight at first leading, and steadily drove the Confederates in his front into their works. Thus unmasked, the Confederate artillery opened with grape and canister, but our batteries, following the infantry as closely as possible, soon took commanding positions within 200 and 300 yards of the [rebel] works that enabled them to keep down the enemy's fire. The whole fight took place in a dense forest of magnolias, mostly amid a thick undergrowth, and among ravines choked with felled or fallen timber, so that it was difficult not only to move but even to see.... Soon after Weitzel's movement began [Brigadier General Cuvier] Grover, on his left, moved to the attack at two points, but only succeeded in gaining and holding commanding positions within about two hundred yards of the works. This accomplished, and no sound of battle coming from his left, Grover determined to wait for further orders, and Weitzel conformed his action to Grover's.[4]

The uncertainty and hesitation of Grover and Weitzel were the results of Banks's slipshod planning. In his haste to launch the assault Banks had neglected to coordinate the movements of his forces, leaving commanders to move on their own as they saw fit. One of them, Sherman, who had opposed making the assault and who commanded on the far left of the Union line, had not moved at all, and when Banks rode over to Sherman's position to find out why, he found Sherman in his tent lounging over a late breakfast, or early lunch—and perhaps a few drinks. Convinced that the assault would fail, he had decided not to participate. Banks relieved him of his command on the spot, but Sherman dashed away, sprang up on his horse and led his troops on an advance across an open area called Slaughter's Field, on the southeast section of the Confederate line.

The consequences of his charge against the rebel works were as bad as he had expected. As his troops neared the rebel line, advancing across the open field, they were struck by intense artillery and rifle fire and took heavy losses. Several hundred of his men managed to make it to the ditch that ran in front of the Confederate works, but they were quickly felled by gunfire or driven back. Sherman himself became one of the casualties, suffering a severe wound that forced him out of the action and sent him to New Orleans to recover. Brigadier General Neal Dow, one of Sherman's brigade commanders, was also wounded.

Elsewhere along the Union line the results were not much better. Weitzel's and Grover's troops were driven back from the Confederates' left side and forced to dig in to hold their line. Augur's advance against the Confederates' center was likewise repulsed. General Banks's insistence that Port Hudson be taken that day had gone for naught but disaster. He summed up the battle in a message to Grant: "The fight was very bitter and our losses severe."[5] Banks's army had suffered nearly two thousand casualties—293 killed, 1,545 wounded (including ninety officers) and 157 missing—and all that his troops had to show for their efforts was a new line, somewhat closer to the Confederates' works. In contrast to the Union losses, Gardner's rebel garrison had lost an estimated 235 men, including killed, wounded and missing.

Among the Union units that had braved the fierce rebel fusillades that day were the First Louisiana Native Guards and the Third Louisiana Native Guards, two regiments of black troops, the First composed of free Negroes from New Orleans and the Third composed of recently freed slaves.

Gardner's vastly outnumbered garrison, with pluck, determination and a botched Union attempt, had withstood and turned back Banks's army, and now Banks decided he would resort to a siege after all. Soldiers and free blacks who were hired for the task began digging rifle pits, gun emplacements, breastworks and zig-zag approaches to the rebel line, while Union artillery relentlessly pounded Port Hudson. Admiral Porter's fleet lying in the river joined the intense bombardment, his mortar boats showering the rebel positions with shells by night, his gunboats blasting them by day.

At the same time, Gardner was strengthening his works and trying to keep ahead of the damage done by Union guns. His artillery, though, was mostly silent, saving its ammunition for a new Union infantry assault. A shortage of ammunition was only one of the problems within the Confederate lines. The situation was slowly deteriorating, the food supply running out and sickness plaguing the beleaguered garrison as it suffered alternating periods of scorching heat and drenching rains. Tons of food were destroyed in a blaze set off by Union shells that hit a storehouse, and Gardner's troops began butchering their horses and mules to feed themselves. Desertions began to increase, the desperately hungry soldiers stealing away during the night. Gardner, defiant in the face of disaster, had told his troops, "The enemy are coming, but mark you, many a one will get to hell before he does to Port Hudson."[6]

For more than two weeks Banks's army dug and waited, dug and waited. Banks finally lost patience and decided to try another assault. He summoned his commanders to meet with him on the evening of June 13 and at the meeting he laid out a new plan of attack, providing more details this time. The plan called for the Union forces to concentrate their assault on two points believed to be vulnerable. One was called the Priest's Cap, a salient on the left center of the rebel line. The other was called the Citadel, a redoubt the rebels had built on the far right of their earthworks, near their line of heavy guns that overlooked the river.

The attack was scheduled for early morning on the next day, June 14, allowing officers and men little time to prepare themselves. Union artillery opened up on the rebel line before the infantry was to rush the rebel positions, and when it did, the rebel soldiers took quick refuge in their gopher holes. As soon as the bombardment stopped, they hurried out of their holes and took their places on the parapets and delivered merciless volleys into the advancing Union ranks. The leading regiments—the Fourth Wisconsin, Eighth New Hampshire and Twenty-fifth Connecticut—of Brigadier General Halbert Paine's division suffered heavy losses in their attack on the east side of the salient, and Paine himself was severely wounded, but some of his troops managed to force their way across the Priest's Cap parapet. All who did, however, were soon killed or captured by the defenders, members of the Forty-ninth Alabama and First Mississippi infantry regiments. More than half of Paine's men, with their nine-month enlistments about to expire, balked at making the charge and stood idly by.

The planned simultaneous attack on the north side of the Priest's Cap by General Grover's troops, after getting off to a late start and emerging from their narrow sap into a forbidding abatis, also failed. Their tardiness in launching their attack had allowed the rebel regiments to shift from the east side, where they had just turned back Paine's regiments, to the north side in time to repulse Grover's men.

At the Citadel the only achievement of the attack by the division commanded by Brigadier General William Dwight, who had replaced the wounded General Sherman, was to capture a high, flat piece of land that became the site of an artillery emplacement from which Union guns could more effectively hammer the Confederate positions.

For the second time Banks's attempt to take Port Hudson by storm had failed. This time his army had lost 1,792 men — 203 killed, 1,401 wounded and 188 missing. The Confederates lost twenty-two killed and twenty-five wounded. Celebrating their victory, the rebel soldiers, accompanied by bugles and drums, loudly sang "Bonnie Blue Flag" as the Union troops pulled back from the Confederate works.

For three days after the assault the bodies of the Union dead and wounded lay where they had fallen, the odor of corpses rotting in the Southern summer sun so strong that the Confederates at last asked for a truce to allow them to take the bodies to the Union lines. Banks agreed, and details of rebel soldiers went out to the bloodied field, picked up the bodies and delivered them into Union hands for burial. Meanwhile Banks's demoralized troops resumed digging the saps that stretched toward the rebel line. And before the saps had been extended very much, Banks issued a call for a thousand volunteers to make a third assault on the rebel line—which proved a futile effort when only about three hundred men answered his call for volunteers.

While the Union soldiers dug, the Confederates kept busy repairing and strengthening their works and dealing with growing hunger and thirst. By the first of July they had run out of meat, the corn supply was nearly exhausted, and cowpeas, difficult to digest, were taking the place of corn, resulting in widespread stomach ailments. Molasses and sugar remained in adequate supply, and the troops used them to brew a sort of beer, which they found easier to drink than the only water that was available to them, putrid as it was. They also came up with substitutes for coffee — parched rye, parched meal, parched sweet potatoes — that lasted as long as the ingredients could be scrounged. When the supply of tobacco ran out, the men chewed or smoked leaves or pieces of bark.

On July 4 the Union troops took the day off from their digging and other toils to observe Independence Day. The observance included a public reading of the Declaration of Independence, the firing of blank artillery salutes, patriotic speeches and the distribution of rounds of wine and whiskey — and an occasional rifle shot at the Confederate line.

Three days later the ram *General Price*, captured by the U.S. Navy from the rebels' River Defense Fleet at Memphis, pulled into shore above Port Hudson to deliver a dispatch from General Grant. Colonel Irwin, Banks's assistant adjutant general, narrated the climactic events that followed:

> At last on the 7th of July, when the sap-head was within 16 feet of the priest-cap, and a storming party of 1000 volunteers had been organized, led by the intrepid [brigade commander Colonel Henry] Birge, and all preparations had been made for springing two heavily charged mines, word came from Grant that Vicksburg had surrendered. Instantly an aide was sent to the "general-of-the-trenches" bearing duplicates in "flimsy" of a note from the adjutant-general announcing the good news. One of these he was directed to toss into the Confederate lines. Some one acknowledged the receipt by calling back, "That's another damned Yankee lie!"
>
> Once more the cheers of our men rang out as the word passed, and again the forest echoed with the strains of the "Star-spangled Banner" from the long-silent bands. Firing died away, the men began to mingle in spite of everything, and about 2 o'clock next morning came the long, gray envelope that meant *surrender*.
>
> Formalities alone remained.[7]

With the noise of celebration resounding in their ears, the Confederate soldiers at last accepted the truth of the message from Vicksburg. Soon hundreds of them clambered over their parapets to join the joyful Union soldiers, grasping their hands to shake, joking and laughing with them, the relief strikingly obvious on both sides. It was not till after midnight that General Gardner made a formal effort to receive the news himself. He dispatched a party of officers to Banks asking for a copy of the message Banks had received from Grant. Banks sent it to him. Satisfied, Gardner then wrote to Banks to arrange a discussion of surrender terms.

At nine A.M. on July 8, Gardner sent three of his senior officers — Colonel I.G.W. Steedman, Colonel W.R. Miles and Lieutenant Colonel Marshall J. Smith — to meet with three of Banks's senior officers, Brigadier General Charles Stone (a member of Banks's staff), General Dwight and Colonel Birge. In the shade of a cluster of magnolia trees, the two sets of officers calmly and cordially discussed the surrender arrangements while sipping from glasses of Bordeaux wine. The surrender was to be unconditional. Gardner would turn over Port Hudson and its garrison and all weapons, materiel and military equipment to Banks. The Confederate officers and men would become prisoners of war, the officers to be held until they could be exchanged and the men to be paroled after they had been processed. The sick and wounded would receive care from Union medical personnel. Personal property could be kept by its owners. The troops were to line up for the formal surrender ceremony at seven A.M. the next day, July 9.

At seven o'clock on the morning of the 9th, Brigadier General George L. Andrews rode into Port Hudson leading a procession of regiments selected from each of Banks's divisions and military bands playing "Yankee Doodle." At the head of his troops General Gardner

The surrender of Port Hudson. On receiving news of the fall of Vicksburg, Maj. Gen. Franklin Gardner, the Confederate commander, realized the fight to hold the fortification was lost, and he agreed to surrender on July 8, 1863. Hundreds of rebel soldiers climbed over their parapets, shaking hands and laughing with the Union soldiers in relief (Library of Congress).

stood waiting. The order "Ground arms" was shouted, and the Confederate soldiers abandoned their weapons in stacks before them. General Gardner then unbuckled his sword and held it out for General Andrews to accept as the ultimate symbol of surrender. Andrews told Gardner to keep it.

The Confederate flag was then lowered and the Stars and Stripes raised to replace it as the Union bands again struck up and Union artillery boomed in triumphant salute. General Gardner, still a favorite of his troops, made a short farewell speech, and after his men had cheered his announcement of their imminent parole, the ceremonies concluded. The rebel officers, including Gardner, would be shipped off to New Orleans or Memphis or a camp in the North to be interned until they could be exchanged. The enlisted men, once they had gone through the records-keeping process, would be free to go home. The total number of Confederates surrendered by Gardner that day was put at 6,340 — 405 officers and 5,935 enlisted men.

The fight for Port Hudson was over. After relentless bombardment, repeated assaults and more than six grueling weeks of siege, the last Confederate stronghold on the Mississippi had fallen. In a terse sentence General Banks announced the historic good news to General Grant: "The Mississippi is opened."[8]

Epilogue

On the same day that General Pemberton capitulated to General Grant at Vicksburg, the assault on Helena by Lieutenant General Theophilus Holmes and his seventy-six hundred rebel troops was repulsed by the outnumbered Union garrison, which, aided by the gunboat *Tyler*, inflicted heavy losses on the attackers and drove them back toward Little Rock, their dead and wounded abandoned on the ground where they fell.

Also on that day, a Confederate force led by Major General Richard L. Taylor, with more defiance than strategy, from the west bank of the Mississippi above New Orleans opened fire on Union transports moving up and down the river and drew the attention of Admiral Farragut, who quickly sent the *Monongahela*, *Kineo* and *Essex* to return the fire of

The Mississippi River steamer *Imperial* is greeted by a cheering throng as it arrives at the New Orleans riverfront on July 16, 1863, having departed from St. Louis on July 8. It was the first freight-carrying civilian steamboat to venture down the Mississippi following the opening of the river after the Union's capture of Vicksburg and Port Hudson (Library of Congress).

the rebels, driving them away from the river, squashing any threat to the environs of New Orleans.

Thus the mighty Mississippi, along its full, 2,350-mile extent, from Lake Itasca in Minnesota to its debouchment into the Gulf of Mexico, once again was possessed by the United States of America. Confederate claims on it had been denied, all serious threats to it had been defeated, all obstacles removed. Now its unending waters would once more flow, in President Lincoln's words, "unvexed to the sea."

In a public demonstration that the river no longer was vexed, the steamer *Imperial*, having shoved off from the wharves of St. Louis on July 8, arrived in New Orleans on Thursday, July 16, making a grand entrance at the riverfront. "The *Imperial*," a reporter for *Harper's Weekly* wrote, "is an immense, showy vessel, one of the first-class river steamers.... But it was not her size nor fine equipments which impressed the eager multitudes who thronged to see her; it was the fact that she was the first freight boat which had ventured down the Mississippi since the fall of Vicksburg and Port Hudson; and every one who gazed upon her proud form saw in her the embodiment of reawakened commerce with the Mississippi Valley."[1]

The Mississippi River had indeed been opened — and the Confederacy constricted, very much as old General Scott had prescribed.

Chapter Notes

Introduction

1. The flag is now in the museum at Fort Sumter.
2. John G. Nicolay, *The Outbreak of the Rebellion*, page 73.
3. Ibid., page 75.
4. Ibid., page 81.
5. Charles Winslow Elliott, *Winfield Scott, the Soldier and the Man*, page 718.
6. Scott to Seward, March 3, 1861. Scott, *Memoirs*, Vol. 2, pages 625–628. Quoted in Elliott, page 696.
7. Scott to McClellan, *Official Records, War of the Rebellion*, Series 3, Vol. 1, pages 177–178. Complete text at www.civilwarhome.com/scottmcclellananaconda.htm.
8. Elliott, page 723.
9. Shelby Foote, *The Civil War, a Narrative: Fort Sumter to Perryville*, page 89.
10. Bruce Catton, *Terrible Swift Sword*, page 226.

Chapter 1

1. Frémont Memoirs, Bancroft Library, University of California, pages 240–241. Catton, *Terrible Swift Sword*, page 27.
2. Ulysses S. Grant, *Personal Memoirs of Ulysses S. Grant*, page 144.
3. Ibid., page 148.
4. Ibid., page 149.
5. Harry Hansen, *The Civil War*, pages 97–98.
6. Ibid., pages 98–99.
7. Catton, *Terrible Swift Sword*, page 31.
8. www.longcamp.com/proc3.html, page 2.
9. Catton, *Terrible Swift Sword*, page 50.
10. Ibid.
11. Foote, page 98.

Chapter 2

1. Joseph H. Parks, *General Leonidas Polk* (LSU Press, 1992), page 125. Steven E. Woodworth, *Jefferson Davis and His Generals*, page 28.
2. Woodworth, page 31.
3. Ibid., page 34.
4. Ibid., page 37.
5. Ibid., page 39.
6. U.S. War Department, *The War of the Rebellion: A Compilation of the Official Records of the Union and Confederate Armies* (Washington, D.C.: Government Printing Office, 1880–1901), Vol. 4, page 181. Woodworth, page 41.
7. Ibid.

Chapter 3

1. Welles to Rodgers, June 11 and 12, 1861, *Letters Sent by the Secretary of the Navy to Officers* ("Officers, Ships of War"), National Archives, Record Group 45. Quoted in John D. Milligan, *Gunboats Down the Mississippi*, page 7.
2. James Mason Hoppin, *Life of Admiral Andrew Hull Foote*, page 161.
3. Ibid., page 160.
4. Ibid., page 179.
5. Henry Walke, "Operations of the Western Flotilla, Part I." *The Century* magazine, Vol. 29, January 1885. www.rugreview.com/cw/cwg1.htm.
6. Ibid.
7. Rodgers to "Dear Sir," June 30, 1861, Rodgers Papers. Quoted in Milligan, page 9.
8. J. Thomas Scharf, *History of the Confederate States Navy*, pages 32–33.
9. Ibid., page 49.
10. Ibid., page 43.
11. R. Thomas Campbell, *Confederate Naval Forces on Western Waters*, page 53.
12. Scharf, pages 249–250.
13. Ibid., page 250.

Chapter 4

1. Clarence Edward Macartney, *Mr. Lincoln's Admirals*, page 83, quoting from Foote's book, *Africa and the American Flag*.
2. Hoppin, pages 171–172.
3. Ibid., page 160.
4. Ibid., pages 177–178.
5. Grant, page 161.
6. Ibid., page 162.
7. Hoppin, page 186.
8. Grant, page 163.
9. Ibid., page 164.
10. Ibid., page 165.
11. Ibid., page 166.
12. Ibid.
13. Ibid., page 167.

14. John S.D. Eisenhower, *The Agent of Destiny*, page 397.
15. Ibid.
16. Ibid., page 395.

Chapter 5

1. Grant, pages 168–169.
2. Ibid., page 169.
3. Ibid.
4. Ibid., page 170.
5. Michael Burlingame and John R. Turner Ettlinger, eds., *Inside Lincoln's White House: The Complete Civil War Diary of John Hay*, pages 191–192.
6. Grant, page 170.
7. Foote, page 184.
8. Grant, page 170.
9. Ibid.
10. Hoppin, page 194.
11. Grant, page 172.
12. Hoppin, pages 196–197.
13. Ibid., pages 197–198.
14. Henry Walke, "Operations of the Western Flotilla, Part I." *The Century* magazine, Vol. 29, January 1885. www.rugreview.com/cw/cwg1.htm.
15. Hoppin, page 200.
16. Ibid., page 203.
17. Ibid.
18. Ibid., page 205.
19. Walke, "Operations of the Western Flotilla, Part I."
20. Hoppin, page 212.
21. Ibid., page 210.
22. Ibid., page 209.
23. Kenneth P. Williams, *Grant Rises in the West: The First Year, 1861–1862* (University of Nebraska Press), page 206. Kendall D. Gott, *Where the South Lost the War*, page 116.

Chapter 6

1. Hoppin, page 218.
2. Grant, pages 173, 175.
3. Ibid., page 175.
4. Ibid.
5. Gott, page 118.
6. Ibid.
7. Ibid.
8. Ibid., page 119.
9. Grant, page 173.
10. Ibid.
11. Gideon J. Pillow, "Siege and Capture of Fort Donelson, Tennessee," Report No. 1, www.civilwarhome.com/pillow1fortdonelson.htm.
12. Gott, page 129.
13. Hoppin, page 232.
14. Ibid.
15. Grant, page 176.
16. Henry Walke, "Operations of the Western Flotilla, Part I." *The Century* magazine, Vol. 29, January 1885. www.rugreview.com/cw/cwg1.htm.
17. Ibid., page 2.
18. Ibid.
19. Ibid.
20. Ibid.
21. Ibid., page 3.
22. Ibid.
23. Ibid., pages 3–4.
24. Ibid., page 5.
25. Ibid.
26. Ibid.
27. Pillow, "Siege and Capture of Fort Donelson."
28. Hoppin, pages 226–227.
29. Ibid., pages 228–229.

Chapter 7

1. Grant, Page 176.
2. Ibid.
3. Ibid., page 178.
4. Lew Wallace, "The Capture of Fort Donelson," www.civilwarhome.com/donelsoncapture.htm, page 5.
5. Ibid.
6. Grant, page 179.
7. Ibid.
8. Ibid., pages 179–180.
9. Ibid., page 180.
10. According to Lew Wallace's account of the capture of Fort Donelson, General Floyd held a war council on the morning of February 14, where he proposed an attack on the right side of the Union line and a retreat to Nashville via Charlotte. Floyd's officers, according to Wallace, agreed, but when it was time to begin the attack, Floyd's order was countermanded by General Pillow. A second war council was held on the night of February 14.
11. Wallace, "The Capture of Fort Donelson," page 9.
12. Ibid., pages 9–10.
13. Ibid., page 12.
14. Grant, page 181.
15. Ibid.
16. Ibid.
17. Wallace, page 13.
18. Grant, page 182.
19. Wallace, page 13.
20. Pillow, "Siege and Capture of Fort Donelson," page 5.
21. Grant, page 182.
22. Pillow, "Siege and Capture of Fort Donelson," Report No. 2, page 3.
23. Ibid.
24. Ibid.
25. Ibid.
26. Wallace, page 14.
27. Gott, page 254.
28. *Clarksville Star*, Clarksville, Tennessee, July 8, 1932, page 1, column 1.
29. Ibid.
30. Ibid.
31. Texts of the three notes are from Grant, pages 183–184.
32. Pillow, "Siege and Capture of Fort Donelson," Report No. 2, page 4.
33. Wallace, page 15.
34. Ibid.
35. Grant, pages 184–185.
36. Ibid., pages 185–186.

37. Pillow, "Siege and Capture of Fort Donelson, Tennessee," Report No. 1, page 6.
38. Pillow, "Siege and Capture of Fort Donelson," Report No. 2, pages 4–5.
39. Stanley Horn, *The Army of Tennessee* (Indianapolis: Bobbs-Merrill, 1941), pages 96–98. Woodworth, *Jefferson Davis and His Generals*, page 84.

Chapter 8

1. Charleston *Mercury*, May 30, 1861. Quoted in T. Harry Williams, *P.G.T. Beauregard, Napoleon in Gray*, page 64.
2. T. Harry Williams, *P.G.T. Beauregard*, page 114.
3. Beauregard to Pryor, February 14, 1862, the Alfred Roman Papers, *Beauregard*, Vol. 1, page 224. Quoted in T. Harry Williams, page 248.
4. Hoppin, page 248.
5. *Harper's Weekly*, March 29, 1862.

Chapter 9

1. Hoppin, page 249.
2. Henry Walke, "Operations of the Western Flotilla, Part I." *The Century* magazine, Vol. 29, January 1885. www.rugreview.com/cw/cwgl.htm, page 7.
3. Hoppin, page 266.
4. M.F. Force, *Campaigns of the Civil War, from Fort Henry to Corinth*, pages 79–80.
5. Ibid., pages 267–268.
6. Ibid., page 268.
7. Walke, "Operations of the Western Flotilla, Part I."
8. Hoppin, page 269.
9. Walke, "Operations of the Western Flotilla, Part I," page 9.
10. *Official Records of the Union and Confederate Armies*, Vol. 8, page 629. Quoted in Kenneth P. Williams, page 397.
11. From the remarks of Confederate Navy Captain C.W. Read, "Reminiscences of the Confederate States Navy," www. civilwarhome.com/reminiscencecsn.htm, page 5.
12. Walke, "Operations of the Western Flotilla, Part I," page 9.
13. Hoppin, pages 273–274.
14. Ibid., page 274.
15. Walke, page 10.
16. Hoppin, pages 282–283.
17. Walke, page 10.
18. Hoppin, page 288.
19. Kenneth P. Williams, page 399.
20. Ibid.
21. *Official Records of the Union and Confederate Navies in the War of the Rebellion*, Series 1, Vol. 22, pages 715–719. Quoted in Kenneth P. Williams, page 399.
22. Campbell, page 49.
23. Force, page 90.
24. Bern Anderson, *By Sea and by River: The Naval History of the Civil War*, page 107.
25. Force, page 90.

Chapter 10

1. Francis Vinton Greene, *The Mississippi*, pages 11–12.
2. Hansen, page 119.
3. Ibid.
4. Force, page 94.
5. Ibid., pages 94–95.
6. Grant, page 193.
7. Ibid.
8. Force, page 95.
9. Ibid.
10. Ibid., page 95.
11. Ibid.
12. Grant, pages 194–195.
13. T. Harry Williams, page 122.
14. Grant, page 195.
15. Ibid., pages 196–197.
16. T. Harry Williams, page 126.
17. Quoted in T. Harry Williams, page 132.
18. Grant, page 197.
19. http://en.wikipedia.org/wiki/Battle_of_Shiloh, page 4.
20. Hansen, page 129.
21. Grant, page 200.
22. Ibid., pages 199–200.
23. Ibid., pages 202–203.
24. Ibid., page 201.
25. Ibid., page 203.
26. Quoted in Catton, *Terrible Swift Sword*, page 224.
27. Ibid., pages 224–225.
28. T. Harry Williams, page 143.
29. Grant, pages 204–205.
30. Ibid., page 205.
31. Ibid., pages 205–206.
32. Kenneth P. Williams, page 383.
33. Ibid., page 384.
34. Ibid., page 386.
35. Grant, page 207.
36. T. Harry Williams, page 145.
37. Grant, pages 209–210.
38. Ibid., page 211.

Chapter 11

1. Robert Underwood Johnson, and Clarence Clough Buell, eds., *Battles and Leaders of the Civil War*, Vol. II, page 24. The quote is reported by David Dixon Porter in the article he contributed to *Battles and Leaders*.
2. Ibid., page 25.
3. The elder Porter took young Farragut under his wing to return an act of kindness done by Farragut's father in behalf of the elder Porter's father.
4. Fletcher Pratt, *Civil War on Western Waters*, page 74.
5. The records concerning Farragut's interview are seemingly contradictory. In a letter to his wife dated September 10, 1862, Welles wrote, "Admiral Farragut did not know that we intended to capture New Orleans and Forts Jackson and St. Philip till the matter was decided upon and he was notified of his appointment, told what was required of him to do."
6. *Battles and Leaders*, Vol. 2, page 26.

7. Ibid., pages 28–29.
8. Pratt, pages 76–77.
9. Ibid., page 77.
10. Charles L. Dufour, *The Night the War Was Lost*, page 129.
11. *Battles and Leaders*, pages 57–58.
12. Ibid., page 58.
13. David D. Porter, *The Naval History of the Civil War*, page 177.
14. Dufour, pages 204–205.
15. Porter, pages 177–178.
16. *Battles and Leaders*, pages 34–35.
17. Ibid., page 35.
18. Ibid., page 60.
19. Dufour, pages 248–249.
20. Log of the *Itasca*, April 21, 1862. Quoted in Dufour, pages 249–250.
21. Loyall Farragut, *Farragut*, pages 226–227.
22. *Battles and Leaders*, page 60.
23. Porter, page 181.

Chapter 12

1. James Parton, *General Butler in New Orleans*, page 240.
2. Ibid.
3. David D. Porter, page 185.
4. *Battles and Leaders*, Vol. 2, page 62.
5. Parton, page 242.
6. Dufour, pages 270–271.
7. Scharf, page 288.
8. Ibid.
9. Ibid., page 287.
10. *Battles and Leaders*, Vol. 2, page 80.
11. Ibid., pages 77–78.
12. Parton, pages 243–244.
13. *Battles and Leaders*, Vol. 2, pages 83–84.
14. David D. Porter, page 185.
15. Ibid.
16. *Battles and Leaders*, Vol. 2, pages 90–91.
17. David D. Porter, page 185.
18. Ibid., page 91.
19. Ibid.
20. Scharf, page 299.
21. David D. Porter, page 186.
22. Ibid.
23. Parton, page 251.
24. Dufour, pages 283–284.
25. *Battles and Leaders*, Vol. 2, page 54.
26. Parton, page 268.

Chapter 13

1. civilwar.bluegrass.net/OfficersandEnlistedMen/davidemanueltwiggs.html.
2. Foote, page 295.
3. Dufour, page 45.
4. Ibid., page 46.
5. Ibid.
6. Ibid., page 57.
7. Ibid.
8. Woodworth, page 25.
9. Dufour, page 68.
10. Elise Ellis Bragg to Braxton Bragg, October 13, 1861, in *Bragg Papers*, University of Texas Archives.
11. Dufour, pages 91–92.
12. *Official Records* (navies), Vol. 6, page 878. Davis to Moore, April 17, 1862.
13. Dufour, page 229.
14. Parton, page 265.
15. George H. Devol, *Forty Years a Gambler on the Mississippi*, pages 118–119.
16. Parton, page 265.
17. Dufour, page 301.
18. George W. Cable in *Battles and Leaders*, Vol. 2, page 21.
19. Parton, page 270.
20. Ibid.
21. Ibid., page 272.
22. Albert Kautz in *Battles and Leaders*, Vol. 2, page 91.
23. Ibid.
24. Parton, page 273.
25. Ibid.
26. Ibid., page 274.
27. Ibid., pages 275–276.
28. Marion A. Baker in *Battles and Leaders*, Vol. 2, page 99.
29. Parton, pages 312–313.
30. Ibid., page 276.
31. *Battles and Leaders*, Vol. 2, page 99.
32. Parton, page 278.

Chapter 14

1. Benjamin F. Butler, *Butler's Book: Autobiography and Personal Reminiscences of Major-General Benj. F. Butler*, pages 375–376.
2. Quotes of Butler and Soulé are from Parton, pages 295–296.
3. Parton, pages 297–298.
4. Butler, page 395.
5. Parton, page 323.
6. Butler, page 418.
7. Parton, pages 327–328.
8. Ibid., page 331.
9. Dufour, page 309.

Chapter 15

1. Chester G. Hearn, *Ellet's Brigade: The Strangest Outfit of All*, page 5.
2. Charles Ellet, Jr., *Military Incapacity and What It Costs the Country* (New York: Ross and Tousey, 1862), page 14. Quoted in Gene D. Lewis, *Charles Ellet, Jr.: The Engineer as Individualist*, page 185.
3. Hearn, *Ellet's Brigade*, page 5.
4. Lewis, page 186.
5. Ellet letter to Stanton dated March 15, 1862. Quoted in Lewis, page 187.
6. Herbert Pickins Gambrell, "Rams versus Gunboats: A Landsman's Naval Exploits," *Southwest Review*, Vol. 23 (October 1937), page 55. Quoted in Lewis, page 187.
7. George C. Gorham, *Life and Public Services of Edwin M. Stanton*, Vol. 1 (New York: Houghton Mifflin, 1899), page 290. Quoted in Lewis, pages 189–190.
8. Hearn, *Ellet's Brigade*, page 7.
9. Ibid.
10. Ibid., pages 292–294. Lewis, page 190.

11. Quoted in Lewis, page 187.
12. Lewis, page 191.
13. Warren D. Crandall and Isaac D. Newell, *History of the Ram Fleet and the Mississippi Marine Brigade: The Story of the Ellets and Their Men* (St. Louis: Society of Survivors, 1907), pages 23–29. Quoted in Lewis, page 191.
14. Ellet to Stanton, March 31, 1862, *Official Records* (navies), Vol. 22, pages 682–684. Quoted in Hearn, page 8.
15. Ibid.
16. Hearn, *Ellet's Brigade*, page 17.
17. Ellet's letter to his wife, dated May 29, 1862, Ellet Papers, University of Michigan, Special Collections Library, Ann Arbor. Quoted in Hearn, page 18.
18. From Ellie Ellet's letter to Charles Ellet, dated May 2, 1862. Quoted in Lewis, page 194.
19. From Charles Ellet's letter to Ellie Ellet, dated May 7, 1862. Quoted in Lewis, page 194.
20. Herbert Quick and Edward Quick, *Mississippi Steamboatin'*, pages 269–270.

Chapter 16

1. Hoppin, page 299.
2. Ibid., page 301.
3. Ibid., page 303.
4. Ibid., page 311.
5. Ibid., page 312.
6. H. Allen Gosnell, *Guns on the Western Waters: The Story of River Gunboats in the Civil War*, page 85.
7. The author takes particular interest in the actions of the *General Sumter*. Aboard it was his great-grandfather, Robert T. Patterson, the boat's chief engineer.
8. Gosnell, pages 87–88.
9. Scharf, page 254.
10. Henry Walke in *Battles and Leaders of the Civil War*, Vol. 1, pages 447–449.
11. Scharf, page 255. From Report of Capt. J.E. Montgomery, *Official Records* (navies), Vol. 10, page 888.
12. Scharf, page 255.
13. David D. Porter, page 166.
14. Ibid., page 167.
15. Scharf, page 256.
16. David D. Porter, page 167.
17. Ibid.
18. Hearn, *Ellet's Brigade*, page 22.
19. Davis to Ellet, *Official Records* (navies), Vol. 23, pages 39–40. Quoted in Hearn, *Ellet's Brigade*, page 24.
20. Ibid., page 41. Quoted in Hearn, *Ellet's Brigade*, page 24.
21. Scharf, pages 256–257.
22. *Battles and Leaders*, Vol. 1, page 449.
23. Ibid.
24. Alfred Ellet in *Battles and Leaders*, Vol. 1, page 455.

Chapter 17

1. Charles Carleton Coffin, *My Days and Nights on the Battle-field*, page 291. The statement was an exaggeration. The boats were built in various cities and converted into rams in New Orleans, their crews coming from many places.
2. Memphis *Avalanche*, June 6, 1862. Quoted in Coffin, pages 291–292.
3. Coffin, page 292.
4. Ibid., page 293.
5. Ibid., pages 293–296.
6. Scharf, page 259.
7. Alfred W. Ellet in *Battles and Leaders*, Vol. 1, page 456.
8. Scharf, pages 259–260.
9. *Battles and Leaders*, Vol. 1, page 457.
10. Chief Engineer Robert T. Patterson escaped and made his way back home to New Orleans.
11. Scharf, page 260.
12. *Battles and Leaders*, Vol. 1, page 452.
13. Scharf, page 260.
14. Ibid., page 262.
15. *Harper's Weekly*, June 28, 1862, page 410.
16. Coffin, pages 306–307.
17. Scharf, page 261.
18. *Harper's Weekly*, June 28, 1862, page 411.
19. These estimates are from Henry Walke, *Battles and Leaders*, Vol. 1, page 452.
20. Ibid.
21. Some sources say Colonel Ellet died of measles contracted while he was hospitalized.

Chapter 18

1. A.T. Mahan, *Admiral Farragut*, page 176.
2. Pratt, page 105.
3. Mahan, pages 181–182.
4. Sarah Morgan, *The Civil War Diary of a Southern Woman*, page 48.
5. Ibid., page 59.
6. Ibid., pages 63–64.
7. Dufour, page 20.
8. William L. Shea and Terrence J. Winschel, *Vicksburg Is the Key*, page 16.
9. *Official Records* (navies), Vol. 18, page 492. Anderson, page 128.
10. Parton, pages 193–194.
11. Mahan, pages 182–183.
12. Ibid., page 183.
13. Morgan, pages 87–91.
14. Morgan's information about the Navy personnel who were fired on contradicts other sources and is apparently inaccurate.
15. Morgan, pages 94–95.
16. Mahan, page 184.
17. Ibid., pages 183–184.
18. Ibid., page 184.
19. David D. Porter, pages 248–249.
20. Ibid., page 256.
21. Ibid., page 255.
22. Ibid., page 256.
23. According to their captains' reports, the *Brooklyn*'s and the *Kennebec*'s orders were confusing, and the *Katahdin* received no orders. Copies of the reports appear in David D. Porter, pages 253–254.
24. David D. Porter, page 250.
25. Ibid., pages 250–251.
26. Anderson, page 132.

Chapter 19

1. Scharf, page 310.
2. David D. Porter, page 249.
3. Scharf, page 309.
4. Isaac N. Brown, *Battles and Leaders*, Vol. 3, page 573.
5. Campbell, pages 113–114. George W. Gift, "The Story of the Arkansas," *Southern Historical Society Papers*, Vol. 12, 1887, page 50.
6. Scharf, pages 310–311.
7. Brown, *Battles and Leaders*, Vol. 3, page 574.
8. Scharf, page 313.
9. Brown, *Battles and Leaders*, Vol. 3, page 574.
10. Ibid., page 575.
11. Ibid.
12. Ibid.
13. Scharf, page 315.
14. Brown, *Battles and Leaders*, Vol. 3, page 575.
15. Scharf, page 312.
16. Ibid., page 313.
17. Ibid., page 314.
18. Brown, *Battles and Leaders*, Vol. 3, page 575.
19. Ibid., pages 575–576.
20. Scharf, pages 319–320.
21. Ibid., page 321.
22. Ibid., pages 321–322.
23. Ibid.
24. Campbell, page 129.
25. Scharf, pages 323–324.
26. Ibid., pages 325–326.
27. Campbell, pages 132–133.
28. Scharf, pages 330–331.
29. Ibid., page 330.

Chapter 20

1. Foote, pages 573–574.
2. Ibid., page 292.
3. Ibid., page 577.
4. Ibid., page 579.
5. Brown, *Battles and Leaders*, Vol. 3, page 579.
6. Ibid.
7. Ibid.
8. Gift, "The Story of the Arkansas," page 207.
9. Lt. Col. Richard B. Irwin in *Battles and Leaders*, Vol. 3, page 583.
10. *Harper's Weekly*, "The Battle of Baton Rouge," September 6, 1862.
11. Ibid.
12. Ibid.
13. Brown, *Battles and Leaders*, Vol. 3, page 579.
14. Morgan, pages 194–197.

Chapter 21

1. David D. Porter, pages 283–284.
2. Grant, page 250.
3. Macartney, page 274.
4. Grant, pages 252–253.
5. Ibid., page 253.
6. Ibid., page 254.
7. Ibid., page 255.
8. Pratt, page 135.
9. National Archives, C225, letter of Stephen R. Mallory to William F. Lynch, August 22, 1862. Campbell, pages 169–170.
10. David D. Porter, pages 284–285.
11. Brown, *Battles and Leaders*, Vol. 3, page 580.
12. David D. Porter, page 285.
13. William T. Sherman, *Memoirs of General William T. Sherman*, Vol. 1, pages 285, 289.
14. Ibid., page 290.
15. John D. Milligan, editor, *From the Fresh-Water Navy: The Letters of Acting Master's Mate Henry R. Browne and Acting Ensign Symmes E. Brown*, page 127.
16. Sherman, page 291.
17. Grant, page 257.
18. Ibid., page 256.
19. Sherman, page 292.
20. Ibid., pages 292–293.
21. Ibid., page 293.

Chapter 22

1. Sherman, page 294.
2. Ibid.
3. David D. Porter, page 289.
4. Sherman, page 296.
5. Ibid.
6. Ibid., pages 296–297.
7. Ibid., page 295.
8. David D. Porter, page 288.
9. Sherman, page 298.
10. Ibid.
11. David D. Porter, pages 289–290.
12. Ibid., page 291.
13. Ibid.
14. Sherman, pages 299–300.
15. Ibid., page 300.
16. Ibid., page 301.
17. Ibid., pages 301–302.
18. Ibid., page 302.
19. Ibid., page 303.
20. David D. Porter, page 292.
21. Grant, page 260.
22. Ibid.
23. Ibid., page 261.
24. Ibid.
25. Ibid., pages 261–262.
26. Ibid., page 264.
27. Ibid.
28. Ibid., pages 264–265.
29. David D. Porter, page 296.
30. Ibid., pages 296–297.
31. Gosnell, pages 184–185.
32. Ibid., page 186.
33. David D. Porter, pages 298–299.
34. Shea and Winschel, page 68.
35. David D. Porter, page 300.
36. Dispatch from General Loring to Major R.W. Memminger, assistant adjutant general, dated March 22, 1863, http://loring-atomicmartinis.com/fortpem ht.
37. David D. Porter, page 301.
38. Ibid., page 303.
39. Sherman, page 306.
40. Ibid., page 311.

Chapter 23

1. John D. Winters, *The Civil War in Louisiana*, page 206.
2. *The War of the Rebellion: A Compilation of the Official Records of the Union and Confederate Armies*, Vol. 15, pages 590–591. Quoted in Shea and Winschel, page 76.
3. Mahan, page 201.
4. Irwin, in *Battles and Leaders*, Vol. 3, pages 588–589.
5. Lawrence Lee Hewitt, *Port Hudson: Confederate Bastion on the Mississippi*, page 39.
6. Ibid., page 40.
7. Mahan, page 222.
8. Ibid., page 213.
9. Ibid., pages 223–224.
10. Ibid., page 224.
11. Ibid.
12. Ibid., page 227.
13. Ibid.
14. *Official Records* (armies), Series 1, Vol. 20, pages 137–138. Gosnell, page 202.
15. Henry O. Gusley, *The Southern Journey of a Civil War Marine*, page 157.
16. Shea and Winschel, page 88.

Chapter 24

1. Shea and Winschel, page 96.
2. *Official Records* (armies), Series 1, Vol. 24, page 735.
3. Ibid., page 730.
4. Ibid., page 745.
5. Ibid., page 744.
6. Ibid., page 780.
7. Grant, pages 279–280.
8. David D. Porter, page 313.
9. Ibid., page 315.
10. Edwin Cole Bearss, *The Campaign for Vicksburg*, Vol. 2, page 313.
11. *Official Records* (navies), Vol. 23, page 610. Shea and Winschel, page 105.
12. Grant, page 284.

Chapter 25

1. Bearss, page 345.
2. *The Pine Bluff Commercial*, December 17, 1904. Quoted in Bearss, page 355.
3. Grant, pages 285–286.
4. Ibid., page 289.
5. Ibid., page 290.
6. Ibid., pages 290–291.
7. Ibid., page 291.
8. Shea and Winschel, page 121.
9. Grant, page 294.
10. Ibid.
11. Ibid., page 298.
12. Ibid.
13. Bearss, page 482.
14. Grant, pages 298–299.
15. Ibid., page 299.
16. Ibid.
17. Bearss, page 574.
18. Ibid., pages 300–301.
19. Ibid., page 579.
20. Grant, page 302.
21. Ibid., pages 307–308.
22. Emma Balfour diary, May 17, 1863. Quoted in Shea and Winschel, page 141.
23. Sherman, page 323.
24. Ibid., page 325.
25. Grant, page 310.
26. *Official Records* (armies), Vol. 23, page 274. Quoted in John C. Pemberton, *Pemberton: Defender of Vicksburg*, page 183.
27. Pemberton, page 184.
28. Sherman, page 325.
29. Ibid., pages 326–327.
30. Grant, page 312.
31. *Official Records* (armies), Vol. 23, page 279.
32. Shea and Winschel, page 173.
33. Grant, page 327.
34. Ibid., page 328.
35. McClernand, whom Grant distrusted, had incurred Grant's wrath when he falsely claimed that his troops were on the verge of carrying the Confederate defenses and appealed to Grant to have Sherman and McPherson renew their attack to prevent the rebels' concentration at McClernand's front, which they did, futilely increasing their casualties during the second assault on Vicksburg. McClernand then wrote a self-congratulatory article that was published in St. Louis and other cities in the Midwest. In it, according to Sherman's account, McClernand "claimed that he had actually succeeded in making a lodgment in Vicksburg, but had lost it, owing to the fact that McPherson and Sherman did not fulfill their parts of the general plan of attack. This was simply untrue" (Sherman, pages 327–328). On June 18, Grant relieved McClernand and replaced him with General Ord.
36. Grant, page 329.
37. Ibid.
38. Ibid., pages 330–331.
39. Ibid., page 331.
40. Ibid., page 332.

Chapter 26

1. Shea and Winschel, page 189.
2. Hewitt, page 127.
3. Ibid.
4. Irwin, in *Battles and Leaders*, Vol. 3, page 593.
5. Shea and Winschel, page 197.
6. Hewitt, page 131.
7. Irwin, in *Battles and Leaders*, Vol. 3, page 597.
8. *Official Records* (armies), Vol. 26, Part 1, page 624. Quoted in Shea and Winschel, page 203.

Epilogue

1. *Harper's Weekly*, August 8, 1863.

Bibliography

Anderson, Bern. *By Sea and by River: The Naval History of the Civil War.* New York: Da Capo Press, 1989.

Badeau, Adam. *Military History of Ulysses S. Grant,* Vol. II. Bedford, MA: Applewood Books. Originally published by D. Appleton and Company, New York, 1881.

Boritt, Gabor S., ed. *Lincoln, the War President.* New York: Oxford University Press, 1992.

Butler, Benjamin F. *Butler's Book: Autobiography and Personal Reminiscences of Major-General Benj. F. Butler.* Boston: A.M. Thayer, 1892.

Campbell, R. Thomas. *Confederate Naval Forces on Western Waters.* Jefferson, NC: McFarland, 2005.

Catton, Bruce. *Terrible Swift Sword.* New York: Pocket Books, 1967.

_____. *U.S. Grant and the American Military Tradition.* Boston: Little, Brown, 1954.

Cimprich, John. *Fort Pillow: A Civil War Massacre and Public Memory.* Baton Rouge: Louisiana State University Press, 2005.

Coffin, Charles Carleton. *My Days and Nights on the Battle-field.* Boston: Dana Estes, 1863.

Commager, Henry Steele, ed. *The Blue and the Gray: The Story of the Civil War as Told by Participants, from the Nomination of Lincoln to the Eve of Gettysburg.* New York: Meridian, 1994.

Cunningham, Edward. *The Port Hudson Campaign, 1862–1863.* Baton Rouge: Louisiana State University Press, 1963.

Davis, William C. *Jefferson Davis: The Man and His Hour.* New York: HarperPerennial, 1992.

_____, and Wiley, Bell I., eds. *Photographic History of the Civil War.* New York: Black Dog and Leventhal, 1994.

Detzer, David. *Allegiance: Fort Sumter, Charleston, and the Beginning of the Civil War.* New York: Harcourt, 2001.

Devol, George H. *Forty Years a Gambler on the Mississippi.* Bedford, MA: Applewood Books, 1996.

Draper, John William. *History of the American Civil War,* Vol. III. Boulder, CO: University Libraries. Originally published by Harper and Brothers, New York, 1870.

Dufour, Charles L. *The Night the War Was Lost.* Lincoln: University of Nebraska Press, 1994.

Eisenhower, John S.D. *Agent of Destiny: The Life and Times of General Winfield Scott.* Norman: University of Oklahoma Press, 1997.

Elliott, Charles Winslow. *Winfield Scott: The Soldier and the Man.* New York: Macmillan, 1937.

Foote, Shelby. *The Civil War, A Narrative: Fort Sumter to Perryville.* New York: Random House, 1958.

Force, M.F. *From Fort Henry to Corinth.* New York: Charles Scribner's Sons, 1903.

Freeman, Douglas Southall. *Lee's Lieutenants.* New York: Scribner, 1998.

Gift, George W. "The Story of the *Arkansas.*" Southern Historical Society Papers, Vol. 12, 1887.

Gosnell, H. Allen. *Guns on the Western Waters.* Baton Rouge: Louisiana State University Press, 1949.

Gott, Kendall D. *Where the South Lost the War: An Analysis of the Fort Henry–Fort Donelson Campaign.* Mechanicsburg, PA: Stackpole, 2003.

Grant, Ulysses S. *Personal Memoirs of Ulysses S. Grant.* Old Saybrook, CT: Konecky and Konecky.

Greene, Francis Vinton. *The Mississippi Campaigns of the Civil War.* New York: Blue and Gray Press.

Gusley, Henry O. *The Southern Journey of a Civil War Marine.* Austin: University of Texas Press, 2006.

Hansen, Harry. *The Civil War.* New York: New American Library, 2001.

Hearn, Chester G. *Admiral David Dixon Porter*. Annapolis, MD: Naval Institute Press, 1996.

———. *Ellet's Brigade*. Baton Rouge: Louisiana State University Press, 2000.

———. *When the Devil Came Down to Dixie: Ben Butler in New Orleans*. Baton Rouge: Louisiana State University Press, 1997.

Hewitt, Lawrence Lee. *Port Hudson, Confederate Bastion on the Mississippi*. Baton Rouge: Louisiana State University Press, 1987.

Hoppin, James Mason. *Life of Andrew Hull Foote, Rear Admiral United States Navy*. New York: Harper and Brothers, 1874.

Johnson, Robert Underwood, and Clarence Clough Buel, eds. *Battles and Leaders of the Civil War*, Vols. II and III. Secaucus, NJ: Castle, 1982.

———, eds. *From Sumter to Shiloh: Battles and Leaders of the Civil War*, Vol. I. South Brunswick, NJ: Thomas Yoseloff, 1956.

Ketchum, Richard M., ed. *The American Heritage Picture History of the Civil War*, Vols. I and II. New York: American Heritage, 1960.

Konstam, Angus. *Mississippi River Gunboats of the American Civil War, 1861–65*. Oxford, United Kingdom: Osprey, 2002.

Lee, Robert E. *Recollections and Letters of General Robert E. Lee*. Old Saybrook, CT: Konecky and Konecky.

Lewis, Gene D. *Charles Ellet, Jr.: The Engineer as Individualist*. Urbana: University of Illinois Press, 1968.

Macartney, Clarence Edward. *Mr. Lincoln's Admirals*. New York: Funk and Wagnalls, 1956.

Mahan, A.T. *Admiral Farragut*. London: Sampson Low, Marston, 1892.

McNeese, Tim. *The Mississippi River*. Philadelphia: Chelsea House, 2004.

Melton, Maurice. *The Confederate Ironclads*. Cranbury, NJ: Thomas Yoseloff, 1968.

Milligan, John D. *Gunboats Down the Mississippi*. Annapolis, MD: United States Naval Institute, 1965.

———, ed. *From the Fresh-Water Navy: 1861–64, Naval Letters Series*, Vol. III. Annapolis, MD: United States Naval Institute, 1970.

Morgan, Sarah. *The Civil War Diary of a Southern Woman*. New York: Touchstone, 1992.

Nicolay, John G. *The Outbreak of Rebellion*. Stamford, CT: Longmeadow, 1996.

Niven, John. *Gideon Welles, Lincoln's Secretary of the Navy*. New York: Oxford University Press, 1973.

Nosworthy, Brent. *The Bloody Crucible of Courage: Fighting Methods and Combat Experience of the Civil War*. New York: Carroll and Graf, 2003.

Owen, William Miller. *In Camp and Battle with the Washington Artillery of New Orleans*. Baton Rouge: Louisiana State University Press, 1999.

Page, Dave. *Ships Versus Shore: Civil War Engagements Along Southern Shores and Rivers*. Nashville: Rutledge Hill, 1994.

Parton, James. *General Butler in New Orleans*. New York: Mason Brothers, 1864.

Patterson, Benton Rain. *The Great American Steamboat Race: The* Natchez *and the Robert E. Lee and the Climax of an Era*. Jefferson, NC: McFarland, 2009.

Pemberton, John C. *Pemberton: Defender of Vicksburg*. Chapel Hill: University of North Carolina Press, 1942.

Porter, David D. *The Naval History of the Civil War*. Mineola, NY: Dover Publications, 1998.

Porter, Horace. *Campaigning with Grant*. New York: Mallard Press, 1991.

Pratt, Fletcher. *Civil War on Western Waters*. New York: Henry Holt, 1956.

Quick, Herbert, and Edward Quick. *Mississippi Steamboatin'*. New York: Henry Holt, 1926.

Scharf, J. Thomas. *History of the Confederate States Navy*. New York: Gramercy Books, 1996.

Semmes, Raphael. *Memoirs of Service Afloat During the War Between the States*. Secaucus, NJ: The Blue and Grey Press.

Shea, William L., and Terrence J. Winschel. *Vicksburg Is the Key: The Struggle for the Mississippi River*. Lincoln: University of Nebraska Press, 2003.

Sherman, William Tecumseh. *Memoirs of General William T. Sherman*, Vol. I. Bedford, MA: Applewood Books, 1875.

Simson, Jay W. *Naval Strategies of the Civil War*. Nashville: Cumberland House, 2001.

Spedale, W.A. *The Battle of Baton Rouge 1862*. Baton Rouge. LA: Land and Land, 1985.

Still, William N., Jr. *Iron Afloat: The Story of the Confederate Armorclads*. Columbia: University of South Carolina Press, 1985.

United States Naval War Records Office. *Official Records of the Union and Confederate Navies in the War of the Rebellion*. Washington: Government Printing Office, 1894–1922.

United States War Department. *The War of the Rebellion: A Compilation of the Official Records of the Union and Confederate Armies.* Washington: Government Printing Office, 1880–1901.

Wideman, John C. *Civil War Chronicles, Naval Warfare: Courage and Combat on the Water.* New York: Metro Books, 1997.

Williams, Kenneth P. *Grant Rises in the West.* Lincoln: University of Nebraska Press, 1997.

Williams, T. Harry. *P.G.T. Beauregard: Napoleon in Gray.* Baton Rouge: Louisiana State University Press, 1955.

Winters, John D. *The Civil War in Louisiana.* Baton Rouge: Louisiana State University Press, 1963.

Woodworth, Steven E. *Jefferson Davis and His Generals.* Lawrence: University Press of Kansas, 1990.

_____. *Nothing but Victory: The Army of the Tennessee, 1861–1865.* New York: Vintage Civil War Library, 2006.

Wright, Marcus J. *General Scott.* New York: D. Appleton, 1897.

Index

Albatross 218–219, 222
Alexandria, La. 217, 221–222, 249–250
Algiers, La. 22, 134
Anaconda Plan 3, 4
Anderson, Maj. (later Brig. Gen.) Robert 1, 16
Anglo-Saxon 226
Arizona 221–222
Arkansas 24, 161, 170–181, 183–184, 189–190, 192, 194
Arkansas Post *see* Post of Arkansas
Arrow 23
Augur, Brig. Gen. Christopher C. 216, 220, 250
Autrey, Lt. Col. James L. 164

Bailey, Capt. Theodorus 110–111, 126–128, 162
Baird, George W. 221
Banks, Maj. Gen. Nathaniel P. 215–218, 220–222, 234–235, 241, 249–255
Baron DeKalb (formerly *St. Louis*) 195, 204, 212–213
Bartlett, Midshipman John Russell 104, 112
Baton Rouge, La. 162, 163–168, 180, 183–187, 189–191, 208, 216, 218, 220, 222, 249–250
Beall, Brig. Gen. William N.B. 249–250
Beauregard, Maj. Gen. P.G.T. 1, 64–68, 84, 86–92, 94–98, 121, 151, 154, 159, 182
Bee 28
Bell, Capt. Henry H. 105, 108–110, 117, 130–133
Bell, Maj. Joseph W. 137
Belle Algerine 114–115
Belmont, Mo. 30–32
Benjamin, Judah 25, 66, 68, 121–122
Benton 20, 37, 52, 75, 77–78, 151, 155–157, 176–177, 197, 203, 224–225, 229–230
Benton, Thomas Hart 9
Bird's Point, Mo. 36, 72
Bissell, Col. Josiah W. 72, 76

Black Hawk 203, 204–205
Blair, Montgomery 99
Blue Wing 202, 205
Boggs, Capt. Charles 116
Bowen, Maj. Gen. John S. 227, 229, 232, 247–248
Bowling Green, Ky. 35–36, 39, 43, 46, 66–67, 84, 86
Bragg, Maj. Gen. Braxton 86–90, 94, 121, 123, 163, 201
Breckinridge, Maj. Gen. John C. 87–89, 182–187, 189, 191
Brooke, Cmdr. John M. 23
Brooklyn 22, 104, 108, 110–113, 117, 169–170
Brown, Cmdr. Isaac N. 171–175, 177–180, 184–185, 189, 194–195
Browne, Ensign Symmes 197
Browning, Orville 9
Bruinsburg, Miss. 230, 232
Bryan, Mayor Benjamin F. 162–163
Buckner, Maj. Gen. Simon Bolivar 35, 56–63, 228
Buell, Brig. Gen. Don Carlos 35, 46–47, 66–68, 84, 87–88, 91–92, 95–98
Butler, Maj. Gen. Benjamin F. 119, 130–139, 164, 168, 180, 191, 215–216

Cable, George W. 126
Cairo 20, 152, 155, 195–197
Cairo, Ill. 5, 7, 11, 14–15, 17–18, 28–30, 32, 35–37, 39, 45–46, 48, 52, 63, 70–72, 74–77, 84, 104, 146, 161–162, 181, 193–194, 196, 220
Calhoun 23, 221
Callender, Elliot 149–150
Cameron, Simon 17–18, 33
Camp Moore 183, 186
Cape Girardeau, Mo. 7, 14, 71
Carondelet 19–20, 39–41, 49–51, 74, 77–82, 150–152, 155, 158, 171–174, 177, 195, 224–225, 229
Carondelet, Mo. 20, 48
Catton, Bruce 4
Cayuga 112, 126, 186

Chalmette, La. 119, 137
Champion 177
Champion Hill 240–242
Charleston, S.C. 1, 64, 66, 99–100
Charlotte, N.C. 23
Cheatham, Brig. Gen. B.F. 32
Chillicothe 212–213
Cincinnati 20, 39, 41, 45, 75, 78, 149–152, 204
Cincinnati, Ohio 18, 71
Cincinnati Pilots' Association 19
City, George W. 184
Clark, Brig. Gen. Charles 185, 187–188
Clarksville, Tenn. 35, 48, 60–61
Clifton 222
Coffin, Charles Carleton 156, 159
Colonel Lovell 147–148, 150, 156–157, 159
Colorado 103, 105
Columbus, Ky. 7–8, 14–16, 28–33, 35–36, 43, 66–69, 73, 98, 171, 198, 235
Conestoga 7, 18, 28–29, 37, 39–40, 43, 50
Confederacy, size of 2
Confederate naval officers 21–22
Corinth, Miss. 68, 76, 84, 86–91, 97–98, 154, 182
Crandall, Lt. Warren 160
Craven, Capt. Thomas T. 113, 162
Crocker, Brig. Gen. Marcellus 236
Crump's Landing, Tenn. 87, 89, 91–92
Curtis, Brig. Gen. Samuel 10

Davis, Capt. Charles H. 146, 148–149, 151–156, 161–162, 164, 167–168, 170–171, 175, 177–180, 192
Davis, Jefferson 2, 12–16, 21, 64, 66, 84, 96, 122, 124, 126, 172, 183, 228, 242–243, 250
Davis, Joe 242

Defiance 106, 118
DeKalb see *Baron DeKalb*
Delisdemier, L.F. 150
Dent, Fred 5
Dent, Julia 5
De Soto 209–210
De Soto Point 168, 170, 226, 246
Devol, George 126
Dick Fulton 144
Dickey 177
Dryden, Lt. David M. 145
Duncan, Brig. Gen. Johnson K. 106, 118
Dupont, Capt. Samuel 99–100
Dwight, Brig. Gen. William 253–254

Eads, James B. 17, 20, 24, 37
Eddyville, Ky. 29
Ellet, Lt. Col. Alfred 144–146, 153, 157, 161, 168–171
Ellet, Col. Charles, Jr. 140–146, 152–153, 155, 157–161, 222
Ellet, Charles Rivers (Charlie) 146, 160–161, 196, 208–209, 220
Ellet, Edward 144
Ellet, John 144
Ellet ram fleet 192
Emory, Brig. Gen. William H. 216, 220
Empire City 226
Era No. 5 209–210
Essex 20, 37–39, 41, 45, 179–180, 186, 189–190, 218, 257
Estrella 221–222
Ewing, Francis 195–196

Farragut, Adm. David G. 101–105, 110–111, 113–114, 117–120, 124–131, 139, 162–165, 167–171, 175, 177, 179–180, 183, 185, 216–223, 257
Farragut, Loyall 220
Florida 22
Floyd, Brig. Gen. John B. 47, 56, 59–60, 62–63
Foote, Flag Officer Andrew Hull 27–30, 33, 36–37, 39–43, 45–46, 48, 50–55, 67–68, 73–78, 80–81, 83–84, 101, 142–144, 146–149
Forest Queen 202, 225
Forrest, Brig. Gen. Nathan Bedford 60, 62, 198
Fort Bisland 220
Fort DeRussy 69
Fort Donelson 35, 38, 40, 42–56, 60–63, 67, 69, 73–74, 84–86, 146, 148
Fort Heiman 35–36, 39, 43
Fort Henry 29, 35–48, 53, 67, 69, 73, 84–85
Fort Hindman 202–206

Fort Jackson 3, 25, 100–101, 105–107, 110, 112–114, 118–119, 122, 124, 127, 131, 138, 162–163
Fort Monroe 141
Fort Moultrie 1
Fort Pemberton 212–213
Fort Pillow 68, 76, 84, 98, 146–148, 152–155
Fort Randolph 154–155
Fort St. Philip 3, 25, 100–101, 105–107, 111, 114–115, 118–119, 124, 127, 131, 162–163
Fort Sumter 1, 2, 5–6, 16, 28, 64, 140, 212, 249
Fort Thompson 72
Fox, Gustavus V. 99–102, 104, 162, 167
Frémont, Jessie Benton 9–10
Frémont, Maj. Gen. John C. 4–11, 20, 28–29, 70–71
French, Col. Jonas 134, 137

Galena, Ill. 5, 6
Gardner, Maj. Gen. Franklin 249–250, 252, 254–255
General Beauregard 147–148, 150, 156–159
General Bragg 147–151, 156, 158–160
General M. Jeff Thompson 147–148, 150, 156–158, 160
General Polk 71, 82
General Quitman 106, 115, 118
General Sterling Price 147–148, 150, 156–159, 224–225, 254
General Sumter 147–150, 156–158, 160; see also USS *Sumter*
General Van Dorn 147–148, 150, 156, 158–160
Genesee 218–219
Gift, Lt. George W. 173, 176–180, 184
Gorgas, Brig. Gen. Josiah 23
Gosport shipyard 23
Governor Moore 106, 114–116, 118–119
Grand Duke 221
Grand Gulf, Miss. 185, 227–230, 232, 234–236, 241
Grant, Fred 229
Grant, Maj. Gen. Ulysses 5–8, 11, 15–16, 18, 28–33, 35–49, 52, 54–59, 61–63, 67, 84–88, 91–93, 95–98, 192–194, 196, 198, 201–202, 206–208, 211–214, 220, 223–248, 250, 252, 254–255, 257
Great Western 177
Green, Brig. Gen. Martin 232
Gregg, Brig. Gen. John A. 236–237
Grover, Brig. Gen. Cuvier 216, 220, 251–253
Gwin, Lt. William 87, 97, 173, 203

Halleck, Maj. Gen. Henry W. 33, 35–37, 44, 46–48, 52–53, 67, 70–72, 76, 81, 83, 85–86, 91, 98, 142–144, 148, 170, 180, 193, 215–217, 220, 222, 235, 241
Hamburg Landing, Tenn. 88–89
Hampton Roads 103, 141–142, 170
Hardee, Maj. Gen. William J. 14, 67, 86–90
Harper's Weekly 211, 258
Harriet Lane 103, 118
Harris, Gov. Isham 14–15, 94
Hart, Capt. J. Henry 156–158
Hartford 103–104, 110–113, 117, 119, 128, 131, 165–166, 169–170, 175, 218–220, 222
Haskins, Maj. Joseph A. 163–164
Havana 22
Haynes's Bluff, Miss. 173, 195, 198–199, 201, 214, 223, 227, 242–243
Heisler, Lt. George 128
Helena, Ark. 196, 211, 246, 257
Helm, Brig. Gen. Benjamin Hardin 185
Henry Clay 225
Henry von Phul 225
Herron, Maj. Gen. Francis 244
Hickman, Ky. 15
Hobbs, Sgt. Charles A. 232
Hodges, John 173
Hollins, Capt. George N. 25, 71–72, 77, 82, 124–125, 151
Holmes, Maj. Gen. Theophilus 246, 257
Horizon 226
Hunter, Maj. Gen. David 10, 33
Hurlbut, Brig. Gen. Stephen A. 92, 96, 206, 227

Imperial 258
Indianola 210, 217
Iroquois 109, 114, 162, 164, 169
Irwin, Lt. Col. Richard B. 216, 251, 254
Island No. 10 70, 72–78, 81–84, 98, 147, 150, 171
Itasca 108–109, 117
Ivy 23, 71, 224, 229

Jackson 23, 28, 106, 118–119
Jackson, Miss. 87, 184, 191, 227, 235–237
Jefferson Barracks, Mo. 5
Jefferson City, La. 24
Jefferson City, Mo. 9
Jessie Benton 155–156, 159
Johnston, Gen. Albert Sidney 12–13, 47, 56, 66–68, 76, 84, 86–88, 90–92, 94, 182
Johnston, Maj. Gen. Joseph

123, 227–228, 238, 240, 243, 246, 250
J.W. Cheeseman 226

Katahdin 169, 186, 189
Kautz, Lt. Albert 113, 128, 131–132
Kennebec 117, 165, 169
Kennon, Capt. Beverley 115–116, 118
Kentucky, politics of 7, 15
Kimball, James 165
Kineo 109, 185–186, 189, 218–219, 257
Kinsman, Lt. J.B. 134–136

Lafayette 224–225, 229
Lake Providence, La. 208, 220
Lancaster 144, 177, 220
Lee, Gen. Robert E. 64, 170
Lee, Cmdr. S. Phillips 162, 164
Lee, Brig. Gen. Stephen 198
Leonard, Capt. W.H.H. 149
Lexington 7, 18, 28, 30–32, 39–40, 43, 87, 94, 201
Lexington, Mo. 9
Lincoln, Abraham 1–4, 7–10, 17, 33, 36, 85, 99, 101, 122, 126, 155–156, 162, 167, 170, 182, 185, 193, 203, 206–207, 216, 235, 239, 258
Lioness 144, 161
Little Rebel 147–148, 151, 156–160
Livingston 71
Logan, Maj. Gen. A. 233–234, 240, 247–248
Loring, Maj. Gen. William Wing 212–213, 239–240
Louisiana 24, 102–103, 114–115, 118, 124
Louisville 20, 50–51, 155, 204, 224–225, 229
Lovell, Maj. Gen. Mansfield 25–26, 106, 123–125, 127, 134, 164
Lynch, Capt. William F. 185
Lyon, Brig. Gen. Nathaniel 9

Mackall, Brig. Gen. William W. 82–83
Magoffin, Gov. Beriah 15–16
Mahan, Capt. A.T. 218
Mallory, Stephen Russell 21–25, 124–125, 177, 195
Manassas 71, 106, 114–115, 117–118
Manassas, Va. 64, 66
Marmora 195–196, 201
Marquesa de la Habana 22
Mary T. 221
Maurepas 71, 82
McClellan, Maj. Gen. George 3, 6, 17–18, 20, 33, 35, 46, 85, 101, 140, 164, 170

McClernand, Maj. Gen. John A. 36–37, 40, 44, 48, 54, 56–58, 63, 92, 96–97, 193–194, 201–207, 223, 226–228, 230, 232–236, 238, 241, 243, 247
McCown, Brig. Gen. John P. 72–73, 76
McDaniel, Zere 194–196
McPherson, Maj. Gen. James B. 208, 220, 222, 226, 230, 235–237, 239–240, 243, 247
McRae 23, 71, 114–115, 118
Meigs, Brig. Gen. M.C. 142
Memphis, Tenn. 13–15, 84, 87, 98, 124, 147, 152, 155, 159–161, 165, 167–168, 170–171, 181, 186, 192, 194–196, 201, 206, 208, 227, 254–255
Memphis & Charleston Railroad 35, 84, 86, 91
Merrimack 23–24, 140–142
Milliken's Bend, La. 202, 206, 226, 246
Mingo 144
CSS *Mississippi* 24, 102–103, 124, 126
USS *Mississippi* 105, 109–110, 117, 132–133, 218–219
Mobile & Ohio Railroad 86, 91
Moderator 226
Monarch 144, 153, 157–159, 201
Monitor 140
Monongahela 218–219, 257
Monroe, Mayor John T. 126–131, 134, 138
Montgomery, Ala. 22, 24, 66
Montgomery, Capt. James E. 147–148, 150–151, 155, 159
Montgomery, Lt. Col. Louis 247
Moore, Gov. Thomas 121–122, 124, 163–164
Morgan, Brig. Gen. G.W. 197–199, 202, 204
Morgan, Sarah 163, 165–166, 190
Mosher 113–114
Mound City 20, 151–152, 170, 224–225, 229
Mound City, Ill. 20, 55
Mumford, William B. 139
Murray, E.C. 24

Nashville, Tenn. 35, 54, 60, 62, 66, 68, 84–85
Natchez 162, 164–165, 210, 232
Nelson, Brig. Gen. William 91
New Carthage, La. 223–227
New Madrid, Mo. 14, 70–74, 76–78, 80–81, 84, 98, 147
New Orleans, La. 3, 24–25, 65, 71, 86, 100–104, 115–134, 136–138, 162–165, 167–168, 180, 183, 185, 191, 215–218, 220–222, 250, 255, 257–258

New Orleans *Picayune* 122, 124, 130
New York, N.Y. 1, 7, 100, 102, 123
New York *Herald* 110–111, 113, 177
New York *Tribune* 180, 209
Nicolay, John G. 2

Oglesby, Col. Richard 29–30, 33, 56
Oneida 164, 169
Opelousas, La. 162, 221–222
Ord, Maj. Gen. Edward 247
Oregon 23
Osbon, B.S. 111–112

Paddy's Hen and Chicks 155
Paducah, Ky. 7–8, 11, 15–16, 18, 28–29, 31, 36–38, 52
Paine, Brig. Gen. Eleazar 36, 82
Paine, Brig. Gen. Halbert 253
Palmer, Cmdr. James S. 162, 164, 169, 222
Park, Mayor John 161
Parke, Maj. Gen. John G. 244
Parton, James 132
Pea Ridge 183
Pemberton, Lt. Gen. John C. 193–194, 196, 198, 201, 212, 219, 227–228, 235, 237–244, 246–248, 250, 257
Pensacola 105, 110, 112, 129
Perkins, Lt. George 126–127
Phelps, Lt. S.L. 18, 28–29, 37, 39–40, 42–43, 68
Pillow, Brig. Gen. Gideon J. 13–15, 32, 47–48, 51, 56–60, 62–63
Pinola 108–109, 169
Pittsburg 20, 50, 78, 81–82, 150–151, 195, 224–225, 229
Pittsburg Landing, Tenn. 87, 89, 91–92, 94, 96, 98, 148, 154
Plum Point Bend 148, 152, 155, 157
Point Pleasant, Mo. 71–73, 81
Polk, Maj. Gen. Leonidas 12–16, 30, 67–69, 90
Pontchartrain 82
Pook, Samuel 17, 20
Pope, Brig. Gen. John 5, 70–78, 80–83, 147–148
Port Gibson, Miss. 230, 232–235
Port Hudson, La. 191, 208, 216–220, 228, 234–235, 241, 249–251, 253–255, 258
Port Royal, S.C. 99
Porter, Adm. David Dixon 100–108, 111, 117–119, 124, 152, 168–170, 172, 179, 192–196, 199, 201–206, 207, 210, 213–214, 216–217, 220, 222–224, 226, 228–230, 245, 252

Porter, Cmdr. William 38, 41, 179
Portsmouth 103
Post of Arkansas 202–203, 206, 228
Prentiss, Maj. Gen. Benjamin 92, 94, 246
Price, Maj. Gen. Sterling 9–10, 29, 71
Prime, Capt. Frederick 245

Queen of the West 144, 153, 157, 171–175, 179–180, 195–196, 201, 208–210, 217, 221–222

Randall, Gov. Alexander 4
Read, Lt. Charles W. 114, 172, 176
Read, Midshipman John H. 128
Resolute 106, 115, 118
Richmond 109–110, 112, 117, 162, 169–170, 216, 218–219
Richmond, Va. 15, 23–24, 64, 66–68, 86, 96, 121, 167, 170, 183–184, 228, 246
River Defense Fleet 25–26, 106, 115, 118, 147, 171, 186, 254
Rodgers, Cmdr. John 17–20, 28
Ross, Brig. Gen. Leonard 211, 213
Rousseau, Capt. Lawrence L. 22, 25
Ruggles, Brig. Gen. Daniel 86, 94, 183, 188
Russell, Boatswain's Mate George 131–132

Sachem 105, 218
St. Louis 20, 39, 41, 45, 50–51, 75, 83, 155–156, 160, 195
St. Louis, Mo. 4, 5, 7, 10–11, 14, 18, 20, 24, 45, 55, 71, 81, 84, 183, 192, 196, 205, 258
Sampson 144
Scharf, J. Thomas 118, 152
Sciota 109, 169
Scott, Thomas 81
Scott, Lt. Gen. Winfield 1, 3–4, 9, 13, 17, 26, 33, 121, 258
Selfridge, Lt. Cmdr. Thomas 195–196
Semmes, Adm. Raphael 22
Shea, William L. 236
Sherman, Brig. Gen. Thomas W. 216, 220, 250
Sherman, Maj. Gen. William T. 68, 74, 92–93, 95–97, 194–199, 201–206, 213–214, 225–227, 235–237, 240, 242–244, 251–253
Shiloh, Tenn. 83, 93–97, 182, 193, 203, 249
Shrodes, Capt. John Miller 161
Signal 195
Silver Wave 225

Smith, Maj. Gen. A.J. 197, 202, 205, 233, 247–248
Smith, Lt. Calvin 239
Smith, Maj. Gen. Charles F. 29, 35–37, 39–41, 54, 58, 85–87
Smith, Maj. Gen. Edmund Kirby 221
Smith, Brig. Gen. Martin L. 122–123, 164, 198
Smith, Brig. Gen. Morgan L. 197–198, 202
Smith, Lt. Cmdr. Watson 211
Soule, Pierre 126, 130–131, 136–138
Spitfire 155
Springfield, Mo. 9–10
Stanton, Edwin 81, 140–144, 146, 148, 152–153, 160–161, 215
Star 115
Star of the West 212
Steele, Brig. Gen. Frederick 196–197, 199, 202–203, 242
Stembel, Cmdr. Roger N. 28, 42, 149, 151
Stevens, Lt. Henry K. 172–173, 175, 184, 189–190
Stevenson, Maj. Gen. Carter 228
Stevenson, Capt. John A. 106
Stewart, Brig. Gen. A.P. 72
Stonewall Jackson 106, 115–116, 118
Strong, Maj. George 134
Stuart, Col. David 92, 198–199, 203
CSS *Sumter* 22–23
USS *Sumter* 177, 186, 189
Switzerland 144, 146, 158, 220, 222

Tangipahoa, La. 183
Taylor 7, 18, 28, 30–32, 39–40, 43, 50–51, 87, 94, 171–175, 177, 197
Taylor, Maj. Gen. Richard 219–221, 257
Taylor, Zachary 13, 70
T.D. Horner 144
Tennessee 24, 161, 171
Thomas, Gen. Lorenzo 85, 141–142
Thompson, Brig. Gen. M. Jeff 14, 71, 151, 159–160, 172
Tift, Asa 24, 124
Tift, Nelson 24, 124
Tigress 92, 202, 204–205, 226
Tilghman, Brig. Gen. Lloyd 38, 42, 241
Todd, Lt. Alexander H. 185
Totten, Brig. Gen. Joseph G. 20, 142–143
Tupelo, Miss. 98
Tuscumbia 224–225, 229

Twiggs, Maj. Gen. David E. 121–123
Tyler see *Taylor*
Tyson, Acting Master Herbert 130

Van Dorn, Maj. Gen. Earl 66, 84, 169, 172, 182–185, 193, 198
Varuna 116–117
Vicksburg, Miss. 87, 101, 159, 162, 164–165, 168–172, 180–181, 183–186, 190, 192–194, 196–198, 201–202, 207–208, 211, 213–214, 216–220, 222–223, 225–231, 236–237, 239–248, 254, 257–258
Villepigue, Brig. Gen. John Bordenave 154
Virginia 23, 140–141
Virginia 2, 3, 23, 64, 66, 140, 215

Wainwright, Cmdr. Richard 169
Walke, Cmdr. Henry 19, 31, 40, 42–51, 74, 76–82, 150, 152–153, 158, 161, 173–174, 195
Walker, Leroy 2, 14–15, 121–122
Wallace, Brig. Gen. Lewis 41, 48, 54–56, 58, 60, 62, 92, 96–97
Wallace, Brig. Gen. W.H.L. 92, 96
Warley, Capt. Alexander 117–118
Warrenton, Miss. 208, 228, 242
Warrior 106
Washington, D.C. 1, 9–10, 18, 25, 85, 132, 162, 170, 193, 203, 244, 250
Washington Artillery 164
Weigel, Lt. Henry 133
Weitzel, Brig. Gen. Godfrey 119, 217, 220, 251–252
Welles, Gideon 17, 27, 39, 42–43, 52, 68, 73–75, 77, 81, 100–102, 104, 140, 142, 148, 151–152, 169–170, 210, 217, 230
Westfield 109
White River 29, 170, 203
Whittle, Cmdr. W.C. 124
William H. Webb 210
Williams, Brig. Gen. Thomas 164–165, 167–168, 170, 180, 183, 185–187, 189, 207
Wilson's Creek, battle of 9
Winona 117, 169
Winschel, Terrence J. 236
Wissahickon 169

Yankee 23, 28
Yazoo City, Miss. 171–172, 194, 212
Yazoo River 159, 170–174, 194–197, 199, 201–203, 206–207, 211–214, 223–224, 227

www.ingramcontent.com/pod-product-compliance
Lightning Source LLC
Chambersburg PA
CBHW081545300426
44116CB00015B/2762